D0214411

Understanding the Modern Culture Wars:
The Essentials of Western Civilization

by

Paul A. Cleveland

Boundary Stone • Birmingham, Alabama

© Paul A. Cleveland, 2001
All rights reserved.
First Printing, March, 2003

No part of this publication may be reproduced, stored in a retrieval system, or transmitted in any form by any means, electronic, mechanical, photocopy, recording, or otherwise, without prior written permission of Paul Cleveland, except for brief quotations in critical reviews or articles.

ISBN 0-9727401-0-4
Library of Congress Control Number 2003090240

Cover art:
Rembrandt Harmensz. van Rijn: *Jeremiah Lamenting the Destruction of Jerusalem*, ©Rijksmuseum Amsterdam, Netherlands. Used by permission.

Cover design: Teresa Brooks

For information about useful reference materials, additional reading lists, and other available resources from Boundary Stone, visit our web site:
http://www.boundarystone.net

Dedicated to Clarence B. Carson, a scholar, author, mentor, and trusted friend.

Table of Contents

Section 3: The Early Modern Era . . . 233

I would like to thank several people whose help was especially valuable in completing this book. I would first like to thank Clarence Carson for his invaluable help in meeting with me and reviewing the manuscript at various stages of the process. Without his guidance along the way, the book might never have been completed. In the process of consulting with Dr. Carson, I gained a great deal of experience that will no doubt serve me well in the future. In addition, I would like to thank Victoria Long, Larry Taunton and Brandon Robbins. Victoria provided many excellent editorial suggestions which greatly improved the readability of the book. Larry provided some excellent insights from his own professional experience. My photograph appearing on the back cover was provided by Brandon. I would also like to thank my wife, Cathe Cleveland, for her help in formatting the final copy. While each of these people provided me with much needed assistance, any errors that remain are my own.

Paul A. Cleveland

Chapter 1: Prologue

From the instant time began, a drama has been unfolding. At just the right moment, human beings appeared on the scene. For the first time in history there was a creature who was not only alive, but who could think abstractly, plan for the future, and act upon his plans. For the first time in the drama of creation, there was a creature who could discern whether his behavior was moral or immoral, just or unjust, right or wrong. Further, for the first time there was a creature who possessed a conscience which tended to bother him when his behavior was immoral, unjust, or wrong. And though there were already social creatures in the animal kingdom, for the first time in history there was a creature who could not only share his dreams for the future with other people, but at the same time he could share the dreams of other people as well. For the first time, there were creatures who could cooperate with one another to realize their individual and collective dreams.

The relationships of people living and working together to achieve common and individual goals give rise to what we call civilization. But, what are the essentials which allow civilizations to develop? And, what attributes of a community of people define a civilization? Also, what factors or essentials define Western civilization? Finally, what factors are at the root of the pervasive conflict that threatens to undermine this civilization? These are the questions to be answered broadly in the following pages.

To begin this exercise, it is first necessary to more fully define what is meant by the term civilization. A civilization is a human society marked by the advanced development of culture to such a point where human interaction is characterized by civility rather than by the grossness of savagery.

The term civilization itself has as its root the word civil. A civil human being is one who is courteous, complacent, obliging, and kind. In addition, a civil individual deals with others honestly and fairly and has respect for their lives, liberty, and property. Such a person is peaceful, good natured, courteous, accommodating, hospitable, polite, tolerant, and tender. In brief, a civil person is not a threat to others, but actually promotes the general well-being of the community even as he promotes his own self-interest.

This is not to say that a civil person would never have an occasion for disturbing the peace or for creating tension in society. Actually, the use of force and coercion is often necessary. For example, it is quite appropriate for a civil individual to use force to either defend himself or someone else from the unjust actions of others. In this case, the duty of civility requires the suppression of injustice. Or again, it may be necessary for the civil person to stand against falsehoods which are generally accepted by others. In such cases, even though compromising the truth might allow for relative peace, the price of making a concession would be too high. This problem is compounded because people disagree about a great many things. And, since a constant battle over every possible point of disagreement would allow for very little cooperation, fighting over every point of conflict is not worthwhile. Therefore, the civilized person must determine which truths are so fundamental that they cannot be abandoned. In short, the civilized person will choose his battles wisely and choose to overlook what appears to him to be a great many shortcomings in his neighbors. The main point here is that total passivity is not a prerequisite of civility, and, further, that the civil person's use of force, or his disruption of the peace of society to wage a battle of ideas, is bounded by limits. As a general rule, therefore, we might say that a civil individual is a person who attempts, as much as is possible, to live at peace with those around him.

On the other hand, the lack of civility is apparent when savagery, criminality, oppression, and rudeness mark the relations among men. An uncivilized individual will lie, cheat, and steal to suit his own ends. Such a person can be described as someone who is sullen, ill-disposed, hostile, impolite, and self-willed. He can be obstinate, belligerent, self-assertive, cruel, and inhumane. The lack of civility leads to murder, rape, stealing, and a host of other immoral acts because the uncivilized person has a lack of respect for others.

Given this definition we must admit that there has never been a time in the recorded affairs among men when perfect civilization existed. Examples of ruthless dealings among people have always been evident. Further, the presence of uncivil behavior at any time in society implies the absence rather than the presence of civilization. No mere human has ever lived the perfect civil life. Instead, human experience is marked by the propensity to lapse into incivility. So much is this the case that our natural condition could be characterized more correctly as uncivil than civil. As such, there would appear to be nothing to write about, for there never has been a pure civilization. Yet, there are varying degrees of civility in human relations which have been manifested in and between communities throughout history. It is the higher degrees of civil interactions among men which mark civilization. Our quest is to discover the essential elements or factors which fostered the development of higher levels of civility in Western communities.

To begin this quest, a consideration of human origin and of human nature must be made. The reason for this consideration is straightforward. As Phillip Johnson writes,

> Every culture must have a creation story as a basis for things like philosophy, education and law. If we want to know how we ought to lead our lives and relate to our fellow creatures, the place to begin is with knowledge about how and why we came into existence.[1]

Thus, a shared explanation of human origin is not only one of the necessary elements for the establishment and continuation of civilization, but such an explanation also serves as a framework within which an analysis of civilization can proceed.

There are two competing explanations of human origin in Western societies today. The first is a traditional view. Until recently, it was the popular opinion held by people in Western societies. And, while it has lost its general popularity, it remains widely believed by many people today. It holds that human existence is the result of the creative act of God. Scripture tells us that God created man in his own image. That is, human beings were created by a purposeful act of an all powerful, infinite, personal Being who has always existed. The creative process is recorded in Genesis 2:7, "And the LORD God formed man of the dust of the ground, and breathed into his nostrils the breath of life; and man

---

[1] Phillip Johnson, *Reason in the Balance*, (Downers Grove, Illinois: InterVarsity Press, 1995), p. 12.

became a living being." Based on this account of human origin, theologians argue that every human being is understood to be constituted from two essential elements: body and soul. The body of a man is material and is made of the same elements found everywhere in inanimate objects in the created order. And yet there is life to the body which is the result of the presence of the soul. In addition, it is the soul which is intelligent, conscious, spiritual, and moral. It is the soul which reasons and wills the body to action.

The alternative view is relatively new, although the materialistic philosophy behind it dates back to the earliest stages of intellectual speculation about such things. It gained academic acceptance in the nineteenth century and has since become the generally accepted point of view regarding human origin in Western societies. Proponents of this view argue that human existence is the result of a naturalistic process. That is, our presence in the universe is a chance occurrence. It supposes that human existence is the result of a mechanical process which has forever been ongoing and will continue on indefinitely. For this reason, we can refer to this view as naturalism. Its chief metaphysical assumption is that nature is all there is, or ever has been, and that nature operates as an entirely closed system with no interference from the outside. Hence, God's existence and actions are viewed as irrelevant at best. As a result, there is no particular reason or purpose for human existence.

Even though naturalism has become the cornerstone of education in Western society, there are nevertheless some serious metaphysical problems with it. As Phillip Johnson has also written,

> The assumption that nature is all there is, and that nature has been governed by the same rules at all times and places, makes it possible for natural science to be confident that it can explain such things as how life began. This advantage comes at a high price, however. Naturalism opens the whole world of fact to scientific knowledge, but by the same token it consigns the whole realm of value to human subjectivity.[2]

---

[2] Phillip Johnson, "Is God Unconstitutional: The Established Religious Philosophy of America", *The Real Issue*, Dallas, TX: Christian Leadership Ministries, 1995, p. 16.

The problem arises because the naturalist has no reason for the existence of life, or the origin of individual personality, or the origin of human conscience. Following the perspective of naturalism, such things are treated as random accidents which have no explanation. In addition, all forms of philosophical materialism fail to offer any adequate explanation of such things as sensation, thought, and volition. These things simply cannot be accounted for in any meaningful way on a material basis alone.

The lack of any foundational basis for moral behavior is particularly troubling. From the naturalist perspective, morality is relegated to the realm of personal preference. Gordon Clark accurately assessed the serious problems resulting from this situation. His argument begins by appealing to common opinion which presumes the immorality of such things as murder, theft, dishonesty, and adultery. He points out that everyone has an innate sense that such human actions are morally wrong. Likewise, people everywhere tend to admire and affirm such moral imperatives as kindness, tolerance, compassion, honesty, respect for property, and chastity. Since these human leanings are shared, we must wonder where they originated. The traditional view has a satisfying answer to this question. Proponents of this view argue that God has declared some behavior as moral and some as immoral. However, from a naturalistic position, which assumes that God does not speak and has not established such moral laws, there is no ground for the prohibition of certain behavior and the admonition of other and, hence, all morality is lost. As Clark writes:

> The empirical method in axiology can only begin with the discovery in experience of so-called values. Art and friendship, health and material comfort, are frequently so identified. The precise identification, however, is not the crucial point. These so-called values are all descriptive facts. [One individual] discovers in his experience a preference for art and friendship. Someone else may not value art at all. Similarly, personal preference varies between monogamy and adultery. And Stalin shows a preference for murder. . . . Thus murder, as much as friendship, is a value because it has been discovered as a value in experience. How then can a theory which restricts itself to descriptive facts provide ground for normative

prescriptions? If the premise of an argument is the descriptive fact that someone likes something, by what logic could one arrive at the conclusion that other people ought to like the same thing? Any syllogism with a normative conclusion requires a normative premise.[3]

At first glance Clark's statement is difficult to understand. Yet the point that he is making is not that complex once the terms that he uses are understood. Several terms in particular may cause confusion. These include axiology, syllogism, and normative. In addition, it might be helpful to explain what he means by empirical method.

Axiology is the study of values. Syllogisms are logical arguments where a conclusion is derived from a series of declarative statements which are often called axioms or premises. For example, consider the following syllogism.

- Stealing is wrong.

- Taking someone else's property by force is an act of theft.

- Therefore, a man has behaved wickedly if he has taken his neighbor's property by force.

In this argument there are two premises from which a conclusion is drawn. The conclusion derived from the axioms is a necessary consequence of them. Therefore, the argument is a valid argument, but its truth depends upon the truth of the premises.

This brings us to the term normative. It is common practice to differentiate between positive statements and normative ones. Positive statements are explanations which describe how things are, while normative statements prescribe how they ought to be. The difference between them is the difference between the phrases "what is" and "what should be." An example of a positive statement is, "Throughout recorded human history we find instances of people stealing from one another." This is a statement of fact about what has indeed transpired. An example

---

[3] Gordon Clark, "Can Moral Education be Grounded on Naturalism?", *Essays on Ethics and Politics*, Jefferson, Maryland: The Trinity Foundation, 1992, pp 7-8.

of a normative statement would then be, "Men throughout history have shown their own wickedness by stealing from one another when they ought to have refrained from such behavior." This is a statement of judgment about the actions of human beings.

Having defined these terms, we are in a position to better understand Clark's statement once we understand the empirical method. The empirical method of discovery is the scientific method which begins by observing, collecting, and organizing facts. Having gathered this information, the process proceeds by deriving conclusions from the facts. There is much value to be sure in this method of gathering knowledge since we must all begin our exploration of this world by employing it. In the course of time, however, naturalists have become so enamored with the empirical method that they have rejected outright the possibility of God divinely revealing himself to mankind in anything beyond creation itself. They also reject the notion that God has given human beings consciences to discern right and wrong. Having rejected these, the naturalist argues that the only thing which can be known is what can be fully documented from experience alone.

Herein lies the problem which naturalists face and which Clark so clearly points out. If there is any sense whatsoever in discussing right and wrong, good and bad, then there must be some standard of norms. That is, "a normative conclusion requires a normative premise." The syllogism given above was constructed in order to make this point. The conclusion of the syllogism implies that men ought not use force to take their neighbors' property. This is a normative conclusion about how men ought to live their lives. But to arrive at this conclusion, I had to state the premise that stealing is wrong. This statement too is normative for it establishes a norm of human behavior. But how do I know that stealing is wrong? I know it because God has declared that it is wrong and my conscience confirms this declaration. In the final analysis such norms can only be founded beyond men themselves if they are really true. If we try to found morality only in human experience, then any behavior whatsoever is moral. In this case morality is solely a matter of personal preference. The problem with this is that personal preference can take almost any turn because men can and do successfully deaden their consciences against the norms of God. Naturalists realize the problem faced and often seek to solve it by appealing to some social demand. But such appeals are useless in avoiding the essence of the problem. If an infinite Creator has not defined acceptable human behavior, then there is no universal definition of justice. Personal preference is all that remains. The appeal to some nebulous social contract is insufficient and, as Clark so eloquently argues, all horrors are permissible as long as they serve to promote some pragmatic end.

Undaunted by the inherent failure of their philosophy to adequately account for morality, or to provide any basis for it, naturalists persist in their view because they presume that science cannot proceed effectively if they make the concession that there is a transcendent and immanent God. But, is this really the case? J. Gresham Machen, a noted Presbyterian theologian, dealt with this objection when he wrote:

> It is sometimes said that the actuality of miracles would destroy the basis of science. Science, it is said, is founded upon the regularity of sequences; it assumes that if certain conditions within the course of nature are given, certain other conditions will always follow. But if there is to be any intrusion of events which by their very definition are independent of all previous conditions, then, it is said, the regularity of nature upon which science bases itself is broken up. Miracle, in other words, seems to introduce an element of arbitrariness and unaccountability into the course of the world.
>
> The objection ignores what is really fundamental in the Christian conception of a miracle. According to the Christian conception, a miracle is wrought by the immediate power of *God*. It is not wrought by an arbitrary and fantastic despot, but by the very God to whom the regularity of nature itself is due–by the God, moreover, whose character is known through the Bible. Such a God, we may be sure, will not do despite to the reason that He has given to His creatures; His interposition will introduce no disorder into the world that He has made. There is nothing arbitrary about a miracle, according to the Christian conception. It is not an uncaused event, but an event that is caused by the very source of all the order that is in the world. It is dependent upon the least arbitrary and the most firmly fixed of all things that are, namely upon the

character of God.[4]

For these reasons, the modern view of human origin represents a regression, rather than an advancement, in thought. Its failure to explain the existence of the mind, of thought, and of moral consciousness seems sufficient reason for rejecting this pattern of thought in favor of the traditional view. It seems clear that naturalism is an error in judgment. When a society embraces any error as truth, it will not lead to civilization. Instead, when error in thinking is embraced, it inevitably leads to conflict because of the natural friction between the truth and falsehood. This is especially true when there is a dispute among the individuals in society over an issue as critical as its understanding of human origin and, thus, the purpose of human existence.

As we shall see later, much of the demise of civilization in modern Western societies in the twentieth century can be traced to the many errors in thought that have been generally embraced. Perhaps chief among these errors is naturalism itself. Therefore, the more traditional view of origin and purpose of human life will be used as a backdrop for this investigation which aims to discern the factors that promote Western civilization.

Therefore, we begin with the observation that human beings are created in the image of God as creatures whose makeup contains both a body and a soul. To be sure, the vital union of the body and soul has escaped full human comprehension. In fact, this union will likely always remain something of a profound mystery to us. Nevertheless, within the traditional conception of human existence, every person is understood to be the combination of a body and a soul: one material and the other spiritual. As Charles Hodge has said, "we do not know how the body acts on the mind, or how the mind acts on the body."[5] What seems clearly apparent though, is that when physical death occurs, the body remains but it no longer possesses the force of life. Therefore, we can be confident that the soul is the source of the individual's life and when it departs from

---

[4] Machen, *Christianity and Liberalism*, (New York: MacMillan Company, 1934), pp 101-102.

[5] Charles Hodge, *Systematic Theology*, (Grand Rapids, Michigan: Eerdmans Publishing Company, reprinted 1993, vol. II), p. 44.

the body the person dies.

In addition to this, experience demonstrates that certain states of the body can produce certain corresponding states in the mind. Though we see, hear, and feel with our minds, we do so indirectly through the operation of the body. The connection between the body and the mind is so close that either can affect the other. For example, a person's emotional state can cause the person to become physically sick, and physical diseases can cause the degeneration of the mind. Finally, while certain bodily actions require no conscious thought, other actions could not occur without it. These things can be understood and even expounded upon, but a complete understanding of the soul will remain elusive. For example, even though our understanding of the physical process of procreation has dramatically improved, the transmission of the soul remains a mystery. This is so because the soul is not material. Therefore, it cannot be observed in the same way one observes the union of a sperm and an egg which gives rise to a new body. Somehow, in the context of the same process, a new soul is created.

All of this information about human origin leads naturally to the following question. If human beings are created in the image of God, and if God is all powerful and is also the source of all good, then why is it that people are not naturally civil towards one another? This question has certainly sparked much debate. In fact, it is perhaps the oldest and most important philosophical question ever raised. Scripture offers a satisfactory answer to the question, although its answer is found offensive by many people. Namely, the Bible argues that evil, and hence incivility, entered the world because of mankind's failure to obey the commands of his Creator.

In particular, the biblical account indicates that God created our first parents as good and civil people. Yet, as creatures subject to change, our first parents did change when they chose to disobey a commandment of God. Specifically, they questioned God's authority. Rather than accepting God's Word as coming from the only original and determinative being who alone could give meaning, understanding, and interpretation to the facts of the world, our parents sought to judge all things for themselves and, as a result, became subject to God's judgment. Having questioned God's authority, Scripture indicates that they fell into sin and that this condition has been passed down to everyone so that all humanity is fallen. Consequently, the human race continues only because

God, in the graciousness of his character, has temporarily delayed punishing human rebellion. The reason offered for this stay of execution is that God has a good purpose for allowing evil to exist for the present time. In particular, that good purpose is the redemption of humanity from sin. In short, though people were created to commune with God, they have been cut off from him. As a result, Scripture characterizes all people as sinners who only deserve punishment for living lives which are offensive to their Creator. In this state of being, people are given over to their own passions and to fits of rage, anger, hatred, jealousy, unkindness, ingratitude, lust, impurity, and malevolence. These follow because people tend to view all things from a self-centered perspective. What some people find most offensive about this explanation is the declaration that all people of all times, including themselves, are sinful and deserving of death for their rebellion against God.[6]

This is not to say that people always behave as badly as they possibly could. Rather, it merely sets forth the proposition that people left to themselves will disregard God and his rules in living their lives. Thus, people may still behave in morally acceptable ways as a matter of personal choice, but are not inclined to do so for the purpose of pleasing God. From the biblical perspective, the extent of sin is complete in the sense that it affects every aspect of life and, therefore, people tend to direct their affections to all types of things rather than to God. Further, human nature is ethically perverted and, though people are not as bad as they could be, evil governs their lives. Nevertheless, people are still creatures bearing the image of God, however marred by sin, and are capable of doing many apparently good things. For example, we can care for our children and provide them with homes where they are nurtured and taught civil and moral behavior. In addition, we can empathize with and have compassion on our neighbors who have been beset by difficult circumstances such as the death of loved ones or the loss of personal property. Or, to go even further, we can sacrifice a great deal personally for the needs of others. What is even more astonishing in light of our innate immoral tendencies, we can be motivated to do these things on the basis of virtues such as love and courage.

One more point should be made regarding the biblical view of

---

[6] G.I. Williamson, *The Westminster Confession of Faith*, (Philadelphia, PA: Presbyterian and Reformed Publishing Company, 1964), p.54.

human origin. Within this view it is assumed that human beings were created with good minds and were thus able to reason, understand, and know in the same way that we reason, study, and learn today. There are two implications of this view which are relevant for us. First, it should not surprise the researcher to find human beings devising quite ingenious solutions to practical problems during every period of human history. This follows because the arrival of human beings on the scene of history is not viewed as a biological accident which gave rise to a new creature who was only slightly different from some already existing animals. Rather, the appearance of human beings is understood as being the appearance of a substantially different order of creature. Specifically, the creation of a new being possessing a mind who is capable of abstract thought. Put bluntly, based on this view, it is presumed that people everywhere have thought in roughly the same manner as we think today.

The second implication is that while people have always had the same mental capabilities, the biblical account of human origin does not suggest that people were given complete knowledge of themselves and of the world around them. Rather, the implication given is that though humans were given good minds, they still had to learn about themselves and about the world in which they had been placed. As such, early people had no storehouse of knowledge upon which to draw. In a sense, they were original thinkers who were discovering everything for the first time. To be sure, in this process they made many mistakes and often accepted as being true, ideas which were utterly false. This is important because it recognizes that we are the great beneficiaries of the accumulation of accurate knowledge accruing from the intellectual pursuits of people from all past ages. In addition, it recognizes that we are also subject to the same limitations and are also guilty of maintaining numerous egregious errors in our own thinking.

This brings us to the focus of our inquiry. Specifically, we are trying to identify the numerous factors which prompt people in society to live virtuous lives. That is, we will be interested in trying to discover the instrumentalities in nature which restrain incivility and promote civility. There are many different cultural arrangements among people. The arrangements of any particular society are largely the result of commonly shared values, beliefs, and ideas. This common perspective is typically reflected in the nature of the culture's politics, its commerce, its religion, and its arts and sciences. It also gives rise to the culture's institutions: its form of government, its market places, its churches, and its schools. The success or failure of a community is largely dependent upon how accurately the shared values, beliefs, and ideas of the people reflect that which is really true.

The task at hand is to describe the institutions, politics, commerce, religion, and arts and sciences of past civilizations in an effort to discern the values, beliefs, and ideas which served to shape those societies. It will then be important to examine which commonly shared viewpoints were erroneously held, since these false views no doubt contributed to the collapse of civilization. This follows because an erroneous belief will be reflected in a society's institutions. In turn, the ongoing operation of institutions founded upon a lie, rather than the truth, will lead to conflict in human relationships. This conflict will inevitably escalate until the lie is generally rejected and the truth of the matter accepted.

This inquiry into the essentials of Western civilization is valuable because human beings are social creatures. We personally benefit from our relationships with others and have the opportunity to greatly benefit them as well. As such, civil relations among people promote the greatest earthly well-being while the lack of civility leads to the greatest misery.

Study Questions

1. Explain the meaning of the word civility and discuss why it is important for civilization.
2. Why is it that no "perfect" civilizations have developed in human history?
3. Why is a shared understanding of human origin important for the development of civilization?
4. Compare and contrast the two competing views of human origin that are present in Western societies today and explain how they conflict with each other.
5. What are the inherent weaknesses of the naturalist explanation of human origin? Explain why that view fails to provide a sound foundation for civilization.
6. Explain what theologians mean when they say that human beings are creatures constituted of two essential elements: body and soul.

7. Modern American commentators often bemoan the fact that morality is declining. Explain how naturalism has contributed to that decline.

8. Distinguish between normative and positive statements and explain how each relates to axiology.

9. What is a syllogism? Construct an example. Define premise and axiom.

10. What is the scientific method? Explain how it operates in expanding human knowledge. How are people today the beneficiaries of those who lived before them?

11. What does it mean to say that God is transcendent and immanent?

12. What is the Christian conception of a miracle? Why do naturalists attack the idea of the existence of such miracles? What is the fundamental flaw in their reasoning?

Section 1: The Mediterranean World

Human beings are social creatures intended to live in communities. This ought to be clearly understood not only from revelation but from the facts of nature as well. All people enter this world in a social setting. Every child has parents whether those parents are there to rear the child or not. Indeed, it is apparent that the family is the primary means for nurturing children to adulthood as children are totally dependent at birth. Moreover, even though people mature, the reality is that they live their lives in interdependence with others even though they gain independence from their parents. To be sure, the life of the most rugged individualist is bound up with the lives of others.

For this reason, it is not at all surprising that communities of people developed in human history. Nor is it surprising that these communities provided the substantial context in which people secured their lives. Therefore, the first section is devoted to an examination of these early communities. In it, we will examine how different communities handled the various details of promoting human life. We will examine their political, economic, and religious structures so that we can see how the issues of life were dealt with. We will also examine some of the underlying problems that plagued these communities and eventually led to their demise. In this regard, we will get a first glimpse at the fundamental problem of human depravity that tends to undermine all civilizations.

After considering early civilizations, the section will conclude with an examination of Christianity. In truth, Western civilization is very much bound up with the Christian religion. A failure to understand the fundamental nature of that religion will result in a failure to understand the essence of Western civilization. In fact, Christianity is the glue that holds Western societies together.

Chapter 2: Obstacles, Diversity and Trade

I. Introduction

We live in a world where goods must be produced before they can be consumed; and because we are material creatures, consumption is necessary for survival. A person cannot live without food, water, clothing, and shelter; yet these must first be produced before they can be consumed. Even if we consider the eating of fruit which grows naturally on trees or vines in the wild, it must be recognized that before the produce can be enjoyed, someone must first expend the energy to pick, clean, and prepare it. This situation is an essential fact of our existence. Work is necessary to produce the goods that people wish to consume. Further, work, and all those things which naturally or artificially hinder the results of work, stand as obstacles to successful consumption. In addition to this reality, we find that the desires which human beings wish to satisfy are endless. That is to say, no sooner does someone find gratification for one particular desire than he discovers a host of others which he would also like to satisfy. For example, someone's desire for food might be so urgent that his consideration of everything else is forgotten. But, once he has eaten, he will quickly become aware of other things that he also desires. Depending on the individual, it might be any number of different things. It might be a warmer set of clothes to wear or it might be a softer bed to sleep on. Whatever should come to his mind, the reality is that something more will be desired. The important point to grasp from these two realities of life is that human beings have many needs and desires which they wish to satisfy and there are numerous obstacles which must be overcome if satisfaction is to be achieved. Since this is true, the goal of all human labor is to overcome these obstacles with as little effort as possible. The reason that this is so is that we all desire to satisfy more of our wants and desires. Toward this end we are always looking for new and more efficient ways of accomplishing our goals.

Frederic Bastiat, a nineteenth century Frenchman, captured an important implication of this reality in one of his many essays. He wrote,

> To go through the long journey of life from the cradle to the grave, man must ingest a vast quantity of food, protect himself from the inclemency of the weather, and guard against or cure himself of a host of diseases. Hunger, thirst, sickness, heat, and cold are just so many obstacles strewn along his path. In a state of isolation he would have to overcome all of them by hunting, fishing, farming, spinning, weaving, and building; and it is clear that it would be better for him if these obstacles were fewer in number, and still better for him if they did not exist at all. In society, he does not personally attack each of these obstacles, but others do so for him; and he in turn removes one of the obstacles confronting his fellow men.[7]

Thus we find from the outset, that all human beings have an immediate interest in cooperating with others. It is on this basis that much social interaction takes place and that civilizations and societies develop. Specifically, people are better off to the extent that they cooperate with each other in overcoming the obstacles they face. Successful cooperation typically involves some form of dividing tasks among the various people of the community. This is done because it is recognized that obstacles can be overcome more effectively by specializing one's efforts. Thus, the numerous obstacles to consumption that people generally face will be overcome more efficiently according to the degree that individuals specialize in the use of their time. In short, people can mutually benefit each other by such behavior. What is needed are mutual agreements that will allow people to capture the benefits of trade by specializing their individual efforts. To be harmonious, these agreements must be cooperative and, as we will see, one of the chief essentials of civilization is the extent to which individuals are free to voluntarily cooperate with one another rather than being forced into some action.

---

[7] Frederic Bastiat, "Obstacle and Cause", *Economic Sophisms*, (Irvington, NY: The Foundation for Economic Education, 1964), p. 16.

II. The Obstacle of Transportation

One of the primary obstacles humans face in achieving their goals is the transportation of resources from their location to the destination where they are desired. For example, a farmer may well desire to water his crops during times when rainfall is insufficient to sustain growth. To accomplish this the farmer must devise a way to transport water from a spring, pond, lake, or river to his fields. The transportation problem involves finding some means of overcoming the natural barriers which separate his crops from the nearest suitable source of water.

In another example, we might think of the farmer who desires to employ some metal tool to work his land in order to increase production of agricultural products. But, suppose that no suitable metals exist in the region where his farm is located. In that case, either the metal must be imported from some other region and then forged into the tool, or the tool must be forged where the metal is found naturally and then transported to the farm. Either way, the desire to employ such a tool can only be satisfied to the extent that the problem of transportation is solved.

The development of water transportation provided an early solution in overcoming many obstacles to achieving human goals by providing a means for transporting both resources and goods from one region to another. As such, it is not surprising that civilizations tended to develop along river valleys and around seas. Such development was particularly evident around what might best be called the Mediterranean World.

Some of the earliest water craft constructed were nothing more than rafts which proved to be unsuitable for many tasks. Problems of buoyancy and the lack of stability greatly limited what might be hauled from one place to another. This limitation led to the development of boats which were much better suited to the tasks of hauling large loads. The first boats were of the flat bottom variety. Over time numerous improvements were introduced, including the use of rudders to guide the craft and the use of sails to capture the wind as a source of power. In addition to sails, oars were also employed to move boats through the water.

Among the ancient peoples of the world, the Egyptians and the Phoenicians are generally credited with making the greatest strides in mastering the art of water transportation. Both of these groups of people accomplished some rather amazing feats of water carriage. The Egyptians were able to transport stones to build the pyramids from a quarry on one side of the Nile to the construction site on the other side. This was quite an accomplishment considering that some of the stones weighed as much as 50 tons. The Phoenicians were even more advanced than the Egyptians. In the course of time they developed quite a reputation as seafaring merchants. Among the many things they traded was tin obtained from the Middle East and the British Isles. They transported tin as well as many other products and resources to a great many destinations around the Mediterranean basin. So great was the Phoenician mastery of navigating the seas, that there is some evidence that they were the first people to sail around Africa. This was a feat that would not be accomplished again until Vasco da Gama's expedition in A.D. 1497.

In addition to using waterways for transporting resources, there were also valuable resources to be harvested from the sea itself. During earlier times, the most pressing human need for survival was food and it is not at all surprising that the largest industries of the ancient world revolved around the production and harvest of agricultural products. The sea, with its abundance of fish, provided a ready source of food and the fishing industry developed very early in the history of the Mediterranean world. Some writers suggest that fishing alone provided the sole reason why men first constructed boats and took to the sea.[8] Whether this is true cannot be known for sure. What is known is that human beings have more needs and desires than that of food alone. Beyond the necessities of life, people have an endless number of desires which they wish to satisfy. It is for this reason that people trade with one another. Hence, as has already been suggested, the motivation to master the sea in order to transport resources and goods remains as compelling an explanation as the desire to catch fish for food. As we look back at early peoples, it appears that both reasons served as important motives for mastering the water ways. The Greeks, for example, generally had little initial interest in trade and much preferred concentrating on fishing, while the Phoenicians appear never to have been too interested in fishing at all. Instead, as far as we know, their primary interest was always in trade. Whichever came first is unimportant. What is important is that men took

---

[8] J. Holland Rose, *The Mediterranean in the Ancient World*, (New York: Greenwood Press, 1969)

to the seas to harvest its resources and to transport products from one place to another. Both uses of the sea represent human action aimed at overcoming the obstacles of life.

With that said, let us return our focus to transportation. The rivers and seas served as efficient means of transporting goods and allowed for the development of trade among many people throughout a large region of the known world. It also allowed for people to move about and to establish new communities. The Greeks in particular established numerous colonies around the Mediterranean, Aegean, Adriatic, and Black Seas. So much was this the case, that Plato would later remark, "Like frogs around a pond we have settled down upon the shores of this sea."[9] The development around such a broad region of the world is significant because of the great diversity of people and resources to be found in such an area. Such diversity gives rise to opportunities for cooperation and trade. It is also an occasion for people to exercise their own depravity by way of envy, strife, jealousy, and greed.

III. Diversity as Both an Opportunity and an Obstacle

Given the centrality of the Mediterranean Sea and the benefits from trade, it will be profitable for us to consider some areas of diversity which give rise to opportunities to enhance the general condition of human beings. The first thing which should be noted about the Mediterranean Sea is that three continents are connected by it. Each of these continents harbors numerous differences in peoples, climate, native resources, and terrain. In turn, the varieties of people give rise to differences in culture, language, manners, religion, and proficiencies in the arts and sciences. In addition, there were differences among their levels of economic and social attainments.

In discussing the various kinds of diversity, let us begin by considering the variations among people. Before about 4000 B.C., the information available is somewhat limited and is subject to a great deal of speculation and debate about its true meaning. This is because peoples of earlier eras had not developed writing and hence left no written records. What we know about them, we have learned from examining the tools,

---

[9] Will Durant, *The Life of Greece*, (New York: Simon and Schuster, 1939), p. 3.

works of art, and other remains which have been found in archaeological discoveries. From this early information we know that human beings generally lived in tribes. An exact explanation of how tribal living developed is unknown, but given that human beings are social creatures who benefit from interaction with others, we can make some educated guesses. Perhaps these tribes were simply the natural outgrowth of the development of extended families which grew larger and larger over time. And perhaps, at times, these extended families merged with other families to capture some mutual benefits that arose from such arrangements. If so, these combinations gave rise to still larger groups of individuals which eventually led to the development of cities and what might be called early civilizations. Whatever the case, throughout history there have always been some groups of people who have lived in a tribal fashion.

The development of ethnic and racial differences can be attributed to isolated community development. In terms of ethnicity, a group of people that live their lives in isolation from others will tend to develop particular ways of doing things and particular ways of seeing the world. These are expressed in their beliefs and in their institutions. To assess the relative importance of cultural differences that develop in such groups, it might be wise to distinguish between moral beliefs and personal preferences. A person's moral beliefs are fundamentally important because they serve as the individual's connection to the ultimate reality. To the extent that some of those beliefs are at odds with true morality, a problem arises. Specifically, to the extent that a person believes a certain action is moral that is actually immoral, it hinders his ability to live in this world as it actually is. It also results in harm imposed upon those living around him. If immorality is generally pervasive in a community, it tends to hinder the prospects of that community achieving the full benefits of civilization and of life.

This is especially relevant in connection with matters of religion. Consider the various religious beliefs of different people. It should be obvious that all of these beliefs cannot be equally valid. There can be only one correct view of God and of the world he created. Thus, if an ethnic group attempts to worship God in some false way, rather than worshiping him as he requires, it suffers the consequences of its misconception. For instance, maintaining a healthy respect for the property rights of others is something that can be deduced from the nature of this world. It is also something the Bible tells us is God's command. But suppose that a group of people decided to disregard the evidence and promote the notion that individual property rights ought to be readily violated. Will things go well for that community? Will it prosper economically? The answer is that such a community would suffer materially for its disregard of the natural order that has been established by God. As a result, an important part of civilization is the effort to discern the true nature of morality and to promote behavior consistent with such morality.

Alternatively, personal preferences are something of a different order. A preference reflects the value that someone places on a particular choice relative to other options. Preferences reflect the person's individual disposition. Comparisons between people with respect to their individual preferences will reveal a wide variety of tastes. Some of these differences are relatively unimportant and may be of interest only to the extent that they provide variety to life. For example, different cultures may grow different kinds of food or prepare a certain food different ways. While these differences may serve to separate ethnic groups, they may also provide opportunities for interaction and trade among various groups of people.

Ethnic variations are thus the combined product of differences in moral beliefs and differences in personal preferences. While variations in preferences are harmless enough, embracing immorality can be disastrous, and creates a fundamental problem that arises from ethnic differences. Specifically, how does one group of people deal with another which maintains moral beliefs diametrically opposed to their own? On the one hand, a culture that had a proper view of the world would not want to be subverted by a culture that maintained error. Alternatively, it would be good if a culture's errors were exposed so that its people might embrace the truth. Therein lies the real problem: all men err and, to some extent, everyone holds some beliefs which are at odds with reality. It is this dilemma which led John Milton to argue that people owe one another a degree of charitable tolerance. In his support of a free press he wrote:

> For who knows not that truth is strong, next to the Almighty; she needs no policies, nor stratagems, nor licensings to make her victorious; those are the shifts and the defences that error uses against another power. . . . What great purchase is this Christian liberty which Paul so often boasts of? His doctrine is, that he who eats or eats

not, regards a day or regards it not, may do either to the
Lord. How many other things might be tolerated in peace,
and left to conscience, had we but charity, and were it not
the chief stronghold of our hypocrisy to be ever judging one
another.[10]

This is not to say that all moral beliefs of individuals are valid
simply because they hold them. Instead, it is a matter of grace to allow
someone to persist in his error. In addition, this policy does not imply an
intent to allow other people to continue to live with their errors in belief
without trying to convince them of the truth. In fact, allowing such
liberty of thought prompts all individuals to endeavor all the more to
present the most effective case for their beliefs so that the truth might be
more widely known. But, in this case, the battle is waged through
persuasion rather than with physical violence. This is the same thing that
the apostle Paul had in mind when he wrote:

> For though we walk in the flesh, we do not war according
> to the flesh. For the weapons of our warfare are not carnal
> but mighty in God for pulling down strongholds, casting
> down arguments and every high thing that exalts itself
> against the knowledge of God, bringing every thought into
> captivity to the obedience of Christ, and being ready to
> punish all disobedience when your obedience is fulfilled.[11]

In addition to variations in ethnic culture, groups of people also
differ on the basis of race. While all human beings come from a common
ancestry, over time a number of obvious racial differences developed. The
genetic makeup of our first parents contained the potential for a wide
diversity of shapes, sizes, and colors of individuals and their features. In
the course of time, within a relatively small number of individuals, the
process of procreation led to certain common genetic features among
isolated groups of people. At some point, these features became so
distinctive that they gave rise to a more or less well defined race of people.
As long as such groups multiplied themselves in separation from others,

---

[10] Clarence Carson, *Basic American Government*, pg. 148.

[11] 2 Corinthians 10:3-6.

the distinctive traits of the race tended to be perpetuated through generations. On the other hand, to the extent that two or more races blended and mixed with one another, the outgrowth was a new type of race which captured some traits of each group in the mixture.

The process continues today and is easily observable in both the offspring of a family whose father and mother are from the same race as well as the offspring from a family whose father and mother are from different races. Whether it is surprising or not, one thing remains certain: a great deal of incivility of man against man has resulted from overemphasizing the importance of these rather superficial differences in human beings. In short, the fact that people who migrated to a particular area of the world where they were isolated from others and over time developed certain common traits, such as a specific skin and eye color, a particular coarseness of hair, or a certain shape of eyes, seems like a rather insignificant matter. Such differences do not change the fact that all human beings ultimately came from the same source. Nevertheless, such differences led to more than a few acts of aggression and violence based upon an irrational prejudice which can never be characterized as civil. All of this violence and aggression against one another on the basis of racial differences can only be viewed as immoral from a Christian perspective. Since human beings were created in the image of God, and since all human beings have the same ultimate ancestry, it is wholly inconsistent for people to affirm the validity of the Scriptures on the one hand while discounting the humanity of other people because of racial differences on the other.

Even from the point of view of a positivist, who tries to argue his case on the basis of perceived benefits to society, no sustainable argument can be made for either racial purity or for racial unification. To understand this we can begin by noting that racial differences may be of great benefit to human welfare. In particular, to the extent that a race of people develops an advantage over all others in the performance of a particular task, such a difference gives rise to an opportunity for trade. The truth of this is found in a fundamental principle of economics known as comparative advantage which demonstrates that people of different abilities can mutually benefit one another by specialization and trade. Thus, to the extent that people are willing to overlook superficial differences in order to engage in cooperative trade, such variations can be viewed as a very good thing.

If this is true, should the individuals of any particular race seek to maintain their racial purity by refusing to mix with other races? Or, should peoples of all races mix together in an attempt to wipe out all genetic differences? The answer to both of these questions is no. On the one hand, the combination of two races may give rise to traits in the offspring which establish some new comparative advantages that were unknown beforehand. In this case, such mixtures might very well improve the general lot of human beings. Alternatively, if some existing race is lost through being absorbed by such mixtures, the world may lose some special advantage it once possessed. In this case, some opportunity for trade which had previously been available would be lost. At any rate, no one can know for sure which is actually true and, hence, there is no reason to press for either the total mixture of all races nor for the complete purity of any particular race. Any efforts to suggest otherwise are confused and we can only conclude that individuals should be free to make the decisions to marry and raise families regardless of racial differences.

This is all relevant to our current consideration because the centrality of the Mediterranean Sea provided an environment in which there was a great deal of ethnic and racial mixing. It was the meeting ground of the world and people from many different ethnic and racial backgrounds converged upon it. They brought with them not only their genetic differences, but also their differences in language, culture, customs, manners, and ways of life. And so, the Mediterranean world became a sort of melting pot. Because of this situation, the high level of diversity among the various peoples of the region was also the occasion of a great deal of strife.

The combination of ethnic differences, coupled with the diversity of natural resources and climates around the Mediterranean, gave rise to a substantial amount of trade. Among the items traded were horses and mules, sheep, spices, wheat, oil, linen, ivory, silver, gold, tin, bronze, and iron to mention just a few. The trade itself was carried on by nomad tribes, caravan and seagoing traders, colonists, and kings who used armies to transport their goods. Over time, this trade among people thrived. Yet, such advancements in human well-being were often short-circuited by the obstacles of ethnic and racial variations among people.

IV. Plunder as an Obstacle to Life

As was discussed in the opening chapter, human nature is most accurately characterized as sinful. Human depravity can manifest itself in any number of ways. One observable way occurs when some people create artificial obstacles for other people to promote their own interests. Sometimes the greatest obstacles that people face are not those which arise because of the natural barriers of effective work, nor even because of the differences among people which limit effective communication with one another, but the more formidable obstacles contrived by human beings for purely selfish purposes. In all such cases, one group stands to benefit personally from imposing some obstacle on another group.

Even though trade promotes the general welfare, it does not necessarily promote the immediate welfare of everyone. And, given the nature of human beings, the advancement of wealth is also an occasion for men to express their depravity. Such depravity is seen in jealousy, envy, and greed. The actions which are motivated by these human passions can be as overt as the act of stealing goods from others by brute force or crafty deception, or as subtle as imposing legal restraints on others to increase their burdens while easing one's own. It is for these reasons that we find people in all times who are willing to subvert the tenets of justice to promote their own immediate interests at the expense of others.

In ancient times, among those engaged in the practice of using power to control trading relationships, we find nomad raiders, pirates, priests and rulers. Perhaps the easiest means of obtaining a desirable product to consume is to take it by force or deception from someone else. For this reason, the most obvious examples of groups of people who promoted their own interests at the expense of others are nomad raiders and pirates. These individuals sought to overcome the obstacles of life by choosing to live off the productive efforts of others while expending little effort themselves. In attempting to satisfy their desires in this way, they sought the most direct path: namely taking the things they desired from other people. Specifically, they were intent on letting other people do the hard work of production while they merely took the subsequent product for their own pleasure. Thus, nomad raiders sought to descend upon unsuspecting caravan traders with the intention of stealing their wares and money, while pirates sailed the seas in search of cargo ships whose bounty they hoped to capture for themselves.

Raiders, pirates and other thieves have been around throughout history. The intent of their actions is obvious. What may be more or less obvious is that those with governing power have also engaged in essentially the same practice. Sometimes their actions are as obvious as that of thieves and sometimes their actions are far more subtle and difficult to detect. Whichever method is used, one thing is sure, there have been kings and princes of this world who have used their positions of power to effectively accomplish the same ends as those of the nomad raiders and pirates. The only difference between them and the thieves is that they used the legal authority and the power of their positions to accomplish the goal. It is most sad to note that historically the most successful thieves in extracting wealth from others have been governmental authorities. Augustine understood the reality of this situation when he wrote his *City of God*. In that book he asked:

> And so if justice is left out, what are kingdoms except great robber bands? For what are robber bands except little kingdoms? The band is also a group of men governed by the orders of a leader, bound by a social compact, and its booty is divided according to a law agreed upon. If by repeatedly adding desperate men this plague grows to the point where it holds territory and establishes a fixed seat, seizes cities and subdues people, then it more conspicuously assumes the name of kingdom, and this name is now openly granted to it, not for any subtraction of cupidity, but by addition of impunity. For it was an elegant and true reply that was made to Alexander the Great by a certain pirate whom he captured. When the king asked him what he was thinking of, that he should molest the sea, he said with defiant independence: 'The same as you when you molest the world! Since I do this with a little ship I am called a pirate. You do it with a great fleet and are called emperor'.[12]

---

[12] St. Augustine, *The City of God*, (Cambridge, Massachusetts: Loeb Classical Library/Harvard University Press, 1963), Vol. II, Book IV, p. 17.

Whether one uses unlawful force or the legal force of the government to steal, the end result is always the same. In particular, the practice of stealing limits production and trade and, hence, limits the growth in wealth. As such it undermines the level of civility that might have occurred. And, yet, it must be acknowledged that government is necessary to oppose the nomad raider and the sea pirate. Without the rule of law, all would ultimately decay into a "might makes right" world of the most successful raiding parties or pirates. Certainly, neither justice nor civility could be achieved in such an environment.

In fact, the use of government by numerous individuals who have used political power to promote their own immediate interests at the expense of the general well-being of the populace has been commonplace throughout history. This situation arises for a rather obvious reason when it is stated succinctly. Once again, Bastiat captured the essence of why this is the case when he wrote:

> The division of labor, which results from the opportunity to engage in exchange, makes it possible for each man, instead of struggling on his own behalf to overcome all the obstacles that stand in his way, to struggle against only *one*, not solely on his own account, but for the benefit of his fellow men, who in turn perform the same service for him. Now, the result is that each man sees the immediate cause of his prosperity in the obstacle that he makes his business to struggle against for the benefit of others. . . . A physician, for instance, does not occupy himself with baking his own bread, making his own instruments, or weaving or tailoring his own clothes. Others do these things for him, and, in return, he treats the diseases that afflict his patients. The more frequent, severe, and numerous these diseases are, the more willing people are. . . to work for his personal benefit. From this point of view, illness. . . is a cause of his individual well-being. . . . It is therefore quite true that each profession has an immediate interest in the continuation, even the extension, of the particular obstacle that is the object of its efforts.[13]

---

[13] Frederic Bastiat, op. cit., pp. 17-18.

It is for this reason that people throughout time have sought to extend the obstacles of others by way of artificial means to promote their own particular well-being. The very essence of such behavior is really no different from that of the nomad raider or that of the pirate. Specifically, such behavior is an effort to gain an advantage at someone else's expense. Civilization is never achieved through these efforts. Rather, such human action tends to destroy civil relationships and makes it ultimately more difficult to cooperate with others in our efforts to overcome the real obstacles that we all face every day.

Study Questions

1. What does it mean when theorists say that human beings are social creatures? Attempt to explain what life would be like if someone attempted to live in complete isolation from all other human beings. Would such a life be possible?
2. What is the basic means by which human beings achieve the satisfaction of the various ends of life?
3. Explain why trade is mutually beneficial.
4. What are the natural barriers to trade? How have human beings systematically approached dealing with those barriers in human history?
5. Why is it that human well-being and advancement are threatened by the inherent diversity of peoples and geography? Is the threat a natural outgrowth of diversity or does it rise from some other source?
6. According to John Milton, what is the prudent response to people of different religious beliefs?
7. According to the apostle Paul, what is the Christian's duty in a world of diverse religious beliefs?
8. Explain why no sound case can be made for either the strict maintenance of ethnic purity or for the complete elimination of ethnic differences.
9. In what ways does human depravity result in the creation of new obstacles to human flourishing and human well-being?
10. How might someone in a democracy use the legal force of the government to steal from others?

Chapter 3: Early Civilizations

I. Introduction

Our study can continue by considering several groups of people and the development of certain cultures in two near-eastern river valleys and along a portion of the Asian border of the Mediterranean Sea. In particular, the groups of people to be considered include the Sumerians, the Semites, the Egyptians, the Indo-Europeans, and the Hebrews. The cultures and means of daily life of each of these groupings of people provide a fundamental base from which we can work. It will be important to examine how they lived within their own communities, as well as how they related to others around them.

Around 4000 B.C., Sumerian and Semitic tribes began to develop city-states along both the Tigris and Euphrates rivers. The annual floods of these two rivers provided a rich soil conducive to a thriving agricultural industry. The Sumerians were groups of people of similar ethnic stock who moved into the valley from the east. As such, they populated the southern region of the valley towards the head waters of the two rivers which emptied into the Persian Gulf. The Semites were a somewhat different ethnic population made up of numerous tribes which entered the valley from the west. The Sumerians were generally more productive and innovative and their practices were quickly adopted by the Semites.

About this same time, a similar situation existed along the Nile river. It too offered an attractive location for organized agricultural activity. As was the case in Mesopotamia, city-states developed as people migrated to this area. The people of Egypt were Hamites and developed a fairly distinctive culture. Over time, the consolidation of political power and rule over the various city-states gave rise to an Egyptian empire.

As already pointed out, the development of industry in both regions was agricultural and this activity set the stage for a change in the unfolding drama of history. In particular, this enterprise was accomplished only by way of greater specialization and division of labor than had ever existed in tribal living. This change is an important factor in the ebb and flow of human progress. In both the Mesopotamian and Egyptian city-states, large numbers of people lived and worked together. In addition, within each, there was relative peace as human effort was coordinated to harness the resources of the river valleys in order to reap a better agricultural reward.

Along with the greater economic complexity of life and the resulting expansion of economic well-being within these river valley communities, came an increased interest in seizing political power. While political control over the entire river valley was achieved fairly early in Egypt, that was not the case in Mesopotamia. It was much more difficult to establish a large and stable political order in Mesopotamia. Unlike Egypt, the peace in Mesopotamia was often shattered by conflicts between the various city-states. In this river valley, kings continually sought to consolidate power by military conquest, but with little lasting success. As a result, conflict between communities tended to be the norm.

In addition to the ongoing warfare between city-states in Mesopotamia, there was also the constant threat of Indo-European invaders. "The Indo-Europeans represented a new racial group in the Near East; they were large men with fair skins and blond hair, in contrast to the small, dark peoples who predominated in ancient Egypt and Babylonia. Their language was also different, being related to Latin, Greek, and most modern European languages."[14] They lived together in tribes and generally made their living by raising livestock. In the course of time they migrated into the Near East where they posed a threat to existing inhabitants. While Egypt was somewhat spared from Indo-European invasions because of the geography of the area, the city-states along the Tigris and Euphrates were common targets. As was often the case, these groups established themselves in the area by way of conquest, even though some developed their own communities. Either way, once they were in the region, they would quickly adopt the lifestyles and mannerisms of the people already in residence there.

In our discussion of people of the Near East, it will be worthwhile to consider a small tribe of people known as the Hebrews. The Hebrews are actually only one of the many Semitic tribes of the Mesopotamian

---

[14] John B. Harrison and Richard E. Sullivan, *A Short History of Western Civilization*, (New York: Alfred A. Knopf, 1960), pg. 30.

valley. The reason for treating them separately is because of the impact this people had on world religion. According to the Bible, the founder of this people was a man named Abraham who had lived in the Sumerian city of Ur before moving his way up the Fertile Crescent to Haran and finally settling in Palestine. Accordingly, Abraham essentially left one of the most cosmopolitan cities of his day to take up a rather nomadic lifestyle. Such a decision would likely have seemed very odd to his friends in Ur. After all, it was far more typical for a nomadic tribe to eventually assimilate into the city-state rather than for an extended family to leave in order to live such an unsettled existence.

At any rate, his path to a new home extended over a well-traveled trade route. During the time in which he lived, around 2000 B.C., there were frequent donkey caravans which moved along the Fertile Crescent to its northwestern fringe, then turned south, down through Syria and Palestine, and finally journeyed into Egypt. In the early years of the developing trade, donkeys, rather than camels, were used because camels were not yet domesticated for such purposes. This is relevant because there were a number of differences in the routes taken and in the related enterprises which supported the trade. These occurred because of the different needs of these two types of animals. For example, donkeys need food and water more often than do camels. This need led to the development of many more travel centers and way stations along the trade route than would later be needed when camels were employed. As a result, there were a number of opportunities to provide for such needs. Based on the archaeological evidence of the time, as well as that from the Bible, it appears most likely that Abraham was one of the individuals who took advantage of these opportunities. In fact, it seems likely that he was engaged in business either as a donkey "caravaneer" himself or perhaps as an operator of a way station to support the caravan trade.[15] Thus, if he were merely a herdsman, he was likely raising donkeys to sell to caravans as well as growing some crops to provide fodder for them. In this case, he would have essentially been operating a way station along the trade route.

Before leaving the consideration of Abraham's vocation, there is one more issue which might be of interest. Later in Abraham's life, he sent his servant to Mesopotamia to find a wife for his son Isaac. The

---

[15] see W. F. Albright, *Archaeology, Historical Analogy, & Early Biblical Tradition*, (Baton Rouge, LA: Louisiana State University Press, 1966), pp. 22-41.

account is given in Genesis 24 and indicates that the servant made the journey using camels as pack animals. The skeptic would typically seize upon such a statement as evidence of an error introduced by some later writer who wrongly assumed that camels were in use when in fact they were not. However, before accepting such a position, a number of points should be made. First, people were not ignorant of camels and in all likelihood kept some in their herds for various purposes even though they might not have been domesticated yet for the purpose of the caravan trading business. Second, someone had to be the first to successfully domesticate the animal for that purpose. If so, such an individual would have to be particularly entrepreneurial. That is, such a person would have to be willing to take some risk. Clearly, Abraham had the necessary characteristics to be such an entrepreneur. Therefore, it might very well be the case that Abraham was one of the first people to ever successfully domesticate the camel for use in caravan trading. If so, such an innovation would have been a source of great prosperity for himself and his family. Scriptures indicate that Abraham became quite wealthy, thus such an explanation would appear to be at least reasonable. Whatever the case, Abraham's occupation is not of fundamental importance. What is important is the monotheistic religion he embraced and passed on to his descendants. Monotheism, in turn, is particularly significant in the development of Western cultures. Of this, more will be said later.

II. Economic Life

As has already been pointed out, agriculture was the primary enterprise in the Tigris-Euphrates and Nile river valleys. Of central importance to the communities of the areas were the annual floods of the rivers which made agriculture possible in what would otherwise be unsuitably dry regions of the world. However, the flooding rivers were both a blessing and a curse for an uncontrolled flood could cause a great deal of destruction. As a result, efforts were made to control the rivers by a series of dams, canals, and levies. These were constructed to control the rivers and to irrigate the crops.

There were, of course, some differences between the two river valley regions. The Tigris and Euphrates rivers both originate in mountainous regions. As a result, the annual flooding of the rivers is largely the result of melting snow in the mountains during the spring.

However, these rivers can and do flood at other times of the year. This happens if it rains too much in either the river valley itself or in the mountains in which the rivers originate.

By contrast, the flooding of the Nile is largely due to tropical rains which fall two times each year. These rains fall in tropical forests a great distance from Egypt which is itself particularly dry. As a result, the flooding of the Nile is far more predictable. Without the flooding of the river, Egypt would be nothing but a desert. In fact, much of the area is a desert. With an extended desert to the west of the Nile, the Mediterranean Sea to the north, and the Red Sea to the southeast beyond the desert, there remains only a small strip of land for traveling to other parts of the world. Given the various means of transportation available at the time, these geographical features generally isolated Egypt from the rest of the world and provided a natural defense against potential invaders. This natural protection was not available in the Tigris-Euphrates river valley which was accessible from almost any direction except the desert to the south. This distinction is perhaps one of the factors that accounts for the differences in the development of Egypt and Mesopotamia.

The early Sumerian cities were theocracies ruled by priests. The same pagan religious beliefs held by the Sumerians were later adopted by the Semites and the Indo-European invaders. The common religious beliefs involved the polytheistic worship of the gods of nature whom the people believed to be vengeful. They thought that these gods would act upon the whim of the moment to satisfy some passing interest no matter how much harm or destruction was brought upon human beings. As a result, sacrifices were regularly offered to the gods and rites of worship were performed to appease them and to bring success and prosperity. Much of life centered around these rituals, so it is not surprising that the priests served as overseers of worship and appeasers of the gods, as well as rulers who oversaw irrigation projects aimed at harnessing the rivers for the good of the community.

Most people were not land owners, but were essentially tenant farmers or sharecroppers. The rules under which they lived made it difficult for them to rise above a subsistence level. In fact, the laws governing their relationship to land owners tended to prohibit much movement beyond a basic means of survival. The terms of trade were spelled out in detail and identified specific prices for specific agreements.

As a result, there was no room for a prospective farmer to negotiate a better deal. With this situation in place, little thought was given to saving resources in the hopes of procuring one's own land in the future. The land owners were typically part of the priestly class or nobility and used their positions to establish the laws of the city-state. As you might imagine, this situation did not favor tenant farmers or other workers.

A wide variety of agricultural produce was grown in these river valleys including wheat, oats, and barley, as well as a wide variety of garden vegetables. In addition, figs, olives, grapes, and pomegranates were also harvested. The fields were prepared by using hoes and plows. Archaeologists have found evidence that oxen were also employed at a very early date to help plow the fields. In addition, sickles were used to harvest the grain and ox drawn sleds were used to thresh it. It was common for the tools used in the very early periods to be made of stone and later on to be made of metal. Stone tools continued in use for a long time because stone was abundant and cheaper than metal alternatives. However, as better processes of producing metal products developed, and as the trade of metals between regions increased, more and more metal tools were employed because of the advantages such tools offered.[16]

While agriculture was the main industry, a flourishing trade in textiles, pottery, jewelry, metal goods, and brick also developed. These industries were generally sponsored by the priests and the nobility. There were artisans and craftsmen of various types who used their abilities in producing a wide variety of goods. But, once again their opportunities were somewhat limited by legal mandates imposed upon them by the ruling authorities.

In addition to these occupations, a mercantile class was also present which engaged primarily in trade among communities. As has been pointed out in the example of Abraham, these people lived essentially nomadic lifestyles. Merchants not only had to be willing to live as nomads, they also had to be militarily able to defend themselves since their caravans were often the targets of bandits and raiders. As one might imagine, this was not an occupation for the faint of heart. Some caravans employed as many as two to three thousand donkeys in their trade and each donkey could in turn carry between one hundred and fifty to two

---

[16] George A. Barton, *Archaeology and the Bible*, (Philadelphia: American Sunday-School Union, 1916), pp. 148-73.

hundred pounds of load.[17] These caravans moved goods, such as metals, to various regions of the world. It was also common to trade via official government caravans which carried not only goods but tribute from vassal kings to their overlords. This trade was carried on over the long trade route stretching from the heart of Egypt, northward through Palestine and Syria, and down the Tigris-Euphrates river valley.

It is worth noting that commerce and trade was expedited by the development of money. Early on, precious metals became widely used as a medium of exchange. As such, a price would be quoted in terms of the amount of some metal, as measured by its weight, which would be accepted in trade for the product. Thus, the use of a set of scales was an important tool in finalizing the purchase of some good or service. This remained true until standardized coins were developed around the seventh century B.C. However, between 1500 and 1300 B.C., gold and silver metal rings and ingots of particular weights were used. The development of these rings and ingots was a forerunner of actual coinage because the concept behind them was the same as that behind a standardized coin. In particular, the rings and ingots could be molded into common sizes representing various weights. By having already weighed and molded the metal into such units, transactions could be completed far faster than by weighing the metal from some raw form.[18]

A final feature of the economic environment which should be mentioned is that slavery was common place. Although it is not entirely clear what the primary source of slavery was, it most likely stemmed in large part from the conquering of one city-state by another and the enslaving of the defeated people into the service of the victors. Slaves were permitted more freedom than we might commonly think. Perhaps this freedom existed because the prospects of life beyond the city were so dim that there was little thought among slaves to leave their masters. Whatever the case might be, slaves were generally allowed freedom of movement around the city and were often seen on errands for their owners.

To sustain this lifestyle, the ruling elite had a vested interest in extending their rule in order to gain greater wealth and recognition.

---

[17] W.F. Albright, op. cit., pp. 32-4.

[18] G.A. Barton, op. cit., pp. 174-82.

Thus, empire building became the mode of operation and the various city-states were often at war with one another. Over time, several strong leaders arose who were able to consolidate power and conquer other city-states to form empires. Yet, the resulting empires were often unstable because individual city-states tended to be fiercely patriotic. Furthermore, the process of empire building itself established the seeds of its own destruction as some new ruler with greater power would inevitably arise to conquer existing empires and lay claim to the available economic bounty.

III. Religious Life

Human beings are religious creatures and have always been in awe of the holy. Along with this awe, people have feared the retribution of God in one way or another. Throughout history, religion of some sort has been common to all people. So much is this the case, that a person is perhaps never more religious than when he believes himself to be void of it. Such individuals tend to be as zealously dogmatic about their unbelief as is any devout believer. Consider for a moment the prominent intellectual view of our day which suggests that the fear of the holy is only a psychological human response to an innate longing for security in an otherwise indifferent universe where chance occurrences result in death and destruction. This view has at its heart the worship of random chance. "Good luck" or "good fortune" are the hallmark expressions of faith in this system of belief. However, when the shroud of scientism is stripped away, this seems just as religious as the pagan's fatalistic view of being subject to the whims of the gods.[19] In the final analysis, this view is dogmatically religious for it proceeds from the unnecessary assumption of a strictly closed universe.

Whatever else might be said about the religious faith of people in the twentieth century, religion was extremely important in the lives of the people who lived in early cultures and its influence dominated most every area of life. This was true in both river valley civilizations and there were similarities and differences between the religions practiced there. In both areas polytheism was at the heart of religious worship. People in both

---

[19] R. C. Sproul, *Not a Chance,*

areas believed that there were many gods who could and did intervene in human affairs. This belief was held so fervently that the religious practices of the time could best be described as pagan fatalism. That is, all of one's life was believed to be controlled by the capricious acts of the gods. In both areas, the gods that were worshiped were nature gods. For example, the Egyptians worshiped the sun god Ra as well as the falcon god Horus, while the wind god Enlil, the sky god Anu, the moon god Sen, and the sun god Utu were particularly prominent in Sumerian city-states. In both locations numerous temples and shrines were constructed to facilitate the worship of the gods to promote peace with them and, hence, to secure protection and prosperity for the people.

There were, of course, differences in the religions practiced in these two river valleys. For example, over the course of time in Egypt the belief in an afterlife and in a final judgment became more important. As this happened, beliefs about one's future prospects became the center of popular religious worship. At the time of one's death, it was believed that the individual would be judged to determine whether he was fit for eternal happiness. If the person's evil was too great, he was thrown to a beast. This belief dominated religious worship in Egypt as is witnessed by the cult of Osiris. Eventually, such beliefs became foundational to all worship. As a result, Egyptians tended to take individual morality very seriously.

While the belief in an afterlife was also prevalent in Mesopotamia, it was mostly seen as being the same sort of experience for everyone. The afterlife was popularly viewed as being cold and dark and there was certainly nothing about it to look forward to. As a result, one's behavior in the present life hardly mattered in the afterlife. Thus, the focus of worship in Mesopotamia was largely an attempt to appease the gods to gain some temporal success in this present life. Based on such a belief, issues of individual morality and the effect it would have on one's destiny were generally ignored.

Religious worship was also at the heart of the development of the greater part of the arts and sciences. Architectural styles and building techniques were developed in the process of constructing temples, shrines, and tombs for the worship of the gods. In Egypt, the use of stones to construct temples and pyramids remain an impressive feat of human ingenuity. In turn, the process of building these structures required the development of some fundamental mathematical relationships. The discovery of these relationships established the foundation for further advancement later. When writing first appeared, much of the literature had some religious theme. For example, the Sumerian *Creation Epic* recounts how the god Marduk won a battle over other gods in the spirit world and, as the result of his consolidated power, created the earth and men. These initial literary efforts opened the door to other efforts and, once again, set the stage for further advancements in written communication. In addition to these advancements, the pursuit of astrology as it related to common superstitions of the time led to some initial developments in the field of astronomy. In short, the pursuit of religious worship had as an unintended consequence the advancement of knowledge about a number of very practical matters.

Despite some of these advancements in knowledge, the general impact of pagan religion was that it limited human progress. The pervasive fatalism of the time greatly restrained individual freedom. In fact, the average person was more or less bound to the city-state and to his position in life. The rules of life imposed upon him stifled his ability to act independently. As a result, he felt little personal responsibility for his life. This situation thwarted the private efforts of the individual to improve his own life and thus undercut the gains that might have been accomplished. Instead of private enterprise, there was an overarching belief that the individual was relatively unimportant. This fact, coupled with the pagan worship that aimed to secure the common good by appeasing the gods through some kind of sacrifice, led to the development of some of the more reprehensible religious practices of the time. For example, it became common practice for worshipers of Molech to burn babies to death to gain his favor. The individual was thus absorbed by the primary goal of securing the common good of the society.[20]

Whatever else might be said, one thing should be rather obvious. A society that so heavily discounts the freedom and responsibility of the individual will not partake in the benefits that individual initiative will likely promote. Since knowledge tends to accumulate over time, we cannot know what discoveries were never made which might have been made by now, nor can we know how long some later discoveries were postponed. What can be known, is that progress is the result of human

---

[20] Henry Grady Weaver, *The Mainspring of Human Progress*, (Irvington, NY: Foundation for Economic Education, 1947, 10th printing).

action and that human action is best promoted by securing individual freedom and responsibility.

At this point in our discussion of religion it is worthwhile considering the Hebrew people and their religion in some detail. Unlike the other peoples of the world, the Hebrews developed a monotheistic religion and rejected the worship or acknowledgment of any other gods. That is not to say that every Hebrew in every period of time confirmed this belief, but merely that it was their official religion. In fact, on various occasions, judges, kings, and prophets would chastise the people for worshiping other gods in the same fashion as their neighbors. The attack against embracing other religious perspectives was so strong that later prophets predicted that the demise of Israel would be due to the general apostasy of the people. The prophets were particularly harsh in their condemnation of political and religious leaders who compromised the faith by embracing polytheism for expedient ends.

In discussing the development of monotheism by the Hebrews, it has become popular to suggests that there is a natural progression in human religious worship from polytheism to monotheism and finally to atheism. While the linearity of this view may certainly be appealing for the Western mind, "historically it cannot be shown that monotheism always comes after polytheism. And there is little foundation for the self-serving belief, popular in Britain in the nineteenth century, that monotheism is everywhere the product of human progress."[21] The evidence simply does not support such a view. In the first place, the Hebrews were certainly not the most sophisticated people of their era. In fact, they remained much less sophisticated than their counterparts and, as was often the case, when they began to adopt more sophisticated ways of life, they often coupled such advancements with a tendency to engage in polytheistic syncretism. In the face of such popular movements in society, only a few voices were heard to object. This was especially true by the time of the Assyrian and Babylonian sieges. In the face of such threats there were only a few prophets among the Hebrews who called for the nation to repent from its worship of false gods and return wholeheartedly to its monotheistic worship of God alone.

By contrast, the most intellectually sophisticated people of

---

[21] Daniel J. Boorstin, *The Creators*, (New York: Random House, 1992), p. 44.

antiquity, the Greeks, maintained a polytheistic view of the world. In fact, the best efforts of Greek philosophic speculation resulted only in a kind of pantheism which is similar to the eastern mysticism of the modern age. The fundamental problem of pantheism is its failure to explain in a satisfactory way the presence of evil. All of these pieces of evidence taken together serve to completely discredit the evolutionary view of religious progression and argue in favor of the fact that the religion of the Hebrews was truly unique and profound.

Thus, it is surprising that such a group of people as the Hebrews would adopt a monotheistic religion. This is especially true when we examine something of their history. Abraham, the patriarch of the Hebrews, came from the Sumerian city of Ur and grew up in a world of polytheistic worship. This is significant because the Hebrews maintained their ties to relatives in Mesopotamia. Having initially settled in Palestine, they moved to Egypt and lived there for several centuries before moving back into Palestine. Thus, they had been exposed to a vast array of religious worship which was all polytheistic. Finally, "in Palestine they were right at the heart of the civilized world, immediate neighbors of the Phoenicians. All trade, all movements of culture passed through or immediately outside the borders of Israel."[22] Given such a history, it would seem all the more likely that such people would have been among the most polytheistic of the world for the pragmatic purpose of getting along with others to advance their own interests. And yet, at the heart of Hebrew religion was the command that they were to remain committed to God alone. Such a commitment of faith alienated them from others because they came to be seen as intolerant. In their rejection of other peoples' gods and faiths, such a message was unavoidable. This is indeed strange since the general predisposition among human beings is to be liked and accepted by others, especially when there are pecuniary benefits from such behavior.

How then did Hebrew monotheism arise? How did such a small and obscure group of relatively unsophisticated people come to such a profound religious conviction? These are important questions because monotheistic religions altered the course of history. In addition, only monotheism can provide an adequate explanation of human existence in

---

[22] W. F. Albright, op. cit., p.14.

its fullest expression. The Bible indicates that the Hebrew religion was the result of the immediate action of God himself. In particular, it began on the premise that God made himself known to Abraham, Isaac, Jacob, and Moses by special revelation. Perhaps the most awe inspiring meeting of God and man was his meeting with Moses. According to Scripture, at this meeting God revealed himself to Moses in a burning bush. Moses was attracted to the bush because he saw that even though it was on fire, nevertheless the bush itself was not burned. As Moses sought to get a better look at this phenomenon, he was confronted by the voice of God speaking to him from the bush. In the course of their encounter Moses asked God what his name was. God responded, "I AM WHO I AM." The entire meeting was quite profound. A fundamental characteristic of God was revealed in the imagery of the bush which always burned, but was never consumed. Consider for a moment the nature of what was being communicated by this revelation. God, the eternal flame, the Being from which all being came, and who always existed, and who always will exist, met with a single man to tell him how he was to be worshiped. Certainly, this was a holy encounter which altered history.

IV. *Political Life*

As already indicated, political life in both river valleys tended to revolve around religion. So much was this the case that the early Sumerian city-states were initially ruled by priests. And, as the rule in Egypt continued, the pharaoh was seen as a god. Thus, religion was central to obtaining and sustaining governmental rule and it became a vehicle by which potential rulers could more effectively consolidate power. Furthermore, since humans have always shown the propensity to exert power over others for their own gain, it was just a matter of time before rulers attempted to use military force to conquer large areas of land for their own personal gain. As city-states developed in both areas, the temptation for government leaders to attempt to build empires to promote their own vested interests proved too strong to resist.

A. *Egypt*

In Egypt, unified political control came very quickly. In a relatively brief period of time the wars between city-states led to the consolidation of power. These struggles led to two empires: the Upper and the Lower kingdoms. Somewhere around 3200 B.C. both of these regions were unified by a particularly powerful king. This unification, and the subsequent succession of rule, is known as the Old Kingdom. It continued until around 2500 B.C.

To sustain the unified state, the pharaoh had to stay apprised of the goings on throughout the Nile valley. This was accomplished by delegating power to trusted friends. These officials became responsible for various regions of the river valley as well as various areas of political concern. The empire was divided into forty-two regions, called nomes, and an official from pharaoh's court was assigned to execute the pharaoh's decrees in each nome.

During this seven hundred year period, the Egyptians accomplished numerous feats which are still marveled at today. For example, it was during this time that hieroglyphic writing first appeared. And, perhaps the best known, if not the greatest achievement of Egyptian civilization, was the building of the pyramids at Giza around 2600 B.C.

It was shortly after this triumph, around 2500 B.C., that the Old Kingdom disintegrated. One lesson to be learned from this is that grandiose public projects, like the pyramids, can serve to tear a civilization apart rather than to bind it together. This conclusion follows when it is recognized that the pyramids required a vast expense of resources. Since all resources have alternative uses, a clear-cut economic choice was being made. As such, the taking of resources for projects as large as the pyramids surely diminished the material well-being of more than a few members of the nobility around the kingdom as well as that of the average person living in the empire. In fact, the resources needed to build them were obtained by the force of law. This kind of impoverishment of the populace in order to build monuments to the egos and legacies of rulers inexorably led to growing discontentment and hatred of the ruling authorities among the citizens of the nation. In due time, a number of powerful, disgruntled, ruling nobles successfully rebelled and were able to set up their own rule in various regions of the Nile valley. As a result, unification of political control over Egypt was lost until around 2160 B.C.

Of course the splintering of the empire did not end the aspirations of rulers to gain and maintain authority. And, between the Old and Middle empires, there were battles to gain supremacy. In 2160 the ruling family at Thebes was able to regain control over all Egypt. This marked the beginning of the Middle Kingdom which was maintained until around 1800 B.C. Although the worship of Osiris was prevalent beforehand, its widespread rise to central prominence came during the Middle Kingdom. Also, it was during this time that extensive trade through Palestine developed. In addition, either just before or sometime shortly after the disintegration of the Middle Kingdom, the Hebrews ventured into Egypt and took up residence there. Whether they moved before or after the fall of the Middle Kingdom remains a matter of speculation. What is certain is that the Middle Kingdom came to an end when local leaders once again exerted their own power. Their success in establishing local rule led to the disintegration of the empire. Unfortunately for them, their actions also made the region vulnerable to outside invaders. The Hyksos, who were either of Semitic or Hittite origin, seized the opportunity and successfully conquered Egypt shortly after the conclusion of the Middle Kingdom. Some have argued that the Hebrews entered Egypt during the reign of the Hyksos. This is plausible since a Semitic pharaoh would have provided the most favorable circumstances for someone like Joseph to be given a high office in government. While it is uncertain what the exact timing was, what is known is that the Hebrew residency in the area spanned the years of the rule of the Hyksos.

It was not until about two hundred years later, around 1580 B.C., that the Egyptians were able to regain power under the direction of Ahmosis I. Ahmosis I was a particularly capable leader who was able to put together an army and drive the Hyksos out of Egypt. This marked the reestablishment of Egyptian rule and the beginning of the New Kingdom. As a consequence of this success, it appears that the Hebrews were likely enslaved because it was a time of great national pride. Since the Egyptian nationals had been subjugated by a people of another ethnicity, the Egyptians themselves would have had a great distrust of people from other cultural backgrounds in general and of Semites in particular. As a result, there were strong incentives present which must have motivated the rulers to enslave the Hebrews to prevent another period of Semitic rule. The Israelites would have, therefore, remained as slaves in Egypt from around 1580 B.C. until their exodus somewhere around 1400 B.C.

The Hebrew exodus from Egypt is important in the development of civilization because of their motivation to leave. It was not simply that the people were oppressed economically. Though there were certainly economic reasons for the exodus, the most important factor was that the people could no longer endure the Egyptian's pagan religion and its influence over the whole of culture. As Paul Johnson writes:

> So the Exodus was an act of political separation; but it was also, and above all, a religious act. For the Israelites were distinct, and were seen and feared by the Egyptians as distinct, precisely because they rejected the whole weird and teeming pantheon of Egyptian gods, and the entire spirit of Egyptian spirituality, which in its own way was as intense and all-pervasive as the dawning religion of Israel. Just as Abraham felt that religion in Ur had come to an impasse, so the Israelites and their leader Moses, who saw more clearly than the rest, found the world of Egyptian religious belief and practice suffocating, insufferable, odious and evil. To leave was to break out not just of physical slavery but of an airless spiritual prison: the lungs of Israel in Egypt craved for a fiercer oxygen of truth, and a way of life which was purer, freer and more responsible. Egyptian civilization was very ancient and very childish, and the Israelite escape from it was a bid for maturity.[23]

This is certainly interesting. In the Hebrews we find a people that on the surface of things would appear to be less sophisticated than those who populated the cities of ancient times, and, yet, it was this very people who were actually more mature in their religious views. At any rate, it was their willingness to leave the security of Egypt and venture into an unknown future in the hopes of a better and freer life that has indeed provided a better and freer reality for humanity today.

Returning now to our consideration of the political climate of Egypt during the New Kingdom, we find the names of pharaohs with which we are probably most familiar. It was during this period that the Setis and Ramses ruled Egypt. In addition, it was during this period of time that Tutankhamen, whom we refer to as King Tut, ruled as Pharaoh in Egypt. One of the most striking attributes of Egypt during this era was that the essential nature of the empire was the same as it had been in earlier times. Egypt was a land dominated by religious fatalism. It affected all areas of life and was used by the ruling class to maintain their power

---

[23] Paul Johnson, *A History of the Jews*, (New York: Harper & Row, Publishers, 1987), p. 30.

and control. In addition, the Egyptian Empire, in periods when it was unified, is best described as a static society. That is, change of any form was generally avoided. It is perhaps for these reasons that there was no codified law in Egypt. Pharaoh was seen as a god and his rule was accepted no matter how arbitrary it was. At any rate, the New Kingdom remained pretty much intact until around 950 B.C.

B. *Mesopotamia*

The unification of city-states in Mesopotamia was not as easy. Instead, there seemed to be perpetual war and conflict between them. Even though the leaders of one city might succeed for a period at consolidating power by conquering others, it was only a matter of time before it would be conquered by some other group. The first successful consolidation of power came around 2400 B.C. when a Semitic ruler named Sargon I of the city of Akkad was able to conquer the Sumerian cities in the lower regions of the valley as well as other Semitic cities to north and west. In all, his overlordship extended from the Persian Gulf, up the Fertile Crescent, extending west to the Mediterranean Sea and north to the Zagros mountains. The Akkadian Empire lasted for about two hundred years and finally fell because of the influx of Indo-Europeans and other Semites from the Arabian desert as well as because of the rebellion of the Sumerians.

With the fall of the Akkadian Empire, several Sumerian cities reasserted cultural dominance. In particular, the cities of Ur, Erech, and Lagash flourished. But, once again, there was no consolidation of Sumerian power. As a result, the stage was set for another Semitic conqueror to establish an empire in the region. The Amorites began such a conquest around 2000 B.C. and successfully established an empire. Babylon became the capital city of this empire. Its most famous leader was Hammurabi, who was the first known ruler to write down a code of laws. One of the significant effects of this action was to break the monopoly of power held by the priests. In writing the law, Hammurabi set himself up as a secular law-giver and judge. That is not to say that religion became unimportant. Instead, religion was used for pragmatic political ends. In particular, it was used to consolidate, build, and maintain political power. Hammurabi proved quite effective in this use of religion by promoting the worship of Marduk throughout the empire.

The written code was also significant because it was an attempt to standardize the law throughout the region. Prior to such a written code it was common for laws to vary from city-state to city-state. This situation had previously served as a troublesome stumbling block for would-be empire builders. Thus, establishing a unified code of law was helpful in Hammurabi's efforts to maintain his political rule.

The code itself was rather lengthy and contained some general laws along with some regulations which were quite specific. For example, there were general prohibitions against stealing, bearing false witness against others, and assault and battery, along with specific punishments for breaking those statutes. And, among the vast number of laws controlling agriculture, we find the following regulation governing the terms under which someone could rent the services of an ox: "If a man hires for a year, the wages of a working ox is 4 *Gur* of grain."[24] This restriction was exact and, in fact, such restrictions in trade were common in the Hammurabi Code. The economic effect of such rules was to limit private initiative and the potential gains from trade that might have occurred had it been legal to negotiate prices. Of course such rules did serve the interests of the privileged class. But, the benefits accruing to this special interest group were far smaller than the potential gains from trade that could have been realized by the general populace had the people been allowed to freely engage in trade.

At this point it is once again interesting to consider the Hebrews for they too had a law code. The complete Mosaic code was centered around the Ten Commandments which were, according to Scriptures, written on tablets of stone by God Himself. These, in turn, were elaborated on in the Pentateuch, with all subsequent rules being more or less an expansion upon the meaning of Ten Commandments. While there are certainly similarities between the Pentateuch and the Hammurabi Code, the differences are pronounced and significant. As Paul Johnson writes,

> . . . though the Mosaic code was in [a] sense part of a Near
> Eastern tradition, its divergences from all other ancient
> codes are so many and so fundamental as to make it
> something entirely new. Firstly the other law-codes, though

---

[24] G. A. Barton, op. cit., p. 364.

said to be inspired by God, are given and worded by individual kings such as Hammurabi or Ishtar; they are thus revocable, changeable and essentially secular. By contrast, in the Bible, God alone writes the law–legislation throughout the Pentateuch is all his–and no Israelite king was ever permitted, or even attempted, to formulate a law-code.[25]

While the Mosaic law followed the accepted norms of prohibiting such things as theft, murder, adultery, and bearing false witness, it did not add to such laws specific details of trading relationships which were apparent in other codes. In addition, the Mosaic code was intended to apply to everyone equally. All people, no matter how rich or poor, were to be treated impartially under the law. This was quite different from other codes which contained provisions that allowed rich people the opportunity to buy their way out of a situation in which they had violated the law. The Mosaic law was, therefore, astonishing. It was general and appealed to everyone's innate sense of justice, it was impartial and applied to everyone equally, and it was permanent and could not be changed by the whims of men with power. This is truly significant for it was the Ten Commandments which, until recently, served as the base of legal thinking in Western societies.

V. Conclusion

People benefit from their relationships to others and their attachment to communities. The reality of this fact was not lost on people of ancient times and by 4000 B.C. we find the development of complex communities in which human effort was more or less coordinated for the general good. It was in everyone's best interest to divide tasks among themselves to achieve greater gains from trade. Along with this, the use of tools and the development of capital was extremely helpful in expanding production, and the proliferation of such tools required further specialization and division of labor. On top of the expansion in trade that was taking place, numerous discoveries allowed for improved production of goods and services which enhanced the quality of life. As a result, from

---

[25] Paul Johnson, op. cit., p. 32.

about 4000 B.C. to 1000 B.C. there were substantial developments in production and trade in both the Nile and Tigris-Euphrates river valleys.

While the development of these civilizations was a matter of the historic record, it should be clear that the advancements made during this period were limited by the religious views of the people and by the political controls imposed by the ruling class. The fatalistic view of life at the heart of most of the religions during this time limited individual freedom and responsibility. As we will see later, such freedom is fundamental to economic progress. In addition, as has been the case throughout history, the ruling elite established rules of life which tended to work in their best interests and at the expense of the interests of others. As such, it was common for kings to use their positions of authority as well as the religious views of the people to further their political control. These factors greatly reduced the level of general well-being which could have been attained. It also limited the speed at which progress was made in many areas.

In the midst of these problems, a small but very important people, the Hebrews, appeared on the scene. Through this people, monotheism was established and a vastly superior view of the law was provided. The differences in their religion and in their understanding of the nature and purpose of the law have had profound effects on civilizations ever since.

In religion, while other people were worshiping a multitude of gods who ruled over the lives of humans by whimsy and caprice, the Hebrews worshiped one God. They worshiped the God who created the universe and held that universe together according to his own providential care. And, while the God they worshiped was seen as sovereign over history, they nevertheless affirmed man's freedom to choose his own course of action and his responsibility to act in accordance with the commands of God. It was this understanding that was at the very foundation of their thinking about the law. The law was given by God according to his character. As such, it was a permanent standard of behavior which could never be altered or added to and which should always be applied impartially. These ideas were so revolutionary at the time that the Hebrews were seen as outcasts in the broader world around them because those who were consistent in their religious practices would not compromise their faith. Some people, then and now, view such behavior as intolerant. However, it was the fundamental religious and moral views of the Hebrews that have provided for the development of

Western civilization as we know it.

Study Questions

1. Describe the people groups that developed the Mesopotamia and Nile river valleys: Sumerians, Semites, Hamites, Indo-Europeans, and the Hebrews.
2. What was it about the river valleys that attracted people to develop communities there? How did trade help the people who populated these early communities to make economic progress? Describe what life was like in these communities.
3. Discuss the importance of religion in the early communities of the river valleys. What role did religion play in government?
4. How did religious beliefs differ between the people who populated the Nile Valley and the people who populated the Mesopotamia Valley? What was the significance of these differences?
5. Explain the process by which governing authorities sought to expand the territory over which they ruled.
6. What hardships resulted from the increase in political power? How did these hardships hinder human progress? What outcomes eventually followed from these political impositions? Is the same process at work today? Explain.
7. How did the building of the pyramids contribute to the disintegration of the Old Kingdom? What lesson can be learned from this? Can you think of any modern examples?
8. Describe the development of the Hebrews. What importance can be attached to their monotheistic religion and why did it so radically separate them from the other peoples of that era?
9. Which Babylonian ruler is known as the first ruler to have a written code of law?
10. How was the Mosaic law different from other early written codes?
11. How would you refute the view that there is a natural progression in the development of human religious worship as a culture progresses from polytheism, to monotheism,

and ultimately to atheism?

12. Define: syncretism(51), pecuniary(52), nomes(54), hieroglyphic(54).

13. Differentiate between: Upper Kingdom, Lower Kingdom, Old Kingdom, Middle Kingdom, and New Kingdom.

14. Locate on a map: Tigris, Euphrates, and Nile Rivers. Also, Mesopotamia, Egypt, and Babylon.

Chapter 4: Building Empires

I.   The Assyrians

The Assyrian people were of Semitic origin and established themselves along the upper Tigris River around 3000 B.C. As a people, they were not particularly creative. Instead, they merely adopted the practices of other peoples living nearby. Although they were conquered by the Babylonians during its first empire, they never lost their own identity. When the Babylonian Empire fell around 1750 B.C., the Assyrians reasserted their full independence. During the next 750 years the Assyrians were repeatedly attacked by various groups of people and as a result developed a strong military force to defend themselves. As it turned out, the Assyrians were particularly capable in battle and their military forces became known as the best in the Near East.

The Assyrians, however, were not content to use their military might to protect their immediate interests. Eventually, the prospects for increasing their own wealth by plundering their neighbors proved too attractive and they began their own conquests of surrounding areas. Their adoption of new iron weapons and other military tactics gave them a great advantage. In addition, they had well-trained soldiers and an excellent cavalry. For these reasons they were quite successful in expanding their empire. In fact, when the Assyrian army camped outside the walls of a city, little resistance was typically offered against them. That is because the Assyrians had developed a reputation of slaughtering anyone who opposed them. As a result, most of the peoples conquered by the Assyrians quickly offered to pay almost any amount of tribute to avoid being cruelly wiped out.

It should be pointed out that the Assyrians were not only inept in economic creativity, but were also not particularly adept at using the inventions of others to produce wealth. Their own limitations, magnified by the human passions of envy and greed in the presence of the success of others, led the Assyrians to use their strength to plunder the wealth of their neighbors. The initial aggressive tendencies of the Assyrians can be likened to a street gang which arbitrarily establishes its territory and requires some compensation from residents and passers-by to be left alone to live in peace. Or, we might think of it as a payment to a mafia family to insure that one's place of business or home was not suddenly destroyed. In a word, the Assyrians were about the business of extorting wealth from others. However, because the territory over which the Assyrian army marched was so wide, it was difficult to collect continuous tribute from defeated cities. A city might well pay whatever was asked if the Assyrian army was on its doorstep, but once the army moved on, the people saw no compelling reason to continue to pay the extortion. Only the return of the army could stir them to do so and since the army was not large enough to rule everywhere at the same time, the practice of forced tribute was rather ineffective.

Because of the numerous rebellions, King Tiglath-pileser III (reigning from 746-727 B.C.) instituted a new policy. Instead of marching the army around on simple raiding expeditions, the Assyrians began a policy of destroying the ruling classes of the states which developed a history of rebellion. Toward this end, large numbers of the upper-class of the conquered peoples were exiled from their homes to other places in the empire. The aim of the policy was to destroy the leadership. Thus, deporting the nobility was intended to limit the conquered state's ability to mount an effective rebellion against the Assyrians so that the bounty gleaned from vassal states might flow continuously to Nineveh. It might be noted that this same policy has been used in the twentieth century by the Russians. After World War II, Stalin exiled large numbers of people from their homes and moved them to various remote locations throughout the Soviet Empire. The purpose of such action was essentially the same as that of Tiglath-pileser.

Paul Johnson effectively captures the picture of the Assyrian policy as it was used upon the Hebrews of the northern kingdom in his, *History of the Jews*:

> For a time Israel bought the Assyrians off, or formed coalitions of other small states to halt their advance. But in 745 BC the cruel Tiglath-pileser III ascended the Assyrian throne and turned his warlike race into a nation of imperialists. He inaugurated a policy of mass deportation in

conquered territories. . . . Stricken internally by the religious and social divisions, the northern kingdom of Israel was in no condition to resist. In 734-3 Tiglath-pileser conquered Galilee and Transjordan, leaving only Samaria. Tiglath died in 727, but his successor, Shalmaneser V, took Samaria in the winter of 722-1 and the following year his successor, Sargon II, completed the destruction of the northern kingdom, removing the entire elite and sending in colonists. . .[26]

As might be imagined, though the policy appeared to achieve the desired end of securing their rule over conquered peoples, it actually fostered an even greater hatred of the Assyrians that eventually led to their downfall. Furthermore, the practice did not stop the numerous insurrections and there were still continuous rebellions against the empire. At its height, the Assyrian Empire extended from the Persian Gulf to Syria, down through Palestine, and into Egypt. Among the various peoples forced to pay tribute to the Assyrians were the Hebrews. Nevertheless, Judah was able to maintain a nominal degree of independence. Judah was the southern kingdom of the Hebrews and it managed to keep its independence even as the northern tribes of Israelites were being conquered. In fact, their relative independence arose when Israel fell victim to Tiglath-pileser. By refusing to join a coalition of states aimed at rebellion, Judah was able to win the temporary favor of Assyria. Rather than join the confederation aimed at opposing the Assyrians, Ahaz, king of Judah at the time, sought protection from Assyria and agreed to become a loyal vassal king by paying tribute.

Although this action may have saved Judah's superficial independence, it was gained at a heavy price. As a vassal king, Ahaz was forced to make numerous concessions and compromises. The most problematic of these were religious. Ahaz was forced to bow down and honor the Assyrian god, Molech, and to erect an altar to his worship. For the faithful monotheistic worshipers of Yahweh this action was unthinkable since they believed there was only one God and he alone was to be worshiped. Ahaz, however, did not share the traditional faith of Israel and to him it was merely a pragmatic political choice which secured

---

[26] Paul Johnson, op. cit., pp. 69-70.

not only the immediate peace of Judah but his reign as well. In addition to compromising the faith, the regular tribute that had to be paid resulted in a heavy burden of taxation. The evidence indicates that this burden fell harder on the poor even though they gained less from the payment than did the wealthier landowners. This happened because the tax revenues for the tribute were collected by levying a head tax on the people. These taxes fell more heavily on the poorer people of Judah. Such actions gave rise to the prophetic utterances that God would judge the nation for its oppression of the poor. The prophets during this time repeatedly spoke out against the rulers for promoting favoritism within the law.

During the reign of Hezekiah, Judah eventually rebelled against Assyria and stopped paying tribute.[27] In response to this action, the Assyrians laid siege to Jerusalem. There is some debate about whether there were two such historical instances in which Assyrian troops marched against Jerusalem. If there were two cases of siege against the city, then the first took place in 701 B.C. According to the two campaign theory, Hezekiah avoided catastrophe the first time by agreeing to pay Sennacherib the desired tribute. Eventually, however, he again rebelled against Assyria prompting a second military campaign. If this is the correct order of events, the second campaign would have occurred in 688 B.C. The Assyrian king, Sennacherib, would have again been the leader of his troops marching against Jerusalem. In his second campaign he would have come with the intention of destroying the city completely because of Hezekiah's insolence in rebelling again. Another possibility is that there was but one military campaign in 701 B.C. In this case, even though Hezekiah paid the tribute, Sennacherib continued his onslaught against Judah to make an example of the Hebrew king.

Whichever account is accurate, Sennacherib was unable to take the city. The biblical account of the siege indicates that a miraculous deliverance took place. Scripture instructs us that during the siege the angel of the Lord went into the Assyrian camp during the night and killed one hundred and eighty five-thousand soldiers. The Greek historian, Herodotus, attributed the deaths to an epidemic. On this basis, some have suggested that it must have been the bubonic plague which was

---

[27] John Bright, *A History of Israel*, (Philadelphia: The Westminster Press, 1946), pp. 251-287.

carried into the Assyrian army camp by field mice or rats. In any event, the Assyrian troops were providentially depleted and were forced to return home. Interestingly, after this incident neither Sennacherib, nor any later Assyrian king, returned again to lay siege to Jerusalem even though the empire continued for another eighty or ninety years. This is perhaps due to the fact that after Hezekiah's death in 687, his son Manasseh gave up the rebellion and revived the payment of tribute. Nevertheless, it was quite unlike the Assyrians to allow a single state to rebel without experiencing the full force of its military retribution.

Another example of the ongoing problem of internal turmoil might help provide a better picture of the monstrous task the Assyrians faced in attempting to successfully maintain an empire whose primary aim was the general extortion of wealth from others. In 721 B.C., at the beginning of the reign of Sargon II, Merodachbaladan, a Chaldean, was able to successfully overthrow the Assyrian rule in Babylon and was able to establish his own rule there until 709. At that time Sargon was able to retake the city, but Merodachbaladan escaped southward to the Persian Gulf. After Sargon died, Merodachbaladan returned to Babylon and once again mounted a rebellion against Assyria. Sennacherib, Sargon's son, repeatedly tried to suppress the Babylonian rebellion with no success. Exasperated, he finally sent the army to destroy the city. Once more, this action reminds one of the action that a street gang might take with respect to an uncooperative victim or that of a mafia family against a business owner who refused to make his extortion payment.

Despite their success in conquering various peoples throughout the Near East, and their success in destroying local leadership by deporting instrumental people, the Assyrians faced serious problems. The intense hatred of them by subject peoples led to constant turmoil in the empire. As a result, the military was continually called upon to put down rebellions. Over time this led to the depletion of the Assyrian army. In addition, enemies beyond the boundaries of the empire were always a threat, and the military was often needed to secure the borders. Internal turmoil and external enemies eventually brought the empire to an end. In 625 B.C., Ashurbanipal, who ruled Assyria from 668 to 626, died. He was the last of the great kings of Assyria. Though the kingdom continued, its final end was clearly in sight.

The final destruction of the empire was due primarily to an increase in the military power of the Babylonians and the Medes. In the same year that Ashurbanipal died, Nabopolassar, a Chaldean, gained Babylonian independence from Assyria. Over the next few years he consolidated his power and began to expand his own borders. Likewise, the Medes began the same process. In 612 B.C., the Medes and the Chaldeans came together to lay siege to the capital city of Nineveh. Their forces were overwhelming and they successfully captured and destroyed the city. It was the blow which immediately ended Assyrian rule.[28]

It should be evident from all of this that rather than promoting civilization, the Assyrians destroyed it. They behaved very poorly with respect to others and made it all the more difficult for people to live at peace with one another. If they accomplished any good at all, it was through the deterrence of potential raiders who were prone to attack and rob caravan traders moving through the area. By limiting their opportunities to plunder traders, the Assyrians allowed trade to flow more freely than it might have otherwise. But this argument is weak in that it only replaces one raider with another. Still it was trade, coupled with the ability of the people of conquered states to produce wealth, which provided the incentive for plunder in the first place. The Assyrians fundamentally knew that it was in their interest to maintain trade and production as much as possible. Otherwise, there would be nothing to steal. However, such benefits to the general populace of the region were obviously far below the amount of wealth taken from them. They would have been better off defending themselves from the raiders than paying the heavy tribute to the Assyrians.

II. The Resurgence of Babylon by the Chaldeans

To the winner goes the spoils and so it was that the Chaldeans, Medes, and Egyptians each attempted to consolidate their power following the fall of the Assyrians. The Medes were content with building their empire to the east and north and left the Babylonians and the Egyptians to fight over who would control Mesopotamia, Syria, Palestine, and Egypt. The Egyptians pressed northward in an attempt to expand their rule and to establish themselves as the dominant power in the region. However, the Babylonians were ultimately successful in capturing

---

[28] George A. Barton, op. cit., pp. 65-69.

Mesopotamia, Syria, and Palestine by defeating the Egyptians and pushing them back into Egypt itself. Thus, with their victory over the Assyrians and the Egyptians, the Babylonians developed their own empire in the very heart of what was formerly the Assyrian Empire.

The Chaldeans were also of Semitic origin and took up residence in Babylonia during Assyrian rule. Throughout the Assyrian Empire, the Chaldeans had resisted the Assyrians with greater or lesser degrees of success. Eventually, with the aid of the Medes, they brought the Assyrian Empire to an end. With the fall of Assyria, the new Babylonians began to establish their own rule fashioned after the same pattern as that of the Assyrians before them. In 604 B.C., the battle for control of the region with the Egyptians reached its peak. The Egyptians attempted to march against the Babylonians and Nabopolassar sent his son, Nebuchadnezzar II, to engage them. The crucial battle took place at Carchemish. It was there that Nebuchadnezzar defeated the Egyptians and pursued them towards Egypt. Perhaps he would have pressed the attack all the way into Egypt and conquered and subjected it to Babylonian rule had it not been for the death of his father. When Nabopolassar died, Nebuchadnezzar returned to Babylon to be made king. Nevertheless, his success established a new Babylonian Empire which extracted tribute from the small states in Mesopotamia, Syria, and Palestine. Using the earlier analogy, a new street gang had taken over the territory and claimed all payments of extortion for itself.

Nebuchadnezzar was an effective empire builder. He successfully pieced together an empire which stretched from the Tigris-Euphrates river valley to Syria/Palestine. Among his accomplishments was the successful conquest of Judah which had remained relatively independent for so long. The Babylonians adopted the Assyrian practice of deporting the leaders of a conquered state. When they captured Jerusalem in 597 B.C., they exiled large numbers of Hebrews to various places in the empire. The city was later destroyed in 586 B.C. because of a rebellion led by Zedekiah whom the Babylonians had set up as a vassal king.

The fall of Jerusalem and its subsequent destruction are recorded in 2 Kings 24 and 25 and in 2 Chronicles 36. These two accounts of the situation provide insight into what took place. When the Babylonians seized control of Palestine by pushing the Egyptians back into Egypt, they forced Judah to pay tribute in the same way that it had paid Assyria. Judah complied with the Babylonian demands initially. However, in time they refused to continue payments. When Judah refused, the Babylonians accomplished what the Assyrians had been unable to do: they successfully laid siege to Jerusalem.

In the period of time from 597 to 586 three Judean kings are prominent: Jehoiakim, Jehoiachin, and Zedekiah. It was Jehoiakim who refused to pay the tribute. This action subsequently resulted in swift Babylonian reprisal. At that time, Nebuchadnezzar attacked and captured the city of Jerusalem ending Judean independence. Evidently, during the siege Jehoiakim died and left his son, Jehoiachin, as king. Jehoiachin was eighteen years old at the time and served as king for only three months before the siege was complete and he was carried into exile with his mother and a large number of other members of the ruling class.

At this time Zedekiah was made a puppet king by the Babylonians. As such, he was expected to loyally carry out every order from Babylon. He ruled for eleven years. At the end of this time he mounted a rebellion of his own which was quickly rebuffed by the Babylonian military. Once they recaptured the city, they looted it and destroyed its walls and temple. Zedekiah was caught fleeing the city and was forced to watch as the Babylonians killed his sons. Afterwards, they gouged out his eyes, bound him in chains, and transported him to Babylon to be imprisoned. In addition, they completed the process of expatriation by deporting the remaining nobility.

As already stated, Nebuchadnezzar (who reigned from 604-562 B.C.) was a very capable conqueror and empire builder. In addition to this, he took great pride in culture. This led him to engage in numerous public works projects. Perhaps the best known and most spectacular among these were the construction of his palace and the hanging gardens. These projects were funded by the plunder taken from conquered peoples and are examples of what men can do by stealing property from others. Certainly such practices could not be characterized as civil. At any rate, under Nebuchadnezzar's direction the city of Babylon became one of the most impressive cities of the ancient world.

The success of Babylon was short-lived. There are a number of reasons why it failed, but two which seem most prominent are its limited military power and its failure to produce a subsequent leader as capable as Nebuchadnezzar. The combination of these two factors, coupled with the sudden military power of the Persians, set the stage for the demise of the Babylonian Empire. Nebuchadnezzar died in 562 B.C. His son, Amel-marduk, took the throne for two years before he was assassinated. His brother-in-law Neriglissar succeeded him and ruled Babylon for four years until he died. His son was heir to the throne but was killed by Nabonidus who seized it for himself. He reigned until the Persians conquered Babylon in 539 B.C. During the last eight years of his reign, he moved from Babylon to Tema, an oasis in the Arabian desert, and left the day to day affairs of ruling the kingdom in the hands of his own son, Belshazzar. Thus it was Belshazzar who fell victim to the Persian conquest and Nabonidus was subsequently taken prisoner.

III. The Persian Empire

As mentioned earlier, the Medes had more or less withdrawn from Mesopotamia and any immediate conflict with the Egyptians and Babylonians. Having left the heart of the Assyrian Empire for the Egyptians and Babylonians to battle over, the Medes concentrated on building their own empire in the east and north. The king of Media during a significant proportion of this time was Cyaxares. He was the ruler of the Medes when they were allied with the Babylonians in defeating the Assyrians and capturing Nineveh. Even though they were once allies, in the latter part of Nebuchadnezzar's life, Cyaxares and the Medes grew to be his most dangerous rival. During his reign in Media, Cyaxares achieved great success. He expanded his own empire as far west as Lydia. In doing so he conquered all of the territories just north of the Babylonians. As a result, the Medes controlled much of Asia Minor and their presence immediately north of the Babylonians posed the most significant threat.

When Cyaxares died, his son Astyages took over as ruler of Media. It was under his rule that a revolt broke out in the empire. The revolt was led by Cyrus of Persia. In 550 B.C., Cyrus captured the Median capital city of Ecbatana and dethroned Astyages. He them proclaimed himself ruler over all Media and Persia. It was a crucial event that marked the rise of the largest empire known to date. Cyrus quickly expanded his rule westward through Asia Minor to the Aegean Sea by conquering Lydia, southward he captured Mesopotamia, Syria, and Palestine by displacing Babylonia, and eastward he extended his empire to the borders of India by subjugating the peoples of this region to Persian rule.

Although Persia's ultimate aim was the same as that of the Assyrians and Babylonians before them, their conquest of the Near East was generally celebrated. Many people of conquered areas felt as if they had been liberated from oppression. This was because the Persians generally treated conquered peoples far better than those who ruled before them. As an example, the Persians ended the policy of exiling the local leadership and nobility of a conquered state. Instead, they instituted a policy of tolerance and liberty which allowed such people to return to their homes if they so desired. In addition, rather than forcing conquered peoples to worship Persian gods, they allowed them to worship according to their own religious traditions. For the people who endured the rule of the Assyrians and the Babylonians, these policies were likely cause for a great deal of rejoicing.

Of course the personal liberty provided by the Persians was not complete. They were as much interested in exacting the largess from subjugated peoples as were past rulers. This stemmed from the desire to be the strongest bully in town as had been the Assyrians and the Babylonians before them. It is quite evident from the ruins of the palaces they built in Persepolis, Ecbatana, and Susa that the taxes collected throughout the empire allowed the royal family and ruling nobility of Persia to live in extreme luxury. The Persians were not thought of favorably by peoples who had never come under Assyrian or Babylonia rule. In particular, the Greeks of Europe fought vigorously against Persian control and saw no benefit in succumbing to Persian aggression.

Having been established by Cyrus, the Persian Empire endured for almost two centuries. After Cyrus died, his son Cambyses secured the throne for himself by having his brother quietly killed. Cambyses' motive was to eliminate any potential threat of a rival for the throne. It was an action which later became a common practice among the Persian nobility. In fact, later kings were forced to expend a great deal of energy maintaining their rule against a backdrop of numerous schemes among family members and servants who were forever plotting to seize control by eliminating the king. Nevertheless, under the rule of Cambyses and his successor Darius I, the Persian Empire reached its zenith in terms of geographical control. Cambyses conquered Egypt and Darius expanded the empire into India and Europe. Only the European Greeks were able to withstand the onslaught, and for a time it appeared that even they would fall victim to Persian expansion.

John Bright captures for us the point at which the Persian Empire reached its peak in terms of its expansion:

Suffice it to say, under Darius, Persia reached her zenith. Only in one venture, and that his most ambitious, could Darius be said to have failed. This was his attempt to conquer Greece, a project for which he had prepared for some years. After an initial venture had gone awry when a storm destroyed the Persian fleet off Mt. Athos, in 490 Persian troops landed on the island of Euboea. But their stupidly harsh treatment of the city of Eretia roused the Greeks against them. When they crossed to the mainland they were met at Marathon by Miltiades and his Athenians administered a stinging defeat. Darius, forced to defer the project, was unable to resume it before his death.

Darius was succeeded by his son Xerxes (486-465), a man of vastly less ability. . . . Xerxes turned to the invasion of Greece. Bridging the Hellespont (480), he moved with a huge army through Macedonia, overwhelmed the heroic Spartan ban at Thermopylae, captured Athens, and put the Acropolis to the torch. But then came the fiasco at Salamis in which a third of the Persian fleet was destroyed. Xerxes thereupon returned to Asia, leaving the general Mardonius in Greece with an army. But the following year (479) this was cut to pieces at Plataea, while the remnant of the Persian fleet was destroyed near Samos.[29]

These events ended the expansion of the Persian Empire. Following the death of Darius in 486, the empire was ruled by individuals who were not as capable. In addition, from this point on there was much intrigue and conspiracy surrounding the royal family. Xerxes himself ended up being assassinated by his own son Artaxerxes.

Before he died, Darius developed a method of administering the empire which probably allowed it to survive in spite of the numerous murders of rulers. Under his plan the empire was divided into twenty satrapies or regions. A quasi-autonomous ruler, called a satrap, was set up to rule over each of these twenty regions. These men were typically chosen from the ruling family or from the families of other nobles. They

---

[29] John Bright, op. cit., pp. 357-358.

were closely watched by means of a series of checks and balances to ensure that they remained loyal to the king. Of course there was precious little loyalty in the royal family, but there was always the threat of immediate retribution should someone be caught in the act of conspiring against the crown.

John Bright is once again helpful in capturing the intrigue which beset the late rulers and members of the royal family of the Persian Empire:

> A vigorous but savagely ruthless man, Artaxerxes III [358-338] ascended the throne over the bodies of all his brothers and sisters, whom he slew as possible rivals. Then, having put down revolts everywhere with an iron hand, he turned to the reconquest of Egypt. In the course of an initial attempt, which failed, he burned the city of Sidon down upon thousands of its inhabitants. By 342, the goal had been reached, and Egyptian independence ended. Yet the empire, though seemingly as strong as ever, was in fact on its last legs. Artaxerxes III was poisoned and succeeded (338-336) by a son, Arses, who was himself poisoned and all his children slain. The fact that the next king, Darius III Codomannus (336-331), was a grandson of a brother of Artaxerxes II shows clearly how the Achaemenian house had virtually wiped itself out by its gory intrigues.[30]

Whatever the Persians offered the rest of the world by building roads which improved trade routes, or any of its other accomplishments, the example of its royal family and their relationships with one another is certainly not to be admired. The Persians were little better than the empire builders that preceded them. At the heart of their rule was the desire to exercise power and influence over a countless number of other people and to extract vast material resources from them in order to live in luxury. This is exploitation. Empire building in this vein is the height of incivility in human relationships. It destroys, rather than creates civilization. The Persian Empire came to an end when Alexander the Great conquered much of the known world.

---

[30] Ibid, p. 392.

Study Questions

1. Explain how the Assyrian Empire developed. In what way did the Assyrians redirect their military power from a just end to an immoral one? Why did they do so?

2. What was the inherent limitation that tended to destabilize the Assyrian Empire? How did the Assyrians attempt to handle the problem? What are modern examples of the same policy?

3. Describe the circumstances in which the Assyrian Empire fell. Discuss the development of the Babylonian Empire that replaced it.

4. Describe the circumstances in which the Babylonian Empire fell. What change in policy helped the Persians secure their rule of the Near East?

5. What biblical events were occurring during the rise and fall of the Assyrian, Babylonian, and Persian Empires?

Chapter 5: Greece

I. A Brief History

As was discussed in the second chapter, numerous peoples ended up populating much of the area around the seas of the Mediterranean world. Among those establishing colonies, no group was more prolific than the Greeks. That is not to say that all Greeks had exactly the same heritage, but they did share a more or less common religion and language. Nevertheless, the Greeks were generally independent minded and sought to maintain their own separate city-states. They were aided in this by the natural barriers that existed between cities. These obstacles made aggression more difficult. While there were occasions when one city-state might force others to submit to its rule, the Greeks, more than any other peoples to that date, prized freedom. That is not to say that they necessarily prized individual freedom. In truth, they really did not because they thought that the value of the individual was largely determined by the degree to which he profited the state. Nonetheless, the Greeks treasured the independence of their city-states and fought to keep them that way. But, as we will see, even the Greek respect for the self-determination and freedom of the city-state would fade over time as the prospects for economic gain by political action became apparent.

The level of culture in the Greek city-states ebbed and flowed over time. About 2500 B.C., a rather impressive community developed on the island of Crete. As this culture developed, its form was adopted by the communities along the mainland. This dissemination resulted from the rise in trade which was, in turn, due to the opportunities created by the Cretan culture. Thus culture and wealth flourished until nomad raiders brought such activity to an end around 1200 B.C.

After the invasion of the raiders, culture declined for about 400 years. Cultural activities reemerged around 800 B.C. This rise in activity was evidenced by the writings of Homer and by numerous other efforts in the arts and sciences. From his work, as well as that of many others, we have learned a number of things about life in Greek communities. What we know is perhaps best illustrated by a comparison of the lives of people who lived in the two most impressive city-states of Greece: Sparta and Athens.

Sparta was established amid an invasion of Indo-Europeans into the Peloponnesian peninsula around 1000 B.C. These invaders settled a number of cities in that region of Greece. As was true of much of Greece, the land was ill-suited for producing much wealth by farming. This reality forced the inhabitants of Greece to look to other productive efforts by which they might make their living. Rather than developing other enterprises, the Spartans opted for a plan of obtaining wealth through conquest. Much like the Assyrians before them, they saw the opportunity to exploit the sweat of others as the best means by which to obtain the things that they needed to survive. Therefore, they used their strength to take what they wanted. They were quite successful in plundering the bounty of others and were able to capture and enslave many of the neighboring peoples.

Once they started down this road, it quickly became apparent to the Spartan leaders that certain measures were necessary to sustain a society so dependent on the work of slaves. In particular, they realized that they must be greatly feared if other people were going to continue to submit to their rule. As a result, Sparta developed a strict code of life for its citizens which was meant to develop their military prowess. Much of this code is attributed to the ruler, Lycurgus, who instituted a number of reforms. His reforms were intended to rigidly control community life to foster certain attributes in the Spartan citizenry.

The Spartan code aimed to train men for war and conquest. As such, it sought to inculcate in the people courage and valor as the highest virtues of life. In addition, they prized the physical body which they thought was to be strong, able, and perfect. To accomplish this, the individual was expected to endure a harsh upbringing and to bear up under extremely unfavorable circumstances. This kind of training began at a very early age. The Spartans were so preoccupied with the body that some children never lived long enough to enter their training program. At birth, if a child had some physical defect he was immediately killed. Of those who survived, when a boy turned seven years of age he was placed in a military camp to be raised by the state. At these camps, the children were taught the ability to endure pain as they were exposed to intense emotional and physical stress. Those who endured without complaint were praised while the others were severely chastised for their weaknesses. The driving motivation behind all of this was to raise men who were strong, unemotional, and courageous.

Little time or effort was expended on intellectual pursuits because the Spartans were determined above all else to develop the kind of character suitable for war. Therefore, it was not surprising that the Spartan people as a whole spent little time reading or writing and the arts and sciences were generally ignored. But, their army was highly feared and their stoicism was often admired. For example, Plato thought so highly of their regimen that his utopian plan for a republic was based in large measure upon the Spartan way. However, Plato never had to live in a place where individualism was so thoroughly disdained. If he had been forced to live with them, he would have quickly realized that in addition to their valor and courage on the battlefield, the Spartans were also cold, selfish, and cruel. The Spartans lived a narrow existence. When viewed critically, there was very little happiness, joy, or fulfillment in their lives. There was nothing much about this kind of life which made it worth the living. So much was this the case, that some Greeks often remarked that the reason Spartans were so fearless in battle was that death was preferable to the rigors of daily life in their culture.

Athens, on the other hand, was quite the contrast to Sparta. It too was the result of an Indo-European invasion. Athens developed as the central city of a region of Greece known as Attica. Instead of being ruled by a king, it developed a government of the aristocracy. The aristocracy was made up of the wealthier landowners of the region. Like the members of the upper class in other regions of the world, the Athenian aristocrats often used the power of the state to further their own ends at the expense of others. As a result, as is true in all places where this happens, there was tension between them and the rest of the people living in the city-state.

However, the tension in Athens took on a different form from that which occurred in other places. The nature of the difference is best understood when it is recalled that the region was not very well suited to farming. In fact, other than the cultivation of olives and grapes, the land was generally ill-suited for growing much else. Therefore, the Greeks turned to other endeavors. The development of new means of producing wealth resulted in the dispersion of power. In the course of time, business owners of various types came to hold as much power as did the aristocrats. While the Spartans concentrated on forcing others into servitude as the main means of securing a living, the Athenians developed a number of other industries. As a result, the making of wealth there was generally the result of production and trade. Mining, metallurgy, shipbuilding, stone cutting, and textile manufacturing were among the industries that developed. Of these, mining proved particularly significant. The region of Attica was rich in a number of resources including marble, iron, zinc, silver, and lead. The various uses of these minerals, was becoming better known and this provided the opportunity to mine and sell both the raw materials and the products which could be made from them. As a result, businesses aimed at extracting and refining these resources blossomed.

However, would-be mining entrepreneurs faced one significant problem. Specifically, the Athenian government claimed for itself the ownership of all resources located underground. As such, any mining operation had to obtain a state license. This tied much of the potential wealth which could be created in the region to politics and set the stage for much abuse. It also generated large sums of money for government use. While some of the funds were spent for legitimate functions of government, such as building military defenses for protection against the Persians, much was either squandered by politicians who spent the funds for their own pleasures and egos or for financing huge government projects that were not particularly useful. Even though these projects were impressive to look at, it is doubtful that they added to the general level of Athenian well-being.

Nevertheless, the new opportunities of creating wealth through production and trade set the stage for tension between those made rich by trade and the old aristocracy. The political life of Athens vacillated as each group gained relatively more political power. Even with the restrictions imposed on one another by way of legal obstructions, there was still a far greater degree of freedom among the people of Athens than in any other Near Eastern civilizations.

While the Athenians, like the Spartans, prized the physical attributes of agility, athletic ability, and strength, they also valued the mind and sought its development. An emphasis on the development of the mind was not unique to Athens. Rather, the Athenian ideal was far more common in the Greek world than the total devotion to physical abilities that was dominant in Sparta. Therefore, education in Athens, as well as in most other Greek city-states, focused not only on the development of athletic skill, but also on writing and arithmetic. The ideal Athenian was both physically fit and mentally astute. It should also be noted that between the development of the mind and the body, Athenians thought that mental sharpness was more important. While some physical defect might be ignored, stupidity was not tolerated.

Having briefly compared these two city-states, it is possible to better understand the history of the region, especially the defeat of Persia. In the last chapter we considered the growth and the decline of the Persian Empire and noted that its expansion was checked by the Greeks. It is not necessary for us to examine all of the details of the Persian Wars beyond what has already been said there. But it is important for us to highlight the role of the Athenians in that conflict. The Athenians were at the forefront of leadership of the Greek confederacy which had been formed to resist the Persians. This coalition of independent states, known as the Confederacy of Delos, was established with voluntary contributions and had as its chief aim the defeat of the Persians. The Greeks readily recognized that it would take a united effort to resist the awesome power of the Persian army. As such, the individual states were generally willing to join forces to protect themselves from the Persian aggression. There were of course some who thought that fighting Persia was a fool's errand and refused to participate. Some of these even went so far as to betray the confederacy by supporting the Persians. But the pessimists remained in the minority. As it turned out, the Confederacy of Delos was overwhelmingly successful. Through their joint efforts, the Greeks were able to defend themselves. They were able to drive the Persians back into Asia and, since the Persians had so many problems internally, the Greeks were able to secure their borders from the threat of further Persian aggression.

Throughout history there has been a tendency for government bureaus and institutions to live on beyond the purpose for which they were established. Once formed, these institutions often develop lives of their own and pursue activities far beyond those for which they were created. Because such institutions accomplish their activities by way of coercion, they often end up being used for any number of evil purposes beyond the good for which they were originally established.

Such was the case of the Confederacy of Delos. After the threat of the Persians abated, the usefulness of the coalition was questioned by many of its members. However, because of her leadership in establishing the organization, Athens had a vested interest in its continuation. Therefore, rather than allowing the dissolution of the organization, the Athenians used their force to sustain it. Not only did they force existing members to stay in the confederacy, they also forced others to join it. Rather than being a means of voluntary defense against an outside aggressor, the Confederation of Delos became an instrument of the forced exploitation of other Greek city-states for the primary benefit of Athens. The Athenians essentially used their leadership in the war against the Persians as the rationale for establishing their own empire in the region.

Over the next fifty to sixty years this created hatred among the people of the other Greek city-states for the Athenians. While the citizens of Athens recognized the value of freedom, they failed to apply their belief consistently. Instead, they compromised their principles by enslaving others for temporal gains. In the end, they had participated in exactly the same behavior as that of the Persians. The ill-will resulting from the pompous arrogance of Athens led to the Peloponnesian War. Ironically, the other Greeks came to view Sparta as a potential liberator from the oppressive rule of Athens. In time, Athens was defeated and Sparta emerged as the most powerful city-state in Greece. But of course the Spartans were far more overbearing than their predecessor. As Will Durant has written:

> Sparta now assumed for a spell the naval mastery of Greece, and offered to history another tragedy of success brought low by pride. Instead of the freedom which she had promised to the cities once subject to Athens, she levied upon them an annual tribute of a thousand talents ($6,000,000), and established in each of them an aristocratic rule controlled by a Lacedaemonian harmost, or governor, and supported by a Spartan garrison. These governments, responsible only to the distant ephors, practiced such corruption and tyranny that soon the new empire was hated more intensely than the old.[31]

Given the enmity this created with the rest of the Greeks it was just a

---

[31] Will Durant, *The Life of Greece*, (New York: Simon and Schuster, 1939), pg. 459.

matter of time before Sparta too would fall. They were subsequently defeated by the Thebeans in 362 B.C.

It appeared that independence for the various city-states could be maintained following the demise of Sparta, but that was not to be. The resentment that resulted from the abuses of the Athenians and the Spartans had destroyed the trust among the various city-states of Greece. They were no longer able to join together to defend themselves for the common good. When the need arose, each city sought to defend its own interests independently of the others. As a result, Philip of Macedon was able to conquer Greece by 338 B.C.

II. Philosophy

Before moving on to discuss Alexander the Great and the Hellenization of the Mediterranean world, it will be worthwhile to consider the development of philosophy. This will serve two purposes. First, Greek philosophy has had a significant impact upon Western civilization. And second, an understanding of the development of Greek philosophy will provide a better understanding of the historical events taking place in Greek history.

Thales of Miletus, who lived in the sixth century B.C., is thought to be the first philosopher.[32] What made him the first philosopher was that he was the first person, as far as we know, to successfully predict a natural event. That is not to say that people before him were ignorant of the regularity of many natural events, but simply that Thales was the first to predict an event of a different sort. He correctly predicted the eclipse of the sun. More importantly, he made this prediction on the basis of a universal law he had formulated about the cosmos. This was quite a departure from the religious beliefs of the people of the Near East who attributed all such occurrences to the capricious acts of the gods. For the first time, someone had examined a vast amount of information and had deduced from it some precise order which allowed him to accurately predict a future event.

This led Thales to speculate about other things as well and he began to search for a logical explanation of the cosmos. In so doing he

---

[32] Gordon Clark, *Thales to Dewey*, (Jefferson, Maryland: The Trinity Foundation, 2nd edition, 1989), pp. 3-180.

conjectured that all the universe was made up of a single substance. Today we classify this type of philosophical speculation as corporeal monism. That is, he was speculating that all things, including rocks, animals, trees, stars, and human beings, were made of the same material substance. In Thales examination of the evidence, he suggested that all things were ultimately made of water. His speculation caught the imagination of others. Several philosophers following his lead argued in the same fashion. While they proposed other substances as being the sole ingredient from which everything else comes, there was some agreement that the world was, in fact, composed of a single substance.

This speculation ended when Parmenides pointed out the absurdity of the proposition. He correctly deduced that if it were true, then nothing could be said to distinguish one thing from another. That is, all predication would be logically lost if everything was made of the same thing. If substantive distinctions can actually be made between dogs and cats, rocks and animals, men and women, and anything else, then it cannot be the case that everything is made of the same material substance. For this reason he posited an alternative. In particular, he suggested that the universe exists as a corporeal pluralism. This view promotes the idea that all things in the universe are merely the different combinations of a fixed number of underlying elements. Parmenides' work started a new philosophical quest to identify the underlying elements of reality. This quest continues today by some through the study of chemistry.

However, Parmenides' thinking suffered from a serious flaw too, for he had no explanation for the multitude of ongoing admixtures and the motion of elements that regularly occur in the universe. Specifically, if the underlying set of atoms from which all else came were immutable, why did they move or mix at all? While some philosophers attempted to answer this question by way of numerous contrivances, in the end it was shown that corporeal pluralism was unable to provide a satisfactory answer to the question.

As the philosophical search for truth progressed, the inherent problems of explaining the universe on a material basis alone gave rise to a growing skepticism among the Greeks. More and more, people doubted that any explanation was possible. In such an environment, people naturally turned their interests away from the search for truth to the practical issues of day to day life. For this reason, the Greeks became more interested in learning the art of persuasion in order to gain for themselves what they wanted. To instruct them, a number of men became teachers. These men had developed the art of rhetoric and they had the ability to make poorer arguments appear to be better than they really were. They dispensed with moral restraints and argued that man was the measure of all things. In their view, any opinion was as good as any other and what was needed was an impressive way to present one's position. Therefore, they offered to teach their methods to others so that they too could gain political success. These teachers came to be called sophists because they were offering people what they believed was the wisdom needed to get ahead in this world.

With the growing level of skepticism among the general populace, the sophists were generally well received. Parents, who desired that their children succeed in the world, were willing to pay the fee the sophists charged in the hopes that their children would develop an advantage over others. The primary focus of their teaching was on making witty or clever arguments, regardless of how shallow they might be upon further inspection. The goal of the training was to teach the student to effectively influence and persuade others to a particular course of action. The underlying philosophy of the sophists might well be called pragmatism. Like its twentieth century counterpart, the main emphasis was placed on the desired goal to be accomplished without regard to the legitimacy of the means used to achieve that end.

The rise of skepticism and the success of the sophists occurred over the course of the fifth century B.C. This timing is important because it was during this century that Athens redirected the Confederacy of Delos to achieve its own ends at the expense of its neighboring city-states. Thus, skepticism allowed the Athenians to justify their abuse of power in their own minds as long as it accomplished some immediate end they desired to achieve. Since they saw no foundation for truth or for justice and morality, no one had pangs of conscience in using political power for certain expedient ends. As was already noted, the Athenians used their position of leadership in the coalition to exploit others. This exploitation gave the illusion of prosperity in Athens. However, it was only prosperous in the sense that money unjustly extracted from other city-states was used to fund various public and private projects that enhanced the well-being of the residents of Athens. But, all of this was accomplished at the expense of the well-being of many people elsewhere who had been forced to pay taxes for the pleasures of the Athenians. To be sure, such largess funded the construction of many magnificent buildings and purchased many goods for those who were politically connected, but such behavior could hardly be called civil.

Toward the end of the fifth century, when corporeal pluralism had failed to provide a sufficient answer and skepticism was so thoroughly entrenched that it seemed that no one would endeavor to search for truth again, three philosophers appeared. The second was the student of the first and the third was the student of the second. They were Socrates, Plato, and Aristotle. Each was a tower of philosophy in his own right.

Socrates (469-399) was the first among them. As far as we know he never wrote anything of consequence, and in his discussions with the sophists he often claimed that he knew nothing in particular. He had the annoying habit, however, of asking an endless stream of questions directed toward the sophists who presumed themselves to be teachers of men. By these questions he probed for the foundation upon which their teachings were based. In the course of such dialogues, he would show that in fact no foundation existed and that their arguments were superficial and unwise. The result of such discussions revealed the intellectual shallowness of the sophist philosophy of life. Though they presumed themselves to be wise, they were fools. This type of behavior did not sit well with those who had risen to positions of influence on the basis of sophistry. The threat he posed to people of position led them to bring spurious criminal charges against him. Having been found guilty of certain supposed crimes against the city, he was offered the choice of exile or suicide. He chose suicide.

It was Plato (427-346) who wrote down the dialogues of Socrates for our benefit. It cannot be known how much attributed to Socrates was really his and how much was added later by Plato himself. Notwithstanding, these dialogues revealed the total intellectual destruction of sophistic thinking. Chief among the popular concepts to fall was the notion that man was the measure of all things. Such a concept was shown to be completely unreasonable against the intellectual onslaught of Socrates as retold by Plato. In various dialogues that Socrates had with a sophist by the name of Protagoras, Plato exactingly revealed the utter folly of sophism. Gordon Clark captured the essence of this attack for us:

If man is the measure of all things, then every opinion is true; in fact Protagoras says explicitly that whatever seems true to anyone is true for him to whom it seems so. Now, everyone, even Protagoras, believes that some men are wiser than others; but the difference between most men and Protagoras lies in the fact that most men believe the wise are wise on account of the truth of their opinions, and the unwise are ignorant on account of their false opinions. But if all opinions are true, as Protagoras says, and if the majority holds the opinion just now attributed to them, then this opinion–namely that some opinions are false–is true; and thus Protagoras is convicted of contradicting himself. What is most embarrassing: most people believe that Protagoras' theory is false, and since he admits that their opinion is true, he admits that his theory is false. . . . The next step in Plato's refutation of Protagoras concerns the physician or statesman who changes bad appearances to good. Let it be granted that one medical theory and one political proposal is as true or just as any other. . . .If opinion made it so, then everyone would always be healthy and prosperous. No plan would ever fail. . . .[T]he logical absurdity of Protagoras' admitting the falsity of his thesis and the *ad hominem* reply based on Protagoras' claim to greater accuracy in prediction, may be taken as sufficient refutation not only of the ancient doctrine that all opinions are true but also all the modern dilettante relativism that dismisses important controversies as merely a matter of opinion. Superficial minds still think that a proposition can be divested of its authoritative truthfulness and reduced to the innocuous level of all nondescript beliefs by castigating it as somebody's opinion.[33]

Having successfully refuted the sophists, Plato developed an alternative understanding of ultimate reality. He recognized that the ultimate reality must be incorporeal rather than corporeal. That is, reality is not a material substance. In place of the former philosophic materialism of the pre-Socratics, Plato offered his philosophy of ideas. He argued that everything in the universe was nothing but an imperfect representation

---

[33] Ibid, pp. 66-67.

of a perfect idea. For example, there are many types of physical objects that are each called chairs. In Plato's understanding there must, therefore, be a perfect idea of a chair after which all the actual examples of chairs are patterned. Thus, Plato argued that there is a spiritual world of ideas which parallels the physical world.

Aristotle (384-322) was one of Plato's students and while he shared Plato's criticism of the sophists, he did not share his philosophy of ideas. He thought that a parallel world of ideas was simply superfluous and argued instead for a philosophy of forms which are put into motion by an Unmoved Mover. Aristotle believed that the universe was the result of a First Cause. In the process of making his argument, Aristotle focused on the use of logic as a means of gathering knowledge about the universe. He viewed logic as a structure of coherent thought, not as a science in and of itself. It was logic which forced him to propose the necessity of an ultimate, immutable Being. Greek philosophers attached several names to such a Being, including First Cause, Unmoved Mover, and Logos.

In arguing for such a Being, it would appear that Aristotle shared a conception of God that paralleled that of the Hebrews earlier and of the Christians later. However, this was not true. His conception of a First Cause was more closely linked to an impersonal and immutable force which provided an order to nature rather than to a personal God who created and sustained the universe providentially. In our present discussion, there are several important points. First, Socrates, Plato, and Aristotle effectively demonstrated that the material universe cannot be explained from itself but must be explained on an immaterial (spiritual) basis. While Plato and Aristotle disagreed as to the nature of this reality, they both affirmed that it must be.

Second, when people disregard some spiritual explanation of the physical universe and despair of knowing the truth, it results in the proliferation of pragmatism, which pays lip service to issues of justice, fairness, and morality. In the midst of such pragmatism, civilization inevitably declines. This is extremely important because in our own day skepticism, and its resulting pragmatism, has flourished. For this reason, the prospect for the continuation of Western civilization would seem to be bleak.

Of final importance was Aristotle's discovery of logic. Consistent, orderly thought is crucial in intellectual advancement. Throughout time, before Aristotle himself, logical thought was fundamental to a sound education. This is as true today as it was then. If we are to have a proper understanding of things, then our thoughts cannot be confused, chaotic, and contradictory. Instead, a proper understanding of reality is ordered, concise, and clear.

III. *Alexander and the Spread of Hellenism*

Philip II of Macedon was king from 359-336 B.C. During that period of time he developed a well-trained army and set his sights on the conquest of Greece. Philip was enamored by Greece. He was fascinated with Greek culture, philosophy, and life and sought to unify the region through military means. In his book on Greece, Will Durant captured a bit of Philip's character for us:

> He was strong in body and will, athletic and handsome, a magnificent animal trying, now and then, to be an Athenian gentleman. Like his famous son he was a man of violent temper and abounding generosity, loving battle as much, and strong drink more. Unlike Alexander, he was a jovial laugher, and raised to high office a slave who amused him. . . .He had a subtle intelligence, capable of patiently awaiting his chance, and of moving resolutely through difficult means to distant ends. In diplomacy he was affable and treacherous; he broke a promise with a light heart, and was always ready to make another; he recognized no morals for government and looked upon lies and bribes as humane substitutes for slaughter.[34]

By 338 he completed his conquest of Greece. Rather than rule it directly as a large empire, he formed the Hellenic League which theoretically gave each city-state its independence under the terms of membership to the organization. Of course, the terms of membership greatly limited the freedom of the individual city-state to truly have the liberty of self-determination. Nevertheless, such an organization was not wholly foreign to the Greeks and was likely a wise decision for maintaining governance.

---

[34] Will Durant, op. cit., pp. 475-76.

One of the first acts of the league was to declare war on Persia. In doing so, Philip hoped to include all of the Greek city-states of Asia Minor in his loosely structured empire. However, he never had the opportunity to engage the Persians because he was assassinated in 336 before the confrontation could begin. His son Alexander ascended to the throne instead.

Alexander was only twenty years of age when he took over his father's position. Earlier in Alexander's life, Philip had procured the services of Aristotle as his tutor. For most of Alexander's life the two remained on friendly terms. "Physically, Alexander was an ideal youth. He was good in every sport: a swift runner, a dashing horseman, a brilliant fencer, a practiced bowman, a fearless hunter. . . .He liked hard work and dangerous enterprises, and could not bear to rest. . . .He was abstemious in eating, and, until his last years, in drinking, though he loved to linger with his friends over a goblet of wine."[35]

When Philip was killed, many Greeks thought it would be a good time to reassert their independence. In their view, Alexander posed no threat because they thought he was too young and too inexperienced. They assumed it would be an easy thing to reject him as their ruler. Acting upon this belief, many of the city-states chose the occasion of Philip's death to rebel against Macedon. To their chagrin, Alexander proved to be a far more capable leader than they had anticipated and in the first two years following the death of his father he put down the rebellion.

Having secured the kingdom, Alexander began his famous conquest of the Persian Empire. His army crossed the Hellespont in 334 and overpowered the first Persians at the Granicus river. After working his way down the coast of Asia Minor, he turned into the hinterland and then back down toward the coast where he met the main body of the Persian army at Issus. His military strategy in battle proved successful against what had appeared to be overwhelming odds. Darius III was able to escape Alexander's grasp at Issus. However, he was not so fortunate when he tried to escape again at Gaugamela. At that confrontation, the Macedonians once again proved to be superior in battle. As the situation grew worse, many Persians fled from the fight. Darius was among the first

---

[35] Ibid, pp. 538-39.

to do so. His decision to flee for his life prompted his own generals to assassinate him for cowardice. It was the decisive blow. The Persian Empire had come to an end and Alexander subsequently took control of the cities of Susa, Persepolis, and Ecbatana. From there he pushed all the way to the Indus River. While he wanted to continue his conquest, his soldiers would go no farther. Just the same, his empire stretched from Greece to India to Egypt.

Alexander's triumph over the Near East and Egypt took nine years. In the beginning, he sought to Hellenize the world. But, after spending such a long period of time in the Near East, he decided to promote unity by joining together the various cultures of the world. In his pursuit of unity, he attempted to thoroughly mix all cultures and all peoples. He thought that this would put an end to conflict. By eliminating the differences that separated people from one another, he thought that hostility among them would cease. That is not to say that Greek culture was to take a back seat in the process. In fact, Alexander intended to make Greek culture fundamental to achieving the necessary change. He married the daughter of Darius III as well as the daughter of Artaxerxes III in order to promote his plan to achieve cultural unity. In addition, he encouraged his military leaders to do likewise and take for themselves wives of other cultures.

The military campaign took a heavy toll on Alexander. In the two years following the campaign, Alexander's best friend died and he began to drink heavily. The combination of these factors led to his own death at an early age. His death left a vast empire without an heir to the throne. The result was a power struggle among the highest ranking military men in his army as each sought to seize control. In the course of this struggle, three kingdoms emerged: the Egyptian, the Seleucid, and the Macedonian.

While Alexander's conquest set the stage for the spread of Greek culture around the Mediterranean world, the fusion of races to produce one unified race of people never materialized. The Greeks were more or less tolerated depending upon how badly they oppressed the various subjugated peoples. In the Seleucid Empire, which encompassed the territory of the main part of the Persian Empire, there were cities of predominantly Greek influence amidst the larger mass of people who remained mostly Oriental in their thinking, speaking, and acting. The Ptolemaic Empire of Egypt was still dominated by Greek culture even though Alexandria was a melting pot of sorts. In addition, there were distinct separations of people by heritage. The peoples conquered in these regions saw no compelling reason to accept all things Greek. To understand some of the dispersion of Greek culture and the tensions of life which it sometimes created, two examples are perhaps worthwhile. First, we will consider the case of the Jews in Judea and next the rule of Egypt by the Ptolemies.

A.   The Attempt to Hellenize Judea

In seizing control of portions of Alexander's empire, Ptolemy I succeeded in establishing rule over Egypt, Palestine, and Phoenicia. Thus Judea, which had been repopulated by Jews who had returned there from their Babylonian exile during the Persian Empire, was initially under the control of the Ptolemies. This situation was never well accepted by the Seleucids and in 198 B.C., during the reign of Antiochus III, they gained sway over the region by driving the Ptolemies back into Egypt. The change in governance was at first celebrated by the Jews in Judea. Over time, however, this celebration ended and the Jews developed a deep hatred for the Seleucids. This occurred when Antiochus IV attempted to fully Hellenize the region.

Governing Judea was always a challenge. The peculiar religious practices of the Jews separated them from the Greek melting pot. For a ruler bent on assimilating all people under his control into a unified whole, these differences were a formidable obstacle. For example, Jewish law forbade marrying non-Jews. It also prohibited worshiping any god but Yahweh. These statutes, coupled with their dietary laws and other restrictions in daily life, separated them from other people. It was, therefore, impossible to assimilate the Jewish people into a common culture. In fact, the end could not have been accomplished unless all the other cultures had been willing to adopt the Jewish way of life. This, of course, was not what the Greek rulers had in mind. As a result, the Jews remained somewhat of an enigma and there was always tension between them and other people with whom they had contact.

Given this situation, Antiochus III wisely granted the Jews the right to worship in their prescribed manner and to carry on life within the context of their faith, as long as they continued to pay their taxes and tribute. Antiochus remained an ambitious man who sought to expand his sphere of influence. He did this, but overstepped his bounds by invading Greece. The Macedonian Kingdom had fallen victim to Rome, and Greece was under Roman control. Thus, when Antiochus trespassed upon their domain, the Romans immediately declared war on his nation and drove him back into Asia. Having defeated him, the Romans made a number of specific demands to which he acquiesced, because he was in no position to resist. As a result, the Romans took his son, Antiochus IV, hostage as part of the terms of settlement.

It was an embarrassing defeat and left Antiochus in serious financial difficulty. In 187 he was killed trying to rob a temple. His other son, Seleucid IV, took the throne and reigned until 175 when he was assassinated. At the time of his assassination, his brother was in the process of returning from Rome. When Antiochus Epiphanes discovered that his brother was dead, he took control of the Seleucidian Empire. Having been held hostage in Rome, and thus knowing the extent of Roman power, Antiochus sought to further unify his kingdom. To do this he imposed new rules aimed at furthering the Hellenization of the region. In Judea, he made Jason, a Greek sympathizer, high priest, because he promised not only to secularize the Jewish religion, but to funnel Temple funds to the royal palace as well. In his further efforts to bring unity, he replaced Jason with Menelaus, who was even more fervent in his support of Hellenization. During this time, the Temple was turned into a place for the secular worship of Zeus, and the Jews were prohibited from continuing the practices of circumcision and the maintenance of their dietary laws. Antiochus sought to unify his domain so completely that he used whatever force was necessary to bring it about. As a result, he mandated the death penalty for anyone who violated the law. He burned copies of the Scriptures and executed a large number of Jews who continued to practice their religion.

Antiochus was intensely hated by those who were faithful to the Jewish religion. Because of his intolerant stance, there was a great deal of bloodshed. Those unwilling to submit to Hellenization were sought out, persecuted, and killed. As the violence grew, an underground resistance movement erupted into the Maccabean rebellion led by Judas the Maccabee. From 166 to 164 his forces succeeded in driving the Greeks out of Jerusalem and the surrounding area. In December of 164 the Jews rededicated the Temple to the worship of Yahweh. This event is still celebrated by Jews today as Hanukkah. In 163, Antiochus died as the

Seleucids were preparing military action to retake Jerusalem. Given the financial difficulties of the Seleucid Empire, the threat of Rome, and the high cost of subduing the rebellion, the new ruler wisely allowed the Jews to resume their religious freedom.

This example demonstrates that the attempt to unify culture, race, religion, and language through the use of force is a doomed enterprise. In fact, such efforts, rather than promoting civilization, contribute to the destruction of it. From this we see the profound wisdom that Jesus demonstrated when he refused the temptation to set up his kingdom by the use of force. When the devil offered to make Christ the king over the whole earth if he would but worship him, Jesus made it clear that he would only worship God. Furthermore, before his crucifixion, when Pilate questioned him about being a king, Jesus responded that his kingdom was not of this world. In fact, the apostle Paul laid out the importance of this in his second letter to the Corinthians when he wrote, "For though we walk in the flesh, we do not war according to the flesh. For the weapons of our warfare are not carnal but mighty in God for pulling down strongholds, casting down arguments and every high thing that exalts itself against the knowledge of God, bringing every thought into captivity to the obedience of Christ. . ."[36] The significance of this is that the founder of the Christian religion, which seeks unity in Christ's kingdom, assumes that his kingdom is established not by force but by persuasion of human minds and hearts. That is not to say that followers of Christ have never succumbed to the temptation to use force. Rather, it is to make clear that Jesus' followers cannot act in such ways and be consistent with his teaching.

B. The Ptolemaic Empire

As mentioned above, the Ptolemaic Empire of Egypt was established by Ptolemy I, son of Lagus, who was one of Alexander's generals. When Alexander died, Ptolemy brought his body to Memphis and placed it in a coffin made of gold. While other men of power fought each other in the Near East in an effort to seize control over all of Alexander's empire, Ptolemy consolidated his power and rule in Egypt

---

[36] 2 Corinthians 10: 3-5.

and, thus, broke away from the empire. He established the city of Alexandria as the seat of his new domain.

Under the Ptolemies, Egypt was ruled as a despotic state. The royal family assumed the ownership of all land and of everything that was produced on it. Thus, the royal family decided how much produce the average person was allowed to keep and consume. Tyranny of this type was possible because of Egypt's long tradition of believing that the king was a god. As a result, the ruling family maintained a state monopoly over every form of enterprise, and a large bureaucracy developed to manage the kingdom. Controls were so extensive that the state reserved for itself the right to requisition the use of any and all property throughout its province.

Government officials instructed farmers about which fields to cultivate and which crops to grow. They controlled all mining operations and every major industry in the region. While minor industries were left in private hands, they were heavily taxed. Large tariffs were imposed on foreign products which might otherwise compete with state products and all trade routes through the region were monitored by state officials to extract heavy tolls from trade.

These parasitic practices allowed the royal family to amass a huge fortune. With this extracted wealth, they were able to undertake massive public projects and dabbled in a host of personal interests. As a result, the capital city of Alexandria flourished. As evidence of this, the Ptolemies established both a museum and a library that contained extensive collections. In addition, state funds were used to support an army of scholars and writers for the purpose of advancing the arts and sciences. By such heavy expenditures, Alexandria became a cultural mecca. A visitor to the city in those days would have been most impressed by the magnitude of the visible accomplishments of the rulers.

But these accomplishments were somewhat superficial. They existed for a relatively brief time by the extensive oppression of the Egyptian people. The bureaucratic system put in place by the Ptolemies resulted in rampant favoritism, partiality in matters of justice, and the exploitation of a vast number of people. The capricious acts of bureaucrats destroyed the incentives of the average individual to participate in production. In time, workers banded together and refused to work unless they received higher pay or better working conditions. In addition, racial tensions mounted because the bureaucrats were largely

Greek, while the workers were either Egyptian or Jewish. Beyond these difficulties, more and more resources were devoted to financing military campaigns. To maintain their position, the Ptolemies gradually compromised to appease the people. Nevertheless, conditions worsened.

Even in the arts and sciences, socialism led to deterioration rather than advancement. As Will Durant observed:

> It was above all an age of intellectuals and scholars. Writing became a profession instead of a devotion, and generated cliques and coteries whose appreciation of talent varied inversely as the square of its distance from themselves. Poets began to write for poets, and became artificial; scholars began to write for scholars, and became dull. Thoughtful men felt that the creative inspiration of Greece was nearing exhaustion, and that the most lasting service they could render was to collect, shelter, edit, and expound the literary achievements of a bolder time.[37]

On the surface, it appeared that huge monetary expenditures were advancing the arts and sciences, but below the surface many possible advancements were delayed for years. One of the prime examples of this was the earth-centered theory developed by the Ptolemies. Though the theory was inconsistent with the facts, the researchers made it plausible by increasing the complexity of the theory itself rather than looking for another option. Such complexity gave the theory an appearance of being intellectually superior even though it was wrong. Over time, this error in thought was promoted so strongly that it was dogmatically held. So much so, that it came to be seen as part of the Holy canon of the Christian religion.

This case raises the question as to whether such state expenditures for scholarship can actually produce anything of lasting value, or whether they more often result in the proliferation of some error which suits the interests of those in charge. In the example considered, the more correct conception of the order of the cosmos had to develop in spite of the fact that the authorities persecuted the scientists for challenging the canon of faith. That the actual advancement arose in this way suggests that

---

[37] Will Durant, op. cit., pp 602-3.

coercive efforts to advance the arts and sciences are as much folly as the attempt to stifle them.

From this example, we learn something else of the limitations of force. As Henry Weaver has stated so clearly,

> Force and fear have their uses. . . but they are ineffective in stimulating ambition, initiative, creative effort, and perseverance. Threats of the concentration camp or the firing squad might make a man run a little faster or work a little harder—at least for a time—but fear reduces endurance and hastens fatigue. It also works at cross-purposes to mental development and moral growth. It depresses the higher nerve centers, and its continued use tends to paralyze the normal processes of thought.[38]

Study Questions

1. Describe what life was like in Sparta. Compare and contrast life there to that in Athens. What underlying beliefs about life account for the differences?
2. What was the Confederacy of Delos? How was its purpose altered after the threat of a Persian invasion subsided? What resulted from this change in purpose?
3. What is philosophy and how did it develop in Greece?
4. What was the underlying impasse in the early corporeal philosophies? How did this impasse result in the rise of sophism?
5. How did Socrates challenge the sophists?
6. Compare and contrast the philosophies of Plato and Aristotle.
7. What motivated Alexander the Great to set out to conquer the world?
8. What was Alexander's emerging plan to Hellenize the world?
9. How did Hellenization change after Alexander's death?

---

[38] Henry Grady Weaver, *The Mainspring of Human Progress*, (Irvington, NY: Foundation for Economic Education, 1947), pp.57-8.

10. Why were the Jews a more or less constant problem for the Seleucids? In what ways did these rulers attempt to deal with this problem?

11. Discuss the way in which the Ptolemies ruled Egypt.

Chapter 6: The Roman Empire

I. The Roman Republic

The people who populated Italy were a mixture of two groups that migrated there from different places. The first group came from Africa. They were short and dark-skinned people who were later joined by Indo-Europeans who came into Italy from the north. Together, these people settled down and mixed with one another to form the local ethnic stock. In time, other groups of people settled on the peninsula as well. In particular, Greek and Etruscan colonists migrated there around 900 B.C. They introduced new ideas and new cultures to the locals.

As was true of other regions of the world, city-states developed from the congregation of local tribes in certain areas. Rome was one such city. When the Etruscans colonized the west coast of the peninsula, they were not content to establish their own city-states. Instead, they conquered and subjugated other cities to themselves. Rome fell under Etruscan rule in this process and their dominance of the region continued for quite some time. Eventually, in 509 B.C., the people of Rome rebelled against the Etruscans. They successfully overthrew their rule and gained independence. In setting up their own rule, the Romans developed a unique governmental form. They established a senate and a couple of assemblies which were each controlled by various factions of the population. In addition, instead of having a king, they elected two consuls to handle the daily duties of administration. This marked the beginning of the Roman Republic.

Before discussing the development of Rome further, it will first be valuable to discuss two schools of philosophy that emerged after Plato and Aristotle, Stoicism and Epicureanism. The tension between these philosophies had a significant impact on the way in which the Roman Empire developed. As a fundamental point of reference, both schools tended to reject the belief that the ultimate reality was immaterial. This left the door open for the resurgence of philosophical materialism. Beyond this common point of reference, both schools used their respective understanding of nature to develop ethical systems of behavior. That is, each sought to provide a map of how people should live their lives in this world.

The Stoic point of view is generally traced back to Zeno of Citium, while the Epicurean philosophy is associated with Epicurus, from whom its name derives. Since both of these philosophers lived around 300 B.C., their resulting schools of thought were associated with this date. However, the ideas behind their teaching were not entirely new and can be traced back to pre-Socratic philosophers. This is important because as we begin to consider the development of Rome, we will classify the people of the early era as Stoic, even though Stoicism as a school of philosophy had yet to make its appearance. This is not a problem because what is important are the ideas that the philosophy taught and not the philosophy itself. Since the ideas upon which this philosophy was built were not new at Rome's founding, it follows that it is quite possible to classify the Romans as proponents of Stoicism, since they professed and lived more or less consistently with its major tenets.

With that said, let us examine some of the fundamental principles of Stoicism and Epicureanism. Stoicism was a materialistic view of the world which assumed that change occurred in a deterministic manner. Alternatively, Epicureanism assumed that motion and change were indeterminate. This was the major distinction in thought between the two philosophies. Surprisingly, this distinction led to dramatically different conclusions as to what was important and valuable in this life. Because Stoics believed in mechanistic determinism, they also believed in fatalism. Their view of fate was not so much that a man could do nothing to affect his situation, but that whatever he did would have predetermined results. In their view, the results of any action were determined beforehand by natural laws that establish boundaries for human action. Based upon the Stoic point of view, the ideal of life was virtuous and moral. Put briefly, moral behavior was seen as the kind of behavior that fit best within the context of the rules of nature. Vices were to be avoided because they were unnatural and a person was supposed to live his life by adhering to moral principles, conforming his life to the natural laws of behavior. Therefore, a Stoic tended to promote the virtues of building a strong family life and of fulfilling his social and civic duties. Stoics encouraged people to be patriotic, prudent, temperate, and judicious. They believed in self-discipline and moderation and frowned on wantonness and self-indulgence.

Alternatively, the Epicureans rejected determinism. They argued instead that the world was more free flowing than deterministic. Therefore, they rejected the notion that the results of human action were those that followed necessarily from some predetermined design. As for the soul, they believed that it died when the person died and so assigned no particular meaning to it. In their view, the greatest good, was the pursuit of pleasure and the avoidance of pain. They concluded this because all men naturally gravitated towards pleasurable things and were repulsed by things which caused pain. Furthermore, the enjoyment of this life was the important thing and this end was for them the wise man's guiding force. For this reason, Epicureans of all ages have tended to avoid activities that involved pain. It was also why Epicurus, himself, argued against having a family. He thought that a wise man would not have one because it would be a hindrance to his own enjoyment. While Epicurus argued vigorously against participating in gross immorality, preferring instead an ascetic life which avoided the human pain of a guilty conscience, many adherents of his philosophy eventually disgraced themselves by participating in a number of grossly immoral activities while pursuing some immediate pleasurable end.

The importance of distinguishing between Stoicism and Epicureanism is that a better understanding of the history of Rome can be gained as one observes the level of acceptance of the points of view offered by each school. As stated above, the early Romans were most accurately classified as Stoic. There was a common understanding that human laws ought to be consistent with natural laws if peace and order were to result. This concept provided the basis for Roman society and established the foundation upon which it developed its institutions that were intended to secure the development of civil relations among men. It was this understanding that resulted in the particular form of republic government which the Romans formed. This showed much wisdom, because men can never develop peace and order among themselves if they disregard the natural order in regards to their relationships with each other by legislating laws to suit the interests of those with political power. In turn, the dispersion of power amongst the factions of the population was prudent and provided certain checks on individual behavior. Regrettably, in the course of time, Rome discovered the truth of this proposition when she began to abandon the principles upon which she was founded.

The fact that Stoic ideals were prominent in Rome is not meant to suggest that the Roman people had abandoned the pagan polytheism and the superstitions it engendered. Such a conclusion is wholly unwarranted. In fact, the Romans maintained the same kind of paganism as that held by the people of Greece and the Near East. They believed in a pantheon of gods, who more or less controlled their destinies. What was new in their beliefs was the notion that there was some order in the administration of divine rewards and punishments. This idea became so prevalent among Roman philosophers, that some of them rejected the pantheon in favor of a sort of monotheistic pantheism. For them, the Greek concept of the Logos, which divinely ruled over nature, crowded out the notion of multiple gods. Of course, those who held this view were the exception rather than the rule among the general populace.

Based upon this system of beliefs, the Roman Republic began as well as any state before it and much better than most. Given their strong commitment to moral living, the Romans developed strong family ties and, as has already been pointed out, established a rather remarkable form of government: a limited democracy which fostered wide civic participation but limited the abuses of mob rule. The people of Rome were generally patriotic, loyal, honest, and strong. Like the Spartans, they could also withstand adverse circumstances because they were raised to revere the virtues of courage and perseverance.

While these traits of character bode well for Roman civilization, there were a number of negatives. As has always been true, given the depravity of men, the demise of the Etruscans was also the occasion for conquest. Indeed, attempts to conquer Italy quickly followed. Rome defended herself well and other communities began to look to her for protection. This she provided, but as her strength grew, she became a threat rather than a protector. Finally a series of wars broke out among the nearby city-states. In 336 B.C. the conflict ended with the Roman conquest of the area. Though Rome was still many years from its future glory, this success marked the beginning of the decline of civilization.

The first problem to be dealt with was the issue of how to treat subjugated peoples. To their credit, the Romans showed much wisdom by refraining from sharp brutality and even extended citizenship to some people. Just the same, they did not offer such benefits to everyone whom they had conquered. Far from it, in fact, because some people were reduced to slavery. The result of this activity was to intensify the separation of classes under Roman rule and to increase the strife between classes. This was compounded by the fact that the resources of conquered communities were seen as a ready means of financing the public interests of Rome. As such, foreign wealth was often tapped for military purposes and used to finance public projects.

Rome's rise to power during this time became a threat to the Carthaginian control of Mediterranean trade. Carthage was established by the Phoenicians on the northern coast of Africa very near modern day Tunis. As pointed out in an earlier chapter, the Phoenicians were excellent seamen and made their living by trading with others throughout the Mediterranean world. To facilitate this trade, they developed numerous ports to supply their ships which traversed the seas hauling goods and resources from where they could be found to where they were desired. Carthage was one of the ports that they founded.

Carthage grew in importance as wealthy Phoenicians fled from Asia during the empires of the Assyrians, Babylonians, Persians, and Greeks. As a result, the population of Carthage swelled and the city flourished. These people brought with them as much wealth as they could and reestablished their businesses out of the reach of both the empires they left behind and of the heavy taxes those empires levied. Estates were established and numerous enterprises grew.

The Phoenicians were secretive about their trading practices. They did not want to compete with any other merchants and thought it best not to divulge any information that was useful to them in their business activities. They were able to maintain their monopoly so long as no one else ventured into their domain. In earlier times Carthage had reached agreements with Rome which limited the scope of Roman enterprise. These agreements were made when the Romans had little choice but to accept the arrangements because they were ill-equipped to challenge Carthage's control. However, as Rome grew stronger, she became more of a threat to the Carthaginian dominance of Mediterranean trade. Rome's desire to expand by trade and conquest eventually led to conflict between these two powerful city-states and to the Punic Wars.

The first Punic War was fought between 264-241 B.C. The main issue of the conflict was over who would control Sicily. Rome initially sent a sizable army to Sicily, but was never able to achieve victory because of Carthage's control over the sea. Given this situation, they were able to continue to supply their soldiers and maintain their presence on the island. This prompted the Romans to build a navy. After completing construction of a number of ships and learning to sail, the Romans set their sights on Carthage itself. Unfortunately, this first effort failed when the fleet suffered serious losses in a storm. After rebuilding her navy, Rome was able to cut off Carthaginian supply lines and Carthage withdrew from Sicily.

The second Punic War was fought between 218-201 B.C. While the first conflict ended with the Carthaginian withdrawal, they never really conceded defeat and were constantly looking for a way to regain their advantage. In the first Punic War, Hamilcar had been a Carthaginian hero. After being defeated by the Romans, he went to Spain to strengthen the Carthaginian presence there and to establish a base from which he could attack Italy. He was killed in Spain while trying to secure his position. His son, Hannibal, eventually emerged as the new Carthaginian leader. Since he had sworn as much to his father, he was intent on vengeance against Rome. In 218 B.C. he made his famous crossing of the Alps using elephants as pack animals. It was a treacherous journey and many of his men and animals died along the way, but he finally made it across the mountains. The first groups of people he met along the way, were tribes of Gauls who welcomed him. Over the next two years Hannibal was unbeatable and defeated numerous Roman armies. As a result, the Romans withdrew to Rome and left the rest of Italy to Hannibal. For the next fifteen years Hannibal had his way on the peninsula. Meanwhile, the Romans decided to launch a counteroffensive. They deployed armies to Spain and Sicily. The Roman leadership believed that if they could control these two regions they could cut Hannibal off from any support. After securing victories in these places, they pressed their attack against Carthage itself. It was the decisive move in the war. Hannibal was called back to Carthage to protect his home, but it was too late, and the Romans defeated the Carthaginians. While the Carthaginians attempted to revive their fortunes, Rome emerged as the undisputed master of the Western Mediterranean.

Victorious in conquest, the Romans continued their pursuit of riches at the expense of their neighbors. Over the course of the next few generations, the virtues of Stoicism were traded for the pleasures of

Epicureanism by the Roman people. Having secured the Western Mediterranean, the Romans turned their attention eastward: in 200 B.C. Rome declared war on Macedon. In four years of conflict she defeated Macedon, and all of Greece fell under her influence. Initially, Rome withdrew her army from the region, but that left the door open for Antiochus III to invade Greece, as we have already seen. This prompted the Romans to return to the region to defeat Antiochus. Afterwards, a constant Roman presence was maintained in Greece.

In time, the Roman Empire expanded throughout the Mediterranean world. As the empire grew, the fortunes of war flowed back to Rome. Money and slaves poured into central Italy. The owners of businesses bought slaves to do their work. Slaves were used in agriculture, manufacturing, mining and many other economic activities. In fact, slaves displaced most all of the local free laborers, and these lower and middle class Roman citizens found themselves unemployed. They were more than a little dissatisfied with this turn of events. As discontentment grew, new political opportunities grew as well. Some political leaders began to use public funds which had been gained by the exploitation of conquered peoples to provide food, clothing, and entertainment for the now idle Roman populace. These wasteful expenditures set the stage for further political infighting and rebellion.

Much of the entertainment was provided at public games. These games were primarily athletic events. For example, foot racing, discus throwing, wrestling, and boxing were among the competitions held. In addition to these, there were also gladiatorial exhibitions. These might involve a duel between two men or a fight between two groups of men. Or, they might also have involved fights between animals or fights between animals and men. The gladiators themselves were usually criminals who had been convicted of capital crimes. These crimes included murder, robbery, arson, mutiny, and sacrilege. It was this latter crime which was used by later emperors to persecute the Christians, because they refused to worship the pagan gods of Rome. As a result, a large number of these people were killed at that public games. Most people justified the brutality of these spectacles by various rationalizations. However, some of the more committed Stoics remained repulsed by them and saw in them no redeeming value.

Other forms of entertainment were chariot races, horse races, theatrical performances, and exhibitions of exotic animals. Gambling on the chariot and horse races was commonplace. More and more Roman life revolved around these activities and the demand for them increased. Government authorities responded to the demands by putting on more events and by constructing buildings in which they could be held. Over time, many such facilities were built including the Circus Flaminus, the Circus Maximus, and the Colosseum. While the Colosseum was the venue for many events, its primary use was for gladiatorial competitions. The important point is that this was how idle Romans spent their time. Regrettably, the pleasure they took in seeing people die in mortal combat fed the more debased passions of the human heart. These things were the symptoms of the breakdown of civilization which Rome was experiencing because of her increasing disregard of the divine commands of God and of the endowed rights of people in general. The republic was in decline.

II. Revolution and the Rise of the Emperors of Rome

Plunder, pillage, and slavery was becoming the source of Roman wealth rather than private production. Those with political connections used their positions to gain control over more property and used slaves to work it for them. Slavery became more barbaric than it had ever been before. Prior to the Roman Empire, slaves throughout the world had been treated relatively well and had freedom to move about the communities in which they lived. However, as the empire progressed, slaves were more and more viewed as simple property, to be fed and clothed only in order to secure their labor for some intended purpose. Since political position was a means by which people acquired wealth, bribery, perjury, and corruption were rampant. People sold their votes to the highest bidder, and politicians took out large loans to buy them. The politician knew that once the political position was secured he could exploit it for more than enough money to repay the loan and make himself wealthy at the same time.

A successful politician sometimes found it worthwhile to curry the favor of the idle masses by promising them some new reform aimed at taking the property of the wealthy for their benefit. Among the first politicians to use class strife to further their own ambitions were Tiberius and Gauis Gracchus. These brothers emerged upon the political scene with the promise to redistribute land for the benefit of the lower classes. They were, of course, opposed by the wealthier landowners who controlled the Senate and, in the end, had both men killed. Still, there was growing discontentment among the people. They were becoming so focused on their bellies and on their own pleasures that they failed to consider the importance of morality. Increasingly, they ignored matters of justice. Instead, the two classes of Roman society, the *optimates* (the ruling elite that controlled the Senate) and the *populares* (the poor and middle classes), debased themselves for immediate pleasures provided by the efforts of slaves and by the oppression of subjugated peoples. Political power and control were seen as the instruments of fulfilling personal desires, and this resulted in near constant conflict between the *optimates* and the *populares*, whose individual interests were now at odds with one another.

The struggle for power went on year after year, and Rome appeared to be heading for certain collapse as a result of internal strife. It was in the midst of this situation that men like Julius Caesar and Pompey rose to positions of power and prestige. Each of these men was overly ambitious and sought to rule Rome as a dictator. In time, Caesar emerged victorious over Pompey, but in turn, he was assassinated by Brutus.

This is not to say that the Stoic philosophy which had been the tradition of Rome was completely abandoned. Actually, there were a number of people who watched with disgust the abuses made of government power. They were repulsed by the political action that advanced the interests of the well-heeled. Perhaps chief among them was a man named Cicero. He was a man of resolute courage and conviction who led the resistance against the military leaders who were undermining the Republic. In addition, he disdained the Roman games, and pointed out repeatedly that such events brought out the worst in human character. Cicero was a man of moderation and moral fortitude in the midst of an exceedingly corrupt environment.

When the showdown between Caesar and Pompey occurred, Cicero sided with the loser. Nonetheless, Julius Caesar did not press the issue and allowed Cicero to retire from political life. Thereafter, he spent a number of years writing down his ideas about human nature, natural laws, and the fundamentals of government. When Caesar was murdered, Cicero returned to the public stage to denounce the upstart Mark Antony. Antony purposed to use the opportunity of Caesar's death to seize the throne for himself. Cicero rightly saw him as just another overly ambitious man who would subsequently use the power of government to secure his own egotistical desires. He, therefore, opposed Antony. In so doing he sealed his own fate, for Antony successfully pressed the government for Cicero's life. Mark Antony's soldiers apprehended him at his coastal villa and killed him there.

While Cicero's efforts to stem the tide of debauchery and injustice in his country were unsuccessful, his writings had a profound impact on the nature of the United States government. In devising the government of the United States, the framers of the American Constitution sought to emulate some of the better qualities of the Roman Republic. They knew Cicero's writings well and drew upon them frequently in their efforts to form a new government. In particular, they were very much impressed with his views about separating the powers of government in order to limit the potential for abuse. They understood from Cicero that a monarchy is only as good as its king, that an aristocracy is only as good as its nobility, and that a democracy inevitably turns into mob rule because of the depravity of men. As such, the American Founders attempted to construct a government which was limited in its scope but which could still carry out the functions for which it was needed. Specifically, they sought to secure for all citizens the protection of life, liberty, and property. It seems somehow strange that it took so long for such a government to be created, but given the current state of affairs in the United States, perhaps the natural course of events is that all governments tend to operate as systems of corruption and injustice. At any rate, during the fall of Rome, the government was increasingly corrupt.

Caesar's death brought about a renewed struggle for the empire and Mark Antony was at the forefront of the fight for power. In addition, Caesar's adopted son, Octavian, joined the contest. The resulting conflict between Octavian and his adversary Antony was the determining factor in Rome's future. In this struggle for power, Octavian was victorious and defeated Antony at Actium. Having defeated him there, Octavian pursued Antony to Egypt. It was there that Mark Antony committed suicide, leaving Octavian in the unquestioned position of power.

When he returned to Rome, Octavian showed remarkable wisdom by abandoning rather than seizing control. Nevertheless, the Senate conferred upon him the title Augustus, which many in history have mistaken for his name. Augustus Caesar was also given the authority to rule Rome as an emperor, which he did from 27 B.C.- A.D. 14. He was a most capable ruler. During his reign, Rome enjoyed a time of peace which had not existed for many years. He settled many of the conflicts which divided the classes. As a result of the intelligence he showed, Roman stability returned. Also of interest is his admiration of Cicero and of Cicero's writings. He thought highly of the man and of his view of life. Perhaps this accounts for some of his success.

Of course, there were some negatives. During his rule he greatly expanded the money supply by aggressively mining precious metals and minting them into coins. In and of itself this activity was not troublesome, except for the fact that he, as others before him, assumed ownership of all precious metals and used slaves to mine them. The combination of these two factors led him to deplete these resources at a rate far faster than warranted by economic conditions. Initially, the rapid increase in the money supply created the appearance of prosperity. However, as time passed, the mines began to play out, and a strong incentive to debase the coinage arose. Such fictions as debasement could not be maintained forever. When it became known that the money was devalued, the empire suffered a number of economic hardships. In essence, by rapidly mining the resource for his own benefit, Augustus set the stage for later emperors to defraud the people in an effort to maintain their own financial success. In addition to these future monetary problems, it should also be noted that Augustus spent the money he coined for his personal use as well as the numerous public projects that were constructed. This type of governmental arrangement inevitably skewed the makeup of economic activity toward that most favored politically. In Rome, this had the effect of penalizing the private efforts of those who were not politically connected. Further, he made this condition permanent by virtually guaranteeing that Rome would never be ruled as anything other than an imperial state. The significant downside of imperial rule was that stability always depended upon how well or how badly the emperor ruled. In Rome's future there were both good and bad rulers.

It was not long before Rome suffered under the poor rule of both corrupt and incompetent emperors. Before his death, Augustus decided to make his position hereditary as imperial rule had been throughout the past. When he died, his step-son and son-in-law, Tiberius (A.D. 14-37), became emperor. While Tiberius shared Augustus' Stoic ideals, he was much less capable. To his credit he did recognize the internal damage being done in Rome by continuing the rapid mining and coinage of money which was begun by Augustus. Therefore, he cut the rate of production which reduced the money supply. The natural result was a recession in the Roman economy as business activity promoted by the government declined. Yet, his decision was still a wise one, because it extended the resource and slowed the growing Roman reliance upon monetary reserves as her sole contribution to the rest of the world. He realized that as the mines played out, the Romans' position would be threatened. But, Tiberius was never particularly adept in dealing with people. In time, he was manipulated by those closest to him. In addition, Tiberius was a solitary man, and as the pressures mounted, he withdrew more and more from public life. As a result, there were a number of plots to seize power by those around him. While none were successful, the circumstances and details of his reign left an unfavorable impression. When he died, Gauis, who is better known as Caligula, became emperor of Rome.

Caligula (A.D. 37-41) was a young man obsessed with the power of his position. He quickly lost touch with reality and behaved like a mad man. He thought himself above reproach and disregarded the Stoic virtues of moderation and restraint. Instead, he pampered his every lustful whim. He had no respect for others and thought people existed solely for his amusement. In the pursuit of enjoyment and entertainment, Caligula spent public funds freely. He was so extravagant that he rapidly depleted the treasury. To find other sources of funding, he aggressively raised taxes. Because of his short fuse and unstable character, no one questioned him as he increased his tyrannical hold. More and more he became a lunatic who took great pleasure in inflicting pain on others. While he tried to buy popularity, most people simply hated him, and at the age of twenty-nine one of his own guards took his life in the palace.

After Caligula was murdered, Claudius (A.D. 41-54), who was fifty years old at the time, was made emperor. Claudius had a number of physical aliments, some of which were due to an intemperate lifestyle. Public office was not his aspiration. Rather, he spent most of his time in private intellectual pursuits and enjoying the pleasures of idle merriment. He viewed the demands of an administrative position as too confining for his tastes. For this reason, it was widely believed that he was little more than a harmless buffoon. As such, he was readily accepted as the new emperor. Everyone was glad to be rid of the psychotic Caligula and Claudius seemed harmless. As it turned out, Claudius' mind was exceptionally sharp and he moved swiftly to secure his position by ending many of the oppressive policies that Caligula had started. While his political policies were normally favorable, his own Epicurean tastes proved to be his downfall. He loved wine, women, and song and allowed himself many pleasures. His indulgences ended up costing him his life. His fifth wife married him for the practical purpose of securing the throne for her son. When he found out about the plan, he was determined to name someone else as his successor, but before he could do so his wife poisoned him with mushrooms. When he died, her son Nero (A.D. 54-68) rose to power.

Though it took him somewhat longer to sink to the depths of depravity which Caligula reached in so short a time, Nero nevertheless equaled, if not surpassed, those excesses. He was, perhaps, the worst of the lot. At an early age he gave himself over entirely to sexual license. He participated in the most perverse practices imaginable and found himself given over completely to his vile passions. Nero was not only sexually immoral, but was malicious, deceitful, and unmerciful; he even had his own mother and two wives murdered. In addition to this evil, he actively persecuted those who were just coming to faith in Jesus Christ for their refusal to acknowledge him as a god. So wicked was he that he had many of these people covered with pitch and burned atop poles as luminaries at night. Like Caligula, he drained the public treasury to pay for his dissipation, while pressing the citizenry for ever more money to finance his extravagant tastes. It is even thought that he may have had the city of Rome set on fire so that he could rebuild it according to his own design. Whether or not this is true, he used the occasion to blame the Christians for starting the fire so that he could step up his persecution of them. He was cruel and wasteful. His vanity and arrogance preceded him everywhere. When the people could stand him no longer, he was forced from his position and only avoided assassination by committing suicide.

With Nero's death, a competition among the military leaders for the throne ensued. The winner of the contest was a man named Vespasian. He and his two sons, Titus and Domitian, ruled Rome from A.D. 69-96. Vespasian ruled for the first ten years. He was a man of strong will and practical learning, though he was not particularly known for his great intelligence nor his keen foresight. In fact, he probably had neither. Nevertheless, he worked diligently to restore the financial stability of the empire whose funds had been drained by the excesses of past emperors and by the depletion of monetary reserves as production of gold and silver from the mines slowed. However, his Spartan tastes were certainly not shared by many of the aristocrats. Instead, they thought he was as oppressive as Nero, because he imposed a heavy tax burden upon them to restore the public treasury and to pay for a number of public works projects. These were necessary for the status quo of the empire to be maintained, but not necessarily justified on a rational basis. It would have been better had he recognized and addressed the failures of Roman rule, rather than continuing with what was wrong with it. Vespasian, however, did not see it that way.

His lack of vision was also revealed by his rejection of technological innovations which might have resulted in productivity gains. But, rather than pursue these, he acquiesced to the myth that such inventions create unemployment. He saw the well-being of people linked to the amount of effort employed in work rather than to the amount of produce resulting from it. Therefore, he hindered economic growth and the creation of wealth. While the upper class suffered under his rule, the poor and middle classes were also hampered, although they might not have realized it. The economic success of the provinces around the Mediterranean world, and the tax revenues taken from them, served to conceal the harm caused by his misguided economic policies. They also served as a source of revenue to restore the public treasury. For this reason, many view Vespasian as generally competent. To his credit he did not participate in the debauchery of Caligula or Nero, but in his administration he was far from competent.

When he first came to power, Vespasian sent his son, Titus, to put down the Jewish rebellion that was occurring at that time. In this process, he destroyed the Temple in Jerusalem in AD 70. For the rest of Vespasian's reign, Titus was groomed for succession. When Vespasian died, Titus became emperor. His career was only two years long because he died at the age of forty-four. Unlike his father, he was a bit of a spendthrift and during his brief reign he depleted the treasury that Vespasian had worked so hard to restore. When he died, he was succeeded by his brother Domitian. The history of Domitian's career was also mixed, as might be expected given the power of the Roman emperor. He ruled the empire fifteen years before he was assassinated by his own household.

Domitian's death marked the beginning of what many historians regard as the peak of the Roman Empire. It has been referred to as a "golden age" of sorts during which Rome was ruled by a number of "good" potentates. This "golden age" extended from A.D. 96-180. During this time there were five rulers: Nerva (96-98), Trajan (98-117), Hadrian (117-138), Antoninus (138-161), and Marcus Aurelius (161-180). Numerous writers have praised these men for ushering in the *pax romano*, or Roman peace. During their reigns, significant public projects were completed, and daily life was carried on with as much stability as anyone could remember. They each made contributions which improved the efficiency of the Empire and were generally well liked by the people. None of the five became as drunk with power as had Caligula or Nero and each refrained from participating in excesses. Each had both strengths and weaknesses, and, on the whole, it is quite understandable why some writers referred to the time of their rule as a golden age of peace and prosperity.

While these rulers were certainly much better than some of the imperial magistrates of the past, they were far from perfect in their administration of justice. As already mentioned, the Christians were persecuted by past emperors and these five certainly did not stop that practice completely. During Trajan's reign, Christians were regularly slaughtered at the games for their refusal to worship the emperor as a deity. To his credit, however, he did institute a more lenient policy of not actively searching them out. He decided, instead, to punish only those who were made known to the state and who refused to recant their positions. Nevertheless, under this policy many were executed for no sound reason save that they would not honor the emperor as a god. Hadrian and Antoninus continued Trajan's policy. As an example of how the policy worked in practice, the case of Polycarp can be used. He was martyred for his refusal to proclaim Caesar as Lord. His execution took place in A.D. 156 during the reign of Antoninus. Furthermore, "Marcus Aurelius. . . gave renewed force to the law against strange religions. . ., and initiated a sharper period of persecution which extended into the reign of Commodus. . ."[39] This kind of lapse in judgment suggests that it is unwise to praise these men too highly. While it is true that they practiced a good deal of moderation compared to the egregious wrongs of past emperors, they were nonetheless guilty of abusing their positions of

---

[39] Williston Walker, *A History of the Christian Church*, (Edinburgh: T.&T. Clark, 1959), p. 43.

authority and in using their power to have men put to death unjustly. As Edward Coleson observed:

> While the persecution of the Christians by Nero and Domitian may properly be classed as the ragings of unsound minds which struck out at others also, the fact remains that often the best emperors persecuted the Christians most systematically while the less competent ones neglected this "duty" along with all their other responsibilities. This tragic misunderstanding between upright, honorable heathen and noble, saintly Christians illustrates how thoroughly good men may misunderstand each other.[40]

In retrospect, it is indeed ironic that Marcus Aurelius renewed the systematic persecution of the Christians. He was, after all, a Stoic philosopher who believed strongly in God and in man's need to live morally upright in this world. This same point of view was shared by the Christians themselves as they strived to live virtuous lives for the glory of Jesus Christ. "God has designed a natural order for this world,' Marcus Aurelius wrote. 'The duty of every man is to do his part in this order; to live willingly in community, helping others. . . "[41] Strangely enough, it was this man who executed a great many people who sincerely sought to live according to these very words. "Would many of the best pagans, who were really 'not far from the Kingdom,' have become Christian had they actually understood Christianity in its true light?"[42]

Following Marcus Aurelius to the throne was his incompetent son, Commodus (A.D. 180-192). Under his reign the condition of the Empire returned to a precarious position. While the rulers of the second century extended the length of the Empire, they could not save it from its inevitable downfall. The truth that a nation governed by a monarch is only as good or as bad as the person in power became very well known to the Romans of the third century A.D. Commodus participated in some

---

[40] Edward Coleson, *The Harvest of Twenty Centuries*, (Spring Arbor, Michigan, 1967), p. 18.

[41] Russell Kirk, *The Roots of American Order*, (Washington, DC: Regnery Gateway, 3rd edition, 1991), p. 123.

[42] Coleson, op. cit., p. 18.

of the same excesses which had oppressed the people of the empire in the first century. As a result, military leaders assassinated him after twelve years of rule. This event resulted in military despotism which marked the rule of Rome throughout the third century. Political intrigue and plots of assassination occurred regularly, and rulers often sought to secure their positions by soliciting the support of the military with bribes. This favoritism was quite costly and drained the public treasury, forcing the emperors to find new sources of revenue. Taxes and controls increased throughout this period of time, and more and more people became acutely aware of the confines of tyranny and oppression. In this environment, the people lost their desire to fight to preserve the government because they could not imagine an alternative worse than the one they are living under. When such attitudes are widespread, civilizations collapse under their own weight. Rome was rapidly moving to this end.

III. Some Other Issues of Life in Rome

During the history of Rome, agriculture remained the primary industry, and the tools used were the same ones which had been employed for centuries. In particular, the plow, spade, hoe, pick, pitchfork, and rake were all utilized. As already noted, the use of slaves to do the actual work of tilling the ground and cultivating the plants was commonplace. This arrangement, however, had its drawbacks. Chief among them was the fact that slaves were not innovative since their position was not likely to change even if advancements were made. As a result, they tended to be slow and never searched for any means of reducing the costs of production. An increase in the number of free laborers might have changed this situation if they were allowed to participate in the profits generated from their ideas. However, even where free men displaced slaves, there was little hope of profiting greatly from one's own ideas, and so progress was exceedingly slow.

Instead, production of all types shifted to large estates. These estates not only had mills which were used to grind the grains grown there, but they also manufactured a number of other products. It was common to find furniture being made, cloth being woven, and clothes being pieced together. In fact, these estates tended to be more or less self-sufficient. Even when some slaves gained their freedom, they continued to work on these estates as essentially serfs since they did not have any options that were more attractive by which to earn a living. The increase in serfdom foreshadowed the coming of the Middle Ages.

This is not to say that all production was carried on in this way, but merely that the employment of slave labor tended to move it in that direction. There were still numerous artisans who practiced their trades in villages and served the needs of many estates. The incentives of these artisans to improve their crafts and of merchants to make a living by way of trade would eventually erode as feudal society replaced it, but that would be many years in coming.

Trade remained a substantial feature of life throughout the empire. There were many products which simply could not be produced on large estates and which had to be acquired in exchange, if they were to be enjoyed at all. In fact, there was widespread trade during the Roman Empire throughout the Mediterranean world. Among the items traded were corn, cattle, hides, wine, wool, furniture, statuaries, jewelry, ivory, olive oil, tortoise shells, spices, pearls, metals of all types, fish, silk, linen, vegetables, poultry, fruits of all kinds, nuts, paper, and glass. This is just a small list of the much larger catalog of items which were traded. The Romans facilitated trade by building roads which overcame many of the natural obstacles of land travel and by controlling the seas to prevent pirates from plundering merchants.

Mining for metals and minerals was done solely with slaves and criminals. As had the Greeks before them, the Roman government assumed ownership of all resources below the surface of the ground. As such, it controlled the extraction and distribution of all precious metals which were used as the common commodity of exchange. Once extracted, the metals were used to make coins which the emperor used to pay for things he wanted and to finance public projects and military campaigns. As a result, these coins were dispersed throughout the empire. Mining was, thus, the chief source of revenue for both the emperor and the government. Emperors became very wealthy from their coinage of money as noted previously in the example of Augustus. While the public control of precious metals resulted in politically manipulating the direction of economic activity, the most insidious temptation for the emperors was to increase their wealth by debasing their coins to expand their purchasing power beyond what mining alone provided. This was particularly attractive as it became more difficult to mine the known reserves of gold and silver. As Will Durant observed, "Nero lowered the silver content of the denarius to ninety percent of its former quantity, Trajan to eighty-five percent, Aurelius to seventy-five, Commodus to seventy, Septimius Serverus to fifty."[43]

Intense mining operations using slave labor, coupled with the debasing of the money, resulted in the proliferation of Roman coins and a corresponding rise in the prices of goods. The emperor, and those closest to him, benefitted most from controlling the money supply. When the emperors began the process of debasing the coinage, it served as a means of taxing wealth generally from all the people throughout the empire. The damage of this was masked somewhat by the expansion of trade, which tended to promote the general interest of everyone. But the clear reality was that the Romans began consuming goods which were essentially bought without having to offer anything in return except impure gold or silver coins. As a result, the numbers of goods imported into Rome greatly exceeded those exported from it. Over time, Roman industry all but ceased to exist. The Romans became complacent and gave up producing anything of value themselves. The mischievous debasement of the money caused more than a little disruption in the lives of many people as the Roman leaders sought to continue their way of life by essentially defrauding others for what they wanted. But as the old saying goes, you cannot fool all of the people all of the time. Eventually, the flow of goods into Rome declined and prices rose to exceedingly high levels. When the emperors tried to control those prices, the flow of goods all but stopped. The end which had been foreshadowed long beforehand finally arrived.

Before closing our discussion of the Romans, it might be profitable to discuss several other items of interest. First, they were exceptional builders, and the ruins of many of the things they constructed survive today. In fact, some things are still in use. They employed a number of engineering innovations which allowed them to design and build things intended to endure the test of time. From the Ptolemies, they learned how to use hydraulics and made extensive use of this knowledge. While it is obvious that the emperors' control over the money supply allowed them to prosper at the expense of others, it is also true that some of the

---

[43] Will Durant, *Caesar and Christ*, (New York: Simon and Schuster, 1944), pg. 330.

projects they financed promoted the general well-being. The construction of Roman roads is a prime example of this fact. At the height of the Empire there were 51,000 miles of paved roads as well as a substantial network of secondary roads. These provided a better means of both communication and transportation than had ever existed and served to promote trade, which benefitted people in general. However, the benefits proved far too small to outweigh the heavy costs of tyranny.

Study Questions

1. Describe the process by which the Italian peninsula was settled.
2. Compare and contrast Stoicism and Epicureanism.
3. Describe how Carthage was founded and how it developed over time.
4. Who were the combatants of the Punic Wars and why were they at odds with each other? Describe how the conflict progressed in time and its final resolution.
5. What was life like for citizens of the Roman Empire? . . . for slaves?
6. How did Julius Caesar rise to power in Rome? Describe the circumstances of his death and the process by which Rome changed from a republic to an empire.
7. What is the inherent problem of imperial rule? Use examples from the Roman experience to make your case.

Chapter 7: Christianity

I. The Fullness of Time

Christianity began "when the fullness of the time had come."[44] In many respects, it was the perfect time for a new religion to spring forth into this world. Greek thought and culture permeated much of the world. As such, the intellectuals of the age rejected the pagan belief in polytheism. Instead, they gravitated towards either skeptical Epicureanism or pantheistic Stoicism. The masses, on the other hand, continued in their polytheistic beliefs and were generally convinced of their need for divine forgiveness. Further, they believed in an afterlife of rewards and punishments which were bestowed on people according to the individual's merit in this present life.

The time was also ripe for the Jews. They longed for their political independence and eagerly awaited the coming of the Messiah. The prophets had spoken of him. He was the one who would sit on David's throne and rule forever. Thus, they believed that when the Messiah came, he would gain for them political freedom and establish Jewish rule worldwide. Given the fact that the Jews had been subjugated to the Romans, from their perspective it was the perfect time for the Messiah. Before considering the details of Jesus' life, it is worthwhile to examine some of the peculiarities and circumstances of the time into which he was born.

As already developed in our discussion of the Hellenization of the world, the Jews successfully rebelled against Antiochus IV. When he died, the more urgent threat posed by the Romans led the Seleucid ruler to grant the Jews a large measure of freedom rather than risk squandering his resources in an attempt to bring Judea back into submission. In turn, under the leadership of the Hasmonean family, the theocratic Hebrew

---

[44] Galatians 4:4.

state was reestablished. However, over time the Maccabean rulers proved that they too had been influenced by Hellenistic ideas. They became more interested in practical political issues than in religious concerns; the practical problems of daily life seemed more pressing than the proper worship of God. As a result, their worship became more secularly motivated.

"Under John Hyrcanus, the Maccabean ruler from B.C. 135 to 105, the distinction between the religious parties of later Judaism became marked. The aristocratic-political party, with which Hyrcanus and the leading priestly families allied themselves, came to be known as Sadducees."[45] While the Sadducees held to the traditional ceremonies of Judaism and sought to promote moral behavior among the people through obedience to its laws, they nevertheless rejected the spiritual dimensions. They did not believe in a resurrection of the body or in an afterlife. They also rejected the idea that good and bad spirits or angels inhabited creation. For them, the primary purpose of religion was to secure the good things which could be had in this life by adhering to certain principles of behavior.

While this point of view was readily accepted among the upper classes, most people rejected it and sought to maintain the purity of the Jewish faith. The strongest opposition to the Sadducees came from the Pharisees. They sought to keep the Jewish religion free from all outside influences. The Pharisees themselves were highly educated men who spent many years studying the law of God. They understood the fine details of the law and taught that it was necessary for the individual to keep it exactingly to have any hope of gaining divine favor. In a word, they tended toward legalism. Jesus later criticized them for this position because they had forgotten the many passages of Scripture that point to the fact that God is merciful. Just the same, their focus on obedience to the law served as a point of agreement between them and the Sadducees. Unlike the Sadducees, the Pharisees believed in the resurrection of the body, in an afterlife of divine rewards and punishments, and in a Messianic hope.

Because of these differences in belief, there was conflict between the two groups. These differences inevitably led them to dispute among

---

[45] Williston Walker, *A History of the Christian Church*, (Edinburgh: T.&T. Clark, 1959), p. 13.

themselves the appropriate degree to which the Jewish nation should remain separate from the rest of the world. The Pharisees sought strict separatism while the Sadducees pragmatically leaned towards developing closer ties with others. Therefore, among the religious leadership there was a distinct split in opinion over this issue. The general populace tended to side with the Pharisees and favored separatism.

Jewish independence came to a sudden end in 63 B.C. when Pompey conquered the entire area. Will Durant provided a short synopsis of the events that led up to the conquest and explained what they meant.

> Recognizing the weakness of the little kingdom, the Hasmoneans spent two generations widening its borders by diplomacy and force. . . . The descendants of those brave Maccabees who had fought for religious freedom enforced Judaism and circumcision upon their new subjects at the point of a sword. At the same time the Hasmoneans lost their religious zeal and, over the bitter protests of the Pharisees, yielded more and more to the Hellenizing elements in the population. Queen Salome Alexandra (78-69 B.C.) reversed this trend and made peace with the Pharisees, but even before her death her sons Hyrcanus II and Aristobulus II began a war of succession. Both parties submitted their claims to Pompey, who now (63 B.C.) stood with his victorious legions at Damascus. When Pompey decided for Hyrcanus, Aristobulus fortified himself with his army in Jerusalem. Pompey laid siege to the capital and gained its lower sections; but the followers of Aristobulus took refuge in the walled precincts of the Temple and held out for three months. . . . When the ramparts fell 12,000 Jews were slaughtered; few resisted, none surrendered, many leaped to death from the walls.[46]

While Pompey made Hyrcanus priest and ruler, there was clear understanding among the people that Judea was subject to Rome. Hyrcanus was simply a vassal king accountable to the Romans. From the Jewish perspective, the situation became worse when Herod, a half-Jew, was made ruler over the region in 37 B.C. "His character was typical of

---

[46] Will Durant, *Caesar and Christ*, (New York: Simon and Schuster, 1944), pp. 530-531.

an age that had produced so many men of intellect without morals, ability without scruple, and courage without honor."[47] In fact, Herod showed himself capable of loyalty to anyone in power so long as it might secure his own position. For this trait he was highly praised by Augustus, but deeply hated by the Jews. It was in this environment that the contest for dominance between the Sadducees and the Pharisees over the religious affairs of Judaism continued. As this struggle persisted, the general populace continued to side with the Pharisees. On top of all of this, because of their subjugation to Roman rule, there was also a renewed interest in the Messianic hope. In fact, a heightened sense of anticipation that the time was right for the coming of the Messiah swept the region.

In addition to this activity, a number of sectarian groups generally referred to as the Essenes, had also formed. They lived their lives out of the mainstream of society in a more or less monastic fashion. They lived ascetic lifestyles denying themselves numerous material pleasures in order to devote themselves to meditation and prayer. Not only did they separate themselves from the outside influences of the broader world, but from the mainstream of Jewish life as well. Yet, much like the majority of people of the time, they also looked for a coming Messiah to bring an apocalyptic end to the age.

In the broader world outside, we have already seen that the Roman populace was increasingly Epicurean. Generally speaking, they were more interested in feeding and entertaining themselves than in discerning the ultimate truths of life. While this focus of life was widely accepted, it nonetheless sparked a counter movement among a number of conservative intellectuals who sought to enumerate the virtues of Stoicism. Their efforts resulted in an ongoing debate about the ultimate nature of the universe. Repeatedly, the Stoics pointed to the Logos, which they conceived of as an impersonal force that provided for the natural order of all things and determined the destiny of all people. Their belief in such a force was the fundamental reason they gave for virtuous living in this life. This was significant, for while Greek philosophy pointed to an impersonal force as the essence of universal order, Christians would point to Jesus Christ. As the apostle John wrote at the beginning of his gospel message to the world:

---

[47] Ibid, p. 531.

> In the beginning was the *Logos*, and the *Logos* was with God, and the *Logos* was God. He was in the beginning with God. All things were made through Him, and without Him nothing was made that was made. In Him was life, and the life was the light of men. And the light shines in the darkness, and the darkness did not comprehend it.[48]

By starting his gospel message with this statement, John took a philosophical concept of an impersonal force and filled it with personality. Basically, he argued that Jesus Christ, a person he had known, was in fact the incarnate God who created the universe. In addition, he argued that this person was the very source of all life and all truth, and that his purpose in taking on a human nature was to provide redemption for everyone who trusted in him for salvation. By applying the term Logos to Jesus, John also pointed out that providence and destiny were the work of a personal Being rather than the result of impersonal mechanical forces or of random chance events. In doing this, he spoke against both Stoicism and Epicureanism.

When this message was proclaimed, it was startling. The Jews were looking for a Messiah who would come as a political leader. They thought the Messiah would overthrow Roman rule and establish the Jewish nation over all the earth. Jesus, whom John pointed to as the Messiah, was much different. While John argued that the Messiah's rule was indeed universal, he also pointed out that his throne was in heaven rather than on earth. He argued that the true Messiah suffered and died on a cross as a propitiation for sin and that Christ's rule was accomplished by changing human hearts. Moreover, he argued that Jesus' kingdom would be built as his subjects became obedient to his moral commands as a matter of love and gratitude. This was certainly not the way the average Jew envisioned the Messiah.

Likewise, on the basis of Greek philosophy, which tended to lead people either to pantheism or to skeptical materialism, the notion that God became incarnate for the purpose of saving human beings from their sins was not particularly thinkable. From the pantheistic perspective, it was inconceivable that pure Being was personal, or that Being would take

---

[48] John 1: 1-5

on a human nature and a human body since pantheism invariably attempted to find the greatest good in the spiritual realm alone. From the skeptical point of view, which fundamentally assumed that man was the measure of all things and rejected the idea of an order outside of man, not only was a personal Being inconceivable, but that he would be the source of all justice and truth was unthinkable. Even so, John identified Jesus as God incarnate; the One who created the universe: "to the Jews a stumbling block and to the Greeks foolishness. . . "[49]

Whether one believes John's testimony or not, the fact remains that Jesus is the most significant individual in history. His life and teaching transformed the world and he continues to influence the lives of millions upon millions of people around the globe today. Western civilization would not be what it is apart from Christianity. Therefore, an examination of Jesus life and teaching must be made if we hope to understand his impact on the world.

What we know of Jesus comes mainly by way of the gospel messages that were written during the first century A.D. Because these were written by followers of Christ, some modern skeptics have questioned the historical reliability of them. However, such criticism is unwarranted. As F. F. Bruce has pointed out so well:

> It is only natural that men who were closely associated with the movement should be more interested in writing about its Founder than outsiders would be. It would be odd if anyone dismissed John Morley's *Life of Gladstone* as worthless for the factual information because the author was Gladstone's friend, political ally and cabinet colleague. . . . Nor would any historian ignore Sir Winston Churchill's *The Second World War* or Mr. Harold Wilson's 'personal record' of *The Labour Government, 1964-1970*, on the ground that the authors occupied the position of Prime Minister during the periods covered respectively by these works and would therefore present biased accounts.[50]

---

[49] I Corinthians 1: 23

[50] F. F. Bruce, *Jesus and Christian Origins Outside the New Testament*, (Grand Rapids, Michigan: William B. Eerdmans Publishing Company, 1974), pp. 14-15.

Thus, the New Testament provides our best and most complete source of information about Jesus' life and about his teaching.

Even admitting Bruce's argument, some critics nevertheless continue to heavily discount the information provided in the gospels by suggesting that the authors biased their work too much because of their religious motivation. However, this argument is weak. Gerstner, Sproul, and Lindsley provided an adequate refutation of it.

> But even if the Bible was written for a particular religious purpose, this does not thereby make it unreliable as history. It may be even more reliable because of the religious concern. The three writers of this book, for example, admit that what they write and say is religiously motivated; but we insist that precisely because we are religiously motivated we try to be reliable. Insofar as we become careless, over-zealous, engage in special pleading, or in any other way vitiate accuracy and truth, to that degree we are *not* religiously motivated.[51]

Their point is well taken. To the degree that the writers were confident that what they believed was the very truth, that Jesus was in fact God incarnate, they would endeavor all the more to provide a completely accurate account of his life in order to avoid all possible criticism. In addition to all of this, the research of a number of academicians points to the veracity of the New Testament documents. F. F. Bruce and William F. Albright are foremost among these researchers. While their work is beyond the scope of our present consideration, each, after a thorough examination of the facts, concluded that the Bible was generally reliable and, while some problems remain unaccounted for, they were convinced that much of the criticism against it was nothing more than poor scholarship.[52]

---

[51] John Gerstner, R. C. Sproul, and Arthur Lindsley, *Classical Apologetics*, (Grand Rapids, Michigan: Academie Books, 1984), pg. 142.

[52] By referring to "problems which are unaccounted for", I do not mean to suggest that the Bible contains errors. The Bible was written over a two thousand year period and uses all the various forms and styles of writing which are common today. In addition, there are a number of literary techniques which were common to the culture in which the Scriptures were written. The resulting document is intended to be more than an historical account of the period. In the

With this said, we can begin our examination of the life and teaching of Jesus Christ. According to Matthew and Luke, Jesus came into this world in an extraordinary way. He had a human mother like everyone else, but no human father. Instead, his mother became pregnant as an act of the Holy Spirit. The virgin birth was significant for a number of reasons.[53] First, it reflected the fact that salvation from sin can only come from God himself. Human beings who have rebelled against a holy and just God cannot devise a means by which to save themselves, and the virgin birth reflected this reality. Second, it reflected something about the very nature of Jesus which was unique to him. In particular, the church has always taught that Jesus was a single person who was both human and divine. This teaching has always been a mystery for us because we have no other experience of it. Yet, it is ultimately important to the entire Christian position. If Jesus were not fully human, then his perfect life and atoning sacrifice would not satisfactorily fulfill the requirements of God's law. On the other hand, if Jesus were not fully God, he could not have borne the full penalty for sin and overcome death. Moreover, it reflected the fact that Jesus was sinless and kept from sin. If history shows anything, it is that people everywhere and in every time period have been sinners. That is, all people have failed to live up to even their own moral standards of behavior. It has always been the case that every person has lived his or her life in some form of depravity to a greater or lesser degree. The Bible teaches that this situation is no accident. Rather, it attributes the inherited sinful nature of all mankind back to an original test of our first human parents; a test which they failed and in so doing consigned all

---

course of close examination of the Scriptures, some writers discovered what they thought were either inconsistencies or statements of fact which conflicted with other sources. Most of these supposed problems fade away upon closer inspection. Some remain unresolved. For anyone who has come to the conclusion that the Bible is the Word of God, these are best accounted for by the limits of our present knowledge. God does not err and so our understanding of the situation must be in error if at some point there is a clear conflict between the Word of God and some other source. Further, our understanding of Scripture must be flawed if it results in an internal inconsistency within the Bible itself. Whether all of these presumed problems will be resolved in the future remains uncertain. For those interested in examining a proof that the Scriptures are in fact the very Word of God, I recommend *Classical Apologetics* by Gerstner, Sproul, and Lindsley.

[53] Wayne Grudem, *Systematic Theology: An Introduction to Biblical Doctrine*, (Grand Rapids, Michigan: Zondervan Publishing House, 1994), pp. 529-532.

of their future offspring to a life of sin. The final significance of the virgin birth was that it demonstrated the fact that Jesus was kept from the pollution of original sin.

Following his birth, we know very little of his childhood except that his adoptive father was a carpenter and that he grew up in the town of Nazareth in Galilee. He was brought up in a very ordinary Jewish household. We know further that he was extremely bright and amazed the religious scholars by his understanding of the Scriptures and, like Joseph, that he learned and practiced the trade of carpentry.[54] Beyond this we have no other information of his early life and all else is just irrelevant speculation.

As a young man Jesus began his mission. While some writers have tried to deny it, even a casual perusal of the gospel accounts points to the fact that he saw himself as the Messiah. In short, Jesus thought that he was, in fact, God incarnate. Such a conception was at the very heart of all of his teaching. One cannot read the gospel messages without understanding that Jesus everywhere claimed to be one with God and, thus, claimed to be God himself. As C. S. Lewis pointed out so clearly, he could not have meant that he was a part of God as if he were adhering to some pantheistic notion. As a Jew such a conception of God was wholly foreign.[55]

Throughout his ministry, Jesus forgave sins, healed people from their various diseases (which he did on many occasions), interpreted the Scriptures, and readily received praise and worship from men as only God could rightly expect or deserve. There can be no doubt that he thought of himself as God, and either he was telling the truth or he was not. Once again, C. S. Lewis rightly observed the situation.

> I am trying here to prevent anyone saying the really foolish thing that people often say about Him: "I'm ready to accept Jesus as a great moral teacher, but I don't accept His claim to be God." That is one thing we must not say. A man who was merely a man and said the sort of things Jesus said

---

[54] see Luke 2: 41-50.

[55] C. S. Lewis, *Mere Christianity*, (New York, Macmillan Publishing Company, 1952), pp. 54-55.

would not be a great moral teacher. He would either be a lunatic–on a level with the man who says he is a poached egg–or else he would be the Devil of Hell. You must make your choice. Either this man was, and is, the Son of God: or else a madman or something worse. You can shut Him up for a fool, you can spit at Him and kill Him as a demon; or you can fall at His feet and call Him Lord and God. But let us not come with any patronising nonsense about His being a great human teacher. He has not left that open to us. He did not intend to.[56]

Lewis was absolutely correct in his assessment of the situation. The only respect owed to Jesus Christ was owed to him if he told the truth. If he was telling the truth, he was, in fact, the Lord God and people owed him all praise and all worship. As evidence that the proclamation was true, his disciples pointed to the miracles that he performed. An illustration of this can be found in the method by which Nicodemus approached Jesus. Nicodemus rightly understood when he came to Jesus that only a messenger from God could do the things which Jesus did. Thus, the miracles that Jesus did, provided evidence of the validity of his relationship with God and indicated his divinity. From the beginning of the religion, Jesus' followers argued for the Christian religion on this basis.

Human beings have always had trouble with issues of morality. On the one hand, everyone desires to be treated fairly by other people. People prefer to be treated kindly, compassionately, and fairly by their neighbors. On the other hand, no one wishes to be told what to do. Everyone desires to make his own decisions in life and to pursue his own happiness. Herein lies the problem, because the very nature of God defines what is moral and what is not. People hate this about God because they think that his rules are intended to ruin their opportunities for pleasure. But such notions are completely false. God's moral requirements are directions given according to the very nature of the universe that he created. If his requirements are ignored, the fullest extent the pleasures that he intends will not be enjoyed. Since men do not believe this, they have a fundamental problem. Though they know that moral behavior is needed in general, they deny that it is needed in their own lives. But, how can a

---

[56] Ibid, pp. 55-56.

moral society exist without its being made up of individuals who are themselves moral?

In vain people have sought to establish morality in society by making laws. Unfortunately, laws cannot change human hearts. To be sure, laws may restrain certain kinds of behavior, but they can never produce the kind of good society that people truly desire. "You cannot make men good by law: and without good men you cannot have a good society."[57] For this reason, if there is to be any hope for humanity at all, it must come by way of a fundamental change in the individual human heart. This is precisely what Jesus claimed he would do.

The fundamental problem that must be dealt with first is that human beings start from a deficit situation. They are in effect morally and spiritually bankrupt from God's perspective. To be sure, people may outwardly conform to the rules, but if their hearts are not in it, such behavior could not accurately be described as moral. Jesus made this clear in preaching his Sermon on the Mount. He pointed out that it is not enough to refrain from the physical act of murdering or stealing, but that it is also man's obligation not to hate or covet. This teaching is especially troublesome because it implies that all human beings have already failed, because everyone has harbored such sin in his heart at one time or another. So much so, that when they try to behave outwardly moral, they condemn themselves when they hate others or covet their possessions. Everyone must confess that he needs help. But, where is that help to come from?

Jesus claimed to be the help that mankind needed. Since he was both human and divine, he was able to suffer the consequences which human immorality deserved. C. S. Lewis was helpful in illuminating this when he wrote:

> But supposing God became a man—suppose our human nature which can suffer and die was amalgamated with God's nature in one person—then that person could help us. He could surrender His will, and suffer and die, because He

---

[57] Ibid., pg. 72.

was a man; and He could do it perfectly because He was God.[58]

Recognition of this fact, that Christ died for sinners, allowed the individual to die to himself and to his own will so that he might live for Christ. A truly moral life became a possibility, not because one was trying to live a life to gain God's approval or to gain approval from men, but because God made it possible. God was thus able to change the life of the person from the inside out. Repentance was made possible: the recognition that one had been disobedient to the commands of God and the acceptance of his all wise solution was at hand. Instead of forging ahead according to one's own ability, men could now approach God in Christ Jesus. Therefore, the Christian religion made it plain that the attempt by someone to go it alone, was to hope beyond hope that he might actually live a good life on his own merit. But, this simply could not be done. Whatever else we might say, and it could be substantial indeed, this was Jesus' basic mission as he conceived of it and which he fulfilled. That Jesus died on the cross as an atoning sacrifice for sin, that he rose from the dead as clear evidence that sins are forgiven by trusting in this atonement, and that he was enthroned in heaven and is today interceding for everyone who calls on his name, was the fundamental message of his closest associates, and they proclaimed it to the world.

II. Early Church History

When Jesus completed his mission on earth, he ascended into heaven. This astonished even his own followers, because he made it clear that he intended to build his kingdom and church through the efforts of ordinary men. In fact, he entrusted the success or failure of spreading the message to twelve men. Eleven of these twelve were his followers prior to his crucifixion, while the twelfth man was chosen by Christ later. The last man chosen was Saul of Tarsus, or better known to us as Paul. On the surface, it might appear foolish to entrust such an important message to these men. It is especially amazing that Jesus did this when the abilities and training of the twelve are examined. Other than Paul, they did not begin their missionary careers with much educational training. Rather,

---

[58] Ibid., pg. 60.

they began only with the conviction that what they had seen with their own eyes was true. Even Paul discounted his own education against the experience he had on the road to Damascus.

However, from God's perspective, the spread of the kingdom in this fashion was not foolish at all. In fact, the success or failure of the church did not ultimately depend on these men but upon God, who guaranteed to empower them with the Holy Spirit so that they would accomplish the task to which they were called. Indeed, as we examine *The Acts of the Apostles* written by Luke, we find that one of the first events in the early church was Pentecost. On this occasion the apostles were endowed with spiritual power so that they could accomplish the task that had been left to them. During their individual ministries there were accounts of their healing people of various diseases and other handicaps, of raising at least one person from the dead, of casting out evil spirits, and of speaking in foreign languages which they had not learned previously. In addition, accounts were made of their being miraculously freed from prison to continue their work. Nevertheless, in time most died as martyrs. Chief among the assignments completed during their lifetimes, was the production of the various New Testament books. These were crucially important to Christianity because they pointed to the life and work of Jesus.

The fact that the apostles performed miracles of the same type as those performed by Jesus, was meant to provide sufficient evidence that they were in fact God's messengers because only God could have done the things which they did. This pattern of proof was used in the Old Testament by the prophets and continued on through Jesus and the apostles. There is much discussion about whether or not miracles continue today. On one hand, Protestants argue that the Bible is complete and that there is no longer a need for a messenger of God to show himself as a true prophet by possessing the ability to perform miracles. In their view, miracles have ceased in that sense. This is not to say that Protestants disavow modern day miracles. Many continue to believe that God still acts in ways that are beyond our understanding or out of the ordinary. Just the same, on the basis of this view there is no need for anyone to possess the power to perform a wide variety of miracles in order to establish his credentials. Rather, they would assert that people today can only suppose to speak for God by making a proper presentation of the Scriptures which are viewed as being complete in themselves. No further proof is needed for them for they are already established by the former miracles.

Alternatively, the Roman Catholic view of the matter is that God continues to speak to his church through apostolic succession. That is, Roman Catholics believe that the apostolic order has been passed on and did not end with the death of the last of the original apostles. As a result, they hold that the Christian religion is informed by both the Scriptures and by church traditions that have been accumulated over the course of time. This difference in belief serves as the chief barrier between the two groups of Christian believers and more will be said of this later.

The church grew very rapidly following the day of Pentecost. Beginning in Jerusalem, the apostles preached the message of salvation provided by Jesus Christ as often as possible and many came to believe in him. The growth of this new religion led the Jewish leaders to fear Christianity as much as they had feared Jesus himself. They tried various ways to keep the apostles from proclaiming the message, but putting them in prison proved unsuccessful. The persecution of the followers of Christ was intensified when Stephen was martyred for blasphemy. Following his death many of the converts were dispersed from Jerusalem throughout Judea and Samaria. Still, they continued to proclaim the gospel message wherever they went and many people in these other regions converted to the new religion.

It was during this period of time that Paul was converted to Christianity. Before his conversion, Paul was a member of the Pharisees and was one of the chief proponents of persecuting the followers of Jesus. However, in his encounter with Jesus on the road to Damascus, he was confronted with the truth of the gospel message and his life was changed forever. Instead of persecuting the church, he became one of the most influential of the apostles. Not only was he a gifted missionary who planted churches throughout a great deal of the Roman world, but his vast understanding of Scriptures, coupled with the guidance of the Holy Spirit, allowed him to write numerous letters which provided clear doctrines of Christianity. This was much needed as various doctrinal disputes arose very early in church history.

With all of this said, the fundamental message that the apostles preached is found in the *Apostles' Creed*, which is still recited today.[59] This creed reads as follows:

> I believe in God the Father Almighty, maker of heaven and earth; and in Jesus Christ, his only Son, our Lord, which was conceived by the Holy Ghost, born of the Virgin Mary, suffered under Pontius Pilate, was crucified, dead, and buried: he descended into hell; the third day he arose again from the dead; he ascended into heaven, and sitteth on the right hand of God the Father Almighty, from thence he shall come to judge the quick and the dead. I believe in the Holy Ghost; the holy catholic church; the communion of saints; the forgiveness of sins; the resurrection of the body; and the life everlasting. Amen.[60]

This short statement of faith contains the elements that were taught as the fundamental tenets of Christianity. In addition to the elements of faith, they also taught the practice of certain sacraments, including baptism and communion.

Among the early disputes of the church was whether or not the Jewish ceremonial laws still applied. This became a point of contention when many Gentiles converted. Since they were not circumcised, the question was raised whether or not they should be. Paul argued vigorously against such a practice and pointed out how Jesus fulfilled the various aspects of the ceremonial law. Nevertheless, some of the Jews, known as "Judaizers", continued in their efforts to impose these restrictions upon Gentile believers. Over time, the efforts of the Judaizers led to nothing and Paul's position was canonized.

As Christianity spread, it drew more government attention. This was especially true because of the disputes that erupted in various places where more and more people came to believe that Jesus was indeed the Christ. The Jewish leaders in such places feared losing their positions of

---

[59] The *Apostles' Creed* was not written by the apostles themselves, but was nonetheless the essence of the message that they preached. It was developed later to counter numerous heresies that were being preached as if they were Christianity.

[60] The Presbyterian Church in America, *The Confession of Faith*, (Atlanta, GA: Committee for Christian Education & Publications, 2nd edition, 1986).

authority, while the pagans feared the loss of trading opportunities because people who converted to Christianity gave up the many pagan rites of worship and pagan superstitions. The converts no longer spent their money on items for pagan worship and those engaged in trading those items feared for their financial future. For these reasons, there was a great deal of disruption in daily life wherever the gospel was readily accepted, and this caught the attention of the governing authorities. As a result, the Christians were often persecuted for causing social unrest even though such disturbances were mainly initiated by others. In an effort to restore the "peace" of the communities involved, the authorities treated the Christians as criminals and, as already pointed out in the previous chapter, they were dealt with as if they were traitors deserving the death penalty.

The apostle John died at the end of the first century A.D. He was the last of the twelve to die. However, following the example of Jesus, the apostles had invested themselves in teaching other men to lead the church forward in history. One such man was Polycarp of Smyrna. He was a disciple of John. Polycarp first met John when he was 30 years old. He studied under him and spent the rest of his life teaching other people about Jesus Christ. As already mentioned in the chapter on Rome, he died a martyr during the reign of Antoninus when he was burned at the stake. When asked if he would recant his Christian faith to save his life he replied, "Eighty and six years have I served Him, and He hath done me no wrong; how then can I blaspheme my King who saved me?"[61]

In addition to Polycarp, there were a number of other early church leaders, including Ignatius, Justin Martyr, Tertullian, and Origen. During their lives a number of heresies developed which threatened the church. These men generally stood against these heresies, though their own thoughts were not perfectly consistent with orthodoxy. Nonetheless, Christianity spread. Among the leading heresies that arose were Gnosticism, montanism, and manichaeism.

Gnosticism was rooted in pagan philosophy and Eastern mysticism. The gnostics promoted the concept that all material things were inherently evil. They believed that Jesus did not have a real body but only presented one as an illusion. As a result of this teaching, they

---

[61] A.M. Renwick and A.M. Harman, *The Story of the Church*, (Grand Rapids, Michigan: William B. Eerdmans Publishing Company, 2nd edition, 1985), pg. 28.

became fixated either on pursuing sensual desires with wild abandon or on pursuing an ascetic lifestyle of deprivation.

While montanism was in general agreement with much of the orthodox position of the church, it nevertheless embraced the gnostic heresy so strongly that it promoted an overarching kind of asceticism that could not be conformed with Scripture. As a result, the proponents of this heresy tended to deprive themselves of material blessings to gain favor with God.

Finally, manichaeism was a compilation of a number of pagan philosophies with numerous elements of Zoroastrianism. It viewed the world as if all was a cosmic struggle of good and evil. True Christianity rejected this view and argued that God was sovereign and was in control of the entire universe. As such, he was bringing his plan of redemption to a fitting conclusion in due time and allowed evil to continue in this world only to the extent that it served his good purpose. Therefore, even though there were those who opposed God, their opposition was seen as being nothing but folly that actually served God's end.

Other heresies could be mentioned, but the significant point is that heresies forced the church community to state its official position on a number of matters. The tension to do so led to the New Testament canon and to various creeds which were intended to state the tenets of genuine Christian faith and doctrine. The importance of developing and maintaining a sound Christian theology became exceedingly clear. Theology is the science which teaches the existence, character, and attributes of God, his law and government, the doctrines that ought to be believed, and the duties that people are responsible to practice. It was and is crucial to the Christian religion.

Among the theologians who emerged, perhaps none was greater than Augustine (354-430). Augustine was born in Numidia. Though his father was a pagan, his mother was a devout believer in Jesus Christ. As a young man he studied at a school in Carthage and became a follower of manichaeism. During this time, he gave himself over to sensual pleasures. Yet, he was a careful thinker and the inconsistency of astrology (which was a part of manichaeism) drove him to skepticism. In due time he visited Rome and Milan. While he was in Milan, he became enthralled by the sermons of St. Ambrose. In these sermons, he was confronted with the gospel message and its implications for his life. He converted to Christianity and became a priest in 391. Four years later he was ordained as the bishop of Hippo in North Africa.

Augustine spent the rest of his life preaching the gospel and writing books in defense of orthodox Christianity. Pelagianism, manichaeism, and donatism were among the heresies that he spoke out against. One of the primary focal points of his work, was his strong support for the idea that salvation was the sole act of God. He argued that everyone saved, would be saved by the grace of God alone. In addition to this, Augustine wrote a book titled, *The City of God.* It was an important book about the nature of civilization which he wrote as the Goths were taking control of Rome itself. Even though his book came on the scene at a point in time when civility and order were in decline, he remained hopeful. He saw a brighter future because he anticipated the spread of the gospel message which would continue to change human hearts throughout the world. He believed that as Christ's kingdom was being established on earth, greater civility would eventually reign. Beyond this world, he saw the real celestial city of God as the heavenly city inhabited by God's saints who were raised incorruptible. Only there would people be fully civil towards one another; only there would perfect justice reign. Therefore, he admonished his readers not to fix their ultimate hope on this world. In his view, the suffering endured by God's people providentially served God's purpose of building his kingdom. Therefore, in time, he believed that greater civility would arise among men as God's Word progressed. But, whatever was obtained in the present world, it was only a poor foretaste of what was to come in heaven. This view profoundly affected the thinking of Christians down through the ages as they sought to preach the gospel.

Study Questions

1. What significant circumstances worked together to make Jesus entrance into this world ideal?
2. Compare and contrast the beliefs of the Sadducees and the Pharisees.
3. What was the general Jewish sentiment towards Roman rule?
4. Why is the opening passage of John's gospel shocking to both Jews and Gentiles? Interpret I Corinthians 1:23 in light of your answer.

5. What arguments can be made to support the validity of the gospel accounts of Jesus' life?

6. Why is the virgin birth an essential doctrine of Christianity?

7. Why is it impossible to describe Jesus as merely a good man?

8. What is the fundamental problem of achieving a "good" society? Is it possible to secure it by adopting the right laws? Why or why not?

9. What is the Christian message?

10. Explain how the Christian church expanded following Jesus ascension into heaven.

11. What were some of the problems the early church faced?

12. How were doctrinal disputes resolved? Why were creeds important? Are they important today? Explain.

Section 2: The Middle Ages

After the fall of the Roman Empire, Western civilization was set back for quite some time in Europe. German barbarians took control of Western Europe and established a form of rule that greatly limited the extent to which civilization could develop. While the Christian religion was accepted among these people, they nevertheless embraced all sorts of vain superstitions and accepted as appropriate a number of perverse ideas of securing the order of society.

The early part of the Middle Ages was particularly backward. Illiteracy was pervasive and most people lived in abject poverty. The underlying politico-economic system at the time tended to thwart the prospect of gaining any significant economic improvement. As a result, what was left of civilization was largely secured through the efforts of churchmen. In fact, apart from their efforts, culture might have died altogether in Western Europe. Nevertheless, the church kept alive the Christian conception of civility, and that idea eventually flowered into the kind of society that we call Western civilization.

It was not until the feudal structures that hampered economic advancement began to break down, that this civilization began to revive. This occurred in part as a result of the revival of trade with the East which set in motion a series of events that allowed for the renewal of culture. In particular, it led to the accumulation of wealth which freed people from the tyranny of subsistence living and allowed them to pursue activities that increased learning and provided for a renewed interest in the arts. Prior to this, these things remained out of the reach of most people.

Chapter 8: The Early Period

I. The Fall of Rome

As already noted in the chapter about Rome, the empire was declining and numerous internal and external problems eventually led to its ultimate demise. However, the process of destruction was slow and painful and, upon reflection, a number of reasons for Rome's failure can be identified. As Will Durant has observed:

> A great civilization is not conquered from without until it has destroyed itself within. The essential causes of Rome's decline lay in her people, her morals, her class struggle, her failing trade, her bureaucratic despotism, her stifling taxes, her consuming wars. . . Barbarian inroads, and centuries of mining the richer veins, had doubtless lowered Rome's supply of precious metals. In central and southern Italy deforestation, erosion, and the neglect of irrigation canals by a diminishing peasantry and a disordered government had left Italy poorer than before. The cause. . . was no inherent exhaustion of the soil, no change in climate, but the negligence and sterility of harassed and discouraged men.[62]

While some writers blamed the downfall of the Roman Empire on the spread of Christianity, closer inspection demonstrates the failure of that argument. Rome collapsed because of her own excesses and immorality. Christianity's main impact was to extend the empire for longer than it would have lasted otherwise. The evidence that this was true can be found in the behavior of the Christians themselves. Christian converts exhibited a renewed zeal for moral living. Following the

---

[62] Will Durant, *Caesar and Christ*, (New York: Simon and Schuster, 1944), pg. 665.

teachings of their new faith, they sought to treat other people justly and to practice a personal piety that had long been discarded by the Roman populace. By doing this, they tended to temper the immoral extremes of the people around them. As a result, they seasoned society with a degree of virtue that had all but disappeared.

Some historians discounted the benefits of Christianity by pointing out that some Christians stopped working because they thought that Christ's return was imminent. Others discounted the benefits of the religion because they found numerous examples in history of Christians committing both immoral and unjust acts. But, these criticisms are not really sufficient to prove their case. It was true that many early believers thought that Christ's return was imminent and this prompted some of them to stop working in anticipation of that event. However, it was also true that the apostles chastised such people for this kind of behavior. In his second letter to the Thessalonians, Paul specifically reprimanded his readers for this practice. Paul wrote:

> But we command you brethren, in the name of our Lord Jesus Christ, that you withdraw from every brother who walks disorderly and not according to the tradition which he received from us. For you yourselves know how you ought to follow us, for we were not disorderly among you; nor did we eat anyone's bread free of charge, but worked with labor and toil night and day, that we might not be a burden to any of you, not because we do not have authority, but to make ourselves an example of how you should follow us. For even when we were with you, we commanded you this: If anyone will not work, neither shall he eat. For we hear that there are some who walk among you in a disorderly manner, not working at all, but are busybodies. Now those who are such we command and exhort through our Lord Jesus Christ that they work in quietness and eat their own bread.[63]

The latter criticism of Christians in society was also insufficient to warrant the conclusion drawn from the facts. To be sure, Christians in every time and in every place can be found participating in both immoral

---

[63] 2 Thessalonians 3: 6-12.

and unjust acts. But, this was not unique to Christians alone. This was the common human lot. Such evidence substantiates the basic message that the religion preached. Rather than serving as suitable evidence that the spread of Christianity promoted the empire's downfall, the fact that the Christians fell short of moral perfection was abundantly consistent with the religion itself. Such moral failures were never condoned. The apostles never tired of speaking out against the immoral and unjust actions of converts. Everywhere they went, they admonished their listeners to refrain from evil and immorality. Many of their converts had freely engaged in such behavior before becoming Christian converts and it was no small matter for them to completely change what had been their former way of living. As Paul wrote, "Owe no one anything except to love one another, for he who loves another has fulfilled the law. For the commandments, 'You shall not commit adultery,' 'You shall not murder,' 'You shall not steal,' 'You shall not bear false witness,' 'You shall not covet,' and if there is any other commandment, are all summed up in this saying, namely, 'You shall love your neighbor as yourself.' Love does no harm to a neighbor; therefore love is the fulfillment of the law."[64] Thus, as a matter of practice, Christians were instructed to live both morally and justly with respect to others. That is not to say that they always did so, but then this was the very point of the religion. All people were declared to be immoral sinners and were in need of salvation.

Even though Christianity became widespread, it could not reverse the ultimate direction of Roman society. The population of Rome declined as citizens chose to have fewer children and because of pestilence, disease, and warfare. In addition, the amount of actual work performed declined. Many farms were simply abandoned. The masses preferred to enjoy the pleasures of living off the government dole as spectators at the circuses rather than to experience the rigors of a productive life. Moral standards deteriorated steadily as divorce, sexual indulgence, and unbelief dominated society.

Increasingly, the government's promise to provide the citizenry with all aspects of an easy and pleasurable life proved empty. In its efforts to cater to Roman citizens, the government virtually destroyed the economy. The government tied the economic livelihood of the nation to

---

[64] Romans 13:8-10.

mining for gold and silver and, as the mines played out, so did the prospects of securing the "good life" that was vainly promised to the citizenry. Undeterred by the dismal outlook of continuing its policies, the government tried to sustain itself through increased taxes and debased coinage. The new taxes simply destroyed opportunities and further depressed an already weak industrial base. The fraud of debasing the coinage only resulted in raising product prices and in worsening the economic conditions of the empire generally. The results of both policies were that fewer goods flowed into Rome and even less were produced there. If all of this were not bad enough, more money was spent on public works projects in the hope that these would lead to renewed economic prosperity. In fact, these programs simply depressed production even further by destroying precious capital. All of the policies that were intended to maintain the status quo led instead to new layers of government bureaucracy that tended to undercut economic activity. Greed, envy, complacency, slothfulness, sexual immorality, despotism, maliciousness, conceit, negligence, tyranny, confiscatory taxation, busybody meddling, and jealousy, were some of the key factors that led to the demise of Rome.

"Roads injured by war, neglected by poverty, and endangered by highwaymen, could no longer maintain adequate communication and exchange. State revenues declined as commerce contracted and industry fell; impoverished governments could no longer provide protection for life, property, and trade. The obstruction of commerce compelled the villas to seek economic self-sufficiency; many manufactured articles formerly bought from the cities were—from the third century onward—produced on these great estates."[65] The productive activities that continued in Italy became more and more localized.

The decline in trade and the rise of self-sufficient estates is significant because they were the forerunners of feudal manors that dominated economic life in Western Europe during most of the Middle Ages. The clear disadvantage of self-sufficiency was that it sacrificed the gains in material well-being the people might have enjoyed, had they specialized their productive efforts and traded with each other. In truth, greater specialization and more division of labor in the production of

---

[65] Ibid, pg. 552.

commodities gives rise to more material wealth. Specialization of resources was an important factor in increasing material wealth. Productive resources were diverse and, as an essential fact of nature, always will be. Some resources were generally ill-suited for certain endeavors, and when they were employed in them the results were far poorer than the produce that could have been had from the employment of other resources in that line of production. That did not mean that the poorer resources were not good for anything. On the contrary, their relative disadvantage in one kind of production created an advantage in some other use. This truth was the very basis for expansion of trade in the Roman Empire. It was the reason why people traded. Namely, both parties to trade benefitted. But, as trade decreased, so too did material prosperity. No single estate could have ever hoped to produce all of the things that made life easier because no estate was diverse enough in its resources to produce efficiently the products which could be produced in the Mediterranean world.

As the obstacles to trade increased, less of it occurred. People were left to rely on their own limited devices to make a living. As a result, there was a tendency for them to concentrate on subsistence production. This limitation greatly reduced the average well-being of the people who were consigned to live and work on such estates. As the Germanic tribes overran the western portion of the empire, local self-sufficiency became more and more entrenched. People worked harder and obtained less for their efforts. The decline in well-being, was accompanied by a corresponding decline in literacy as there was little free time to devote to reading. The arts and sciences largely survived in the churches and the monasteries. For these reasons, the early Middle Ages are often referred to as the Dark Ages.

Before moving ahead too quickly to a discussion of the Middle Ages, some additional background information to the collapse of the Roman Empire and of what remained afterwards will be instructive. It bears repeating here that the third century was marked by much political intrigue. In addition to its internal problems, the empire was besieged by numerous groups of people beyond its realm. Continual battles were fought on the frontiers to keep these people in check. Toward the end of the third century, the situation of the empire was desperate. At the same time, even though it was continually persecuted, the Christian religion continued to expand.

It was in this environment that Diocletian (285-305) became emperor. In some respects he was a clever man and sought to solidify his rule by appeasing all parties. In reality, however, Diocletian's greed and arrogance led him to initiate policies that ripped the empire apart. At the time he came to power, the city of Rome had fallen into disrepair. Diocletian opted to move the capital to Nicomedia in Asia Minor. He justified the move for military reasons, but in reality, he was most likely fleeing the decay of Rome. The prospect of tapping the wealth being produced in the East was too great to pass up. From Diocletian's perspective, moving the capital closer to the source of the wealth that might be had made good sense. To consolidate his power and seize this wealth, Diocletian attempted to initiate policies to more thoroughly control the economy. Instead of relying on the mere regulation of production and trade to generate revenues for the state, he implemented policies in which the state actually took control of numerous industries. In an effort to curb rising prices which resulted from Rome's long history of debasing the money, he fixed wages and prices. This action had the inevitable consequence of creating shortages of all types of goods and services. Products became more scarce than ever. The hardships that followed erupted into riots. As a result, Diocletian was forced to relax his price controls.

To support his government reforms, Diocletian raised taxes and collected them in-kind rather than by way of monetary payments alone. Government warehouses were established and bureaucrats traversed the empire collecting produce of every kind from the many business enterprises. This action pushed industry into a mold like that of feudalism which later developed in Western Europe. To ensure payment of taxes, he sought to limit the mobility of the people by binding them to the land on which they worked. This effectively consigned people to certain types of activities and established serfdom as the model of economy. It is uncertain whether or not feudalism would have arisen anyway, but it is clear that such policies greatly aided its establishment in Western Europe. These decrees were nothing short of brutal despotism. The oppressive nature of Diocletian's actions plunged what remained of the empire into civil war. Eventually, he abdicated the throne and spent the last eight years of his life in his palace in Asia Minor. Constantine emerged from the chaos of the time with the most power and planned to have Diocletian killed in order to establish his position as emperor; but before this happened, the former emperor took his own life.

Constantine was perhaps one of the more utilitarian and pragmatic men in history. By 324 he gained control over the whole empire. He accomplished this by strengthening his army and by turning the empire into a military state. Once he gained control, he ruled from both Rome and Nicomedia. This was temporary because in 330 he moved the capital to Constantinople (modern day Istanbul). Like Diocletian before him, Constantine was motivated by the wealth that existed in the East. Constantine was "[c]rafty, unprincipled, and merciless, he destroyed all rivals to his might, among them such members of his own family as made him uneasy."[66] Despite his behavior, he claimed that he converted to Christianity. Whether his profession was genuine or not, he used it to consolidate his power. Whatever his beliefs, Constantine recognized the power of religion for furthering his political purposes. He legalized Christianity and this move paved the way for it to be made the state religion at a later date. While he never outlawed other religions, it was quite clear that Christianity held a favored spot.

While the union of the church and the state provided Christianity with a freedom it had never known before, the marriage itself was an unholy one. In the temptations that Jesus faced during his forty-day fast, he specifically rejected the opportunity to gain a worldly kingdom by political means. He desired people to worship and serve him from their hearts and not as a matter of government compulsion. Such worship and devotion occurred only to the extent that the hearts of people were changed. This was the fundamental message of the gospel. As Paul wrote, "Therefore, if anyone is in Christ, he is a new creation; old things have passed away; behold, all things have become new."[67] Followers of Christ submitted to his rule on a voluntary basis and changed their behavior because they choose to and not because they were forced to. The state could not force such a change. At best it could only elicit some particular response from its citizens to the extent that they feared punishment. Yet this was a poor substitute for a kingdom that embraced not only justice, but mercy and charity as well. A nation established by political coercion

---

[66] Russell Kirk, *The Roots of American Order*, (Washington, DC: Regnery Gateway, 1991, 3rd. edition), pg. 156.

[67] 2 Corinthians 5: 17.

was not the kind of kingdom which Jesus had in mind.

Whatever initial aid Christianity may have gained from being embraced by the state, it also led to a number of long term problems. This was especially true in cases where doctrinal error served some state purpose. In addition, it also provided the church with a source of power that has regrettably been used on numerous occasions in an attempt to force people into Christ's kingdom. Both misuses of power and authority have caused more than a little mischief.

Constantine died in 335. After his death, continual assaults on the empire from outside invaders eventually resulted in the loss of territory. At the beginning of the fifth century, the Visigoths, a people of Germanic origin, sacked Rome. In addition, the Vandals conquered Spain and North Africa, while the Persians were a constant problem in the east. In the middle of the fifth century the Vandals themselves sacked Rome. The result of all of this was that imperial rule in Western Europe came to an end. All that remained of the empire was located in the east and was centered around Constantinople. This empire became known as the Byzantine Empire and it endured until 1453. In the west, a number of different ethnic groups battled for land. In this ongoing struggle, a full blown feudal system, where power was vested in land holdings, emerged as the dominant means of economic survival. Trade in the west came to a virtual halt and life was carried on at a near subsistence level.

II. The Byzantine Empire

The Byzantine Empire was essentially governed like the old Roman Empire from which it came. As already pointed out, it continued until it was conquered in 1453 by the Ottoman Turks. Occasionally, efforts were made to extend its boundaries in order to recapture the territory controlled by the old Roman Empire. For example, in the early sixth century Justinian attempted to do so. Justinian was a man of a humble background who came to the throne through his uncle, whose name was Justin. When he was a small boy, his uncle brought him to live with him in Constantinople. Justin was politically well-connected and Justinian obtained an excellent education growing up in his house. Justin usurped the throne in 518 upon the death of Anastasius and handed over much of the responsibility of government to Justinian, who by this time was a young man. Justin's reign was a short one since he died in 527 leaving Justinian in control.

Like Alexander before him, Justinian had a compelling urge to unify things. He sought unity with great fervor even when it took force to do so. Among the things he tried to unify was his rule over the Mediterranean world. In essence, he was trying to reestablish the Roman Empire. While he successfully took North Africa from the Vandals and Italy from the Ostrogoths, his plans to regain all of Western Europe failed. It was perhaps just as well, because even where he succeeded he did not possess the military wherewithal to quell the numerous conflicts and gain peace. In addition, the Persians remained a constant threat. In light of these circumstances, the likelihood of reestablishing the successful rule over all the peoples of Western Europe was slight.

In addition to his attempt to unify the Mediterranean world under one government, Justinian also sought to provide a common body of law to govern that world. The uniting of church and state, along with the vast amount of laws prescribed by pagans over many years had resulted in a confused legal code. It was quite common for one law to be at odds with another. Thus, given Justinian's inclinations, such a task was long overdue. His efforts resulted in what has been called the Code of Justinian. The central focus of the code made orthodox Christian faith mandatory and outlawed all other forms of religion. In addition, it outlawed a wide variety of behavior considered immoral and established penalties for those who violated the code. The penalties were often harsh by today's standards. For this reason, the code is often criticized by modern writers. Further, it is also criticized because of its intolerance of pagans and of other forms of religion. Nonetheless, under the general precepts of this code of law the Byzantine Empire flourished.

It should be remembered that the union of the church and state began in the early fourth century. Prior to that time, Christianity grew in spite of the more or less continual persecution it endured at the hands of state officials. In this hostile environment, the church spread and the number of people professing faith in Jesus Christ increased dramatically. As churches were planted, an organizational structure eventually developed. Rome became the important center of this organization which was quite natural since it was the seat of Roman rule. However, when Constantine made Christianity legal, the capital city of Constantinople also became prominent. This city became even more important when Christianity was made the official religion of the state. This led to the development of tension between church leaders in these two cities and seeds were sown for Christianity to be split into two visible organizations. At first, there were simply two church hierarchies that competed with one another over doctrinal issues. The two groups often sought unity in matters of doctrine and for quite some time the entire organization was seen as a united whole. Eventually, however, there was a separation between them because the emperor of Byzantium set himself up as both the political ruler of the empire as well as the head of the church. This situation, coupled with some marked disagreements about doctrine, led the leadership in Rome to assert their own prominence over the Christian religion. The result was the formation of two church organizations: The Greek Orthodox Church in the east and the Roman Catholic Church in the west. While the two organizations maintained contact, there were important differences. For example, the Roman Church remained independent of the state although it used its position to influence the political sphere. Still, matters of doctrine were resolved by the church leadership and not by political rulers. Over time theological schisms were created because of political dictates by the emperor. When the doctrinal differences became too great, the Roman Catholic and Greek Orthodox Churches went their separate ways.

In the early years of Christianity, doctrinal disputes arose for a number of reasons and political issues were sometimes behind the debates. Both in the east and the west, the close connection of the church with the state led to laws that attempted to force people to become Christians. To avoid punishment, people worshiped the symbols of Christianity without ever recognizing Jesus as the Christ. In addition, many people simply sought to mix their pagan beliefs with Christian doctrines in order to make their acquiescence to the law more palatable. In short, making Christianity the legal religion resulted in a situation where people simply went through the motions of ritual for the purpose of getting along in society. In this atmosphere, the fundamentals of the Christian faith were far more threatened than they had ever been by the persecution of the state. There are two points that should be noted about this situation. One, Christianity was sometimes used and perverted for political purposes of rulers. Two, because of this, it faced some new obstacles if it was to adhere to its historic position of faith.

Justinian's own life is perhaps a prime example of the problems created for Christianity. On the surface it would appear that Justinian was a Christian. However, a close examination of his own beliefs reveals that conclusion is not necessarily warranted. Towards the end of his life, he embraced the position that Christ did not possess a human body and, therefore, could not have suffered the kinds of afflictions that are common to all human beings. The affirmation that Jesus did indeed possess a human body was by this time a central tenet of the Christian faith. To deny it was to essentially deny the atoning sacrifice of Jesus Christ. Therefore, Justinian's position was at odds with traditional Christianity. While numerous clergy warned him against persisting in his position, as far as we know he maintained it to his death in 565. Therefore, there remains some question as to whether or not Justinian's Christian testimony of faith was genuine. The importance of this is that it indicates that a great deal of what passes as being Christian in the minds of people can often be very far from it indeed.

III. The Rise of Islam

Five years after Justinian's death, Mohammed was born in Arabia. He founded a new religion that resulted in the rise of the Moslem Empire in the late seventh and early eighth centuries. In retrospect, this was very surprising given the circumstances from whence it came. As Edward Coleson has written:

> If you and I could have visited the Arabian Peninsula some six hundred years after the birth of Christ, could we have discerned the "makings" of a mighty movement which would soon sweep the world and even threaten the very existence of the Church? Indeed, had we seen those few flea-bitten, emaciated Arabs wandering from water hole to water hole with their scrawny flocks and herds, we would no doubt have rated these people as the "least likely to succeed." Yet in one short century they would sweep over much of three continents and conquer an empire greater than that of Rome at its height. Impossible, yes! But it happened.[68]

---

[68] Edward Coleson, *The Harvest of Twenty Centuries*, (Spring Arbor, Michigan, 1967), pp. 76-77.

As a young man, Mohammed made a living as a merchant trader. In the course of this activity he came into contact with various people who embraced a wide range of religious beliefs that were common during that time. Included among them were Christianity, Judaism, and Zoroastrianism. It is hard to know exactly what motivated him to do so, but at the age of forty he claimed that he was God's prophet and began to preach a new monotheistic religion. The new religion he espoused was essentially an admixture of the various religions that he had been learned about in the course of his life. This was something quite new for the people of Arabia who were still very much polytheistic in their thinking.

In the early years of his preaching, Mohammed was not particularly successful in winning converts; his efforts were often met with intense opposition. Most of the people living in his hometown of Mecca rejected his message, and he was eventually forced to flee from Mecca and move to Medina. For a time it seemed that nothing would come of his efforts. Then he began to preach the need to bring God's kingdom to earth via a military campaign. It is uncertain why this new message was more successful, but the circumstances of the time might have aided this new vision. Of particular importance was the fact that Medina's food supplies had been strained when Mohammed and his few followers moved to the city. As a practical way of providing food for the people, Mohammed recommended that they raid the caravans that moved though the area as a means of gaining their living. Therefore, it was possible that the new vision was just a religious justification for robbing others. If so, the success of living at the expense of others might well have been very attractive to potential converts. At any rate, this course of action was taken and the ground was established for transforming the religion into a theocratic state directed by Mohammed himself. Rather than preaching salvation through the vicarious atonement of Christ or by way of living a moral life, Mohammed preached that each man must earn his salvation through a strict lifelong regimen of careful obedience to his own "revelations." More and more he focused his "revelations" on political and social legislation which aimed at promoting Arab activism and used this activism to destroy his opposition. In brief, Mohammed aimed at creating a warrior nation. Eventually, the new faith became widely accepted in Arabia and was seen as a reformation of an older religion. As a result, it became the base upon which the people of Arabia justified their active aggression against other people of the world.

Mohammed died in 632. After his death, the warrior nation that he had laid the groundwork for burst forth upon the world with a number of impressive military victories. It never occurred to Mohammed that the nation he formed would attempt to conquer the world, nor was it necessarily on the minds of the Moslem leaders who took control when the prophet died. Just the same, through a series of events, the Arab nation began its conquest. The Moslems first took Syria, then Palestine. From there they defeated the Persians and the Egyptians and moved across North Africa and into Europe through Spain. Having conquered Spain, their progress was stopped only when they were defeated by Charles Martel in 732 at Tours in central France. Though they continued to try to capture France and the rest of Europe, this defeat marked the end of their expansion. From the east, Europe was secured by the Byzantine Empire which held its position successfully against the Moslem onslaught. Still, the empire they created was impressive. It stretched from the Indus River Valley to Egypt, through North Africa and included Spain.

To their credit, the Moslems were not as ruthless in conquest as they could have been. Rather than giving people the option of converting to their religion or being put to death, they offered a third alternative. They allowed conquered people to continue to worship as they wished as long as they were willing to pay an annual tribute for this privilege. This policy provided some degree of religious tolerance during a time when there was little of it to be found in most of the world. As a result, it allowed people from diverse backgrounds to live together in relative peace. However, there was never a complete toleration of other religions, and the civil peace was broken on numerous occasions because of the disputes that arose. While Christians were free to worship as they pleased as long as they paid the required tax, they were not free to criticize Islam. Quite the reverse was often true. They were frequently forced to endure the ridicule of Christianity by Moslems, but if they spoke negatively of Islam it might cost them their lives. Notwithstanding, the Moslem practice of this era was still more tolerant than the religious restrictions imposed in many other places.

In addition to providing for some religious tolerance, the Moslems had the good sense to refrain from using political power to control trade. Instead, they allowed more or less free movement of goods throughout their empire. This decision led to the rapid rise in economic prosperity that was unknown in the feudal society entrenched in Western Europe. This prosperity allowed the Moslem world to engage in numerous activities to advance the arts and sciences. Because of their conquests, they had access to books on Greek thought and philosophy. Ironically, on the foundations of Western thought, the Moslems engaged in various pursuits that led to numerous advancements in the arts and sciences. One advancement which is used universally today was the Arabic number system. Even though this system was borrowed from India, it might not have come to be used in the west for quite some time had it not been for the Moslems. They used this numerical system to develop algebra and to make numerous other mathematical advancements. In addition to this, the Moslems made strides in medicine, astronomy, geography, and physics. "They introduced an impressive list of new farm crops from rice and sugar cane to watermelons as well as new fruits such as oranges and lemons. Toledo blades, Morocco leather, muslin and damask also recall their manufacturing skill."[69] At the same time the Moslems, also known as Saracens, were making advancements, western Europeans were losing their grip on civilization and struggling to survive.

IV. Western Europe

When the Roman Empire fell in the west, the territory was divided up among the various tribes of peoples that had overrun the region. As a result, there was little lasting order in Western Europe. Instead, leaders maneuvered for political control. The dissolution of the political order resulted in the decline of trade. It was no longer safe for merchants to move their goods in that region of the world. Thus, many simply gave up the effort to do so. As trade diminished, cities declined and economic hardships increased. The decline in the general level of economic well-being led historians to refer to the period as the Dark Ages. But this term is somewhat misleading. In the midst of the darkness of the time, many changes were taking place and a new kind of civilization was being formed. While this new civilization was based upon numerous Roman principles, it was more than that. Some institutions were destroyed and others reshaped. Men who had lived on the fringes of

---

[69] Ibid, pg. 85.

the Roman Empire became "Latinized" so to speak. This had already happened for many Europeans who had been part of the empire. In Spain, Gaul, Britain, and Italy the people had adopted many of the Roman customs. They had learned Latin and had given up many of their own customs to copy those of the ordinary Roman citizen. When the empire collapsed, the process was slowed considerably, but it did not stop. Rather, it continued by way of the Roman Catholic Church which not only converted the barbarians to Christianity, but exposed them to the Latin culture of Rome as well. In the meantime, there was competition for power among the various peoples who populated Europe.

As already noted, the political instability of Europe led to a situation where production was primarily consigned to large estates. The possession of land became a fundamental necessity for survival. Leaders of the various tribes of peoples vied for land because it provided what wealth could be obtained and served as a foundation for extending one's rule. The politico-economic system that arose in this fashion was known as feudalism. The details of this system will be elaborated in the next chapter.

With no clear cut political order intact, the Latin Church emerged as an important institution. Christianity had already made inroads into the various barbarian tribes of people that were competing with each other for land. However, the faith was quite weak and was often mixed with numerous superstitions. Nevertheless, the elders of the Roman Church were committed to nurturing these people in their faith despite their poor behavior. It was partly because of the high degree of immorality among these people that led some to seek a higher level of piety in monasticism. As a result, monasteries became a component part of Christianity.

It was in this environment of civil wars and near constant conflict over land between competing interests, that a sort of hierarchy of rule began to emerge. Feudal rule took shape rapidly in France which became a model of political rule throughout Western Europe. One of the more famous ruling families was the Carolingian family. By the end of the seventh century, this family had gained significant political power in France when Charles Martel gained a key mayoral position. Charles was the illegitimate son of Dagobert. His efforts at repelling the Moors at Tours will be forever remembered as the key event in stopping the spread of Islam in Europe. His subsequent campaigns against Moslem Spain secured Western Europe from the threat of the Islamic invasion.

The most notable individual of the Carolingian family, however, was Charlemagne. He was the greatest of the feudal kings of Europe. He was born in 742 and became king in 771 at the age of twenty-nine. He was a large man, over six feet tall. He enjoyed swimming, horseback riding, and hunting. Charles was temperate in both eating and drinking though he was never fond of fasting and thought that it hurt his health to do so. He mastered the Latin language and could speak it as well as his own. He also could understand Greek, but he was never able to speak it very well.

He was motivated to unify Europe by extending his government. During his long rule (771-814) he organized and directed a series of military campaigns that successfully established a European empire of sorts. In the course of accomplishing all of this, he proved himself a man of vision who possessed the practical ability to marshal resources to his cause. In addition, if ever there was a man who sought to bring about Christ's kingdom by force, it was Charlemagne. This was quite evident in the example of his conquest of the Saxons. Upon defeating them he offered "a choice between baptism and death, and had 4500 Saxon rebels beheaded in one day; after which he proceeded to Thionville to celebrate the nativity of Christ."[70] In the course of time, as Charles campaigns continued to be successful, he established an empire that stretched over most of Western Europe including modern day France, Belgium, the Netherlands, Germany, Switzerland, Austria, and much of Italy.

Charles regarded himself not only as a secular ruler, but also as the head of the Roman Catholic Church. He saw it as his personal business to direct the affairs of the church in order to continue the spread of Christianity. He was fond of reading the writings of the church fathers. Among the works he treasured, Augustine's *City of God* stood out as a favorite. This explains much of his behavior. He was endeavoring to build God's City on earth and saw himself as God's appointed agent for the task. Based upon his understanding of these things, it was clear that he conceived of his government as a theocracy similar to that of Israel which was established by God in the Old Testament.

His success was temporary, however. While he understood the

---

[70] Will Durant, op. cit., pg. 462.

vast benefits of living in God's City, he was nevertheless confused over how to obtain it. Political force was no substitute for the love of God, and only the love of God could change the hearts of men. Without regeneration of the soul, men were destined to live in various degrees of incivility relative to each other. The problem of humanity was that sin separated men not only from God, but from one another as well. In vain, Charlemagne attempted to remedy the situation by using the force of state power to compel people into submission and into conversion. Compassion, mercy, fraternity, and good were never, and never will be, achieved at the end of a sword. This is not to say that some things are not worth fighting and dying for, but that a good civilization is a matter of voluntary good will and not a matter of behavior under compulsion. To be sure, under duress and persecution the truth is always worth fighting and dying for. But, the truth cannot be promoted by force. This was known by the early Christian martyrs who gave up their lives rather than recant their faith in Jesus Christ. The test of whether or not something is worth standing for regardless of the consequences is whether or not it is true.

At any rate, Charlemagne misunderstood something fundamental about Christ's Kingdom and thought that it could be had by force. He was certainly not the only person in history to have made that mistake. In fact, it has been quite common for men in all ages to succumb to this temptation. Charlemagne stands out because he was so successful in gaining the military victories which provided the outward unity that he sought. So much so, that Pope Leo III declared him Roman Emperor on December 25, 800. In the remaining years of his life, Charles sought to solidify his authority under this title. At his death, he left a very large, unified European Empire for his children to rule. Still, it was an empire that would not last because his offspring did not share his vision or his abilities. In addition, it was primarily set up on a more or less contractual basis with many landowners. Since each of these possessed varying degrees of power themselves, the continuity of the empire depended upon the abilities of the king. Charlemagne's descendants were not his equals in this task. The result was the fragmentation of power within the context of feudal society. While we will discuss the details of feudalism in the next chapter, it would be profitable for us to consider another prominent figure that rose to power in that system.

In 1026, before becoming the Duke of Normandy, Robert I was

riding through the country side when he happened to see a girl washing clothes in a stream. The girl's name was Arlette and she was the daughter of a local tanner. He was fascinated with her, and would perhaps have sought to marry her regardless of the difference in their classes had he not already been married at the time. Still, he pursued a relationship with her and made her his mistress.

In 1028, Robert became the Duke of Normandy. In the same year he also had a son by Arlette and named him William. In 1035, Robert decided that he needed to go on a pilgrimage to Jerusalem as penitence for his many sins. Before he left to do so, he made William his heir. Robert died on his journey and, at the age of seven, William became the Duke of Normandy. Because he had acquired such a high position at such an early age, he would have hardly been able to maintain it without the aid of the king and of other noblemen who supported him. The problem of his rule was further compounded by his own background. During his life, he was often referred to as William the Bastard. On occasion he was able to accept his illegitimacy with a sense of humor, but he could also be quite sensitive about it. When he came of age, William demonstrated to everyone that he was able to manage his own affairs. In one case, "a rebellion tried to unseat him, but he put it down with dignified ferocity. He was a man of craft and courage and farseeing plans, a god to his friends, a devil to his foes."[71] In the course of time, he used his position to increase his power, control, and influence over more land.

William married Matilda who was the daughter of the Count of Flanders and it was recorded that he remained faithful to her all his life. The marriage expanded his influence and later put him in a position to vie for the throne of England. This he did in 1066. In that year Edward died and left the throne to Harold of Wessex. However, earlier in his life he had promised the throne to William. It was a promise that William had not forgotten. In addition to this fact, Harold had earlier in time pledged his fealty to William. For these reasons, William claimed the throne for himself. When Harold refused to step down, William sought and obtained the blessing of the Roman Church to claim the throne by force.

In October of 1066 he sailed across the English Channel with his

---

[71] Ibid, pg. 481.

forces and met Harold's army at Hastings. Harold's army had already been depleted by a previous encounter with Norse invaders. After repelling the Norsemen, Harold led his forces southward to meet William. On October the 14th the two armies fought against one another all day. At the end of the day William's forces were victorious. "Harold, his eye pierced by an arrow, fell blinded with blood, and was dismembered by Norman knights: one cut off his head, another a leg, another scattered Harold's entrails over the field. When the English saw their captain fallen they fled."[72] William went on to become the King of England and was crowned on Christmas day of that year.

William's ascendancy was an excellent example of the kinds of conquests that occurred within feudalism. This system of private government through contractual pledges of loyalty had developed in Western Europe and was the way in which numerous men both gained and lost power. Upon his victory, William consolidated his power and passed out favors to his friends in the feudal manner. He reduced most of the freemen of England to serfdom and established the feudal system there more fully than it had ever been before. Understanding the characteristics of this form of government and the kind of economic activity that it fosters is crucial not only to comprehending the actions and successes of a person like William, but to understanding some of our own practices today. Therefore, this is the topic of the next chapter.

Study Questions

1. What factors led to the collapse of the Roman Empire?
2. As a result of this collapse, what happened to life in Western Europe?
3. Where did the Byzantine Empire come from?
4. Who was Justinian and how did he attempt to revive the Roman Empire?
5. Explain how the religion of Islam developed. How did it give rise to the Moslem Empire?

---

[72] Ibid, pg. 495.

Chapter 9: Feudalism

I. The Political Environment

The barbarian invasions of the various German tribes throughout Western Europe destroyed the political structures there. The collapse of government resulted in the decline in commerce. Merchants could no longer transport their goods safely or find ready markets to sell their wares. As Will Durant explained:

> The results of the barbarian conquest were endless. Economically it meant reruralization. The barbarians lived by tillage, herding, hunting, and war, and had not yet learned the commercial complexities on which cities thrived; with their victory the municipal character of western civilization ceased for seven centuries.[73]

Land became the indispensable element for producing what wealth that could be had and the competition for it intensified. In this kind of environment, the use of force was necessary either to exploit the property of others or for personal protection from the aggression of others. It quickly became apparent to those merely protecting their interests, that they needed some kind of order to marshal sufficient resources for the purpose of maintaining adequate defenses against aggressors. The political system that developed was referred to as feudalism.

The seeds of feudalism lay in the common practices of the Roman Empire towards its decline and in the customs of the tribes that invaded the region. Among the features of Roman law which provided a footing for feudalism were the following. First, it was a common practice in Rome for a wealthy man to surround himself with a group of dependent followers. Such a man offered these followers favors in return for their

---

[73] Will Durant, *The Age of Faith*, (New York: Simon and Schuster, 1950), pg. 43.

labor. For example, someone might agree to enter into the service of a wealthy man and agree to give him his military expertise or his labor services to secure food and shelter for himself and his family. Such arrangements were mutually agreeable because of the benefits both received.

The barbarians made a living primarily from hunting, herding, and plundering other people. Therefore, they had no need of such contractual arrangements. Nevertheless, they did have a similar practice by which an older man would gather around him a group of youth who would fight in his behalf. For their efforts the older leader allowed the younger warriors to share in the spoils of war. This kind of arrangement, coupled with the contractual practices of the Romans, provided the foundation for the feudal hierarchy of political control that developed in Europe during the Middle Ages.

A second Roman practice that was important in forming the feudal system was binding free men to work certain plots of land. Recall that Diocletian began this practice in order to effectively institute in-kind taxes on produce. This decree had the effect of limiting the mobility of people in general and of slowing the amount of trade. It furthered the development of consigning production to large estates. In the feudal system, the mass of people were bound to the land in like manner.

The feudal system grew in the following way. As a landowner controlled more and more land, he reached a point where the amount of his property was more than he could manage himself. In this case, he secured the services of a vassal to oversee the land for him. The arrangement could be initiated from either side, and the property to be managed might be something other than land. Whatever the circumstance, the vassal agreed to certain conditions and made a pledge of his loyalty in return for the benefits granted to him. In time, these arrangements multiplied and were the basis of various military alliances.

These contracts also resulted in a developing hierarchy of rule. At the apex of this hierarchy was the king who, in theory, was the final arbiter of all matters of justice. Under him were numerous vassals who entered into various agreements with him and pledged their loyalties to him. Lesser nobles directly under the king could be quite powerful in their own right and, likewise, might have vast properties of their own. In turn, these men entered into agreements with a variety of other men who owed them their loyalty. In this way, land was divided among people to be worked for the fruits it would produce. Typically, the property was partitioned so finely that the lord over a particular piece of it was able to maintain himself, his family, and the serfs bound to it. Such properties were known as manors.

Within this framework, an overlord who needed help to protect his interests, called upon his vassals to honor their agreements and come to his aid in accordance with the contracts that they had entered into. Depending upon the relationships, these vassals, in turn, called upon their own vassals for assistance in the matter. In this way, a rather large army could be marshaled by the king for the purpose of either defending his kingdom or for conquering new territories. In addition, fairly small armies could be called upon to handle minor disputes. In a sense, the feudal system was a private form of government which established a complex system of loyalties for governing purposes.

The system had a number of drawbacks which eventually led to its demise. First, it was common practice for a man to enter into more than one overlord/vassal relationship. As a result, a man might owe his loyalty to a rather large number of overlords to whom he was bound. The problem with this arrangement occurred when a dispute would erupt between two of the man's overlords and both called upon his services against the other. In such cases the vassal faced a clear dilemma. These situations led to more complex contracts by which vassals pledged their loyalty to others. But these were of little help in solving the fundamental problem.

The second problem was the inconsistent theory upon which the entire system was based. Feudalism presupposed that the king was the final human authority in matters of law and justice. "Theoretically the king was the vassal of God, and governed by divine right in the sense that God permitted, and thereby authorized, his rule. Practically, however, the king had been elevated by election, inheritance, or war. Men like Charlemagne, Otto I, William the Conqueror, Philip Augustus, Louis IX, Frederick II, and Louis the Fair enlarged their inherited power by the force of character or arms; but normally the kings of feudal Europe were not so much the rulers of their peoples as the delegates of their vassals."[74] Thus, the evident conundrum of feudalism. If the king succeeded in

---

[74] Ibid, pg. 564.

consolidating the kind of power needed to be the final authority (as some did), a governmental monarchy arose and feudalism ceased to exist. In time power was consolidated as nations emerged in Europe. Nevertheless, the feudal system did recognize the value of the individual more than in the past, but the importance of the individual only extended to the nobility and the clergy and not to the peasantry. While this fell far short of today's concept of individual liberty, it was an advancement from what had been conceived of as liberty in the past.

In this light, we find the basis of some of the principles of modern day Western civilization. For example, if a vassal were accused of violating his contractual agreement with an overlord, he had the right to be judged by his peers. From this we obtained our own practice of giving the individual the right to be tried by a jury of his peers in civil and criminal judicial cases. Further, we find in such an observance the ground for not penalizing anyone without the due process of law. In addition to these things, revolutionary theory was formulated within the conceptual framework of contractual government. In particular, it was commonly understood that the king's authority was valid only so far as he continued to uphold his contractual agreements. Should he fail to do so, it was understood that he had violated the terms of contract and could not expect submission to his authority. As a result, the people under his control could legitimately reject his rule by way of revolution. It was this kind of thinking that was behind the American and French revolutions.

Government was thus established on the basis of private contracts. Wars broke out between people in the region when someone refused to honor the terms of a contract, or when there was a dispute about the terms of a contract. In addition, military action was taken to defend the region against outside aggressors who threatened to invade the area, or for the purpose of conquering new territories. For all these purposes a lord might call upon his vassals to come to his aid. Local wars were typically small and generally involved a limited number of people. Because of the use of armor, relatively few knights were actually killed during the conflicts. Nevertheless, a great deal of damage was done. Feuds between lords occurred with great frequency, and in the course of these conflicts, it was common for the knights of one lord to destroy the property of his enemy. They would typically kill the livestock and burn the grain in the fields of the lord that they were warring against. For this reason, serfs usually suffered most from the feuds as their livelihoods were destroyed. Having lost their livestock, they were forced to plow the fields without the help of oxen and many starved from the poor success of such meager means. These disturbances led the Roman Catholic Church to denounce such practices. In addition, by setting forth guidelines, the Roman Church sought to limit the timing and scope of battles to protect people from the ravages of continual warfare.

Due to the frequency of conflict, the construction of castles became commonplace. The castle was constructed to provide an adequate defense against one's enemies. They were typically erected in locations which were difficult to reach; many were built on hills. In addition, it was common for the castle to be surrounded by a moat, which was difficult to cross whether it was dry or filled with water. In an actual conflict, those wishing to enter the castle sought to either scale the walls with ladders or with siege works, or to come through the gates with battering rams. Those defending the castle sought to keep out their foes by shooting arrows at their enemies and by throwing rocks and pouring boiling oil on their heads. While a castle might sometimes serve as the residency of the lord, many maintained manor houses in which they lived most often and only used the castle in cases of emergency or for various ceremonies.

Life among the aristocracy was far from what we might call luxurious by today's standards. Nevertheless, it was significantly better than that of the peasants. While food was generally plentiful, it was rather plain. Spices were normally rare, though as trade increased in the latter part of the Middle Ages they were more prevalent. The typical foods eaten included cabbage, turnips, carrots, onions, beans, peas, apples, pears, various kinds of bread and grains, meat, and fish. In addition, they ate cheese and drank both wine and ale. There was no coffee or tea and milk was usually used to make butter and cheese. The food was typically prepared by being cooked over a wood or charcoal fire. Meats were roasted on spits or with vegetables in large boiling pots. While table manners eventually developed, for the most part people ate with their hands and used their own knives to cut their meat. It was not until the eleventh century that forks made their way to Europe from the East.

In the castles and manor houses, the furnishings were sparse and primitive. The structures themselves were heated by large fireplaces and were usually devoid of windows because of the need to keep out the cold, as there was no glass in general use for such purposes. Until the Crusades, the floors and walls were cold and bare. Afterwards, rugs and tapestries became fairly common. As far as clothes were concerned, most were made from wool. In addition, animal skins were also made into tunics and overcoats and worn to keep the person warm in the winter.

The nobility engaged in a number of pastimes. Among these, hunting was the most common. In fact, most lords took great pride in perfecting their skills as hunters and spent most of their leisure time engaged in the sport. In addition to hunting, they were also very interested in horse breeding. This makes much sense when it is recalled that the nobility was often called upon for military service. The instruments of such service included their weapons of war and the mounts upon which they rode. Therefore, it was important for them to develop their skills of marksmanship and agility. Further, they needed to possess a stock of horses capable of the demands that would be placed upon them in times of battle. In such times, a good horse might very well have been the difference between life and death.

Due to the pressures imposed by the Latin Church, and the general interests of the nobility at large, a code of conduct for knights developed. This code of conduct is commonly referred to as chivalry. It provided a framework within which private warfare was to be waged. James Thompson and Edgar Johnson provided us an excellent explanation of this code.

> It would be strange had there not arisen in feudal society some system of training the young noble to hunt and fight on horseback, to render service to his lord, and to govern his inferiors; some system of inculcating in him the ideals and virtues that bound him to the privileged class of which he was born a member. Such a system was chivalry, which we might define as the institution or profession of knighthood. It would be strange, too, if in the development of such an institution the Church had not come to exert a large influence. Since chivalry may be said to have been the attempt of the medieval aristocracy to formulate and to realize its highest ideal, the institution that undertook to pronounce the proper aims of the good life could not possibly be left out. . . . [U]nbridled private warfare was clearly recognized by the better elements in society as a menace that must be abolished or curtailed. [Without a central government,] the task was. . . left to the Church

[which spoke out against certain activities and sought certain limitations]. . . .The movement was taken up to some extent by lay lords, who formed associations to maintain peace. . . . [Finally,] these checks upon private warfare were reinforced by the growing power of the kings and the great feudal lords. . . . [In response to their efforts], training for knighthood [became]. . . something very different from the rough, simple training of earlier days. . . . At seven a vassal's young son might be sent to the court of his father's lord to serve seven years as page or valet, under the care of the women of the household. Here his duties were those of a servant, since the knight must learn to serve before being served. He received religious instruction and learned the "rudiments of love"; he was trained in grace of carriage and in courtesy and deportment, especially in the proper way to enter and leave a room in which his superiors were and in the proper forms for addressing them. . . . "A truly perfect, gentle knight" was bound "to fear God and maintain the Christian religion; to serve the King faithfully and valorously; to protect the weak and defenceless; to refrain from wanton giving of offence; to live for honour and glory, despising pecuniary reward; to fight for the general welfare of all; to obey those placed in authority; to guard the honour of the knightly order; to shun unfairness, meanness and deceit; to keep faith and speak truth; to persevere to the end in all enterprises begun; to respect the honour of women; to refuse no challenge from an equal and never to turn the back upon a foe."[75]

While this list of virtues is certainly evidence of a movement toward greater civility, we must not think that it was strictly adhered to by all knights. Some diligently sought to emulate the ideal knight in everyday life. However, most did so only when it was to their immediate advantage. In practice, "the same hero who one day fought bravely in tournament or battle might on another be a faithless murderer. . . .He might prate of protecting the weak, and strike unarmed peasants down

---

[75] James W. Thompson and Edgar N. Johnson, *An Introduction to Medieval Europe: 300-1500*, (New York: W. W. Norton & Company, Inc., 1937), pp. 319-324.

with a sword; he treated with scorn the manual worker on whose labor rested his citadel of gallantry, and with frequent coarseness and occasional brutality the wife whom he had sworn to cherish and protect. He could hear Mass in the morning, rob a church in the afternoon, and drink himself into obscenity at night. . . "[76] This is to be expected given that human nature is what it is. Just the same, in the course of time, the influence of both Christianity and the women of the age did moderate many of the excesses of barbarism practiced by the knights. But, while a more civil lord might result in a better life for the peasants subject to him, such an increase in well-being was marginal at best. As we shall see, the life of the serf was quite harsh, and they were always treated as little more than slaves.

The knight was, above all else, a soldier of war and was expected to be ready to fight for his lord when called upon to do so. It was out of this need to be prepared for war that the tournament developed. Tournaments were festive occasions which provided knights the opportunity to test their skills against other knights. They might last a day or for an entire week. Such events were set either in a town square or in a large open field with bleachers set up for spectators. Contests included jousts between a pair of contestants or a staged battle between two competing groups of knights. In the jousts, the competitors began on horseback and rode against one another with lances. After one party was knocked off his mount, the contest continued on foot until one party gave up or was knocked unconscious or killed, or until the noble presiding over the event called the match off. In the staged battle, the warring groups of knights would fight each other, sometimes to the death, in the same manner. The winners or survivors of the event celebrated their victory and enjoyed the praise of the spectators who witnessed their bravery and skill.

With all this said, the life of the average noble was not one of enjoying a great deal of wealth at his leisure. Quite the opposite was true. As overseers of manors, they had the job of managing the production of all the goods upon which their lives and the lives of the serfs depended. In addition, it fell upon them to protect their property from all aggression with whatever help they might be able to call upon from those who

---

[76] Will Durant, op. cit., pg. 575.

pledged them their loyalty. If they possessed more than one manor, they traveled from place to place to assure their control and to handle the affairs at each location. It was up to them to provide the rule of law, such as it was, on their various properties.

"According to one point of view, feudalism was the cause of the sorry state of affairs during the 'Dark Ages.' Others hold that the feudal political structure was an attempt to bring some semblance of order to a distracted world."[77] The first of these views can be understood by way of analogy to the activity of street gangs in the cities of America today. These gangs mark out boundaries and claim control over certain territory. Conflicts arise when one gang ventures beyond the confines of its domain and trespasses upon that of another group. These confrontations can erupt into gang wars which can spill over and affect other people who just happen to live in the neighborhoods involved. To be sure, there are numerous parallels between this analogy and feudalism. It is also quite true that this kind of behavior is detrimental to civilization. But, before concluding that this is all that feudalism amounted to, some consideration of an alternative view is warranted.

"Now feudalism was not the cause of the chaos in the medieval world, according to the contrary view; it was rather the consequence of attempts to stabilize the social and political order to avert chaos."[78] Proponents of this view point to the contractual arrangements that were created among the various parties and to the fact that these were intended to outline a man's responsibilities. In this view, the chief aim of feudalism was to promote the acceptable behavior of men in relation to one another. While numerous flaws in the system prevented it from ever working very well, those who embrace this perspective point out that the arrangements made did bring about some order in an otherwise chaotic environment. And, in the course of time, it did tend to temper some of the grosser forms of barbarism and eventually brought a degree of order from which nations would be formed.

---

[77] Edward Coleson, *The Harvest of Twenty Centuries*, (Spring Arbor, Michigan, 1967), pg. 91.

[78] Ibid, pg. 92.

II. Life on the Manor

As mentioned in the previous chapter, toward the end of the Roman Empire production was more and more confined to large estates in Europe. These large estates are commonly referred to as manors. They operated as self-sufficient as possible given the conditions in which they were located. There were of course many differences among the various estates due to variations in terrain and climate. As a result, some things simply could not be produced locally and had to be traded for if they were to be obtained at all. As a result, some trade continued in the Middle Ages. However, it was substantially reduced from what had been known during the rule of the Romans and the more or less self-sufficient manor served as the normal means of production.

The ordinary manor generally included an area that was between 900 and 2000 acres of land. Small landowners usually held only a few manors under their control, and some had only one. Larger landowners might own many of these tracts of land. The typical tract of land on which a manor existed was somewhat varied to sustain the many economic activities. It included some pasture and meadow land, a forest, a stream and a pond, and a large amount of arable land. These variations allowed for numerous activities and the production of as wide a variety of goods as possible. From growing vegetables in the fields to hunting game in the woods, a diversity of land was most suitable to the self-sufficient ideal which was the feudal manor.

The work of producing the things needed for survival generally fell on the backs of the peasants or serfs. Serfs were bound to the land for life. They spent their entire lives living in one location and rarely ventured beyond the confines of their own manor except to visit a neighboring village. Any extended travel to see the world was unthinkable. What the serfs knew of the outside world they learned from brief encounters with merchants and traveling bands of entertainers who might come through their village from time to time. This was the extent of their knowledge of the broader world around them and they could know little else because they could not read. The primary sphere of their knowledge encompassed that of a practical sort. They knew the fundamentals of various agricultural endeavors and used this understanding, such as it was, to sustain the lives of themselves and their families.

The typical working day began at sunrise and ended at sunset.

While each peasant was responsible for the produce of particular strips of land, the community labored together to do the work of plowing the land and planting, cultivating, and harvesting the crops. Each serf possessed strips of land in each of three fields which were employed in rotating fashion to produce summer grains, or to raise winter grains, or to be left fallow. In addition to growing food, the serfs also had to take care of their livestock and the numerous other chores associated with farm life. In short, they were farmers who spent their lives in this enterprise without the benefit of the capital equipment that modern day farmers use to make their efforts more productive. Their equipment was limited to a few hand tools and a plow which was pulled by oxen. With these, they worked long hours to grow crops and raise animals. Beyond the work they performed for themselves, they were required to work the lord's land as well and to make themselves available for other projects that the lord saw fit to pursue. These other projects might involve building a bridge over a stream, improving a road, or digging an irrigation canal.

Once the crops were harvested, the serfs were forced to pay the lord his due and were forced to tithe to the church. In addition to fulfilling these obligations, they were also required to use the village mill to grind their grain, the village press to crush their grapes, the village brew house to brew their beer, and the village bakery to bake their bread. For each of these services they paid additional fees to the lord of the manor. Because the lord possessed a monopoly in providing such services, it was not uncommon for disputes to erupt over the quality of the work performed by the miller, the wine maker, the brew master, and the baker. To avoid the payment of the fees to use the lord's facilities and to avoid the sometimes shoddy work performed there, it was also common for the local villagers to ignore the mandate and grind their own grain, make their own wine and beer, and bake their own bread. Still, to do so was to violate the rules of manor life for which the serf was liable to be fined.

For all their efforts, peasants generally had enough to eat. They ate the same kinds of things that were available to the nobility. In times of famine, their lot was more precarious, but then most people were confined to the margin of subsistence by the lack of trade anyway. In terms of housing, serfs lived in thatched huts. The floors were dirt and the furnishings were sparse. "As often as not the house had only one room, at most two; a wood-burning fireplace, an oven, a kneeding trough, table and benches, cupboard and dishes, utensils and andirons, caldron, and pothanger, and near the oven. . . an immense mattress of feathers or straw, on which the peasant, his wife and children, and his overnight guest all slept. . . "[79] In the winter it was quite common for the family's livestock to join them inside the hut. This practice not only sheltered the animals from the weather, but provided additional heat as well. While it fell to the women to keep the shelter clean, cleanliness itself was not a high priority.

While the peasants worked very hard, there were days of leisure. The spread of Christianity made every Sunday a holy day and a day of rest. While they were required to attend church, they were also able to participate in numerous other activities and games during the rest of the day. In addition to having every Sunday off from work, they also enjoyed numerous other holidays. Depending on his propensity to show kindness to others, the lord of the manor might even break open his own storehouse to provide his peasants with food and drink on certain days of celebration.

By modern standards, the life of a serf was very difficult. He labored long hours with few tools to produce what little wealth he could and then was forced to pay numerous taxes, fees, and tithes to others. Some estimate that two thirds of everything the average serf produced was taken from him through these various impositions. While that which remained was generally sufficient to sustain his life and that of his family, there was no thought of saving to provide for a brighter future. Without the savings of the general masses of people, there was little accumulation of capital and, therefore, little economic progress. The progress that was made was largely confined to the special projects which the lord of the manor initiated. These included such things as building a dam, bridge, or improving a road to a neighboring village. Over time, these projects added up and provided some base for the economic progress that did occur during this age.

While Christianity was making inroads among the populace, most people remained extremely superstitious and continued numerous pagan practices. The result of all of this was to mix pagan beliefs with Christian doctrines. The church leadership worked to mitigate against this, but their general success in doing so depended upon the capabilities of the

---

[79] Will Durant, op. cit., pg. 557.

local clergy. Furthermore, given the low level of scholarship in that day, it was not uncommon to find even men of the clergy adopting numerous superstitions and pagan beliefs. As a result, numerous pagan ideas and practices became generally acceptable.

Among the pagan practices to make inroads in Christian communities was the practice of the ordeal to determine the guilt or innocence of an individual accused of wrongdoing when there was no other evidence. To decide who was telling the truth, custom required either the plaintiff or the defendant to undertake an ordeal to prove his cause. There were many different kinds of ordeals that were practiced. For example, there was the ordeal of hot water. In this test, the person chosen to undertake the ordeal had to stick his hand into a pot of boiling water to retrieve some small object that had been placed there. If his hand healed properly following the test, his position was established as true. In another kind of ordeal, both the plaintiff and defendant battled each other to the death with whatever weapons were available. The winner of the fight established his position by defeating his opponent. To our minds these notions are strange indeed. On the basis of our understanding, such practices prove nothing except that an individual might be more susceptible to infection when injured or that someone might possess greater skill in battle. But, in the minds of the people of the Middle Ages, they were convinced that God would uphold the cause of the just regardless of the natural laws at work. Religiously minded people today continue to believe that God will uphold the cause of justice. However, they generally realize that such judgments will often be made in eternity rather than in the here and now.

This provides a basic summary of what life was like during the Middle Ages in Western Europe. There was a well-defined class system which governed the individual's life pretty much from cradle to grave and, while it sometimes happened, it was uncommon for anyone to move out of the class to which he was born. An individual in a lower class never had any redress in law if he was harmed by someone above him. He could only bring charge against someone from his own class. Illiteracy was common not only among serfs, but also among the nobility and, if it had not been for the Roman Catholic Church, any form of formal education might have ceased completely. Thus, the Roman Church served numerous functions in society beyond its role in preaching the gospel of Jesus Christ and making disciples of all peoples. Since it was such a major institution, we will consider its development in the following chapter.

Study Questions

1. Describe the political environment of feudalism.
2. What was the inherent inconsistency embedded in the political order of feudalism that eventually led to its demise?
3. What role did the church serve in feudal society?
4. Describe what life was like under feudalism.
5. It is sometimes said that during feudalism, "the nobility fought, the clergy prayed, and the serfs did all the work." Explain the meaning of this saying.

Chapter 10: The Church and the State

I. The Spread of Christianity and the Development of the Roman Catholic Church

The importance of Christianity cannot be underestimated if one hopes to understand life in the Middle Ages. In addition, it is important to understand the development of the Roman Catholic Church, because it played such a large role in the daily lives of people during the age. To be sure, the Christian religion played a crucial role in both the history of Western Europe and of the Byzantine Empire. The growth of Christianity in the first century is largely recounted in the New Testament, and we have already considered some of the details about how the new religion began and spread. We know that groups of Christian converts formed small churches in various towns and cities throughout much of the Roman Empire, especially in Asia Minor. The missionary efforts of the apostles were particularly important in establishing these congregations. There was no organized structure that related one church to the others. Instead, they were loosely bound together by a common belief in Jesus Christ and in the gospel message that had been presented to them by the apostles and other disciples.

That is not to say that there was no interaction between these churches. The apostles often called upon congregations in one region to give money and other resources to provide for the needs of congregations in other places. The apostles reasoned that such giving ought to flow out of the common bond of faith they shared with Christians throughout the world. In the view of the apostles, all believers were bound together by Jesus Christ. Thus, while there was no visible church organization at the time, there was a catholic church made up of all true believers. On the basis of this invisible unity of faith, the apostles called believers everywhere to help their brothers in need. The evidence provided in the New Testament indicates that when called upon, various churches readily responded. Nonetheless, the churches in the various cities remained more or less independent of one another.

It was necessary for each of these churches to develop its own organization and the apostle Paul was helpful in providing a structure of how to do so. Each local congregation selected elders and deacons whose job it was to oversee and coordinate the activities of their church. In time, however, two factors worked together to strengthen the connection of local congregations to each other. First, there was a need to coordinate and supervise the broader missionary efforts. As a result, some church leaders were selected to oversee the efforts of churches in particular regions, thus giving rise to a visible organizational structure between congregations.

In addition to the need to coordinate the missionary effort, there was also a need to maintain a consistent message of the faith. Many of the new converts were from pagan backgrounds. As a result, they brought certain superstitions and pagan beliefs with them to their newfound faith in Christ. These beliefs were typically at odds with the teachings of Jesus and his apostles. Nevertheless, it was quite common for such people to attempt to fuse their long held pagan beliefs with Christian doctrine. This resulted in numerous doctrinal disputes. The need to settle such disputes to maintain a clear and consistent articulation of the Christian message further facilitated the move to a single visible organizational structure. While the apostles wrote letters clarifying the faith, church leaders afterwards began to hold councils to settle doctrinal disputes.

The problem of maintaining doctrinal purity intensified when Christianity was made the state religion. This association forced unbelieving pagans into the church. As a result, many people confessed faith in Christ to get along in society and avoid the consequences of vocal unbelief. In turn, these people had a vested interest in introducing their own preferred doctrinal errors. In their way of thinking the successful introduction of doctrines that better suited their own peculiar tastes and preferences made the religious exercise more palatable. This compounded the problem of resolving doctrinal disputes and also increased the number of them. In this process, church doctrines came under steady attack. That is not to say that the Christian religion was eclipsed either in the Byzantine Empire or in Western Europe, but that it was often masked and confused in both places. Though most everyone claimed to be Christian, in reality the actual number who believed was far fewer.

The difference between professing to be a follower of Christ and actually being one was not new. There were false professions of faith ever since the religion began. In the book of Acts, which recounts the history of the initial growth of the church, there is a story of a husband named Ananias and his wife, Sapphira. According to the account provided, though they claimed to believe in Christ, their claim was shown to be empty by their actions. What initially motivated the couple to make a profession of faith is unknown. That they actually did make such a false profession is an example of the fact that such people have been part of the church in all generations. Jesus himself predicted that this would happen in his church when he told his disciples the parable of the wheat growing with the tares.[80] While Jesus' story was given in reference to the world at large, there is no reason to assume that it does not also apply to human institutions as well. In fact, Jesus told his followers that at the time of the judgment there would be people who expected to enter heaven but who would be turned away because they did not know him.[81] Certainly, among people Jesus had in mind here, there must have been more than a few churchgoers. Just the same, the point being made is that maintaining the fundamental teachings of Christianity became harder when it became the state religion. The result of this action was to force many unbelievers into the church and to open the door for politicians to try to manipulate the religion for their own purposes.

To be sure, doctrinal disputes arose before Christianity was made the state religion and would have continued to arise even if it had not been so designated. It was the need to settle disputes about the nature of the Christian religion that gave rise to the early church councils. These meetings of church leaders were formed in order to maintain the purity of Christian teachings. The Arian heresy was a prime example of the doctrinal controversies that arose in this early era of church history and of how they were resolved in the context of council meetings of church leaders. Arius, a presbyter in Alexandria, began teaching against the divinity of Christ. He argued that Christ was not co-eternal with the Father, but instead had been created by the Father. This position went against the teachings of Jesus and his apostles and was refuted by the church leaders at the Council of Nicea. Constantine oversaw the deliberations since he considered himself the head of the church.

---

[80] Matthew 13:24-30.

[81] see Matthew 25: 31-46.

However, his role was secondary and, in this case, the matter was resolved by more knowledgeable churchmen. In fact, his primary interest in the whole affair was that there would be some resolution that would maintain the unity of his empire. As part of the resolution of the debate, the Nicene Creed was penned. This creed was a succinct statement of Christian belief.

While church leaders had rejected the Arian heresy, that was unfortunately not the end of the matter. Constantine's son, Constantius, adopted the position as his own and began to persecute those who remained faithful to the claims of Jesus Christ and to the teachings of the apostles. That the reversal in position came from a governmental ruler's decision demonstrated the political problem that arose when Christianity was made the state religion. In a bitter twist of irony, those most firmly committed to the original teachings of the Christian faith were once again persecuted for their faith, even though their religion was the officially mandated one. From our vantage point, the important point to make here is that the Christian religion became intertwined with state politics and that many unbelievers used the name of Christ to achieve certain pragmatic ends. Notwithstanding, true Christianity continued to spread even when its believers found themselves standing against the official decrees of the state. Finally, as we saw in a previous chapter, such political entanglements between political officials and church leaders eventually led to the split of the church between the east and the west. In an effort to maintain greater doctrinal purity from the heretical positions of political leaders, church leaders in Rome asserted themselves as the official leaders of the church, thus giving rise to the Roman Catholic Church in the west while the Eastern Orthodox Church continued under state rule in the east.

One additional point should be stressed. While there can be only one correct understanding of the Christian religion, that understanding is not perfectly known among men. That is not to say that nothing is known for certain about the religion, but, because human beings err, human knowledge of the truth is incomplete. Some error is due to ignorance, while other error is the result of willful disobedience. This fact should not be surprising since one of the chief tenets of the religion is that all men, save Christ, are sinners who err. The confession itself is a matter of telling the truth. In every period of time, and in the life of every person, whether they are believers in Christ Jesus or not, shortcomings can be found. While the history of mankind is the story of the depravity of the human race, the history of the church is the story of God's work to redeem and sanctify people for himself. By doing this, he demonstrates his perfect justice and mercy. To the reprobate he shows his justice in judgment and his mercy in staying his hand by bearing patiently their sin. To those being saved he shows his justice in the atoning sacrifice of Christ for sin and his mercy by accounting Christ righteousness to them. The church is a representation of the coming kingdom of Christ that will be made up of the saints. In the present age it is made up of people who err. Therefore, the church has never been the perfect reflection of the justice and mercy of God, nor the perfect earthly manifestation of the *City of God*.

The history of the church is a history of the ongoing struggle to remain faithful to the religion begun by Jesus Christ and taught by the apostles. Of fundamental importance in this task is the need to state clearly certain propositions. These include the Trinity of God, the divine and human natures of Jesus Christ, the atonement of sin through Christ's death and resurrection for all who believe, the resurrection of the body, and the future judgment of the world when Christ returns. In addition, there is a whole host of other teachings which arise from the careful study of Scripture. Such study has continued since the religion began and is still ongoing today. While the fundamental tenets of the faith are clear, there is still much dispute over many issues.

Some of the continuing disputes are instigated by people whose purpose is to thwart the church in its mission. Such people mislead others by confusing the issues. They may be motivated by a desire to profess to worship Christ while disregarding his mandates, or they may simply be trying to undermine the church. Other disputes arise between men of goodwill. In this case, there are proponents on each side of the debate who desire to promote the best understanding as they see it. These disputes arise for many reasons. For instance, they can arise because the issue is conceptually difficult or because the context of scriptural passages is unclear. It is recognized in these cases that all points of view cannot be equally true. It should also be recognized that while some issues are so fundamental to the religion that they cannot be compromised without destroying the faith, others can remain debatable because none of the positions taken strays far from the fundamental profession of faith. The point of all this is that some matters will remain debatable. Regrettably, some people have been persecuted too severely for what amounted to marginal differences of opinion.

With this in mind, we can return to our discussion of church history and the split between the east and the west. As already noted, when Christianity became the official religion, the number of doctrinal controversies increased. It was in this era that Leo was born in A.D. 390. When he was fifty years of age, he became the bishop of Rome. At that time, the churches in Rome, Constantinople, Jerusalem, Antioch, and Alexandria were the most influential. Of these, the church at Rome was the only one located in the west. As the barbarian invaders were separating Western Europe from Eastern control, and as the orthodox bishops were battling against the heretical leanings of numerous secular rulers, the need to maintain the purity of church doctrine seemed paramount. It was in this context that Leo asserted his rule over the entire church. This marked a turning point for the western branch of the church. Leo based his argument on Matthew 16:17-19. In this passage, Jesus told Peter that he would be an integral part of building the kingdom. He specifically said, ". . . you are Peter, and on this rock I will build my church. . . " From this passage, Leo reasoned that Jesus had given Peter the authority over the entire church. He further reasoned that this authority had been passed down to the bishop of Rome since it was the widely accepted tradition that Peter was instrumental in starting the church there. While Leo's contention was generally accepted by the church leadership in the west, the eastern churches rejected it. Leo's assertion of apostolic succession was also rejected later in time by the Protestants who asserted that apostolic authority was never passed on and, therefore, ended with the death of John. Just the same, during Leo's life, doctrinal disputes were intense and needed to be settled in order to maintain a message consistent with the basic tenets of the Christian faith.

Whether or not one accepts papal rule, Leo's motives to maintain the purity of church doctrine were admirable. There is always a need to settle disagreements over the meaning of scriptural passages in order to uphold the traditional teachings of Jesus Christ and the apostles. Sometimes the issues debated are unclear in and of themselves and this compounds the problem of maintaining a consistent system of doctrines. Nevertheless, the need to settle disputed matters was and is important to maintaining unity in the faith. Whatever the solutions to disputes were or might be, church leaders have always held that they should be in accord with the traditional teachings of Jesus and the apostles. In the east, the emperor claimed the ultimate authority to resolve debates and this of course led to more than a little political maneuvering. Leo's solution to the problem was to leave the final resolution of conflict in the hands of the highest ranking church leader rather than in the hands of a secular ruler. This may be overstating the case, as popes have generally not exercised such authority without significant input from other high ranking clergy. Nevertheless, it did promote a monarchial form of church government that placed essential control in the hands of the highest ranking churchman. As a result, a difference of opinion about the proper form of church government eventually became a point of disagreement between Protestants and Roman Catholics later.

With all this said, Leo was a capable and faithful man. At the Council of Chalcedon he led the way in declaring the orthodox position regarding the two natures of Christ. The statement drafted at the Council made clear the teaching that Jesus possessed two natures that resided together in a single person such that the natures were neither mixed, changed, divided, nor separated. He maintained a very high view of the Bible and was seen as a man of high moral character throughout his life. Something of his character is revealed in a meeting he had with Attila the Hun. During Leo's lifetime, the Huns were in the midst of invading Italy and had prevailed against numerous military forces of the empire. When this happened, the emperor asked Leo to meet with Attila, and he agreed to do so. Following the meeting, Attila retreated. One writer accounts for his exodus as follows:

> When Attila faced this 'old man of harmless simplicity, venerable in his grey hair and his majestic garb,' and when in addition the apostles Peter and Paul appeared beside him, 'clad like bishops' with 'swords stretched out over his head,' and threatened with death if he did not obey the pope's command, there was nothing for the trembling yellow heathen to do but return with his troops to his wooden palace in Pannonia and his wife Kreka and his linen sheets and embroidered coverlets.[82]

---

[82] James W. Thompson and Edgar N. Johnson, *An Introduction to Medieval Europe: 300-1500,* (New York: W. W. Norton & Company, 1937), pg. 100.

Whether or not this story is true, cannot be known. What is known is that following their meeting, Attila thought it wiser to return home than to continue his conquest, even though he had the clear military advantage by human estimation. What was it about Leo that prompted an otherwise fearless military leader to retreat from battle? Perhaps the quality of his life as a faithful and devoted follower of Christ produced a degree of holiness that a pagan barbarian could recognize and fear. Whatever Attila's reasons for retreating, he returned from where he had come and died within the year. With his death, the mongol threat ended.

Leo served the church faithfully throughout his life. After his death, Christianity progressed by spreading the gospel message according to the capacities of later church leaders. Some proved to be more interested in promoting their own ends than in promoting the cause of Christ. Others were far more faithful and worked diligently to fulfill the mission that Jesus gave the church. In particular, they sought to win converts and make disciples among all the different peoples of the earth. One of the most influential papal rulers of the Middle Ages was Gregory the Great. He was born to a wealthy senatorial family of Rome in A.D. 540. He was a man of great ability and at the age of 33 became prefect of the city of Rome.[83] Although he served the city well in his handling of both civil and military affairs, he was far more interested in religion. After a brief term in secular office, he turned his attention to Christianity. He used most of his family's wealth to establish several monasteries, even turning the family palace into one.

In the initial years of this pursuit, Gregory spent much of his time fasting and praying. He aspired to an ascetic life until he was called into church service. "In 579 Pope Pelagius II sent him on an embassy to Constantinople where he gained invaluable experience in diplomacy. In 586 he became abbot of his monastery in Rome, and in 590 was elected pope. . . Gregory bent his ceaseless energies towards increasing the prestige of his See in lands where it had fallen low, and his efforts were not vain. He clearly saw the need for missions, for more than two-thirds

---

[83] The term prefect refers to a governmental administrative position in the community.

of Europe was still pagan. . . "[84] In addition, he reasserted the claim that the bishop of Rome was the supreme Christian authority on earth and extended papal control over the Roman Catholic Church. He thought very highly of the Scriptures and was profoundly devotional. His theology was most influenced by the writings of Augustine.

Since he was not particularly original in theological matters, he shared both Augustine's clarity and his mistakes. Among his human weaknesses was the fact that he was overly committed to asceticism. In his religious pursuit of God, Gregory denied himself many things that might have greatly improved his health; he chose to fast extensively. Even when he did eat, he imposed such strict limitations on his diet that he caused himself permanent physical harm. "Austerities and responsibilities had ruined his health; he suffered from indigestion, slow fever, and gout."[85] Toward the end of his life, his physical ailments so consumed him that he spent much of his time wishing to die. Had he better cared for himself, perhaps he could have served the church longer and more diligently. Nevertheless, he lived his life in a manner he believed was fitting before his Lord.

In spite of, or maybe in combination with, his asceticism, Gregory was devoted to serving the poor and the destitute. He willingly gave his own money to meet the physical needs of others and directed church funds to this cause as well. "To every poor family in Rome he distributed monthly a portion of corn, wine, cheese, vegetables, oil, fish, meat, clothing, and money; and every day his agents brought cooked provisions to the sick and infirm."[86] For his service to the poor he was well thought of and highly respected. Perhaps this explains the success he had in consolidating papal power. Because of this increase in power, the pope of the Latin Church played an instrumental role in the affairs of the Christian church as well as in political affairs throughout the Middle Ages.

One thing is clear, though the church was by no means a perfect

---

[84] A.M. Renwick and A.M. Harman, *The Story of the Church*, (Grand Rapids, Michigan: William B. Eerdmans Publishing, 1958), pp. 64-65.

[85] Will Durant, *The Age of Faith*, (New York: Simon and Schuster, 1950), pg. 520.

[86] Ibid, pg. 521.

institution, it did serve a very important role. During the barbarian invasions, church leaders demonstrated great courage and valor. They often stood between would-be conquerors and the masses of people who would suffer if they were allowed to continue unchecked. Because of the willingness of church leaders to stand up to military leaders, they gained favor in the eyes of ordinary people. These actions helped the church grow stronger. As with all human institutions, the power that organizations wield can be used for good or evil. And, since human beings are depraved, it was inevitable that on occasion the Latin Church's power would be used for evil. As with any visible organization, the Latin Church was a mixed bag; it benefitted the human condition in a multitude of different ways, but it was also used for expedient political ends from time to time.

II. Monasticism

The development of monastic orders was an off shoot of the spread of Christianity that was sometimes coupled with asceticism. Understanding monasticism is important to understanding the Middle Ages. Ascetic practices were common in a number of religions and philosophies of the time and proponents of them could be found among all types of people including the Indians, Jews, Greeks, and Egyptians. It was particularly important to gnostic philosophies that taught that the material world was evil and that only the spiritual world was good. For this reason, it was common practice of gnostics to either inflict severe bodily hardships upon themselves or to give themselves over to hedonistic indulgences to gain greater spirituality. They argued that such actions were necessary to gain certain spiritual knowledge. Ascetic influences on Christianity can be traced back to the converted people in cultures that were most influenced by these ideas. To some extent, this influence gave rise to monasticism. As Renwick and Harman point out:

> Christian asceticism took its rise from St. Anthony who was born in Egypt in 251 A.D. He forsook wealth and social position, and retired to mountain-caves in order to dedicate himself to lonely contemplation. Later he gathered round him a small group of disciples which he organized into a community in the desert. Members of such communities

were known as 'cenobites', meaning 'having life in common', a more accurate term than 'monk' which really means 'a solitary'.[87]

Following Anthony's lead, other Christian ascetics founded monastic orders in Egypt which became quite popular. The concept of such orders was eventually imported to Europe by individuals who visited Egypt and were impressed by the simpleness of life in these communes. On the surface, it appeared that these communities provided the Christian answer for materialism, a condition in which the individual denies the importance of his spiritual well-being while focusing only on his immediate physical needs and desires. However, such a conclusion is unwarranted. As we shall see, the apostle Paul spoke against some of the worst aspects of asceticism even as he preached of the importance of committing all of one's self and all of one's resources to the cause of Christ. Nevertheless, he understood that a commitment to asceticism alone merely led to some of the worst forms of self abasement with no other particular end in mind. He was convinced that these practices were totally at odds with the message he wished to preach to the world. Paul admonished people to use their wealth for the cause of Christ, not to disdain it entirely. He feared that ascetic practices would be promoted for the sake of asceticism and that such activity would have nothing to do with Christ.

In some cases, Paul's fears were realized. In time, there arose a competition of sorts among those given to asceticism. It was almost as if they competed to see whose ascetic practices were the most austere. Some prided themselves on going long spans of time fasting, while others deprived themselves of sleep or slept in harsh places and exposed themselves to all kinds of natural afflictions. Some monks isolated themselves from all other humans by venturing deep into caves. "Some, like Bessarion for forty, Pachomius for fifty, years, never [laid] down while they slept; some specialized in silence, and went many years without uttering a word; others carried heavy weights wherever they went, or bound their limbs with iron bracelets, greaves, or chains. Many proudly recorded the number of years since they had looked upon a woman's

---

[87] A.M. Renwick and A.M. Harman, op. cit., pg. 73.

face."[88]

What is clear about all these practices is that they miss the most fundamental tenet of Christianity: favor with God cannot be earned but is given to us by grace through faith in Jesus Christ. In a very real way these examples of asceticism are evidence of the depravity of human nature. Men who practiced such austerity simply to demonstrate what they could do without, found reason to be proud of themselves for their self-denial of the pleasures of this world. In doing so they were just as vain and conceited as the worst materialist. In addition, the physical harm that they did to themselves through these practices made them unfit to participate in the real mission of the church.

As already noted, the apostle Paul clearly spoke against ascetic practices which served no purpose in advancing the gospel of Jesus Christ. A church founded in the city of Colosse struggled with the problem of including ascetic practices in their worship of God. Although Paul had not personally visited this church, when he heard of their struggles he wrote them a letter and denounced those who argued for asceticism. He pointed out that one's standing before God was based on faith in Christ alone. The mark of a true Christian, Paul said, was whether or not his trust for salvation was in the atoning work of Jesus Christ. No human action could ever be added to that sacrifice in order to gain justification before God. But, the ascetics in the church argued that converts also had to practice certain acts of self-denial if they were true believers. Paul spoke vigorously against them. In his letter, Paul wrote:

> Beware lest anyone cheat you through philosophy and empty deceit, according to the tradition of men, according to the basic principles of the world, and not according to Christ. For in Him dwells all the fullness of the Godhead bodily; and you are complete in Him, who is the head of all principality and power. . . . So let no one judge you in food or in drink, or regarding a festival or a new moon or sabbaths, which are a shadow of things to come, but the substance is of Christ. Let no one cheat you of your reward, taking delight in false humility and worship of angels, intruding into those things which he has not seen, vainly

---

[88] Will Durant, op. cit., pg. 59.

puffed up by his fleshly mind, and not holding fast to the Head, from whom all the body, nourished and knit together by joints and ligaments, grows with the increase that is from God.[89]

The point that Paul was trying to make with his readers should be clear. Ascetic practices, in and of themselves, have no value whatsoever in gaining favor with God and those who advocate such practices are foolish to do so. That is not to say that Christians are free to satisfy their every craving. To do so would be to give one's self over to gross materialism which would be to make the opposite mistake. Instead, the Christian is expected to dedicate himself to whatever call God has for his life and to use his resources for promoting the glory of God in this world. God has given the church a mission and that mission is to make Christian converts. To accomplish this end, God calls people to be involved in many different ways. Some callings require a large degree of self-denial. For example, a missionary called out of a cosmopolitan environment in order to communicate the gospel message to people in an impoverished nation will have to give up the possibility of enjoying many of the material possessions that he might have had. In this regard, he might also give up his health and perhaps even his life. But, such a sacrifice is not to be compared to the gains made in promoting the gospel of Jesus Christ. Put simply, God's calling requires self-denial to win converts to the Christian religion.

Nevertheless, to do this effectively it is necessary for the believer to take care of himself and maintain his own health and well-being as best as possible if he is to share his faith with others and be of use to them in their times of need. Paul urges Christians to deny themselves in order to follow God's call on their lives. In doing this, Paul tells his listeners that there are great eternal rewards for living one's life for the cause of Christ and that such a life is merely a thankful response to the grace of God and is not the basis for gaining merit with God. This is Christianity. Asceticism misses this mark. To the extent that monastic orders taught people to maintain ascetic lifestyles without furthering the cause of Christ, they erred. Alternatively, to the extent that they turned their limited resources toward the promotion of the gospel message, they

---

[89] Colossians 2: 8-10 & 16-19.

succeeded in furthering the Christian message in this world.

The Bible never condemns marriage, sexual relations, or the abundance of wealth. Instead, it argues that such things are good as long as people maintain the proper view of them. For this reason, a single person should not be so consumed with finding a mate that he neglects his calling. In this case celibacy is the correct behavior. However, if a man and a woman should marry, it is a good thing. Marriage itself was established by God and is intended to reflect the truth about Jesus relationship with his church. Within marriage it is the duty of both husband and wife to engage in sexual relations. In fact, the unity of a husband and a wife is expressed in a loving, sexual relationship. Furthermore, this relationship reflects in some way the believer's union with Christ. To cheapen this act by adultery and fornication is to hold the gospel message in low esteem. Finally, the Bible never condemns wealth; it condemns living one's life only for the things of this world. Such materialism is wrong, but that does not mean that a life of poverty is the ideal Christian existence.

The problem has always been that depraved human beings pervert good things. On the one hand, when someone is living a life of self-denial as a matter of greater communion with God that spills over into benefits for others, we rightly recognize the action as virtuous. However, on the other hand, not all acts of self-denial are actually motivated this way. The decision to live an austere life in and of itself is of no particular benefit to anyone and, hence, this kind of austerity is of no particular use to Christianity. It is true that Christians are asked to live sacrificially. However, the sacrifices aimed at, are those that aid the cause of Christ as established in the Great Commission that is recorded at the end of Matthew.

We can now return to our consideration of monasticism. In Western Europe, it ought to be noted that the asceticism of the monastic orders there was generally mild relative to those of the east. While the monks did withdraw to the monasteries, they never withdrew completely from society. Thus, monasticism in Europe provided an atmosphere in which monks could think about their responsibilities in serving other people. By providing this atmosphere, the monastic orders trained men and women for service in the Latin Church. They also served the needs of the communities in which they were located in a number of valuable ways. For example, monasteries in Europe provided a training ground ·

where people learned moral behavior. Its devotees were often examples to other people. Some of the monks demonstrated in a clear way how an individual might look beyond his own circumstances and have compassion and mercy toward others. The monasteries provided education for people in an era when few intellectual opportunities existed. Other than the official Church itself, they were the only other institutions that offered formal education during the Middle Ages in Europe. In an age of increasing illiteracy, teaching some men to read and write kept the Dark Ages from being even darker. As such, the monastic orders throughout Europe more or less reflected the kind of Christian charity that Jesus had in mind.

The Benedictine order was a good example of monastic life in Western Europe. The order was founded in A.D. 529 by Benedict of Nursia on the hill Monte Cassino. He was not given to severe forms of asceticism and conceived of the monastery as a place where men would be made fit soldiers in Christ's army. He saw worship as the prime duty of every monk. At least four hours was devoted to it each day. In addition, Benedict believed that idleness was a sin and an "enemy of the soul." Therefore, he prescribed a strict regimen of daily activities. Beyond the requirements of worship, the monks were obligated to split the rest of each day between manual labor of various kinds and devotional reading. While this was a simple life, it was not one in which the individual was totally disconnected from life in this world. In fact, these monastic communities provided vital products during a time when people struggled to survive.

The popularity of the monastic life spread rapidly. "In an age of war and chaos, of doubt and wandering, the Benedictine monastery was a healing refuge."[90] While "[t]he monasteries were founded to save the souls of the monks and to set an example of virtuous living to all mankind, [and] not to foster learning, to further craftsmanship, or to improve agriculture, . . . all of these [latter activities] were significant by-products of monasticism."[91] Because of the importance placed upon reading, Benedictine monasteries became significant library depositories.

---

[90] Will Durant, op. cit., pg. 519.

[91] Frederick B. Artz, *The Mind of the Middle Ages*, (New York:Alfred A. Knopf, 1953), pg. 186.

Because of the importance placed upon manual labor, they promoted advancements in farming tools and techniques, developed numerous crafts, and promoted quality workmanship. For these reasons, monasticism was an important component of life during the Middle Ages in Western Europe and in many ways they made life more bearable than it otherwise would have been.

III. The Crusades

Among the nobility, Christian pilgrimages to Jerusalem were fairly common. Even when Jerusalem fell to the Arabs and was no longer in the control of the Byzantine Empire, such pilgrimages continued. As already mentioned, the Arab Moslems practiced a kind of religious tolerance which allowed the Christians to continue to worship God as they pleased, thus they allowed these pilgrimages to continue unhindered. However, in the early eleventh century the Turkish Moslems became a serious threat not only to Christian pilgrims, but also to the Byzantine Empire. They were far less hospitable than their Arab brothers and generally scorned religious tolerance.

The Turkish threat to the Byzantine Empire prompted Alexius, emperor at the time, to seek help from the West Europeans. He pointed out to the western leaders that it made more sense to secure Constantinople than to allow Turkish aggression to continue unchecked. He argued that if Byzantium fell to the Turks, all of Europe would be opened to a renewed Moslem threat. For this reason, he urged them to lend him their military support.

In addition to these factors, several cities in Italy began to flourish from a revival in trade. Among these, Genoa, Pisa, and Venice emerged as trading centers. This expansion in trade led to individual accumulations of wealth in Europe which had been unknown for centuries. Since many of the goods traded flowed through the Near East, businesses in these cities had a vested interest in keeping the trade routes open. The military success of the fanatical Turks posed a significant threat to this prospect. For this reason, they, too, supported western military campaigns.

The combination of these factors resulted in the Crusades. Pope Urban II thought favorably of Alexius' request for military aid. He also thought that such aid could be provided within the context of a plan to recapture the Holy Land from the hands of the Moslems. Therefore, he began to recruit military forces to undertake the mission. He traveled first to France and told the people there that it was God's will for them to reclaim Jerusalem for Christendom. His efforts were successful and thousands pledged themselves to the task. When he returned to Rome, he made numerous decrees which freed men from their other obligations so that they might go to the Near East to wage a holy war. The actual participants in the first Crusade went for a host of reasons.

> Men tired of hopeless poverty, adventurers ready for brave enterprise, younger sons hoping to carve out fiefs for themselves in the East, merchants seeking new markets for their goods, knights whose enlisting serfs had left them laborless, timid spirits shunning taunts of cowardice, joined with sincerely religious souls to rescue the land of Christ's birth and death. Propaganda of the kind customary in war stressed the disabilities of Christians in Palestine, the atrocities of Moslems, the blasphemies of the Mohammedan creed; Moslems were described as worshiping a statue of Mohammed, and pious gossip related how the Prophet, fallen in an epileptic fit, had been eaten alive by hogs. Fabulous tales were told of Oriental wealth, and of dark beauties waiting to be taken by brave men.[92]

Notwithstanding the wide array of motivations, the European conquest of the Near East began. While Urban had made plans to begin the project in August of 1096, a group led by Peter the Hermit and Walter the Penniless, set out for Palestine from France in March of that year. In addition, a group from Germany led by Gottschalk also advanced eastward at about the same time. These groups were composed of people who were hardly trained for military service. Rather, they were little more than haphazard bands of people from various classes of life joined together by a common quest. They were both ill-trained and ill-equipped for the journey. Lacking sufficient supplies to sustain themselves as they progressed up the Rhine valley, they resorted to pillaging Jewish communities along the way. In addition, the length of the journey was

---

[92] Will Durant, op. cit., pg. 588.

much farther than they had expected.

> Arriving at last before Constantinople quite penniless, and decimated by famine, plague, leprosy, fever, and battles on the way, they were welcomed by Alexius, but not satisfactorily fed; they broke into the suburbs, and plundered churches, houses, and palaces. To deliver his capital from these praying locusts, Alexius provided them with vessels to cross the Bosporus, sent them supplies, and bade them wait until better armed detachments could arrive. Whether through hunger or restlessness, the Crusaders ignored these instructions, and advanced upon Nicaea. A disciplined force of Turks, all skilled bowmen, marched out from the city and almost annihilated this first division of the First Crusade.[93]

The failure of this first wave was not the end of the crusade. A second contingent of West European forces formed even as this misguided horde met defeat. Duke Godfrey led the next expedition to the Near East to battle for the Holy Land against the Moslem infidels. As the second wave of the crusaders made their way to Byzantium, it was suggested that they might as well seize Constantinople. While Godfrey dismissed the idea, the news may have reached Alexius, because he exercised extreme caution in dealing with the crusaders once they arrived at the gates of the city. However, his caution might well have been as a result of his earlier experience with the first wave. Whatever the case, Alexius was quick to offer the second wave of crusaders supplies. In addition, he bribed the leaders to swear their loyalty to him. Godfrey and the others readily did so, and Alexius speedily arranged for their transport across the Bosporus to Asia Minor in early 1097.

While there were many factors working against the crusaders, one served in their favor. Turkish aggression had not only threatened the interests of the west, but those of the Arabs as well. For this reason, Moslem unity was fractured and the people who had been conquered by the Turks were in the process of rebelling against them. As a result, the Moslems were unable to present a united front of resistance. Over the

---

[93] Ibid, pg. 589.

course of the next two and one-half years, the crusaders marched toward Jerusalem battling against the Turks and claiming territory all along the way. On June 7, 1099, they reached the walls of the city and were ready to take it for God and country. Before they arrived, however, the Turks had already been expelled from the city by the more tolerant Fatimids. When the crusaders arrived, the Fatimids offered them peace and guaranteed to make the way safe for all Christian pilgrims traveling to the city. Godfrey rejected the offer and the crusaders took the city by force. They foolishly slaughtered both Moslems and Jews. In addition, they took property away from those who survived, whether they were Christian, Moslem, or Jewish. So barbaric was the governance of the victorious feudal knights from the west, that even the Christians of the east longed for Moslem rule.

The news that the Christians had captured Jerusalem was not well received by the Moslems, and they fought back. When it appeared that they might regain control, new crusades were organized. The next two years were marked by near continual conflict between the Christians and the Moslems. Through this period, Islam was successful in reclaiming much of the land that it had previously lost to the Christian invaders. Even Jerusalem fell into their hands. The crusade movement failed and finally collapsed by the end of the thirteenth century. "Men had entered the Crusades with mixed motives. The immorality, pillage and massacre which so often disgraced the movement show that in spite of great zeal in pursuance of an ideal, no true spiritual power had taken possession of them. The effects were mainly political and social rather than religious."[94]

There were at least four consequences of the Crusades. First, after two centuries of warfare, the Moslems became far less tolerant of Christian pilgrims specifically and of religious diversity generally. There was so much bitterness fostered at the time that the animosity between these two religions continues today. Second, the Crusades damaged the feudal relationships of Europe. Many serfs used the opportunity as an excuse to leave their manors. Most of these people never returned. In addition to the exodus of the serfs from manorial estates, the nobility mortgaged their property to finance the war effort. This meant that Western European wealth was diverted to the East. These factors were

---

[94] Renwick and Harman, op. cit., pg. 93.

among those that undermined feudalism in Europe. Third, while the Crusades served the purpose of pushing back the Turks from Constantinople, the capital was only temporally saved. In 1453 the Turks conquered the city and brought the Byzantine Empire to an end. Finally, the reputation of the Roman Catholic Church was damaged by the failure of the Crusades. The public could not understand why God allowed the Moslems to prevail over them in battle. They believed the religious leaders who proclaimed that the conquest of the Holy Land was God's will. Therefore, when their efforts failed they began to question not only Catholic Church leaders but the Christian faith as well. Of course, the failure of the Crusades was no fault of Christianity. Rather, it was the result of the error in judgment of the leadership. The proponents of the Crusades had wrongly tied faith to an unworthy pursuit of men. They had not heeded the example of Christ or the words of the apostle Paul:

> For though we live in the world, we do not wage war as the world does. The weapons we fight with are not the weapons of the world. On the contrary, they have divine power to demolish strongholds. We demolish arguments and every pretension that sets itself up against the knowledge of God, and we take captive every thought to make it obedient to Christ.[95]

The problem was one that we have already seen. Christianity could not be established by force because no amount of physical force could change the hearts of the people. Rather, Christianity was and is built by proclaiming the life and work of Jesus Christ for the salvation of the souls. Only the Spirit of God can change a man's heart so that he might embrace the good news of the gospel of Jesus Christ. The failure of Christians to heed this teaching damaged the cause of Christ and limited the spread of the gospel message. Even to this day, the Christian gospel is not welcomed in Moslem countries.

The past failures of men provide us with lessons for today and should be used to help us to avoid making the same mistakes. They serve as a clear warning not to act in ways which are at odds with the moral teachings of Scripture. We are responsible for whether or not we heed the

---

[95] 2 Corinthians 10: 3-5.

warnings that history has provided. Unfortunately, it appears that we have been unwilling to do so. People are continuing to develop and promote various schemes by which they hope to save the human race by the use of government force. These schemes come to us packaged in both religious and secular forms. For example, state education in the United States began as a scheme to force a particular kind of religious experience upon the citizenry. In the course of time, the educational institution that was created for this purpose was taken over to promote a humanist salvation. Thus, what was intended for a supposedly Christian purpose is ironically being used to produce the exact opposite. Instead of leading people to Christ, it has become an instrument that leads them away from him. A sad result of this is that the educational system is utterly failing in its efforts to educate children in any meaningful ways as it promotes its naturalistic ends. In a later chapter we will examine why state education is contributing to the downfall of Western civilization.

Study Questions

1. Describe the nature of the early church and how it spread.
2. What two factors served to unify the various local church congregations?
3. Explain why making Christianity the state religion intensified the problem of maintaining doctrinal purity.
4. What is the nature of theology and why is it important? What are the reasons for theological error?
5. What was the Arian heresy?
6. What assertion did Leo make when he was bishop of Rome? Why is his assertion a bone of contention?
7. Discuss the life of Gregory the Great.
8. How did monasticism develop? Compare and contrast how it was practiced in Western Europe and in the Near East.
9. Explain how the Benedictine order was founded.
10. What were the underlying reasons for the Crusades? How did they progress? What were the final results?

Chapter 11: Intellectual Pursuits

I. An Overview

The Middle Ages are sometimes referred to as the Dark Ages because the general populace devoted little time and effort to education. As a result, few advancements were made, but the light provided by formal education never went out completely. As we have already seen from an earlier discussion of this time, the economic situation deteriorated rapidly due to the near cessation of trade. This is perhaps the chief reason why the task of educating people was left essentially to the church. The church responded and, between it and the monastic orders, education continued. During the early part of the Middle Ages, these institutions did little more than to train their immediate members. Thus, formal education of the kind which might produce great thinkers was minimal. Nevertheless, the church kept learning alive and in the latter part of the Middle Ages, as economic conditions improved, the opportunity for formal education increased dramatically.

Reflecting upon the religious oversight of education, some writers have argued that the church's control resulted in the sad state of intellectual affairs of the time. These writers maintain that the church ignored the accumulated body of knowledge because it did not fit with Christian theology. On the basis of this viewpoint, it is suggested that many known truths were abandoned. As evidence for their position, proponents point to instances where the church hindered educational advancements. The decline in sanitary conditions is often used as an example. Prior to the Middle Ages, the Romans had made great strides in increasing the sanitary living conditions of people by constructing aqueducts and by placing an emphasis on bathing. While plagues continued, they were reduced in number and extent of hardship. Thus, the advances made provided the basis upon which sanitation could be continuously improved. However, ascetic influences on many Christians led to the development of the view that God is glorified by human debasement. Those who were committed to this perspective paid little attention to personal hygiene and even went as far as to teach others to disregard it as well. For them, being more saintly often meant living in greater degrees of filth and degradation. As this belief prospered, less effort was expended in improving the general level of sanitation in communities. This resulted in an increase in the number and severity of plagues.

While there is some truth to this argument, it is superficial in many respects. For this reason, it tends to promote an essentially false view of the age. To be sure, ascetic influences on the Christian religion led to a number of mistakes. But we cannot conclude from this fact that Christianity was to blame for the situation. In fact, these errors in judgment cannot be reconciled with the Christian religion as it was taught by Jesus and the apostles. Quite the opposite is actually true. Numerous passages can be found in the Bible that teach men the need to pursue personal cleanliness as a matter of daily life. The failure of men to heed these admonitions does not blemish Christianity, but once again points out the surety of human depravity. Thus, while there is some merit to the argument that the teachings of the church led to certain setbacks in the quality of life, and that it delayed some potential advancements, it is pure fiction to believe that such failures undermine the soundness of the religion. In addition, it is also pure fiction to believe that all the evils that men suffered in this age were the result of the errors of churchmen. In reality, there were many reasons why humans suffered hardship in the Middle Ages. Moreover, not only was the church not the primary culprit of inflicting hardship, but it was in fact an important institution that extended numerous benefits to people that helped alleviate some of their suffering. As for the decline in the sanitary conditions of the age, this situation had more to do with the economic decline resulting from the demise of trade than with church teachings.

The problem for the Christian religion is that human beings have a propensity to read a host of inappropriate things into the Scriptures. An illustration of this propensity may help clarify this point. Consider the teaching that the world is flat. When examining such an issue, it is important to note that the Bible was not written to illuminate our understanding about the principles of physical science. Yet, Christians have attempted to use the Bible for such purposes. Edward Coleson provided the details of how the teaching of a flat world came to be viewed as a component of Christian teaching.

The early Christians tended to reject the idea of a spherical earth since they could not imagine a place on the other side of the earth where things may be hanging downwards, trees growing backwards, or rain falling upwards. While there were writers who insisted that the shape of the earth had no connection with the Christian faith there were others who felt it their duty to settle the question for all time by an appeal to Scripture. The resulting controversy was a tragedy for both science and the church. One Cosmas of Alexandria, for instance, writing from a Sinai cloister about 548 A.D., systematically demolished the pagan notion of a round earth by refuting the opinions of some seventy heathen authorities whom he quoted and substituting his own Christian "world view" for their misguided notions. Cosmas declared the world was flat and twice as long as it was wide, basing his cosmic pronouncements on the ninth chapter of Hebrews in which St. Paul. . . compared the priestly office of Christ with the old order of sacrifice under the Mosaic Law. Cosmas read into the phrase, "a worldly sanctuary," in verse one, that the Tabernacle with its enclosing court and furnishings was a miniature and symbolic model of the physical world. . . . [B]ut the reader need only peruse this familiar chapter of Hebrews once more to see how strained and twisted the whole interpretation was. He could have hardly had less basis for his case, yet he helped set the intellectual world back a thousand years. . . [96]

Just as the errors of asceticism eventually cost the church some of her reputation, so too did the flat world dogma result in her being defamed. Coleson pointed out well that this did not need to happen because there was never any basis from divine revelation that established such a position. But, men err! Perhaps the worst error in judgment thus far in human history was not committed by churchmen in the Middle Ages, but by modern day skeptics who have thrown out divine revelation altogether because human interpretations of it have erred.

---

[96] Edward Coleson, *The Harvest of Twenty Centuries*, (Spring Arbor, Michigan, 1967), pp. 75-76.

As we have already seen, the church provided people with many clear benefits and advantages despite the errors its leadership maintained. Furthermore, pagan scientists should not revel in the intellectual failures of Christians. They, too, are prone to gross errors in judgment. As pointed out in the introductory chapter of this book, the philosophy of naturalism, which is so in vogue today among the majority of modern day scientists, will be remembered in history as one of the poorest displays of human judgment known to mankind. It has no firm base upon which to build a body of accumulated knowledge. As a result, from this perspective, all knowledge is subject to open debate no matter how sound an understanding of the subject has already been developed. For this reason, a whole host of useful information is being discarded for the latest fashion trend, even when the latest trend can be shown to be utter intellectual folly. In the same way that the church set back the accumulation of knowledge, these modern day dogmatists are destroying the foundations of learning for the sake of their impotent world view. Unlike Christianity, which can be saved from error by careful adherence to the teachings of Christ, there is no possible salvation for naturalism. As C. S. Lewis remarked about the Bible, "It was never intended to replace or supersede the ordinary human arts and sciences: it is rather a director which will set them all to the right jobs, and a source of energy which will give them all new life, if only they will put themselves at its disposal."[97]

II. Scholasticism

As has already been noted, formal education fell to the church and the monastic orders. In the course of time, cathedral and monastic schools developed. Charlemagne was particularly instrumental in establishing these schools. While many flourished during his lifetime, they fell upon harder times after his death. Nevertheless, some remained opened and education continued. These schools greatly increased in number again during the eleventh century. Logic became the fundamental tool used to grapple with difficult theological issues. This fashion of training had the side effect of developing the minds of students and expanding their intellectual potential. This in turn led to an increase

---

[97] C. S. Lewis, *Mere Christianity*, (New York: Macmillan Publishing Company, 1943), pg. 79.

in creative thinking and set the stage for numerous intellectual developments.

As wealth in Europe increased, more and more students desired to obtain an education. Students from all over Europe moved to the centers of learning in order to enroll in one of these schools. As the interest in education increased, so too did the number of individuals who aspired to become teachers. Universities were organized to manage the process. They provided a means of assessing the merits of potential teachers as well as a place to teach. Many universities were formed during the early part of the second millennium. Some continued, but most were short-lived. Nevertheless, this process of education thrived and this provided the foundation upon which intellectual advancement was built. In addition, the universities that survived and continued to grow eventually sought and gained independence from the church as well as the state.

Latin was used as the language of all learning, even though it had undergone some changes from the classic period. In the church and monasteries, the Scriptures were studied by using St. Jerome's Latin translation of the Bible. While this translation contained some errors and used common rather than formal language, it nevertheless served its purpose in cathedral and monastic schools, and kept the Latin language alive. As would be expected, new words developed to reflect circumstances unknown to the Romans beforehand, and new dialects developed among the many peoples who adopted the language. These changes made it difficult to understand the classic writings of authors like Cicero. Nonetheless, the language used is most rightly classified as Latin because the similarities were substantial enough to open up the classics to the careful readers of the time.

While the Latin classics of the Roman world had been preserved by the Europeans, they had largely been cut off from the Greek classics as well as from the advancements made by the Arabs. The Crusades and the increase in trade brought an end to this situation. As wealth expanded because of trade, the number of Latin translations of Greek classics increased. The combination of the increase in the number of schools along with greater access to classic literature spurred intellectual development.

Education began with preparatory training of a kind that is still highly praised by some educators today. In the initial stage of education the student was trained to think. This was accomplished by instruction in the seven liberal arts: the *trivium* and the *quadrivium*. The *trivium* was composed of instruction in grammar, rhetoric, and logic while the *quadrivium* involved the study of astronomy, arithmetic, geometry, and music. These two areas provided the foundation upon which the rest of one's educational experience was built. The higher levels of learning centered on either theology, canon law, or medicine. Subject matter was taught to students by employing lectures and debates.

Having gained an education of this kind, a number of reputable thinkers developed. For this reason the period is often referred to as the age of the scholastics. Of considerable importance to this age are the positions taken by different thinkers regarding the nature of reality. The different views can be classified into one of three categories. The first is extreme realism. This position is essentially Platonic and holds that universals exist apart from and prior to individual objects. A proponent of this view would believe that all truths could be attained by reason alone. The significance of this position is that all the truths of faith in divine revelation could be demonstrated by reason if this were, in fact, the proper position. The second position is that of moderate realism which is Aristotelian in origin. This position holds that universals exist only in connection with actual objects. Someone who maintains this position also has a great deal of respect for reason, but in matters of faith subordinates it to divine revelation. Finally, nominalism is a view held by someone who argues that universals are only abstract names that humans use to relate to individual objects and that these names have no existence in reality. As such, someone holding to this view would logically tend towards the kind of positivism that is so prominent in the universities today. The tension between these three positions served as the underlying base for much of the intellectual debate of the late Middle Ages and can be illustrated in the lives and teachings of three men: Anselm, Thomas Aquinas, and William of Occam.

A.   Anselm

Anselm was born in northern Italy in 1033. He became a monk at Bec in Normandy and later became the abbot of the monastery. Under his leadership the monastery developed an excellent school which gained widespread attention. In 1093, he became the archbishop of Canterbury.

He held this position until his death in 1109. Throughout his life, Anselm was a man of strong Christian faith. He was a realist who often sought refuge to be alone in order to pray and to meditate on the Word of God.

Anselm is remembered for several pieces of work. In one of these he set forth an ontological proof of God's existence. Ontology is the science that investigates and explains the nature and essence of all beings. Thus, Anselm sought to prove the existence of God as the necessary being by way of a logical argument. He argued in the following manner. Since we can think of a perfect being against which there is no greater being, this proves the existence of such a being. The reason this is true, is that if it were false, we could conceive of some greater being still. In particular, we could conceive of a greater being who does in fact exist.

Opponents to Anselm's argument were quick to reply. They argued that the problem of Anselm's argument was that it did not get beyond the realm of ideas and that people can conceive of many things which do not exist in reality. For example, the idea of a perfect triangle only implies the existence of the concept of such a thing and not of a perfect triangle itself. On this basis, the opponents argued that Anselm had only proved the hypothetical existence of God and not the very existence of God Himself.

While Anselm's opponents were correct as far as they went, they failed to realize that there is a very real difference between the idea of a perfect triangle and the idea of a perfect being. This point was at the heart of Jonathan Edwards argument in the seventeenth century. As Sproul, Gerstner, and Lindsley have stated Edwards' contention:

> We can think of the nonexistence of a perfect triangle, but we cannot think of the nonexistence of perfect being. We cannot think of the nonexistence of perfect, necessary being. Therefore, that being must exist. We simply cannot think of its not existing. We yield by the necessity to the impossibility of the contrary. This is the *only* thing which we cannot think of as existing *merely* as idea.[98]

The point Edwards made is quite insightful. Namely, if we can

---

[98] R. C. Sproul, John Gerstner, and Arthur Lindsley, *Classical Apologetics*, (Grand Rapids, Michigan: Academie Books, 1984), pp. 101-102.

think of the possibility of a necessary being, then such a being must exist or it would not be necessary. In addition, if people are to think at all, they must think of being. This is true because when a person thinks, he must think of something. Putting the matter another way, everyone is able to conceive of being, but no one can conceive of nonbeing. Therefore, a necessary being must be. The same method can be used to prove one's own existence. An individual cannot think of himself as not existing because every time he attempts to think of his own nonexistence it is the person himself that is trying to think of it. Therefore, that individual must exist. In fact, ". . . we cannot think of anything which *now* exists as not *now* existing."[99]

Since Anselm did not discuss the impossibility of thinking of the nonexistence of a necessary being, his argument was left open to the criticism outlined above. However, his effort has remained an important one in the process of thought and his ontological argument served as a basis upon which Rene Descartes in the seventeenth century and Jonathan Edwards in the eighteenth built. It was the later work of Edwards that provided the finishing touches to Anselm's argument that has been presented here.

In addition to his ontological argument for God's existence, Anselm is also remembered for a number of other works. For example, his book, *Cur Deus homo*, is still important. In it he developed the doctrine of the atonement which remains foundational to Christian faith today. While Anslem provided much that is still useful, he too had his failures. As an extreme realist, Anselm believed that all divine revelation could be understood rationally. Presumably, he believed that all Christian doctrines could be deduced from the evidence of nature. As such, he saw no difference between philosophy and theology. For this reason, Anselm attempted to develop a number of arguments from nature for difficult Christian doctrines such as the trinity of God. These efforts were largely unsuccessful.

---

[99] Ibid, pg. 103.

B. Thomas Aquinas

Thomas Aquinas was born in Italy of a noble family in 1225. Despite the desires of his parents, he became a Dominican monk at the age of eighteen. His superior intellectual abilities were immediately recognized, and he was sent to Cologne where he studied under the direction of Albertus Magnus. This was a great honor as Albertus was perhaps the most learned man of his age. Upon receiving his bachelor's degree, Thomas began an impressive academic career of his own. During his career, Thomas devoted himself to both teaching and writing. His greatest work was his *Summa Theologia* which he began in 1265. Thomas died in 1274 and was unable to finish the project. Yet, what he accomplished in it was so significant that it remains an important work in the study of theology.

Like Anselm, Thomas was a simple man who was deeply religious. He spent a substantial amount of time each day in prayer and thoughtful meditation on the Word of God. He, too, argued that God's existence could be logically demonstrated. Thomas was a consistent and rational thinker and, like Anselm, is classified as a realist.

However, rather than adopting the Platonic realism of Anslem, Thomas opted for an Aristotelian version. He rejected the notion that all doctrines revealed in the Scriptures could be deduced from the evidence found in nature. Instead, he argued that while nature reveals much about God, some issues can only be accepted on the basis of faith from Scripture. For example, the doctrine of the trinity is one that should be believed because it is revealed in the Bible. Aquinas argued that knowledge of God comes in two forms: the natural revelation of creation and the special or divine revelation of the Bible. In his view, these two revelations work together without conflict to reveal God because God both created the universe and purposed redemption. As Gordon Clark summarized Aquinas' position:

> Since all truth forms one system in God's mind, it is impossible for reason and faith to contradict; and furthermore it is always possible for us to show the absence

of contradiction; but it is not always possible to prove the truths of faith.[100]

For this reason, Aquinas would be best classified as a moderate realist.

The primary bridge between what can be known of God from nature and what can be known of God from the Bible, was, in Thomas' view, the proof of God's existence. Rather than argue from ontology as Anselm had, Thomas argued from the very existence of nature itself. He followed the form of Paul's argument at the beginning of Romans. As the apostle wrote, "For since the creation of the world His invisible attributes are clearly seen, being understood by the things that are made, even His eternal power and Godhead, so that they are without excuse, because, although they knew God, they did not glorify Him as God, nor were thankful, but became futile in their thoughts, and their foolish hearts were darkened."[101] These verses imply that God's existence was (and is) necessarily implied by creation and Aquinas set out to develop the proof. The result of his effort is called the cosmological argument of God's existence.

The essence of the cosmological argument is the fact that all effects must have an antecedent cause. Since an infinite regress of finite causes would provide no sufficient cause for the individual effects, there must be some sufficient cause. On the basis of this type of argumentation, the existence of the universe and everything in it can only be explained by some infinite self-existing Being. Once the order of the universe is recognized, it must be admitted that this Being is purposeful and, hence, intelligent and personal. Thomas' argument has been the source of much debate and has spawned numerous opponents who have attempted to refute him. Sproul, Gerstner, and Lindsley provide an excellent discussion of both his argument and the many critiques that have been attempted against it in their book on classical apologetics.[102] They conclude that all attempts to refute Thomas have been inadequate and that the argument stands affirmed by clear reason.

---

[100] Gordon Clark, *Thales to Dewey*, (Jefferson, Maryland: The Trinity Foundation, 1985), pg. 271.

[101] Romans 1: 20-21.

[102] Sproul, Gerstner, and Lindsley, op. cit.

At this point, one may ask why the matter continues to be disputed? The answer has to do with the moral condition of the human race. Since human beings are in sinful rebellion against God, they seek to suppress the truth which they know. In other words, sinful men simply will not affirm that which cannot be denied, for to do so is an indictment against themselves. To acquiesce would mean to admit one's guilt before a holy and just God. Proud and sinful men are not about to make this concession. Therefore, people continue to devise elaborate arguments in an endless attempt to refute that which cannot be refuted.

The work of Aquinas is astounding in that he provided a synthesis of philosophy and theology. Within this synthesis, numerous scientific pursuits can proceed more or less without reference to the Scriptures. Nevertheless, those efforts can only proceed rightly to the extent that they are informed by the Scriptures. To the extent that the knowledge proposed by science does not conflict with a sound understanding of the Scriptures, such efforts are useful. Nonetheless, there can never be a clear conflict since both natural and divine revelation proceed from the same God. Therefore, when conflicts do occur, either the Scriptures are being misread or scientists have erred in either the collection of evidence or the judgments they deduce from the facts. In fact, we would expect both of these problems to continue because of the moral depravity of mankind. Specifically, as stated above, men do not wish to reason to the truth in all cases because, at the point of their rebellion against God, it indicts them of their sin. Thus, outright prejudice often influences them to develop clever techniques to cover over sound arguments. This action results in the obfuscation of knowledge and truth.

C. William of Occam

William of Occam was an English Franciscan who was taught by Duns Scotus. While the exact date of his birth and death are unknown, he lived from somewhere around the end of the thirteenth century to the middle of the fourteenth. William is remembered for his teaching that there was no connection between theology and philosophy. His efforts to support this kind of nominalism provided the foundation for later efforts in the same direction. In particular, the work of Immanuel Kant and of the positivists later proceeded from nominalism.

Occam took direct aim at the logical proofs of God's existence.

While it might have been his intention to make room for faith in God, in actuality he made room for philosophic skeptics. As Gordon Clark wrote in this regard:

> Now with Occam even the existence of God was made totally a matter of theology. But what of philosophy? Had it been so restricted that its area was now zero? If so, the nominalist Occam and the realistic Augustinians had come to essential agreement: there is but one area of knowledge, and whether it is called philosophy or theology makes no difference. But this agreement would have required of Occam the admission that no truth can be discovered by reason apart from revelation. By those who do not recognize divine revelation, such an admission is called skepticism. If there is no revelation and if reason can prove nothing, then knowledge is impossible.[103]

Clark overstated the potential agreement between the Augustinians and Occam. While both might have agreed on the same set of knowledge, there is a difference between obtaining knowledge from two sources as asserted by the Augustinians and obtaining it from only one source as argued by the nominalists. Yet, Clark is quite right to point out the fact that if nominalism were true, then nothing can be known for certain by way of scientific pursuits. If science is set free from any consideration of theology, the foundation for knowledge evaporates. In the course of time, the fact that science has produced some accurate but limited knowledge would seem to speak convincingly against the rising tide of skepticism. Unfortunately, the acceptance of this point of view has not been wide, at least not yet. Though it was not his intention, Occam's work provided religious skeptics with a clever intellectual position for continuing in unbelief. This is a substantial problem, for in our own day the complete separation of philosophy and theology threatens the foundations of Western civilization. Just the same, the appeal of religious skeptics to the work of men like Occam fails to establish their intellectual position since the proofs of God's existence continue to speak against nominalism.

---

[103] Gordon Clark, op. cit., pp. 296-297.

III. Science and Technology

Interest in science in Western Europe fell sharply as the Roman Empire disintegrated. As already stated, this resulted largely from the decline in wealth that occurred because of the collapse of trade. People were more interested in securing the practical means of life than in advancing their understanding of the world in which they lived. Thus, there were few scientific advancements, and people tended to view the world in a manner similar to that of the Greeks in antiquity. The popular point of view was, therefore, a mixture of some basic truths overlaid with numerous superstitions.

Some examples of these admixtures will help provide the reader with a better understanding of the times. For instance, the field of chemistry hardly existed in the Middle Ages and what was present was often mixed together with alchemy. The few books available on the subject were limited and usually provided recipes for dyeing cloth or techniques for handling metals. When some interest was shown in the study, it was mainly by alchemists, whose main goal was to turn base metals into gold. They believed that a single substance provided the underlying unity of all matter and that if that substance could be discovered, then it would be possible to turn any metal into gold by following the right process. This false materialistic view of reality led to many worthless pursuits, which generated little new knowledge. However, it also spawned the real science of chemistry in a rudimentary way with its elemental experimentation. Likewise, the field of astronomy was helped in some respects and hindered in others because of its ties to astrology. The superstitions of astrology, namely the notion that events on earth are controlled by the movements of the stars, kept the science of astronomy from progressing as rapidly as it might have otherwise, but the interest in the stars provided a motive for the careful study of them.

In the course of time, actual sciences more and more displaced the various superstitions attached to them. As might be expected, the beginning of this increase in science coincided with the development and growth of schools of learning. It was within these schools that the modern scientific method developed. This method of investigation can be undertaken from two general points of view. The first is from the perspective of faith. This point of view recognizes the Scriptures as a valid source of information. Nevertheless, the researcher is free to investigate the universe in order to gain a better understanding of it. Within this framework there is a balance between experience and authority. On the one hand, it recognizes the limits of our present knowledge and the potential to increase our understanding of the world through the process of experimentation. On the other, it recognizes the authority of God who provides an ultimate point of reference and a degree of certainty to our limited knowledge. It also establishes moral limits on the kinds of experiments that may be legitimately undertaken. On this basis, the researcher understands that he is merely discovering something of the order of a cosmos that is created and maintained by God.

The second perspective of investigation is that of religious skepticism. From this point of view, all authority is questioned, and no moral limits to the scope of scientific experimentation are acknowledged. On the surface, there appears to be agreement between this method and the method of faith, in that both admit that our current knowledge of phenomena is limited. Yet, unlike the method of faith, the method of religious skepticism has no ultimate point of reference and, hence, no hope of ever gaining the certain knowledge of any truth whatsoever. As such, the skeptic is forever consigned to a world of ignorance and eventually despairs of knowing anything. From the point of view of religious skepticism, experimentation is all there is, and data can be organized along any lines that might seem to provide some consistent order. In addition, without moral limits, the researcher views himself free to experiment in any direction that might appeal to his immediate fancy, no matter how his research might adversely affect the lives of others. There is simply no basis for morality, and anything is viewed as legitimate. In the past, as will be the case in the future, skeptical researchers have treated other human beings in some grossly immoral ways for the sake of experimentation.

Roger Bacon (1214-1292) is a good example of someone from the Middle Ages who followed the method of faith in his scientific endeavors. Bacon was a Franciscan monk who was educated at Oxford. Like many from this school, he was influenced by the nominalists and had little time for metaphysical questions. However, in practice, his approach to science is most accurately categorized within the framework of Aquinas. Whether he acknowledged the theistic proofs or not, he approached his scientific studies on the assumption that the Scriptures were the divine revelation of God. In addition, he argued that much could be learned from this world by way of speculation and experimentation. By employing this approach, Bacon made some advancements in optics and in calendar reform, and he envisioned that scientific pursuits would lead to a host of new inventions that would better the living conditions of human beings. Perhaps his greatest legacy was that by his efforts he established a scientific method which balanced experience and authority along the metaphysical path that Thomas Aquinas developed, even if he did not understand or accept Thomas' philosophy.

In terms of pursuing science from the point of view of skepticism, Frederick II (1194-1250) is a good example. Frederick's father died when he was three, and his mother died when he was five. At the age of four, he was made the king of Sicily, and before her death, his mother obtained a pledge from Pope Innocent III to serve as Frederick's guardian. Unfortunately, Innocent agreed to care for Frederick's upbringing for political reasons alone. He, therefore, neglected the boy and left him to raise himself. He provided little formal education and Frederick found himself free to explore whatever he desired. Frederick had considerable intellectual ability and used his freedom to explore all sorts of things that were left open to him. In the course of time, he became a philosopher, a politician, a soldier, a poet, an architect, a mathematician, a linguist, and a zoologist, among other things. As he grew, he rejected the Christian faith as well as any other religion. Instead, he became a rationalist and he is still praised by rationalists today as the "first modern man."

To some extent this praise is well deserved because his interests did extend human knowledge in a number of directions. For example, his book on hunting with falcons was developed on the basis of carefully recorded experience and provides a great deal of sound zoological information. However, his rejection of divine authority, coupled with an increasing lack of conscience, made it possible for him to engage in all sorts of heinous experiments which could never be morally condoned. For example, "he had young children isolated to see what languages they would talk, and found they would talk none. He had men cut open to see how fatigue affected digestion."[104] And, on one occasion, he even had a man sealed in a wine cask and left to die. He later opened the cask and declared that it proved that a human being does not possess a soul

---

[104] Frederick B. Artz, *The Mind of the Middle Ages*, (New York: Alfred E. Knopf, 1953), pg. 246.

because none could be found. These actions were evidence of madness in spite of intelligence. Further, throughout history, some of the worst crimes against humanity have been perpetrated by men who thought themselves free from the moral commandments of God.

The importance of considering the approaches of these two men is that they are representatives of two vastly different views of the world. In our time there is an ongoing battle between the secular mind of naturalism and the mind that maintains faith in God. Further, the twentieth century is marked by the general dominance of secularism. Even people who affirm their faith in God, often live as if he were unimportant in the day-to-day affairs of life. Thus, it appears to some that all faith in God will eventually die away. But, if this happens, then Western civilization will collapse because it was built upon the foundation of this kind of faith.

In particular, two movements that were closely related were of fundamental importance in the development of the institutional structures within which we live. They were the Renaissance and the Reformation. The spread in intellectual activity in the late Middle Ages gave rise to the Renaissance. It was a movement in scholarship that tended to focus its attention on immediate human concerns and needs. The synthesis of faith and reason provided by Thomas Aquinas opened the door for all sorts of scientific endeavors that furthered the well-being of mankind. By making room for both philosophy and theology, the groundwork was laid to explore and discover the principles of the world. Once these principles were understood, they could, in turn, be harnessed for the betterment of the human race. As a result, much interest was turned away from theology and directed toward other areas of inquiry. Initially, such efforts largely promoted the advancement of human understanding and of human well being. The real problems of such studies occurred when theology was made unimportant or neglected entirely. However, some of those problems developed as the nominalists separated the study of theology from philosophy. As this happened, human focus shifted in order to allow for the rise of a thorough going religious skepticism that allowed for scientists like Frederick to proliferate. In such cases, genius was allowed to pursue all kinds of horrible acts in the name of science. Many of the worsts of these acts came much later, therefore, for now, the emphasis can be placed on the early stages of it.

The humanism of the Renaissance was largely Christian. Dante

Alighieri was a prime example. Dante was born in Florence in 1265 and became one of the great writers of the period. His works include *La Vita Nova* ("The New Life") and *Convivio* ("Banquet"). His most famous work was *The Divine Comedy*. The *Comedy* "is made up of three nearly equal parts which are distinct yet carefully interrelated to form a unified whole. Each part moreover is the expression of one Person of the Trinity: *Inferno*, the Power of the Father, *Purgatory*, the Wisdom of the Son, *Paradise*, the Love of the Holy Spirit."[105] Dante's purpose for writing the narrative poem was to glorify God's plan for human history as he understood it. He also intended to show the foolish things that men do to one another because of their disobedience to God's commands. Dante believed that men could enjoy this life if only they developed their abilities in accordance with the guidelines established by God. He believed that much of the misery of this world was self-inflicted and could easily be avoided. In this sense, Dante was a pioneer forging a path for the development of the Renaissance.

The Divine Comedy transcends time and is still widely read in schools today. The depth of the work itself is the primary reason why this is so. As Archibald MacAllister has written:

> Dante had doubtless learned from experience how soporific a long narrative could be. He also firmly believed that the senses were the avenues to the mind and that sight was the most powerful ("noblest," he would have said) of these. Hence his art is predominantly visual. He believed also that the mind must be moved in order to grasp what the senses present to it; therefore he combines sight, sound, hearing, smell and touch with fear, pity, anger, horror and other appropriate emotions to involve his reader to the point of seeming actually to experience his situations and not merely to read about them. It is really a three-dimensional art.[106]

In addition to the Renaissance, Western civilization was profoundly marked by the Reformation. It was a movement aimed at

---

[105] Archibald T. MacAllister, "Introduction", *The Inferno*, translated by John Ciardi, (New York: Mentor Books, 1954).

[106] Ibid.

recapturing the fundamentals of the Christian faith. The reformers believed that certain aspects of the faith had been eroded over time because the Roman Catholic Church had embraced what was believed to be misguided human tradition. Therefore, the reformers thought that certain practices of the church were at odds with the teachings of Christ. These disagreements arose as a result of the spread in intellectual activity in the late Middle Ages. As more and more people began reading the Bible for themselves, they began to see certain passages that they could not reconcile with the Roman Church's official positions. This eventually sparked a movement to return to the purity of the Christian religion as it was expressed in the Scriptures alone. This movement divided the church and led to a great deal of religious conflict. Throughout Europe, people on both sides were persecuted for their faith. Those with the minority viewpoint in a particular area were often victimized for their beliefs by those who held the majority opinion. This kind of persecution led to a struggle for religious freedom that was finally resolved by the abandonment of state religions in Western societies. This was particularly true in the United States which was populated largely by people who fled the religious persecution that was ongoing in Europe. Nevertheless, the Christian religion, in its various forms, remained at the bedrock of institutional structures and of civil law.

One additional problem arose in this era. Namely, the rise of various cults and factions that claimed to be Christian, but which utterly failed to adhere to the teachings of Christ and the apostles in any consistent way. Since the time of the reformation, some of these groups have come and gone, some remain today, and new ones are forming. This problem has served to obscure true Christianity, either giving it a bad name by making it responsible for the actions of men who are anything but Christian, or by diluting the message so extensively that almost anyone could claim to be a Christian. In each case, it provided unbelieving skeptics with fuel for attacking the faith.

The combination of religious skepticism arising out of a separation of philosophy and theology, coupled with this latter problem, led to modern day secularism which, in turn, opened the door for the spread of naturalism. The result has been the spread of immorality as people turn to science alone for answers to the problems of life. But, it is a fool's errand to attempt to separate one's intelligence from his moral behavior. A wise man not only understands something of the universe, but acts upon his knowledge in a morally acceptable fashion. The fool on the other hand scorns wisdom to pursue his own immorality because he believes that his immediate interests are more important than moral behavior. As we will see later, this is a fundamental problem of modern societies.

Nevertheless, the foundation of the scientific method was laid during the Middle Ages, and, as it was more fully implemented in the Renaissance and Reformation, it allowed for the rapid advancement of knowledge about a host of phenomena that affect human life. As a result, technology has improved the circumstances of human life in a variety of ways. This has been especially true in modern times as new inventions dramatically alter the way in which we accomplish most of the tasks of daily life.

Study Questions

1. What happened to education and learning in the Middle Ages? Why?

2. In what way did asceticism result in a general decline in sanitation? What were some of the other factors in the decline?

3. How did religion hinder the advancement of science?

4. Discuss the rise of Scholasticism in the late Middle Ages. What fundamental tool of analysis was employed? What was the common language of learning?

5. Distinguish between extreme realism, moderate realism, and nominalism.

6. What was Anselm's ontological argument for the existence of God? What criticism was made of his argument? How did Jonathan Edwards revive the argument?

7. What was Thomas Aquinas' argument of the connection between divine and natural revelation? How did his argument provide a place for both philosophy and theology? What argument did Aquinas advance to prove the existence of God?

8. Explain the nominalism of Duns Scotus and William of Occam. How did this position give rise to religious skepticism? What is the ultimate problem associated with

this perspective?

9. Discuss how some fields of study advanced in the universities during the late Middle Ages.

Chapter 12: Growth and Development in the Later Period

I.   *The Renewal and Growth of European Cities*

The beginning of the Middle Ages was marked by the depopulation of the cities of Western Europe. While they never disappeared, their importance was limited in an age when rural subsistence agriculture was the basis upon which the bare necessities of life were provided. Yet, some people always remained in the cities and kept alive a variety of crafts and trades. In the course of time, many of the obstacles to trade that existed after the demise of the Roman Empire were overcome and commerce expanded. As a revival in trade occurred, the cities flourished once again and their populations grew rapidly. The result was an accumulation of wealth in Europe that had been largely unknown since the days of the Roman Empire. Increases in wealth led to an increased interest in education, the arts, and the sciences. All of these factors worked together to set the stage for a transition from the Middle Ages to the modern era which spawned Western civilization as we know it.

Among the many obstacles to trade within a feudal structure of society, were the restrictions imposed by feudal lords on merchants wishing to transport their goods. These restrictions included tolls charged to travel on a particular road, cross a bridge, or use a canal or river. In addition, tolls were levied on merchants to enter ports or to sell their goods in markets. These taxes dramatically lowered the potential gains from trade and, hence, limited the amount of it. For this reason, the term "robber barons", was coined and used by merchants to describe the activities of feudal lords and their quest to gain material wealth. However, in time there arose kings who consolidated their power and control over broader territories. Some of these recognized the potential value of trade and used their positions to reduce the number and size of tolls that merchants were forced to pay. They also worked to make roadways and rivers safe for transporting goods and established markets where merchants could sell their wares. For their efforts, trade expanded rapidly which resulted in an increase in wealth for the merchants and for their customers, who benefitted greatly from the less expensive and more abundant goods made available.

Commerce was also promoted by the development of trade associations or leagues. City-dwellers had always understood the potential value of economic trade and so they formed these associations to promote it. These organizations used their collective power to protect merchants from thieves, tax collectors, and feudal lords who would otherwise impose heavy tolls on merchants. They put pressure on the nobility to allow merchants safe transport over their fiefs and to reduce the overall level of taxation imposed. At the same time, they offered their services to apprehend and punish bands of thieves who might disrupt the trade. Finally, they served as institutions of mediation when disputes arose between various parties to trade. The combined activities of these leagues, along with the wiser administration of law by some kings, resulted in the rapid expansion in trade in the tenth, eleventh, and twelfth centuries.

As trade expanded, so too did local production. The role of merchants has always been that of orchestrating the transport of goods from places where they are plentiful and cheap to places where they are scarce and expensive. During the Middle Ages, merchants traveled to a variety of cities and regions and sought to sell goods they carried with them and to buy local wares that they hoped to sell elsewhere. As with all trade, their profits came from buying low in one region and selling high in another. From this activity they made a living for themselves and provided a valuable service to others by making a wide array of products available for consumption. This activity created wealth and established wide scale markets for commerce among the different peoples of the Mediterranean world. Therefore, the people in any particular area or city were freed from the necessity of producing all the things they needed and desired. Instead, they could focus on the production of those things that they could produce most effectively. The end result of this process of specialization and trade was an increase in wealth that allowed people the opportunity to consume a much wider array of products than had been previously available to them.

As production was extended, organizations called guilds began to reappear. Actually, such guilds had existed since ancient Rome, but they were of little importance in the day to day affairs of Europeans during most of the Middle Ages. However, as trade expanded, the guilds were reorganized and became very important. Two kinds of guilds developed. There were merchant guilds, or leagues, that were organizations of merchants and artisans which sought to expand their markets. "The greater guilds became powerful corporations; they dealt in a variety of goods, purchased raw materials wholesale, provided insurance against losses, organized the food supply and sewage disposals of their towns, paved streets, built roads and docks, deepened harbors, [and] policed highways. . ."[107] In addition to these were the craft guilds, which were associations of individuals involved in a specific trade. For example, there were guilds of weavers, tanners, butchers, and goldsmiths to name a few. Craft guilds were established to develop the skills of individuals who sought to work in particular trades. They generally required someone who wished to pursue a particular line of work to serve as an apprentice early in life and to work one's way up to the level of being a master craftsman by learning all aspects of the trade.

The merchant and craft guilds justified their existence by arguing that their efforts served to expand markets by limiting the abuses of the nobility, by thwarting thieves, by developing trade routes and markets, and by reducing the level of shoddy workmanship. If these organizations had limited the scope of their activities to these things, then they would have provided only valuable services to the communities in which they operated. Yet, as has already been seen before, such organizations rarely limited themselves to beneficial activities only. As trade flourished, these organizations grew in power and strength. In time, the political power they gained was used to monopolize trade in their local areas. It is a strange aspect of human depravity that prompts men to behave in this way. Even though the members of these groups were beneficiaries of freer trade, they began to use the power that they had gained to keep trade from becoming freer still. Like many before them, the people of these associations were motivated by greed, envy, and the desire to secure their positions apart from serving the needs and desires of others. Although commerce and trade contributed to their success, they tried to secure their prosperity by restricting any further extension in commerce that

---

[107] Will Durant, *The Age of Faith*, (New York: Simon and Schuster, 1950), pg. 634.

might undercut their known advantage. As the guilds gained political power, the expansion of trade slowed and the growth in wealth leveled off during the thirteenth century. To add to the problems created by the guilds, in the fourteenth century the greed of kings and nobles, along with their need to finance their near continual warfare, resulted in the imposition of numerous taxes and regulations that nearly suffocated trade. The combination of these factors gave rise to a deteriorating economic situation, which in turn provided the conditions for the outbreak of the Black Death. What followed was a rather dramatic setback in the general material well-being of people that continued through the fifteenth century.

Another obstacle to trade that was overcome during this period was the result of the teachings of the church. Through the years the church frowned on merchandising in general and on the charging of interest in particular. Such a position was a significant problem that limited economic growth. Goods must be transported from the producer to the consumer and, thus, merchandising is a fundamental component of economic life. In addition, any business enterprise must be financed. This is true because expenses always precede revenues in any productive activity. Therefore, business expenses must be financed and borrowing money at interest is one of the means of such financing. By condemning these practices, the church took an essentially anti-trade position. Nonetheless, it was a position that had a long history in that it was promoted by many of the early church fathers. Augustine was one of the few who saw the value of merchants, but even he frowned upon the charging of interest. Thus, there was little support for commerce or finance in the church. However, as we shall see, this perspective owed more to pagan Greek thought than to a thorough examination of the Scriptures.

To understand this, we must first consider what the Scriptures say on the subject of charging interest. First, it must be admitted that there is a prohibition of the charging of interest in the Bible in regards to a particular case. This prohibition is found in Exodus 22:25 as well as in a number of other similar passages.

> If you lend money to any of My people who are poor among
> you, you shall not be like a moneylender to him; you shall
> not charge him interest.[108]

One of the first things to note about this verse, and the others like it, is that it is not a general prohibition on charging interest. These verses prohibit the practice in a special case: charging interest to a *poor brother*. Thus, the prohibition only applied to a very select group of people, while the legitimacy of the general practice was never called into question within the context of Old Testament law.

Why did God ban the charging of interest in this particular case? The answer to this question will remain more or less unknown since its answer rests in the mind of God. Unless he chooses to reveal why he prohibited this kind of lending, then the answer cannot be known with certainty and we are left to speculate over the matter. However, we can make an educated guess about the meaning of the prohibition by considering the context in which it was given. It must be noted that this prohibition is listed among a large number of moral, civil, and ceremonial laws that provided the framework for the nation of Israel. That nation was established by God as a theocracy within which God intended to demonstrate his eternal plan of redemption. In particular, many of the ceremonial laws were intended to point to the life, death, and resurrection of Jesus Christ whose purpose was to provide an atoning sacrifice for the sin of his people. The land of Canaan was given by God to the nation of Israel as an inheritance which was meant to represent the inheritance of eternal life that God would freely give to his people. Since the eternal life of salvation is a gift from God, it cannot be lost. It is, therefore, possible that some of the provisions of the legal code given to Israel were intended to give some indication of that truth. In this case, we might understand the civil law that banned the charging of interest on loans to poor Israelites as a law meant to illuminate a larger spiritual truth. In practice, the prohibition would accomplish two things. First, if interest charges on loans to the poor were prohibited, it would keep such people from running the risk of forfeiting their property by defaulting on a loan. This would tend to insure their continued participation in the inheritance. Since the land symbolized the inheritance of eternal life

---

[108] Exodus 22:25. Also see Leviticus 25:35-38 and Deuteronomy 23:20.

through faith in Christ, it would have been important for the people of Israel to continue in their ownership of the land. Second, the extension of a loan without interest to a poor brother would provide an opportunity for someone to show mercy towards his poor brother in recognition of the mercy he had received from God. Both of these messages could have been intended by this particular provision.

Whether or not this is an accurate account of the matter, it is consistent with other passages in Scripture. For example, in Matthew 25:14-30, Jesus tells a parable about a master who entrusts three of his servants with some of his money while he goes on a journey. When he returns and settles accounts with the three he finds that the first two have put the money to work. Each of these individuals is reported to have doubled the amount of money they were given and are subsequently praised for their work. The third servant, however, is condemned. Instead of using the money in some productive act, the third man buried the money and simply returned the same amount to his master. Upon receiving his money back the master rebukes the third servant and goes so far as to chastise this man for not at least lending his money at interest in his absence.

It would be strange indeed for Jesus to tell such a story if he believed that the act of charging interest was an immoral one. In the story, the master represents God the Father and the three servants are meant to be representative of mankind and their relationship to God. Thus, in a very real sense, Jesus was telling his servants to go out and earn some kind of a return on the resources they possess. It seems, therefore, that far from condemning interest rate charges in society, Jesus was condoning the practice. If this were not the case, why did he use a story in which a man is condemned for failing to gain such interest? In light of this fact, it would appear unwise to argue that charging interest on loans should be banned altogether as a matter of morality. Such a position creates a number of interpretive difficulties if we are to understand the whole of Scripture in a consistent fashion.

Why, then, did the church adopt such a strong negative position against usury? The answer is found more in Greek philosophy, than in Christian teaching. The Greek philosophers thrived in an aristocratic environment and were largely influenced by an overarching view of life different from our own. From their perspective, the individual was valuable only to the extent that he was fit for his civic duty. Thus, in

Greek thought, the individual was subordinate to the city-state. In the context of this view of life, these philosophers looked upon making money commercially as morally degrading. In their view, it undermined one's community standing. Further, of the kinds of things that could be bought and sold, they thought that nothing could be worse than the buying and selling of money at interest. While Aristotle supported private property generally, even he shared this low view of merchants. He even argued that money was a sterile creation of the state and that the act of lending it for gain was, therefore, immoral. While this argument has been discarded by modern economists, it was nevertheless quite prominent among the Greeks and among many peoples of later ages.

As we have already seen, Greek philosophy had a profound impact on the way that people throughout the Mediterranean basin thought. While trade flourished in the Roman Empire, merchants were generally held in disdain by the intellectual and aristocratic elite, even though they benefitted greatly from them. Also, as we have seen, there was a propensity to fuse pagan ideas with Christian doctrine as the religion spread. The negative view of charging interest on loans is an example of how the pagan ideas of Greek philosophy were subsequently fused with Christian doctrines in church teachings. The first move towards this situation occurred at the Nicean Council which prohibited the clergy from charging interest. In the course of time, this ban was extended to other groups until the time of Charlemagne when he made the ban complete and tied it to Christian faith. This view of money interest remained in tact until the scholastics of the later Middle Ages began to attack it. Little by little these thinkers picked away at the basis of the ban. As they did, trade was more and more accommodated by the evolving laws of society. But, it wasn't until the Reformation that biblical scholars finally discarded the inconsistency. Even so, there remains among many religiously minded individuals an aversion to the existence of rates of interest that are believed to be too high.

The reality is that charging interest on a loan is an exchange of goods like any other. In the exchange, one party gives up his use of money for a time because he values the prospect of greater future consumption more than the current consumption that he might enjoy. The other individual has some immediate need that he finds more valuable than the future consumption which he agrees to give up. This is particularly important in the case of financing business enterprise where the borrower is motivated by the prospect of creating sufficient wealth not only to return the necessary interest and principal to the lender, but to provide an excess return as well. Borrowing money today for the purpose of financing business activity is one of the fundamental means of facilitating commerce and of expanding the general material well-being of people. Like all other voluntary exchanges, both parties expect to benefit from the trade.

This does not mean that Christians are free to ignore the poor in society. Rather, there ought to be many mercy ministries created for the purpose of meeting the financial needs of the poor apart from providing them with loans they must repay with interest. If the poor were left to fend for themselves in this way, there is no doubt that their situations would continue to worsen because of the interest charges that they would face. That is, the poor are not likely to borrow money for the purpose of investing in capital that will allow them to improve their future well-being. Instead, they are most likely to borrow for the purpose of meeting some pressing need. In this case, while the concern of the moment might be provided for, the long term prospects for success have been diminished. Therefore, Christian charity may well be needed. Such charitable giving is indeed an important function of the church. Nevertheless, the church's condemnation of usury in general was a rather unfortunate error that resulted from the fusion of pagan ideas with the teachings of Scripture.

II. Building Cathedrals

The life of the individual in the high Middle Ages tended to focus on matters of faith and religion. It is, therefore, not surprising that the primary focus of art during this time was Christianity. In fact, designing, building, and adorning churches accounted for the bulk of the work of artists. As John Harrison and Richard Sullivan have written:

> Every church was a complete museum, filled with sculpture, painting, wood carving, glasswork, metalwork, and decorative handwriting. No amount of description can ever convey a true impression of the total artistic effect created by a medieval church in its entirety. Only by seeing monuments such as Norte Dame in Paris and the cathedrals

at Chartres, Amiens, and Rheims can one appreciate the quality and spirit of medieval art.[109]

This focus makes a great deal of sense when it is remembered that most of the important events in the lives of individuals and families took place in church. There were baptisms, weddings, and funerals as well as weekly worship services. In times of war, the people sought sanctuary in churches, and they were often the focal points of the routines of daily life. For example, it was common for traveling merchants to set out their wares in front of the cathedrals or for the townspeople to store the harvest in them. In essence, the church was at the center of life in towns or villages throughout Europe.

Not only were the churches at the center of life, they were also the most impressive buildings constructed in the communities. "Considering the technological and economic backwardness of mediaeval Latin Christendom, its architectural achievements are phenomenal."[110] Indeed, the churches built during this era were impressive. The architectural style, evolved from that used by the Romans. For this reason, the early manner of construction was usually referred to as Romanesque. The form of these buildings was patterned after the Roman basilica. They were long meeting halls which were usually constructed with a lateral aisle called a transept. The result of this mode of construction was a building shaped in the pattern of a cross.

These kinds of structures were first built in the tenth and eleventh centuries. They were often built with stone, which was preferred to other materials because of the threat of fire. In earlier times, when the absence of wealth precluded such construction, churches had been made from wood. Unfortunately, when they burned down, the community lost the church as well as its contents, and this resulted in severe hardships for the people. Thus, stone construction was much favored. Yet, such construction presented numerous problems. A stone building had to support the weight of a very heavy roof. The Roman solution to this

---

[109] John Harrison and Richard Sullivan, *A Short History of Western Civilization*, (New York: Alfred A. Knopf, 1960), pg. 281.

[110] Frederick Artz, *The Mind of the Middle Ages*, (New York: Alfred A. Knopf, 1953), pg. 385.

problem was to build a rounded arch. The medieval designers adopted this solution and used it frequently. However, one problem with a rounded arch was that it distributed weight evenly across its breadth. As a result, construction of this kind required massive columns and thick walls to help support the weight of the roof and this offered little opportunity for the inclusion of windows in the design of the structure. For this reason, Romanesque buildings had few windows and were often quite dark and dreary places.

By the twelfth century, architects began to experiment with other designs in an effort to brighten the interior of the churches. The Gothic style of construction was developed from these efforts. Gothic design relied on pointed arches and ribbed vaults rather than the rounded arches used in Romanesque construction. This design was a vast improvement because this kind of arch and vault system allowed the weight of the structure to be localized at certain key points. The result of constructing buildings in this fashion was that the main part of the structure was built like a skeleton which was finished with thin walls and with as many windows as the designer desired.

As the Gothic style spread, some of the grandest cathedrals ever built were constructed. Stained glass was typically used in the windows and became one of the primary mediums of artistic expression. The addition of these windows increased the amount of light inside the churches and tended to focus the person's attention towards heaven. And, both inside and outside, stone sculptures were made to represent various teachings of the church.

Constructing a new cathedral was a mammoth undertaking. These massive construction projects were typically overseen by a master mason. He was generally a man of substantial knowledge about construction and design and was well compensated for his expertise. His job was to marshal and organize the resources necessary to complete the project. He provided the plans, oversaw the purchase and acquisition of the materials needed, hired and compensated the workers, and supervised the construction. Among these tasks, the master mason likely visited the quarry from which the stone for the building was being cut on a regular basis. In fact, in some instances he might have even been the owner of the quarry.

Cutting the stone from the earth was in itself a monumental feat. The work was very labor intensive and the only available tools were a pick, an axe, and a chisel. With these limited tools, large stones were cut. They were transported to the construction site in either rough or semi-finished condition. Once at the site, whatever additional finishing touches were needed were completed and the stones were set in place. Afterwards, other masons carved out the various details of adornment. In addition to the work of the artisans in erecting the building, various artists and craftsmen were commissioned to paint pictures, carve sculptures, and to decorate the facility with a variety of artwork intended to focus the worshiper's thoughts on spiritual things.

Many of these structures remain standing today. However, they are no longer at the center of community life. In many cases, they are more or less museums of the past. The competition for power among secular and ecclesiastical rulers, and the struggle for power during the rise of nations eventually led to the decline of the church building as the center of daily life in Western Europe.

III. The Rise of Nations

In the earlier chapter on feudalism it was pointed out that a feudal hierarchy was ultimately inconsistent. If the king were powerful enough to have the final say, then the political system collapsed into a monarchy. On the other hand, if the nobility were powerful enough to resist the king, then he was not at the top of the hierarchy and pledges of loyalty were disregarded. Because of this tension, there was an ongoing contest for power between the king and his nobles, as well as among his nobles, and among kings and nobles of different regions. The result of the ongoing struggles for power was the development of national states which ended feudalism. Because this process was important in the transition from the Middle Ages to the Modern Age, it is worthwhile to provide a brief discussion illustrating that development before moving to an examination of the early modern era. While there were many cases of contests for power that could be considered, we will limit our discussion to those that led to the development of England, France, and Spain. Of these three, we can consider England and France together for their individual development was so closely tied.

A. England and France

The destruction of feudalism by the rise of monarchs in England and France centered around an ongoing conflict known as the Hundred Years' War. Tensions between England and France arose during the reign of the French king Philip IV. Philip was a particularly greedy ruler who sought to extend his power and control. In the course of his activities to do so, he became engaged in numerous military conflicts and needed money to finance these campaigns. Murray Rothbard explained the matter quite well:

> [I]n the early fourteenth century, Philip IV, the Fair, king of France (1285-1314), moved to tax, plunder, and effectively destroy the vitally important fairs of Champagne. To finance his perpetual dynastic wars, Philip levied a stiff sales tax on the Champagne fairs. He also destroyed domestic capital and finance by repeated confiscatory levies on groups or organizations with money. . . .Furthermore, at war with the Flemings, Philip broke the long-time custom that all merchants were welcome at the fairs, and decreed the exclusion of the Flemings. The result of these measures was a rapid and permanent decline of the fairs of Champagne and of the trading route over the Alps.[111]

The expansion of Philip's power and the restrictions imposed on trade were of immediate importance to the English kings for two reasons. First, they held feudal control over portions of land in France, and Philip's activities threatened this control. Second, they received a great deal of their own finances from duties collected on exporting wool to the Flemish who used it to make cloth. Third, Philip, as well as later French kings, encouraged the ongoing conflict the English were having with the Scots. The combination of these factors eventually erupted in nearly continual warfare that lasted throughout the fourteenth century and into the early fifteenth.

Most of the actual military battles were isolated and resulted in little harm to the general populace. However, to finance their war efforts,

---

[111] Murray Rothbard, *Economic Thought Before Adam Smith: An Austrian Perspective on the History of Economic Thought*, (Great Britain: Edward Elgar Publishing, 1995, Vol. I), pg. 68.

both sides actively imposed new taxes and regulations on the people to raise revenues. The excesses of the kings in taxing the people left many destitute and tended to undermine the earlier prosperity that had arisen from trade. Furthermore, since the merchant fairs in France had been curtailed, the effects of the conflict between France and England were felt throughout Europe. As economic conditions declined, so too did the sanitary conditions. This resulted in the outbreak of the bubonic plague in the middle of the fourteenth century which wiped out about one third of Europe's population.

Over the course of the ongoing conflict between the two rivals, it was England that gained the initial upper hand. But, the nation's success was not without problems. In order to raise the armies necessary to fight the war, the taxes and regulations imposed on the English citizenry led to internal hostilities, and there was a great deal of strife between the king and the nobility. As a result, problems at home allowed the French to recover from their losses and mount numerous counter-offenses against the English. By the middle of the fifteenth century, the French had virtually driven the English from French soil. This feat could not have been accomplished without the concentration of power in the hands of the monarch. In fact, the occasion of warfare gave rise to the consolidation of power and to absolutism. Charles VII led the way and between him and his son, Louis XI, the nation of France was established under their rule.

In England, the friction between the king and the nobles eventually resulted in a conflict known as the War of the Roses. That struggle was a battle for a way of life that was quickly vanishing. In the end, Henry Tudor was victorious on the battle field. The various noble factions had been decimated by war, and Henry VII claimed the throne of England and established his own absolute rule there. Henry put an end to feudal contracts. The result was the emergence of the nation state under the rule of an absolute monarch.

B. Spain

Spain had long been dominated by the Moslems. However, there had always remained a Christian contingency. In the course of time, various groups of Christians formed and began an assault on Moorish rule. With the blessing of the Roman Catholic Church, these groups began a conquest of the Iberian peninsula in the eleventh century. They achieved great success against the Moslems, and three important monarchies emerged: Aragon, Castile, and Portugal. But, before they could drive the Moors from the continent, war broke out between the competing Christian factions. In the feudal style, these groups fought each another to gain an edge.

> As in England and France, this period saw in Spain both the rise and the decline of feudalism. The nobles began by almost ignoring the central power; they and the clergy were exempt from taxation, which fell the more heavily upon cities and trade; but they ended by submitting to kings armed with their own troops, supported by the revenues and militia of the towns, and endowed with the prestige of a reviving Roman law that assumed absolute monarchy as an axiom of government.[112]

The culmination of the conflict and the establishment of the national state occurred when Isabella, the heir of Castile, married Ferdinand, the heir of Aragon. The marriage brought together two of the largest remaining factions from the ongoing feudal rivals. Portugal was left to form its own nation. For all practical purposes, this event marked the beginning of the new nation state with an absolute sovereign monarch.

Study Questions

1. Why is commercial trade a fundamental prerequisite for the advancement of the arts and sciences?
2. How did feudal lords inhibit merchant trade?
3. How did some kings use their power to expand trade in the late middle ages? In what ways did others limit that expansion and, in some cases, reverse it?
4. Explain the benefits of the guilds and other trade associations in expanding merchant exchange. How did these organizations limit that expansion?
5. What teaching of the Roman Church tended to limit

---

[112] Will Durant, *The Age of Faith*, (New York: Simon and Schuster, 1950), pg. 698.

merchant trade? How was that teaching formulated over time? What were the inherent problems of that formulation?

6. Explain how life revolved around the church during this era? How were the cathedrals of the late Middle Ages constructed?

7. How did the nations of France, England, and Spain arise?

Section 3: The Early Modern Era

In the course of time, the high Middle Ages gave way to the early modern era. In turn, what transpired in this span of time set the stage for the conflict of ideas that so accurately marks our own age. The early modern era was largely shaped by two movements. The Renaissance and the Reformation resulted in profound changes in the underlying structures of society. The renewal of learning in the high Middle Ages resulted in a renewed interest in the classics of Greek and Roman cultures. Religiously speaking, this literature was increasingly informed by paganism which had significant influence on Western culture. The expression of this change was present in the arts. In time, those most concerned about traditional Christianity began to press for reforms in the church. These efforts eventually erupted into the Reformation.

The struggles among various Christian thinkers set the stage for an ongoing conflict in society that is characteristic of the modern era. Namely, the conflicts that developed among the religiously minded opened the door for the attacks of skeptics. These attacks were made easier by the religious wars and by the advancements that were being made in science.

Chapter 13: The Renaissance

The time span known as the Renaissance is so-called because of the increased interest in and the availability of classical literature. There were several key factors which account for this occurrence. First, as previously mentioned, the increase in trade and wealth led to an increased interest in secular learning. The memory of the greatness of Greece and Rome had never quite faded away. In fact, the artifacts of that era stood as a constant reminder of their former glory. For that reason, when Europeans sought secular knowledge they looked for it in ancient Greek and Roman literature. Second, in 1453, the Ottoman Turks captured Constantinople marking the end of the Byzantine Empire. As a result, a number of intellectuals from the east fled to Western Europe for refuge. They carried whatever literature they could with them. This significantly increased the number of classical works available for study. Finally, in 1454, Johannes Guttenberg introduced a workable, movable type printing press into European life that greatly increased the speed at which manuscripts could be printed. The result of this invention was the rapid expansion of the number of copies of books in circulation.

The combination of these factors led to a number of developments that profoundly impacted European life. The changes that occurred during this time affected the region's religion, its art, its literature, and its politics. The changes in culture during the Renaissance began on the Italian peninsula and spread northward throughout Western Europe along the common trade routes. As the Renaissance spread, it spawned another movement of equal importance in understanding our own time. This movement was the Protestant Reformation. But, this is a topic for the next chapter.

I. Challenging the Christian Religion

As is always true, a person can proclaim Christian faith without actually embracing the essential elements of it. To compound the problem, a person who is truly converted to the religion is not made perfect in this life. Therefore, it is difficult to discern by outward appearances who possesses real Christian faith. In addition, because of their continuing imperfections, adherents of the Christian faith are often accused of hypocrisy. But, it is hardly hypocritical for an individual to confess his own sins and point to Jesus as his only hope of salvation. Nor is it hypocritical to strive to live a more consistent moral life, even if one is unable to attain perfection this side of heaven. Indeed, the willingness to confess one's numerous failures to achieve the perfect moral life is evidence that hypocrisy is not present.

Still, there are genuine hypocrites. There are always people who either claim to be more righteous than they really are or who profess an inward faith in the Christian religion that is actually empty. Since Christianity was the state religion of Europe at this time, almost everyone professed the faith. However, the actual number of true believers was smaller than the number of professions of faith that were made. Because of the relationship of the Roman Catholic Church with secular governments at this time, the problem was especially prevalent. As a result, hypocrisy was rampant and immorality was widespread, even among leaders of the Church. While there remained many God-fearing priests and nuns who made it their primary aim in life to promote the gospel message and practice Christian charity, there were also those who used their positions in reprehensible ways. In some places, the conduct of the clergy was so bad that many people developed a strong dislike for the church and its leaders. Furthermore, it seemed that the closer one got to the seat of papal power, the worse was the corruption among the clergy.

As a result of the clerical corruption, the Roman Church's hierarchal structure became more and more viewed as oppressive. There were even occasions when papal authority was used to further political and economic goals rather than the religious ones it was established to promote. Papal taxation and the Roman Church's occasional meddling in the affairs of local congregations alienated some groups of people. To make matters worse, the hierarchy never seemed satisfied with its income. To increase its treasury, the papacy expanded the issuance of indulgences which were sold by traveling priests to provide remissions of sin. It was the practice of selling such "forgiveness" that prompted Martin Luther to nail his Ninety-five Theses to the door of the church in Wittenberg in 1517, marking the start of the Protestant Reformation. Put simply, there was a growing lack of respect for the Roman Catholic Church at this time. The decline in respect for the church in Western Europe opened the door for the revival of the old pagan religions of Greece and Rome, along with the rise in intellectual skepticism. In addition, it also provided the motivation for men like Martin Luther, who aimed to return the Christian religion to its biblical moorings.

A. Petrarch (1304-1374) and Boccaccio (1313-1375)

Two of the forerunners of the Renaissance movement were Petrarch and Boccaccio. They were contemporaries as well as friends. Francesco Petrarch's parents were of Florentine heritage, but had been forced into exile because of a political upheaval of that city. For that reason Francesco was born in Arezzo. From there, his father moved the family to Pisa for a brief time. However, once again because of changes in the political climate, he was forced to flee. The family settled at Avignon in France. It was there that Francesco came to maturity and was sent off to school by his father to study law.

Though his father intended for him to become a lawyer, Petrarch hated the details involved in mastering such a vocation and much preferred to spend his time reading the works of Virgil, Cicero, and Seneca. He was captivated by their style and refinement and hoped to one day imitate them in his own writings. When his parents died, he abandoned the study of law altogether in order to devote his time to reading and writing poetry and romance literature in a classic style.

Petrarch spent his life in this pursuit. He was so interested in extending the classics that he devoted most of his time and resources to collecting classical literature. He also inspired others to search for ancient Latin and Greek manuscripts possibly hidden away in monasteries or carried away by trading expeditions from the east. It was because of his love of classic literature that he is often referred to as the father of the Renaissance.

Beyond Petrarch's love of the classics, he was highly critical of the Roman Catholic Church and its leaders. He was especially critical of

Christian morality because he felt that it was too restrictive. It was said that he was a vain and egotistical man who tended to worship form over substance. Petrarch tried to make religion a matter solely of emotion and passion. He was, therefore, religious primarily in feeling, but rejected the principles of a moral life. As a result, he was one of the first individuals emerging from medieval times who made a conscious break from traditional Christianity. The Christian religion is a comprehensive one involving both the emotions and the mind. Christians are strongly encouraged to live their lives on the basis of certain moral principles of behavior. Petrarch moved away from such a moral life. His break from traditional Christianity was not so complete that he departed entirely from the Roman Church, but it was still enough to mark a radical change in his attitude about religious ideas. This change not only affected Petrarch, but also all those whom he influenced.

Like Petrarch, Boccaccio was deeply moved by classical literature. He was the bastard son of a Florentine father and a French mother. He was raised in his father's home in Florence, but was never accepted by his stepmother. As a result, he had a particularly unhappy childhood.

> "At the age of ten. . . he was sent to Naples, where he was apprenticed to a career of finance and trade. He learned to hate business as Petrarch hated law; he announced his preference for poverty and poetry, lost his soul to Ovid, feasted on the *Metamorphoses* and the *Heroides*, and learned by heart most of the *Ars amandi*, wherein, he wrote, 'the greatest of poets shows how the sacred fire of Venus may be made to burn in the coldest' breast."[113]

In response to his preferences, his father allowed him to study canon law.

It was at this point in his life that Boccaccio became infatuated with Maria d'Aquino. He was so overcome with the thought of her that he pursued her for five years. She finally submitted to his advances and the two engaged in an adulterous affair until Maria got tired of him and moved on to new exploits. Nevertheless, she became the inspiration for Boccaccio to write a number of highly sensual pieces of literature.

---

[113] Will Durant, *The Renaissance*, (New York: Simon and Schuster, 1953), pg. 10.

He later met Petrarch and developed a friendship with him. The two shared much in common, especially their outlook on the nature of this world and the nature of love. "In his [most famous work] *Decameron*, a collection of one hundred tales or novelettes, Boccaccio makes no pretense of using Christian restraint. He relates bawdy romances with skill and grace, condoning and even glorifying the seamy side of human nature."[114] It was this type of work which endeared these men to each other and which pitted them against Christianity.

B. *Erasmus of Rotterdam (1466-1536)*

An idea that is often promoted in discussing the combined movements of the Renaissance and the Reformation is that the first was largely confined to Italy, while the latter was fundamentally rooted in northern Europe. "It has long been said that the ferment was intellectual south of the Alps and religious to the north, but this generalization is not quite satisfactory. . . "[115] A more accurate assessment of the situation is that the increase in wealth that followed the renewal of Mediterranean trade resulted in a revival in intellectual activities that led to the questioning of the Roman Catholic Church's teaching and authority in a number of important respects. However, such questioning exposed the critic to certain hazards. The foremost of these was to be labeled a heretic. Such a determination resulted in harsh punishment. A person so labeled was put to death for his crime. Nonetheless, there were people willing to accept the risk of being found guilty of heresy in order to raise such questions of the Roman Church's teaching and authority. And while the rise of skepticism may have been concentrated among a talented and rather impressive group of writers and artists in Italy, it was by no means confined there. Nor were those interested in reforming the Latin Church of its corrupting influences located only in northern European countries. In fact, there were a number of religious reformers in Italy during the Renaissance and they sought reform with great zeal. Two of the most

---

[114] John B. Harrison and Richard E. Sullivan, *A Short History of Western Civilization*, (New York: Alfred A. Knopf, 1960), pg. 345.

[115] Edward Coleson, *The Harvest of Twenty Centuries*, (Spring Arbor, Michigan, 1967), pg. 179.

notable were St. Catherine of Siena and Savonarola of Florence. Nevertheless, the Renaissance had the bulk of its most successful adherents in Italy, while most of the religious reformers of the day lived in northern Europe. In discussing the Renaissance, an inadequate picture would be painted if none of the humanists from the north were considered.

Desiderius Erasmus is a good example of a northern European who was profoundly affected by the Renaissance. He was born in the Netherlands near Rotterdam and learned to read and write Dutch. As his education continued, he learned Latin and was exposed to the pagan classics. When he was fifteen years of age both of his parents died, and he was sent to live in a monastery. But he was never content there and eventually was granted his wish to study at the university in Paris. As his education continued, he developed a passion for literature. After leaving Paris he had the opportunity to travel in England where he met and befriended John Colet and Thomas More. Colet had been directly exposed to the intellectual climate of Renaissance Italy and served as an inspiration to Erasmus.

In the context of his studies, he was more amused than shocked to discover that pagan superstitions had been infused into several church teachings over the ages. As he reflected on this situation, he developed an underlying disbelief in any miracles. This of course put him at odds with traditional Christianity. While he never left the Roman Church, he was often critical of it. He used his extensive learning and insightful wit to expose superstition, error, and corruption in his day. He believed that a return to the sources of Christian truth was all that was needed to purify the Latin Church and to promote the good society. In a very real sense, he was one of the first proponents of the notion that it is possible to end evil by promoting education. He thought the main problem that humanity faced was ignorance rather than sin.

On the basis of his views, he embarked upon an effort to try to humanize Christ. He thus set in motion a movement that would eventually view Jesus as just a good man, but nothing more. But, as noted earlier, C. S. Lewis correctly pointed out that such a position cannot be reconciled with the historical record of Jesus' teachings. As Lewis stated so clearly, Jesus did not leave that option open. Based on his own testimony about himself, and given his claims to be God incarnate, one would have to conclude that Jesus was either a liar, a lunatic, or the Lord himself. So, in the final analysis, this effort amounts to an attempt to establish the Christian religion without Christ. While such a scheme is certainly religious, it is by no means Christian. Yet, many individuals, both in the past as well as today, attempted to adopt this same point of view.

Many people may claim to be Christian without embracing the fundamentals of the religion. Indeed, the modern liberal theology of today is an extension of earlier efforts. But can a religious philosophy of life, based only upon an admonition to live one's life according to a particular ethic, be called Christian? Christianity is so-called because of the title given to its Founder. The term Christ is the Greek word for the Hebrew word Messiah. Messiah literally means anointed, or Savior of the world. The Jewish people used the word to express their hope in God's promise to bring forth a man who would be anointed by God for the purpose of saving the world. The Christian religion is the religion that finds in Jesus of Nazareth that person. At its foundation, Christianity is a religion whose object of faith is Jesus. At its heart, the religion proclaims the veracity of Jesus' own words. Without a Savior, there simply is no Christianity. All that remains is an ethical philosophy of life that might just as easily be given any number of different names.

On a more positive note, Erasmus engaged in excellent scholarship that inspired others to zealously pursue academic achievement. This was particularly true in the area of biblical scholarship. His interest in classical literature led him quite naturally to promote the study of Scripture in the original languages of Greek and Hebrew. This effort exposed numerous errors that were prominent at the time because the Latin Church used as its main biblical text St. Jerome's Latin translation. In exposing these errors, Erasmus provided a significant amount of ammunition for other church reformers. In particular, his work provided the critical foundation for those who started the Protestant Reformation. As historians Harrison and Sullivan pointed out, ". . . the humanists unwittingly helped to bring about the Reformation by weakening the position of the Roman Catholic Church."[116]

---

[116] John B. Harrison and Richard E. Sullivan, *A Short History of Western Civilization*, (New York: Alfred A. Knopf, 1960), pg. 365.

II. Renaissance Art and Literature

The Renaissance period is perhaps most often thought of as one in which there was a revival of the arts. It is not surprising that the renewed interest in classics occurred first in Italy because that is where trade and wealth revived first. It is also not surprising that Italy was the center of artistic expression. Human beings are never very interested in self-examination and self-expression through the arts until they are well fed, clothed, and sheltered. So, the production and spread of art began in Italy because it was the first area to prosper from the revival of commercial trade. From there, the revival of the arts followed the spread of prosperity and education throughout the rest of Europe.

The number of exceptional artists of the Renaissance era is far too extensive to cover here. Among them we could consider Ghiberti or Donatello and their sculptures or the magnificent paintings of Masaccio or Botticelli. But none of these artists are as well known as two individuals whose work more or less defined the age. Therefore, the consideration of the lives of Michelangelo and Leonardo da Vinci will suffice in providing us with a fairly clear understanding of Renaissance art.

A. Leonardo da Vinci (1452-1519)

Leonardo da Vinci is often referred to as the Renaissance man. His interests were broad and his talents, skills, and insights were vast. Few people in the history of the world have equaled his genius. He was the illegitimate child of a Florentine lawyer. His mother was a peasant girl who lived in a village some sixty miles from Florence, and she gave Leonardo to his father and stepmother to be raised in the affluent surroundings that his father could provide. As a result, Leonardo had the advantage of a good education, and when he was fifteen years of age he became an apprentice of the artist Verrocchio. Under his tutelage Leonardo perfected his skills as an artist. His most noted works of art include *Virgin of the Rocks*, *The Last Supper*, and the *Mona Lisa*.

Perhaps Leonardo's biggest asset was his attention to detail. Examples of his eye for detail are present in all his work. For example, in his painting, *Virgin of the Rocks*, the plants painted are actually identifiable as known species of vegetation. In addition, he was always quite curious about all facets of life and often made careful observations of whatever might seize his attention. Among his extensive and varied interests were painting, sculpture, architecture, engineering, botany, anatomy, philosophy, and geology. His observations of the things were so detailed that it was said of him that he could paint the face of a person from memory as if the person were present during the process. This attention to detail aided him greatly as an inventor as well as a painter and sculptor.

But, perhaps this attention to detail was also a source of weakness. The problem for Leonardo in this regard was that his interests were too widespread for him to adequately handle all the details of each subject he studied. To compound the problem, he was unable to limit his focus to a specific subject long enough to complete its study before moving to something else. As one historian put it, "He passed too quickly from one task or subject to another; he was interested in too many things; he lacked a unifying purpose, a dominating idea; this 'universal man' was a medley of brilliant fragments; he was possessed of and by too many abilities to harness them to one goal. . . .He wrote five thousand pages, but never completed one book."[117]

He did, nonetheless, leave a legacy of great accomplishments that ranged from his numerous works of art to remnants of various scientific pursuits. These latter efforts, no doubt, flowed out of his interest in nature and his curiosity of how things fit together. He pondered the ordering of nature within a pantheistic view of the world. He conceived of God as being essentially an impersonal force, much like the pagan view of the Greek philosophers. This conception of God became fashionable in the intellectual circles of the Renaissance era. For this reason, he developed the idea that reality was a set of universal principles that direct the operations of nature. While such a view separated him from the Christian conception of reality, it still allowed him to examine and comprehend a number of natural laws. The reason why he was successful was that the actual natural order flowed from the providential rule of an orderly God. As such, a careful examination of the universe revealed universal principles established and sustained by God himself.

---

[117] Will Durant, *The Renaissance*, (New York: Simon and Schuster, 1953), pg. 216.

B. Michelangelo (1475-1564)

Michelangelo was born in the small town of Caprese near Florence. At the age of thirteen he became an apprentice of Domenico Ghirlandaio who was a respected painter in Florence. It was during this time that he began to develop his abundant skill as an artist. Like Leonardo da Vinci, Michelangelo had an eye for detail. During his apprenticeship he carefully examined real world objects that he later painted or sculpted. While he was outstanding at both, sculpting was his passion.

Michelangelo's first opportunity to ply his trade came from the Medici family who wished to develop a school of sculpture in Florence. Ghirlandaio recommended Michelangelo as a promising prospect for this endeavor and he was employed by the famous Florentine family to carve sculptures for them. The Medici family was one of the wealthiest families in Florence. They were politically well connected, and often had family members in government positions. As his work gained greater fame, his services were sought out by various Roman Church authorities as well. One of his most notable works for the Roman Catholic Church was the *Pieta*. The piece was an impressive carving of Mary holding the crucified body of Jesus in her lap. It significantly increased Michelangelo's reputation as an artist and expanded his opportunities to work on other projects. Among his many accomplishments, the statue *David* and the fresco painted on the ceiling of the Sistine chapel are the most well known.

For Michelangelo, art was more than a career; it was his passion and his life. When he was once chided for never marrying or having children, he responded that his art was his wife and that his children were the finished pieces of his work. He was a loner of sorts. He never got along well with others and, though he respected the abilities of Leonardo da Vinci and Raphael, he never cared very much for them personally nor did he seek to keep company with them. He had few friends and was well known for being temperamental. Nonetheless, his abundant skills as an artist were obvious to everyone.

In his art, Michelangelo expressed his preoccupation with the human form. In all of his work he paid careful attention to the details of human anatomy. This was especially true when his subject was a male figure. In this case the muscular details of the male anatomy took the place of central importance in his sculptures and paintings. Some writers found in this evidence that the artist sought to express a profound humanism in his work. Harrison and Sullivan, for example, write, "The work of Michelangelo is probably our best example of the Renaissance glorification of man as lord and master of the universe."[118] Their position may have merit. In the details of his work, especially in his youth, there remain apparent bits and pieces of evidence that appear to provide evidence that he rejected at least some of the essentials of Christianity. One example of this was the sculpture *David*. "As a work of art it has few equals in the world. Michelangelo took a piece of marble so flawed that no one thought it could be used, and out of it he carved this overwhelming statue. But let us notice that *David* was not the Jewish David of the Bible. *David* was simply a title. Michelangelo knew his Judaism, and in the statue the figure is not circumcised. We are not to think of this as the biblical David but as the humanistic ideal. Man is great!"[119] While this evidence suggests that the artist embraced a kind of secular humanism, that conclusion likely goes too far. We cannot know for certain what was at the man's heart, we can only examine the art work that he left behind. That work reflects the extraordinary artistic talent possessed by one man.

III. The Changing Political Climate

The development of nation states, as was briefly discussed in the previous chapter, did not occur without the aid of scholarship providing an intellectual foundation for the absolute rule of monarchs. This work was begun in the universities in Italy and was exported to places of learning throughout Europe. A number of scholars began to develop theories to justify the absolute rule of the head of the state. These writers argued that the state was supreme and should always be obeyed. Within the context of this perspective, "justice has no rational foundation; it is purely mystical and solely a matter of faith. God's commands are purely arbitrary and mysterious, and not to be understood in terms of rational or

---

[118] Harrison and Sullivan, op. cit., pg. 351.

[119] Francis A. Schaeffer, *How Should We Then Live?*, (Westchester, Illinois, Crossway Books, 1976), pp. 71-72.

ethical content."[120]

The underlying foundation that allowed for this kind of argumentation was nominalism. One of the chief implications of nominalism was its low regard for natural theology and for the concept of natural law. In other words, nominalism promoted the belief that there was no basis for a philosophy capable of arriving at any essential truth. Those who adopted such a belief held that the authority of revelation was separate from mental comprehension. In other words, the authority of revelation could be arbitrary. Proponents of this view argued that a person was obligated to embrace revelation by faith without any understanding. Thus, laws, both divine and secular, were to be understood as arbitrary decrees with no basis in rationality.

The effect of the spread of nominalism in the universities was that it undermined the natural law synthesis that Thomas Aquinas developed earlier. This was quite unfortunate, because Aquinas' work made room for both theology and philosophy. His work did not condone violating commandments simply because people did not understand them. Rather, he argued that the commands of God were all potentially understandable in a rational way. For this reason, the rule of civil law should not progress in some arbitrary fashion by the decrees of men, but should be established so that they are consistent with the created order as well. Within this understanding, reason and morality worked together in a very definite fashion. God was understood to be both rational and moral. As such, this view promoted the idea that he created and sustained the world in a very definite fashion and that order could be understood by way of intellectual pursuits. In addition, moral behavior too could be discerned from the created order.

On the other side, nominalism destroyed the link between reason and morality. All laws were viewed as being arbitrary. From this point of view, there was no certain understanding of God's law or of secular law. Whatever was decreed should be done simply because it was decreed. While a person could certainly see the wisdom of blind submission to the decrees of God, it did not follow that the decrees of men ought to be blindly followed because men showed the ease with which they decreed evil. But further, even with respect to the decrees of God, such

---

[120] Rothbard, op. cit., pg. 71.

proclamations by nominalists missed the point. Many of God's commands were perfectly understandable on the basis of reason alone. For example, God prohibited theft. But, even without God's command it was apparent that theft as a means of life was a useless economic system.

Consider for a moment an economy based on stealing. If there is but one thief, he may surely benefit from his activity by preying upon the goods produced by others. However, if all cease their efforts at production in order to participate in theft, they will surely starve to death for there will be nothing to steal. Stealing suffers from a logical fallacy of thought known as the fallacy of composition. What is true for the individual is not necessarily true for the group as a whole. Thus, by logic alone we can understand that stealing is a destructive behavior that reduces the general material well-being of people in a community and should be banned on that basis. The consistency between God's prohibition and our reason increases our faith that indeed he has spoken on the subject.

The result of all of this was that a wide array of instruction guides were written with the expressed intention of educating rulers in the most effective means of government. It was assumed that any decree that a ruler might issue should necessarily be adhered to simply because the governing authority had issued it. Hence, the absolute nature of authority's rule was asserted. As these documents multiplied over time, they all tended to proceed from the assumption that it was incumbent upon the ruler to govern the nation within the restraints of Christian virtue. This generally remained true until the humanism of Italy sprang forth full blown in the work of Machiavelli.

Machiavelli was the son of a lawyer in Florence. He was born in 1469 and died in 1527, which made him a contemporary of both Leonardo da Vinci and Michelangelo. His education was similar to that of those of his social class in Florence at that time. As his studies proceeded, he developed a strong interest in Roman history and often related it to the Florentine political upheaval which was ongoing throughout his life. He was profoundly affected by the growing humanism of the Renaissance and replaced Judeo-Christian morality with a morality of state power. For Machiavelli, the end in mind was far more important than the means that might be used to achieve it. Thus, from his perspective, anything that might be done to advance one's political cause could be justified.

As a result of this mind set, it was not at all surprising that he gravitated toward the political arena. In his mind politics were supreme. He held a position in the republican government that existed when the Medicis were out of power, but his position was eliminated when that ruling family recaptured control of the city. It was this situation that prompted him to write *The Prince,* which was his instruction guide on how a ruler should govern his subjects to expand and strengthen his control. He wrote the book, no doubt, in an effort to ingratiate himself to the Medicis and perhaps to gain for himself a new position in their government. In his book, he broke altogether with Christianity by recommending that it was incumbent upon the sovereign of any state to take whatever steps were necessary to expand and strengthen his rule. He abandoned virtuous conduct and made it subservient to the underlying goal of consolidating power. From his point of view, the only reason a ruler had for adhering to Christian morality was to promote some political end. However, if moral behavior were in conflict with the expansion of power, then, in Machiavelli's mind, it should be sacrificed for the "greater good" of maintaining state control.

As Machiavelli's book circulated, it was widely ridiculed by many people as preaching evil. However, some modern writers praised Machiavelli for writing the first "value-free" tome on political theory. In their view, Machiavelli's work set the stage for the positive study of political science in modern times. Murray Rothbard rightly observed that this effort failed to exonerate Machiavelli from the charge of preaching evil:

> In his illuminating discussion of Machiavelli, Professor [Quentin] Skinner tries to defend him against the charge of being a 'preacher of evil'. Machiavelli did not praise evil *per se*, Skinner tells us; indeed, other things being equal, he probably preferred the orthodox Christian virtues. It is simply that when those virtues became inconvenient, that is, when they ran up against the overriding goal of keeping state power, the Christian virtues had to be set aside. . . . Professor Skinner, however, has a curious view of what 'preaching evil' might really be. Who in the history of the world, after all, and outside a Dr. Fu Manchu novel, has actually lauded evil *per se* and counseled evil and vice at every step of life's way? Preaching evil is to counsel precisely as Machiavelli has done: be good so long as goodness

doesn't get in the way of something you want, in the case of the ruler that something being the maintenance and expansion of power. What *else* but such 'flexibility' can the preaching of evil be all about?[121]

Machiavelli was a product of his times. He cared very little for humanity and had little respect for others, save that they might serve him in some way. While his own cynicism afforded him the understanding that human beings are sinful creatures, he chose to revel in his sin rather than seek forgiveness for it. He was an adulterer and was more than willing to slander other people as his own pen confesses.

> Should anyone seek to cow the author by evil-speaking, I warn you that he, too, knows how to speak evil, and indeed excels in the art; and that he has no respect for anyone in Italy, though he bows and scrapes to those better dressed than himself.[122]

While Machiavelli earned for himself a reprehensible name in history, there remain those who are forever enamored by his counsel. What is frightful are the occasions when people who hold these kinds of political views rise to power. Invariably they use such power for destructive ends. In recent memory, the world has endured the likes of Adolf Hitler and Bonito Mussolini, both of whom embraced similar ideas. To consider these men now is to jump ahead of ourselves. Therefore, it is enough to say that the Renaissance, even though there were certainly a number of legitimate points raised, provided the fertile soil for more than a little evil for future generations.

Study Questions

1. What were the factors that led to the revival of classical literature and to its vast dissemination in Western Europe during the era of the Renaissance?

---

[121] Murray Rothbard, *Economic Thought Before Adam Smith*, (England: Edward Elgar Publishing, 1995), pg. 190.

[122] Will Durant, *The Renaissance*, (New York: Simon and Schuster, 1953), pg. 553.

2. Discuss the lives of Petrarch and Boccaccio. How did these writers challenge Christianity?

3. What factors worked together to help critics of Christianity make their case? What factors worked against them?

4. What aspects of Roman Catholicism provided religious skeptics an opportunity to challenge the Christian religion?

5. How was the work of Erasmus of Rotterdam at odds with the orthodox Christian faith? How did his work open the door for the reformers of the sixteenth century?

6. Compare and contrast the lives of Leonardo da Vinci and Michelangelo.

7. What were some of the positive and negative aspects of the Renaissance?

8. What change in the political order was taking place during the Renaissance?

9. What was Machiavelli's advice to the king? How was it received at the time it was disseminated? How has it been received since then?

10. What is absolutism and how does it depart from Christian teachings?

Chapter 14: The Protestant Reformation

I. Introduction

The Protestant Reformation refers to a movement started by a small handful of men whose initial aim, as they saw it, was to restore the purity of the Christian religion. At first the movement was not something particularly new. In previous ages, similar reform movements were undertaken by various individuals whose goal was essentially the same. Sometimes these reform movements were successful and led to reforms in the church and sometimes they failed. On some occasions the failure of a reform movement resulted in the execution of reformists. Such extreme measures were taken because of the ties between the church and the civil governments involved. In those cases the reformers' efforts were deemed tantamount to treason. In Western Europe the Roman Catholic Church commanded a great deal of political power. However, the reform movement sparked by the efforts of Martin Luther and by the work of John Calvin resulted in the end of Roman Catholic dominance over Christianity in Europe. As a result, the church was divided into a number of different denominations.

There were several points of contention that led to this situation. First, the reformers argued that Scripture alone must serve as the final source of authority in Christian doctrine because, in their view, the apostolic age ended with the death of John. For this reason, one of the rallying cries of the reformers was the Latin phrase *Sola Scriptura*, meaning literally by the Scriptures alone. Alternatively, Roman Catholics maintained that apostolic authority had never ended but was passed down through the papacy. As a result, the Roman Catholic Church argued that sound teaching rested in the Scriptures and the traditions of the Church. Contention between the two groups arose when the reformers questioned whether or not some of the traditions that had been embraced accurately reflected the teachings of Scripture.

Another point of controversy that tended to separate the two groups was the nature of salvation. This particular controversy was not new and had arisen in ages past. At issue was the means by which a person would be justified in the presence of God. The reformers held that justification was a matter of faith and that the faith to believe the gospel message was a gift imparted by God himself through the work of the Holy Spirit. In the reformers view, this was a rather direct process and the church's role in the matter was merely to present all people with the gospel message and leave the results to God. This led to two other pronouncements that also marked the reformers. Namely, the reformers held to *Sola Fide* and *Sola Gratia*, meaning by faith alone and by grace alone. The Roman Catholics, on the other hand, believed that the church was far more central in the process and that the sacraments provided an infusion of grace into the souls of the people. To be sure, both groups recognized the central importance of Christ's atoning death on the cross, and both affirmed many of the other central tenets of the Christian religion. Nevertheless, the differences between them were significant, and reconciliation between the Protestants and the Catholics proved impossible at that time. So much was this the case that the division between Protestants and Catholics continues to this day.

As already noted, reformers in previous ages had come and gone with varying degrees of success. But, in all of these cases the Roman Catholic Church remained more or less the only organized church in Western Europe. In fact, the Protestant reformers initially thought that their efforts might result in a similar unity afterwards. That was not to be the case. There are, of course, reasons why the Protestant movement occurred when it did. One of the important reasons was the spread of Renaissance thought. As already developed in the previous chapter, the increase in trade and wealth that spawned an increase in intellectual pursuits set the stage for people to examine Christian doctrines for themselves. The ability to engage in this exercise was extended with the development of the printing press, because it led to a dramatic increase in the number of copies of the Bible that were available. The combination of these factors resulted in a growing number of educated people who could read and interpret the Bible for themselves. As numerous people engaged in this activity, they began to see differences between what they understood from reading the Scriptures and what the Roman Catholic Church was teaching. As this happened, the reform movement gained strength.

To understand the real importance of this movement, it is first necessary to recall some of the important facts that gave rise to the Latin Church and its structure. Before the collapse of the Roman Empire, Constantine had seen the usefulness of adopting Christianity as the only state religion. "To Constantine's essentially political mind Christianity was the completion of the process of unification which had long been in progress in the empire. It had one Emperor, one law, and one citizenship for all free men."[123] Thus, to help insure peaceful control, religious unity was also sought. A common faith was desirable because it tended to eliminate one source of potential conflict that could have disrupted the ruler's control over the empire. Constantine believed he had found in Christianity the common religion needed to secure his control.

Notwithstanding Constantine's aim at unity, there were doctrinal disagreements among Christians. In fact, the church was divided in numerous ways. These differences stemmed from variations in the theology that people held. Variations in theologies arise in the following way. While all Christians affirm that God reveals himself in the Bible, the Bible is itself a written document that must be read and interpreted. Some passages are more easily interpreted than others. In addition, the Scriptures reveal a number of paradoxes and mysteries. For this reason, it is necessary that any particular interpretation given to a single passage be checked for consistency against other verses. The goal of a theology, then, is to develop a complete framework in which to read and understand the Bible.

Another way to look at the problem is to compare it to the process of science. In this analogy, the Bible provides the facts about God and his relationship to his creation. However, while all the necessary facts are given, they are not given in such a way as to provide the individual with an immediate and proper understanding of those facts and their relationship to one another. The pursuit of a sound understanding of God's Word is, then, the science known as theology. "As the facts of nature are all related and determined by physical laws, so the facts of the Bible are all related and determined by the nature of God and of his

---

[123] Williston Walker, *A History of the Christian Church*, (Edinburgh: T.&T. Clark, 1958 revised version), pg. 105.

creatures."[124] It should, therefore, be clear that while our understanding of nature can be improved by a more accurate science, so too, our understanding of Christianity can be enhanced by a more complete and correct theology.

This means that it is evidently God's pleasure that we should continue to grope for a better understanding of religious truth in this world, even while we fall short of it. In much the same way as we strive to understand the created order around us, we must also strive to understand his divine revelation to us. One of the troubling aspects of this reality is that men, by nature, seem to enjoy promoting error in this quest because of their own sin. That is, people embrace a bad theology because they erroneously suppose that ignorance might protect them from God's judgment. This state of affairs will naturally result in all sorts of theologies that radically confuse the facts of Scripture. But, it must be remembered that it is God who decreed this state of affairs and, whether we like it or not, this is the reality in which we live and learn. Therefore, this situation must ultimately be good. Indeed, people who possess true faith in Christ endeavor to gain as sound of a theological understanding as possible. Furthermore, as one might expect, this pursuit yields the fruit of an improved understanding of the Bible. In turn, better theological understandings expose errors and falsehoods. But, that alone does not mean that all differences will disappear among men of good will. That is not likely to happen in this world because of man's immense ignorance as well as his sinful disposition.

At any rate, there were theological differences in Constantine's day as in our own. For his purposes though, this situation was a problem that needed to be remedied by the elimination of any disagreement. As already stated, his main interest was to secure his control over a vast empire and the unification of religious faith was clearly desirable. Therefore, he called upon the leaders of the church from around the empire to meet together for the purpose of settling the various doctrinal disputes. In one sense, meetings of the most astute minded people in any particular area of study are quite a positive thing. When such people get together for the purpose of comparing their thoughts about the subject, it often leads to an improved understanding of the subject by all parties

---

[124] Charles Hodge, *Systematic Theology*, (Grand Rapids, Michigan: W.B. Eerdman's Publishing Company, reprinted 1993), pg. 3.

involved. The initial church councils produced this kind of result.

However, there is an inherent problem with the way in which these councils worked. Such meetings are not likely to settle every doctrinal dispute once and for all. To be sure, it is quite possible for experts in any field to finally settle certain matters in this kind of setting. But, that does not mean that they will be able to settle all matters that might affect their study. As long as their knowledge of the subject is incomplete, some matters will necessarily remain disputable. In other words, the very nature of making progress in any field of study precludes the possibility that all matters related to it could be finally settled. Indeed, as we have already seen, by definition the study of any subject in this world will always be ongoing and incomplete. Furthermore, even matters that are largely resolved will always be subject to debate as others attempt to learn the discovered truths for themselves. As a result, to exclude future debate will eventually lead to the stagnation of intellectual development in the area being considered and may even lead to the perpetuation of error. This consequence is quite natural. Even though a meeting among experts is likely to advance knowledge in some areas, it is also likely to affirm certain prejudices that tend to distort the truth. In this case, error is passed on to future generations and, if no further debate is allowed, the possibility of overcoming that error is reduced. Thus, while professional meetings of experts are generally productive in and of themselves, if future debate is excluded on topics already considered, they will inevitably hamper further progress in our understanding. This becomes especially problematic if the state eliminates all debate by enacting a legal restriction against it. Under the rule of Theodosius in the Roman Empire, the liberty of dissenting opinions was publicly outlawed and anyone holding heretical points of view was made an enemy of the state. While the church has always had an interest in maintaining the purity of the Christian faith, it has done so in a more academic fashion. But, when it became the state religion, doctrinal issues took on legal significance. This tended to stifle any further debate once an issue was resolved whether or not the resolution was sound.

When power is centralized, it is only a matter of time before corruption follows. If human beings were born saints from their mothers' wombs, this would not be a problem. Regrettably, that is not the case. In fact, throughout time, there have been both secular and church authorities who have used the power of their offices for various self-seeking ends. As mentioned in an earlier chapter, after the fall of Rome, the Latin Church gained influence over the affairs of life in Western Europe and the bishop of Rome emerged as the central figure in the Church's organizational structure. In time, the Roman Catholic Church acquired vast amounts of land that were governed by the pope in much the same way as any other feudal lord ruled his own. As a result, governing temporal property became an important aspect of clerical duty in the Middle Ages. In addition, many of the assumptions about the connections between the church and the state that were prevalent in the East were carried over into Western Europe. For this reason, the clergy had important connections to political life as well. At times the combinations of these factors resulted in some of the worst kinds of immorality and corruption among church leaders and this even at the highest level. In fact, some popes engaged in some of the most underhanded and deceitful political chicanery imaginable. That is not to say that every church leader behaved badly, but merely that the opportunity to do so was there, and some took advantage of it. Nonetheless, because of the ties between the Latin Church and secular governments of the day, people tended to submit publicly to the Roman Catholic Church for fear that their lives would be taken on account of heresy. But, as feudalism gave way to the formation of nations, the opportunities to resist Rome grew. It was in this situation that the Reformation took place.

II. Early Reformers

There were various reformers who appeared from time to time prior to the sixteenth century. Two of the most noted were, John Wycliffe in England and John Huss in Bohemia. John Wycliffe lived during the fourteenth century. He was born in the north of Yorkshire in 1320 and studied at Oxford where he later became a professor of theology. He was ordained into the priesthood, but pursued an academic career. Over the years he wrote a number of important scholastic treatises. In this work he adopted the realism of Augustine's doctrine of predestination. The more he studied the matter, the more he thought he saw this doctrine in the Bible. His work was quite unusual, for his realism was at odds with the nominalism that prevailed at Oxford during his day. Yet, Wycliffe was an exceptional scholar, and he continued to press his case throughout his lifetime. The implications of his understanding of predestination began to permeate his thinking. Within this context he recognized God as being sovereign over all the affairs of this earth. Furthermore, he thought that it pleased God to grant men access to himself through Jesus Christ and concluded from this that men can go directly to God by way of the Son. As a result of this position, he found no basis for the Roman Catholic priesthood to serve as an intermediary between God and men. Rather, he believed that the only mediator between people and God was Jesus Christ. As a result, he came to the conclusion that all true believers in Christ had immediate access to God and were, in a sense, priests who need not be ordained.

Wycliffe's position on the priesthood of all believers became a touchstone for Martin Luther and John Calvin, who would later proclaim it as they led the way in the Protestant Reformation. The Latin Church could not tolerate this position because it did not recognize the Roman Church's view of its own administration of the Christian faith. As a result, the rest of Wycliffe's life was spent at odds with the clergy of the Roman Catholic Church. In fact, they found his position was so offensive that they branded him a heretic and sought to have him executed. However, they were unsuccessful in their efforts to put him on trial because Wycliffe's views happened to serve the immediate political ends of the English rulers and the nobility of his time. This situation was a foreshadowing of the later use Henry VIII would make of the Reformation. To promote several political ends, Wycliffe's services were sought to develop a case in which England might divorce itself from Roman Catholic control. For various reasons this never materialized, and Wycliffe went back to teaching. During the remaining years of his life, the embattled reformer translated the Bible into English and continued his other academic work at Oxford. He died following a paralytic stroke at the end of December 1384. While a number of groups adopted some of Wycliffe's views, no thoroughgoing reformation occurred until the sixteenth century. Nevertheless, his ideas continued to influence various people in various places throughout Europe. Thus, Wycliffe was an example of an early reformer who was much like Luther and Calvin. The major difference was that the social upheaval following his reformation efforts was not so widespread as that flowing from the work of the later reformers.

Wycliffe was not alone in his criticism of the Latin Church's teaching. John Huss was another man who was moved to protest against the Latin Church's structure. In the course of his own studies, he too became convinced that there were certain errors in the Roman Catholic Church that he could not reconcile with what he conceived to be the true nature of the Christian religion. As a result, he felt compelled to take a stand against the Church regarding these issues.

Huss was born in 1369 and was executed for heresy in 1415. In 1390 he came to Prague as a student and earned his way by performing services for the local church. His initial goal was to pursue ordination and the priesthood, but he enjoyed himself so much in school that by the time he finished his master's degree he decided to teach. In 1401, he became the dean of the faculty of arts and was also ordained into the priesthood. Nevertheless, he continued to pursue his teaching and administrative duties at the university. During this time, he undoubtedly read Wycliffe's work which had become very popular in Prague by 1403. This popularity was largely the result of an emerging relationship between Bohemia and England that developed when Anna, a Bohemian princess, married King Richard II in 1383. This event opened the door for a number of Bohemian students and scholars to study at Oxford. It was during this time that they were exposed to Wycliffe's work which they subsequently brought back to Prague. In turn, the way was opened for Huss to read the works of the English reformer.

Huss' admiration for Wycliffe brought him into conflict with the Roman Church in much the same way as Wycliffe. The Church ordered him to stop teaching along these lines, but he continued to do so. Huss, like Wycliffe, enjoyed the favorable support of the Bohemian king which allowed him to continue with his work in spite of the Roman Church's mandate that he stop. Just the same, he was excommunicated by the local archbishop and summoned to appear before a papal court. He initially refused to go and intensified his attack on the papacy by preaching against the sale of indulgences. In particular, he targeted his criticism toward the pope, who had recently offered the indulgences to raise money to finance a campaign against the king of Naples. In denouncing the pope's actions, Huss went so far as to refer to the pope as the Antichrist. In response, the pope excommunicated the reformer.

While King Wenzel of Bohemia attempted to protect Huss, the escalating tensions caused him to direct the reformer to seek asylum elsewhere. During his exile, Huss wrote his most significant book. It was mainly a reiteration of Wycliffe, but it served as an additional tool in the spreading discontent among the populace with the Roman Church. Meanwhile, the papacy continued its efforts to force Huss to stand trial before Church authorities. He was even offered a safe-conduct to do so. Though he doubted the veracity of the promised safety, Huss nonetheless believed that it was his duty to bear witness to his position before the Church council and so he agreed to present himself. When he arrived at the designated place, he was imprisoned and condemned to death. He was subsequently burned to death on July 6, 1415. It was said that he died with courage, singing hymns to the praise of the glory of his Lord even as the flames engulfed him.

The two main points of examining something of the lives of these two men are as follows. First, it was not true that Martin Luther and John Calvin were the first people who felt it necessary to stand up against the official Roman Catholic Church for matters of conscience. As the lives of Wycliffe and Huss demonstrate, there were other learned men who simply did not condone the official teachings of the Roman Church. As these men examined the Scriptures for themselves, they reached certain conclusions about the meaning of them that they thought were at odds with the Church's teachings and they simply could not acquiesce to a point of view they considered to be false.

Second, among the various points of contention that were raised, none was more significant than the issue of authority over the church. Those who came to the conclusion that the primary authority for directing Christian faith in this world was the Bible, invariably questioned papal rule. This kind of questioning was especially prominent in periods of time when clerical corruption was widespread. While corruption was always present in human institutions, it was especially prominent in the Latin Church in the fourteenth and fifteenth centuries. During this time, worldliness among the clergy was widespread and church offices were often used for monetary and political gain. In addition, it was not uncommon for the papacy to sell church offices to the highest bidder or grant them to friends and family members. This is not to say that there were no dedicated clerics during this era. Even in the midst of the corruption, there were always some churchmen who resisted it. These individuals were often appalled as much as the reformers at the amount of corruption present among church leaders.

But the Protestant reformers went further. They believed in

certain principles that did not support the notion that Christianity was intended to spread within the context of a single visible church organization. In particular, they believed that the authority of the church rested in the Scriptures alone and not in the Scriptures plus Roman Church traditions. The views of these reformers were cemented as they meditated on such verses in the Bible as II Timothy 3:16-17. This passage reads, "All Scripture is given by the inspiration of God, and is profitable for doctrine, for reproof, for correction, for instruction in righteousness, that the man of God may be complete, thoroughly equipped for every good work." Another important passage from Scripture for the reformers was Revelation 22:18-19 which reads, "For I testify to everyone who hears the words of the prophecy of this book: If anyone adds to these things, God will add to him the plagues that are written in this book; and if anyone takes away from the words of the book of this prophecy, God shall take away his part from the Book of Life, from the holy city, and from the things which are written in this book." Based upon such pronouncements, the Protestants took Scripture to be the final authority of their faith and they assumed it was incumbent upon each individual to become a student of the Bible. In addition, they came to see the church as being the totality of all people who placed their trust in Jesus Christ for salvation rather than those who were members of a specific organization. This position was later adopted in a certain sense by the Roman Catholic Church that now concedes that Protestants are "weaker" brothers in Christ.

In defense of their position on the Bible, the reformers refuted the Roman Catholic Church's papal structure by offering a different interpretation of the scriptural passage used to support it. The passage that Catholics used was a familiar one. On one occasion, Jesus asked his disciples if they knew who he was. When Peter confessed that Jesus was the Son of God and the Savior of the world, Jesus blessed him for the faith that he had. He went on to make the following statement: ". . . you are Peter, and on this rock I will build My church. . . "[125] On the basis of this passage, the Roman Catholic Church argued that Peter's apostolic authority was to be passed along in time to future church leaders. In their view, it has been passed down to successive popes on the basis of this mandate. But the Protestants argued that the statement meant something

---

[125] Matthew 16:18.

entirely different from what the Catholic Church asserted. In particular, the Protestants argued that Jesus was telling Peter that his faith in him was true and that it was the kind of faith that would be the very substance upon which his church would go forth in the world. In addition, they argued that Jesus was telling Peter that it would be his responsibility to testify to others about his faith in Christ. They believed that this interpretation fit well with Peter's own testimony that was provided in his first letter. In it he argued that Jesus was the cornerstone and that believers were individual stones being fashioned together by the Lord according to his grand plan of construction.[126]

Whatever else might be said, it should be clear that there were a number of forerunners to the Protestant Reformation. The examples of Wycliffe and Huss illustrate this fact quite well. In both cases we find men who were motivated by conscience to take a stand against what they each believed to be error. And, while these individuals might not have lived to see what they had hoped for, they, nevertheless, provided an example that encouraged later Christian reformers.

III. Martin Luther

In the early years of the sixteenth century, a major reform movement radically divided Christians in many countries. Among the reformers of that age was a man by the name of Martin Luther. Martin Luther was so important that his actions were generally credited with sparking the Protestant Reformation. The Reformation splintered European Christianity and resulted in the rise of numerous denominations. Professor Thomas Lindsay aptly captured the significance of Luther's life with the following words:

> History knows nothing of revivals of moral living apart from some new religious impulse. The motive power needed has always come through leaders who have had communion with the unseen. Humanism had supplied a superfluity of teachers; the times needed a prophet. They received one; a man of the people; bone of their bone, and flesh of their flesh; one who had himself lived that popular religious life

---

[126] See I Peter 2:4-10.

> with all the thoroughness of a strong, earnest nature, who
> had sounded all its depths and tested its capacities, and
> gained in the end no relief for his burdened conscience;
> who had at last found his way into the presence of God, and
> who knew by his own personal experience, that the living
> God was accessible to every Christian. He had won the
> freedom of a Christian man, and had reached through faith
> a joy in living far deeper than that which humanism
> boasted. . . . Men could see what faith was when they
> looked at Luther.[127]

Martin Luther was born on November 10, 1483 in Eisleben. His father made a living in the mining business and in operating a number of furnaces. The Luther family struggled to make ends meet in the early years, though, in the course of time, his father became a member of the village council of Mansfeld. Thus, Luther grew up in a hard-working family. His parents taught him the fundamentals of the Christian faith and among the things they had him commit to memory were the Apostles' Creed, the Ten Commandments, and the Lord's Prayer. In addition, he learned many Christian hymns.

Luther was educated according to the common fashion of his day. In 1501 he entered the University of Erfurt and began his college studies. Nominalism dominated the thought of most European universities at this time, and Erfurt was no exception. He began his studies by focusing on the law and intended to become a lawyer. By 1505, he had completed both his bachelor's and master's degrees.

Everyone expected Luther to become a lawyer, but, instead, he decided to enter an Augustinian monastery. There is much speculation as to the exact reason why this abrupt change in direction occurred. Luther said that he made the change because he doubted himself. But what was the nature of this doubt? One line of reasoning proposed that Luther doubted his ability to merit entrance into heaven. The foundation for this kind of speculation was the fact that one of Luther's close friends died just prior to his entering the monastery. This event possibly caused Luther to ponder his own mortality. While this explanation is plausible,

---

[127] Thomas M. Lindsay, *A History of the Reformation*, (New York: Charles Scribner's Sons, 1928), vol. 1, pp. 190-191.

it remains uncertain what actually motivated the young man's action. Whatever the case, Luther did, in fact, become a monk.

As a monk, Luther was greatly concerned about his own salvation. He incessantly toiled in his quest to live a perfect and righteous life. Yet, the harder that he worked at it, the more he realized his own shortcomings. He continually saw himself falling short of the goal of perfection. His failures drove him to the confessional over and over again where he spent hours confessing even the smallest of his sins. Rather than gaining a sense of peace, however, Luther's mental anguish increased. The situation grew worse and worse until finally Luther was directed to study Paul's letter to the Romans. In the opening of the letter, Paul made the bold proclamation that, "the just shall live by faith." As Luther studied the meaning of this statement in the context of the entire letter, he realized that salvation was God's gift to man and that it could not be earned or merited. This new understanding revolutionized his life and completely changed his approach to religion.

In 1508, Luther was assigned to work in Wittenberg and by 1512 he had completed his doctorate degree in theology. Upon completing this work he became a professor of theology at the university in Wittenberg. As a professor, Luther was very popular with the students and he might have continued teaching salvation by faith alone without raising any serious repercussions if it had not been for John Tetzel. Tetzel had been commissioned by Pope Leo X to sell indulgences for the purpose of raising money to build a basilica at St. Peter's Cathedral in Rome. Tetzel claimed that the indulgence would absolve any one of any sins committed, as long as the sin was confessed and the indulgence purchased.

From Luther's point of view, this proclamation was a distortion of the truth. In fact, he believed it was not only false, but offensive to the gospel message of salvation by faith in Jesus Christ alone. Therefore, when Tetzel arrived in Wittenberg on his money raising expedition, it motivated Luther to action. On October 31, 1517, Luther nailed his ninety-five theses to the church door in Wittenberg for the purpose of calling for a debate about the doctrine of indulgences. His purpose in doing so was to show that they had no effect on the salvation of the soul. Luther did not foresee what was to follow on the heels of his action. His case against indulgences led to an ongoing debate that lasted two years and ultimately resulted in his excommunication from the Roman Catholic Church. In those years and the ones which followed, a social upheaval occurred that profoundly altered religious worship in Europe. The result of this upheaval was the development of a number of new Christian sects. Luther himself became a leader of one such group of Christians. Many people across Europe were no longer willing to toe the Roman Catholic line. Having been cast out of the Roman Catholic Church, he and his followers had the task of forming a new church so that they might worship Christ in a fashion they believed was taught in the Bible.

Luther lived the rest of his life under a death sentence issued by the Roman Catholic Church authorities. Yet, the sentence was never carried out because he had the protection of royal forces in Saxony as well as the popular opinion of the German people. For Luther, the Scriptures were the ultimate earthly authority. He attempted to base the rest of his life upon them and to found a church which made them the basis which would direct their worship of Jesus Christ. Following this line of reasoning, Luther found no basis in Scripture for either the monastic life or for celibacy. He, therefore, rejected both and took an ex-nun to be his wife. As for the church he founded, Luther never believed that it was the only Christian church. From his perspective, the church had always been made up of those who had placed their trust in Jesus Christ for the remission of their sin.

IV. John Calvin

John Calvin was born in France on July 10, 1509. His father was a lawyer and a legal advisor to nobility. His mother was noted for her deep affection for her children and her religious piety. Because of his father's position, Calvin was educated with the children of a noble family that his father counseled. Calvin's training was one of the best available during his day. As he grew, Calvin learned to reason carefully and systematically. In addition, he developed the kind of social grace prevalent among the noble class of the age.

When Calvin was fourteen years of age, he entered college in Paris. While he was there, he had the privilege of studying under the direction of some of the most prominent professors of the city. It was during this time that he learned well the languages of French and Latin. He also learned formal logic and argumentation. Calvin excelled scholastically. At the age of nineteen, Calvin left Paris to begin the study of law in Orleans in accordance with his father's wishes. While Calvin had probably already begun to question papal authority, during his time in Orleans he was further exposed to Protestant ideas. When his father died in 1531, Calvin decided to pursue a career in academics rather than the law and moved back to Paris. It was during this time that he became a thoroughgoing Protestant.

His views were reflected in both his lectures and in his writings. For this reason, it was not long before he was forced to flee Paris. He found refuge in Basel in 1535, and there he completed work on his famous, *Institutes of the Christian Religion*. Even though Calvin carefully revised this work in 1539, and made subsequent revisions throughout his life, the fact that he completed the initial text at such a young age is impressive. The *Institutes* is one of the most thorough theological treatments of the Christian religion ever written and demonstrates the intellectual capacity of Calvin. Indeed, John Calvin possessed one of the finest minds known in human history. He thought and wrote with exacting precision and forceful logic.

Calvin's purpose for writing the *Institutes* was twofold. First, he thought it necessary to provide people with a sound introduction to the Bible so that they could read it and understand it for themselves. Second, he wrote it as a vindication of previous reformers. Calvin organized his work around the Apostles' Creed in order to demonstrate that the Protestant religion was not something new. Rather, he thought, it was a religion that more closely followed the teachings of Scripture than did the religion offered by the Roman Catholic Church of his age.

Calvin intended to make his home in Strassburg and to invest his life in studying and writing. But that was not to be. While passing through Geneva at the age of twenty-seven, he was introduced to William Farel. Farel was a committed Protestant who urged Calvin to pastor the local church and to make Geneva his home. Though it went against his personal desires, Calvin was finally convinced that he should accept the offer. Calvin began his work in Geneva by lecturing daily on the letters of St. Paul.

In addition to lecturing and preaching, he also sought to promote the purity of the local congregation. He adopted the pattern of church government that he thought was laid out in the Scriptures and sought to discipline unfaithful church members. Calvin looked to the local government for its support in enforcing the church's decision to censure its members. For this reason, a great many modern writers have argued that Calvin established a heavy-handed, puritanical rule over Geneva. Such writers suggested that Calvin was largely responsible for the local legal code and that he was, therefore, responsible for the oppressive actions taken by the local authorities. But such accusations cannot be upheld by the facts. As professor Lindsay has written:

> When historians, ecclesiastical or other, charge Calvin with the [puritanical regulation of private life], they forget that there was no need for him to do so. Geneva, like every other mediaeval town, had its laws which interfered with private life at every turn, and that in a way which to our modern minds seems the grossest tyranny, but which was then a commonplace of city life. Every mediaeval town had its laws against extravagance in dress, in eating and in drinking, against cursing and swearing, against gaming, dances, and masquerades. . . . To make them ground of accusation against Calvin is simply to plead ignorance of the whole municipal police of the later Middle Ages. To say that Calvin acquiesced in or approved of such legislation is simply to show that he belonged to the sixteenth century.[128]

Calvin's main mistake in his attempts to establish proper church government was to continue in the medieval belief that it was incumbent upon the secular authorities to enforce the church's censures. But, the idea that Calvin was at the center of secular rule in Geneva is hardly sustainable. The fact of the matter was that Calvin often met with obstacles in his work, and his vision for the church was never fully realized. Thus, it is inaccurate to argue that he singlehandedly ruled the city and always got his way with the town council. In many instances the city council stood against him.

John Calvin was an immensely important man, even though, like any other human being, he made his share of mistakes. He was one of the most brilliant men ever to have lived, and his work in Christian theology will remain a treasure house for years to come. On the basis of John Calvin's work in theology, several denominations in the Christian religion were founded. Among these groups of Christians are the Swiss and Dutch

---

[128] Ibid., vol. 2, pg. 108.

Reformed, Scotch-Irish Presbyterians, and the English Puritans. Many modern day American denominations were also heavily influenced by Calvinism, including the Congregationalists, the Presbyterians, and the Baptists. Over the years, Calvinists have become known for their strong interest in evangelism and education. Their interest in each is easy to explain. Like the Lutherans, the Calvinists are convinced that people are saved by faith in Jesus Christ. That is, people are saved from their sin as a matter of God's grace and mercy. In addition, since that gospel message is found in the Bible, which is seen as the final authority, it is, therefore, incumbent upon each individual to submit himself to its rule. This means that each man ought to be able to read and to correctly interpret the Bible. For this reason, education is fundamentally tied to the Christian religion because men need to be able to read and to think with logical consistency if they are going to have the fullest access to the Word of God.

V.   *The Reformation and England*

Religious conditions in England took a different turn than in other parts of Europe because the break with Roman Catholicism came about primarily as a result of a political problem that Henry VIII faced. Henry VIII became king of England in 1509 following the death of his father. He married Catherine of Aragon (Aragon is a region of Spain) for political reasons in order to secure his power. His marriage to Catherine tied the English crown to the Hapsburgs generally and to Spain specifically. In 18 years of marriage, Catherine had borne only one surviving child, a girl named Mary. Henry desperately desired a son who would be his heir, so he sought to annul the marriage. However, Catherine's nephew, Charles V of the Hapsburgs, was the Holy Roman Emperor of the time. Charles was very displeased with Henry's decision, and he used his influence with the pope to prevent the proceedings. The situation eventually led to England's secession from the Roman Catholic Church and to the excommunication of Henry.

All of this transpired at the same time that the reformers challenged papal authority; the time was right for Henry to take his expulsion from the Roman Church in stride. Henry was far from a reformer, but needed to promptly address the problem of ruling a Christian nation without a church. He established the Church of England with a doctrine that was essentially Roman Catholicism minus the pope to remedy the problem. After the annulment of his marriage to Catherine, he married Anne Boleyn, who bore him a daughter named Elizabeth. Dissatisfied with this outcome, Henry continued to seek the right mate to fulfill his desires. While all of this was happening in the political realm, numerous English Protestants left England to study under various reformers on the continent. Many learned their theology directly from John Calvin himself.

When Henry died in 1547, his son, Edward VI, became king at the age of ten. He had been educated by a staunch Protestant, Archbishop Thomas Cranmer. During Edward's rule, Cranmer wrote a book of common prayer and developed a forty-two-article creed of faith that was largely consistent with Calvin's theology. Thus, the reformed doctrine became the established rule of faith in England. The situation was short-lived however, because Edward died of an unknown disease at the age of 15.

When Edward died, there was no other male heir, so Catherine's daughter Mary became queen. Catherine was a devout Catholic and had raised Mary likewise. As a result, she sought to reestablish English ties to Roman Catholicism and make it the official faith of England once again. This move resulted in an assault against the Protestant clergy and some 300 leaders were burned at the stake (Archbishop Cranmer himself being one of the victims). Many reformed minded men fled the country, and Mary became known as "Bloody" Mary. To make matters even worse, she married her cousin, Philip II, king of Spain (son of Charles V). This marriage tied England even tighter to the Hapsburgs and to Spain. The religious strife and the political issues were counter to popular opinion, and most believed that Mary was taking the country in a direction they did not wish it to go. As a result, she was very unpopular with the people. She was never particularly healthy and died of an unknown illness in 1558 after a brief five year reign.

Elizabeth, the daughter of Anne Boleyn, followed her to the throne. Unlike Mary, Elizabeth was a very popular ruler and is still remembered today as Good Queen Bess. She ruled England from 1558-1603. Many terms have been used to describe her, including high spirited, astute, cynical, pragmatic, politically minded, and shrewd. Religiously, she sought to consolidate her position as queen by finding a compromise position between the reformers and the Catholics. During her reign, the

Anglican Church developed a moderate reformed stance that satisfied the majority of the people. However, the decidedly reformed minded theologians remained critical of the compromises and believed they could not accept the position in good conscience. The problems associated with this situation were enhanced by the Puritan movement. Nevertheless, the moderate position taken by Elizabeth worked reasonably well and was favored by the masses. As a result, a general peace over religious matters was maintained during her reign.

After Elizabeth died, the underlying religious differences came to the fore again because of political changes being made. Elizabeth's death marked the end of the Tudor reign over England. James Stuart, king of Scotland at the time, became James I of England and ruled England from 1603 to 1625. He was a thoroughgoing absolutist and believed that it was granted to him to rule England in God's stead. He, more than any of the Tudors before him, embraced the belief in the divine right of kings. As a result of his autocratic rule, he alienated many groups of people including the middle classes of citizens as well as the Puritans, and his general popularity waned. Particularly disturbing was the peace he made with Spain which had remained the nation's arch rival throughout the sixteenth century. James' overtures toward Spain at a time when the English people were still basking in the nation's victory over the Spanish Armada did not serve to further his popularity. James often disregarded Parliament when it stood in the way of his plans. This, more than anything else, resulted in the bulk of the political strife and turmoil that marked his reign. By ignoring Parliament, James stood opposed to the English form of government whose roots went back to the signing of Magna Carta.

The struggle intensified when James' son, Charles I, came to power. He followed in the footsteps of his father, and saw himself as being divinely appointed to rule in autocratic fashion. In addition, Charles increased tensions by attempting to reinstate many features of Roman Catholicism into the Anglican Church. His many struggles with Parliament members and religious leaders eventually led to an open revolt against his rule.

Oliver Cromwell, a well-known Puritan and a member of Parliament, led the fight against Charles. The revolutionary group seized control and it was during this time that reformed theologians were brought together to develop a complete statement of faith (1643-1647).

The result of this gathering was the publication of the Westminster Confession of Faith along with the catechisms to expound the doctrines presented there. These documents were decidedly Calvinistic. The Westminster Confession still serves as the confession of faith of some denominations. In 1649, the fight against Charles was complete, and he was executed. Cromwell ruled England via the Parliament for the rest of his life, but fighting among the various factions of Parliamentary members precluded its continuation. When Cromwell died, the people were generally tired of the instability of government and welcomed Charles' son, Charles II, back from exile to rule as the nation's monarch. Nevertheless, the Civil War succeeded in altering the view of the English monarch and made all rulers thereafter strictly limited by Parliament.

VI. The Catholic Reformation

The schism in Christianity and the mounting tension between the various factions, resulted in a reform movement within the Roman Catholic Church. Devout churchmen in the Latin Church were very much aware of the problems of corruption and immorality within the hierarchy and knew that some kind of reform was necessary. For example, Ignatius Loyola was very much concerned about the church's condition. Loyola was born in Spain in 1491. During the upheaval of the reformation he pledged his loyalty and devotion to the Roman Catholic Church. He founded the Society of Jesus, most commonly known as the Jesuit Order, for the purpose of promoting the purity of the Church and its cause.

There was also a strong interest in the reunification of the Christian community. Among those who sought for reforms, two men stand out as being immensely important. They were Gasparo Contarini and Giovanni Pietro Caraffa.

Contarini came from Venice and was a renowned statesmen in that community. He was considered a broad-minded, upright man who dealt fairly with everyone with whom he had dealings. He was well educated and thought that there was room enough in Catholicism to allow for Protestant theology. He believed that the best way to unify Christendom was to find some sort of compromise. In this effort, the pope made him a cardinal of the Roman Catholic Church, and he led a team of church representatives to meet with several key leaders of the reformation in an effort to achieve reconciliation. There were, however, a number of points of controversy that could not be overcome in these meetings. They included the Protestant affirmation of the priesthood of all believers and the Roman Catholic teaching of transubstantiation. This latter belief is that in the process of the Mass, the wine and bread of communion are transformed into the body and blood of Christ which is the means by which the grace of God is infused into the believer. This teaching was rejected by the Protestants. Protestants believed that the grace of God was imparted to the believer via the indwelling presence of the Holy Spirit who united the person in communion with Christ and that sacrament of communion was a celebration of that fact. Likewise, the notion that all believers were priests offended Roman Catholic sensibilities because it tended to undercut the governing structures of the Church. For these reasons, the efforts of Contarini and his supporters did not yield the reconciliation they sought. However, their efforts did model a kind of Christian charity that all sides should have followed.

While Contarini sought reconciliation by way of compromise, Caraffa saw the matter differently. He strongly upheld the traditional teachings and doctrines of the Roman Catholic Church and thought that the best way to deal with the Protestant Reformation was to state the Roman position more clearly. Caraffa was born into a family of nobility in Naples. At an early age he expressed a strong interest in pursuing the life of a clergyman. Like Contarini he was well educated, though he tended to believe that ends could be better achieved by more heavy-handed tactics than did his counterpart. Though they were friends seeking much the same end, Caraffa believed that it could be most readily obtained by treating all Protestants as heretics. As a result, he was unwilling to compromise with them in any way.

In the course of time, Caraffa became Pope Paul IV and moved to implement his own plans for reforming the Roman Catholic Church. This he did by calling for an extensive council meeting to review and to articulate the acceptable faith of the Roman Catholic Church. This meeting, known as the Council of Trent, was held over an eighteen year time span from 1545 to 1563. While the result of the meeting codified many of the differences separating Protestants and Catholics, it also addressed the problems of corruption within the Latin Church.

VII. The Impact of the Reformation on Life in Continental Europe

The most obvious impact of the Protestant Reformation on life in continental Europe was that it resulted in a great deal of bitter conflict. Catholics and Protestants could not agree upon doctrine. This division was especially problematic because it was generally accepted by both sides that secular governments had a role to play in enforcing church decrees. As a result, throughout Europe Protestants and Catholics struggled against one another for political control. As Russell Kirk has written on the subject:

> What commenced as a debate about theological questions and church discipline soon made an open breach in Christendom; and there followed a century and a half of devastation, the Wars of Religion, Catholic against Protestant and one Protestant sect against another. In the name of the Son of Man, the Redeemer, zealots took the sword against other Christians, illustrating the Christian dogma that all men are sinners.[129]

The events that unfolded in France throughout the sixteenth century provide a vivid picture of this struggle. Calvin himself fled from Paris for safety because of the persecution that the state began imposing on reformers. While there were a significant number of noblemen who favored Protestantism, the crown had determined to rid all of France of the reformers. Many Protestants were apprehended and burned to death in Paris. In one case, an entire ethnic group who populated the Alpine region of France were attacked. These people, known as the Waldenses, held religious views in line with those of the reformers. Even though they had previously been given the right to religious liberty, the Catholics pressed the crown to bring them in line with the teachings of the Roman Catholic Church. The Waldenses refused and appealed to the crown on the basis of the earlier promise that had been granted to them. The king refused to recognize this liberty and ordered that these people should be exterminated. In 1545, an army was put together for that purpose and

---

[129] Russell Kirk, *The Roots of American Order*, (Washington, D.C.:Regnery Gateway, 1991, third edition), pg. 232.

they destroyed between twenty and thirty villages and slaughtered between three and four thousand people. During the siege a number of these people fled for their lives to Switzerland, and some found refuge in Geneva.

In spite of this persecution, the numbers of Protestants in France grew. In fact, the brutal nature of the persecution resulted in a swing of popular opinion in favor of the Protestants and against the crown. Also, even though the Protestants initially accepted their suffering and endured it willingly, eventually they fought back. As the persecution intensified, they wrestled more and more with the question of when it was appropriate to revolt against the authorities. In one case, a group among them devised a plan of killing two brothers, the Duke of Guise and the cardinal of Lorraine, because these men were most fervently behind the extirpation of the Protestants. However, the news of the plan was learned beforehand, and the attempt was foiled.

Some of the top leaders of the nobility on the Protestant side would have been executed except that the king of France, Francis II, died before this happened. While the Guise brothers had been his closest advisors, they lost this connection when Francis' brother, Charles IX, took the throne. Charles was only eleven at the time and his mother, Catherine de Medici, ruled in his stead. She descended from the famous Florentine family of Italy and was also an avowed Roman Catholic. She married into the ruling family in France earlier and now found herself at the seat of power. She was unscrupulous, self-serving, and sought to play both sides against one another for her own gain. Initially, this resulted in a decree aimed at easing hostilities between the Catholics and the Protestants. While falling short of sanctioning the Protestants' right to worship, it would have ended the government's attack upon them.

Unfortunately, this decree did not bring about peace but, instead, led to open conflict between the competing factions. Some Catholics were incensed by the decision and took matters into their own hands. They saw it as an open affront to their religion and felt that the Protestant reformers had to be suppressed. In turn, their actions were followed by reprisals among the Protestants who stormed Catholic churches in areas where they held clear majorities. In addition, the Protestants increasingly demanded the right to worship as they wished. As the tensions between the two sides increased, warfare broke out on all sides. In Switzerland, Calvin urged the Protestants to refrain from violence out of Christian charity, but his call was ignored as both sides showed their proclivity to cruelty and brutality. After two years of conflict, an effort was made to negotiate an end to the fighting.

Regrettably, no final agreement could be reached, and what followed was nearly a decade long span of intermittent fighting. A peaceful settlement was finally in sight when the government recognized the Protestants. This situation resulted because of the leadership of Charles. During the years when he was growing up, he had largely left the responsibility for ruling France to his mother, Catherine. Interestingly, Catherine's maneuvering to sway key Protestants to promote her own political goals appeared to promote the Protestant cause. The main leader of the French Protestant movement was a man named Coligny. He had initially spurned Catherine's advances toward him, but in time saw the potential for furthering the Protestant position and presented himself to the royal court. It was there that Coligny and Charles developed an alliance. The two became more or less friends, and Charles came to see the Protestant cause as an opportunity to avenge a grudge he had been carrying against Philip II of Spain. Together, they planned to help each other. Yet, all was not well, for political intrigue shattered the short-lived peace that had developed through this relationship.

Politically, the relationship between Charles and Coligny threatened to alienate France from Spain. Philip II was staunchly Roman Catholic and was engaged in a plan to extend Spain's control in order to reassert the prominence of Catholicism throughout Europe. Toward this end, he sought to conquer England and to subdue the Netherlands. The Netherlands was an inherited possession that he had received from his father. Reformation thinking had made considerable headway in that region. The resulting religious diversity led to an expansion of religious tolerance there. Practically speaking, the peace such tolerance promoted served as a means of fostering the economic trade that was rapidly developing around the world. Philip's strong religious convictions would not allow him to tolerate such a situation.

As has already been noted, Protestantism made inroads into England, but largely for political reasons. During this time, Elizabeth's moderate position was unacceptable to the more devout Roman Catholics on the continent. She especially alienated Philip, whose marriage proposal she earlier rebuffed. She also rejected Catherine de Medici's efforts to secure English support for France against Spain by refusing to marry either one of her sons. Thus, England was more or less taking a single-handed stand against Spain which was then the richest and most powerful nation in Western Europe. Unable to secure control over England by marriage, Philip had it in his mind to invade the island nation and make it part of his empire. He thought it would be possible to secure his rule over the Netherlands at the same time. It was in the context of this political wrangling that the religious wars in France were played out and in which the alliance between Charles and Coligny was forged.

Based upon his friendship with Coligny, Charles moved towards throwing France's support behind the Netherlands and against Spain. The prospect of this position was particularly troubling to Catherine who had no desire fight against Spain without the assured support of England. She seriously doubted that France could stand up to a Spanish invasion. As a result, she hatched a plot to have Coligny killed. The plot failed, and Charles was furious. Nonetheless, she quickly developed another plan to achieve the desired results. On August 24, 1572, St. Bartholomew's Day, Catholics were incited to lay siege to Protestants throughout the country, and thousands of people were killed. It was one of the bloodiest displays of religious intolerance in an intolerant age, and led to the renewal of open hostilities.

Even though most of the leading Protestants in the country were killed in the massacre, there remained some who quickly banded together to defend themselves and to press their own reprisals against the Catholics. Sporadic religious wars erupted once again and continued throughout the rest of the century. To be sure, the Protestants showed little charity in their efforts to avenge the dead as both sides attempted to secure their positions by violence. It was not until 1598 that peace was finally achieved again, but that would be short lived for the Thirty Years War was looming on the horizon. At the end of the sixteenth century, a modicum of religious peace came when the government granted the people of France freedom of religion and the right to worship on the basis of individual conviction. While there were many factors that led to this peace, perhaps none is more important than England's successful defense of itself from attack by the Spanish Armada in 1588. Philip determined to conquer England and ordered his fleet to take the lead in the invasion. The Spanish fleet was the glory of the seas, but the smaller, more maneuverable English ships successfully defended the English coast and forced the Spanish Armada to retreat for home by sailing northward around the British Isles. The defeated Spaniards met with harsh weather along the journey, and what was left of the fleet was decimated along the Atlantic coastline. It was one of the most striking victories in all of history and marked the decline of Spain and the rise of England in terms of world power.

The main point illustrated by the French history of the sixteenth century, is that the Protestant Reformation led to numerous transformations in society. Old political structures gave way, and modern nations emerged. Unfortunately, this usually occurred in the midst of a great deal of violence and bloodshed sparked by sharp religious differences. Nevertheless, the concept of religious liberty began to make some headway in Europe as people sought for some peaceful civility in a world of religious intolerance. In the midst of the upheaval of the age, numerous religious refugees sought their peace in the newly discovered Americas. For those willing to leave all behind and to start a new life elsewhere, which meant enduring the extreme hardships of pioneer life, a new world awaited and those traveling to it embraced religious tolerance. Despite the hardships involved, many willingly undertook the journey to construct a new social order.

Study Questions

1. What persistent problems in the Roman Catholic Church motivated reformers?
2. Who were some of the earlier reformers and how did they approach the task of reforming the Latin Church?
3. Compare and contrast the lives of Martin Luther and John Calvin.
4. Explain how the reformation movement in England was different from the one in continental Europe.
5. How did the Catholic response to the Reformation lead to an impasse between Protestants and Catholics?
6. What role did the Protestants play in reinforcing this impasse?
7. What were the consequences of the impasse and how did these provide an opportunity for religious skeptics to expand their influence in society?

Chapter 15: The Advancement of Science

I. Introduction

One of the important developments of the early modern period was the rapid advancement of scientific inquiry that resulted in the expansion of knowledge about the nature of the universe. In turn, the increased scientific knowledge was used in many practical ways. These applications of knowledge resulted in substantial material benefits for mankind. As fundamental science continued to increase human knowledge about the universe, it sparked significant controversies that challenged the underlying fabric of Western civilization. One of the main points of contention was the identification of the proper connection, if any, between science and religion. While earlier scientists acknowledged a clear relationship between the two, many modern scientists embraced a view that rejected even the possibility of any connection whatsoever. This latter development serves as one of the factors that erodes the foundation of civilization itself. On this point more will be said, for now, it is enough to consider how the general understanding of the relationship between science and religion changed as we moved into the modern era.

II. The Essence of Scientific Inquiry

At its root, science is an effort to ascertain the laws that determine the facts of experience. If those laws can be discovered by way of investigation, they can be applied beyond the facts investigated to provide a sound basis for the prediction of future outcomes. For example, the chemist, on the basis of his previous experimentation, can tell with a degree of prior certainty the effect of combining certain chemicals. Likewise, the astronomer, on the basis of his careful observation of the movements of heavenly bodies, can give us a specific date and time when the next solar eclipse will occur. There are two methods that are used in scientific pursuits. They are the *a priori* or deductive, which argues from the cause to the effect, and the *a posteriori* or inductive, which argues from the effect to the cause. The latter of these two is generally understood as the natural starting point for all scientific inquiry. This follows from the fact that we are necessarily forced to begin our exploration of the universe where we are. Since this is true, any understanding of nature must proceed from the process that begins by the collecting, comparing, combining, and categorizing of data. Data are the facts as they present themselves to our senses. From these, the researcher looks for an underlying causal relationship to understand how the facts observed are determined. Thus, "in every science there are two factors: facts and ideas; or, facts and the mind."[130]

With this much said, it follows that science is founded upon certain underlying assumptions. Three necessary assumptions are fundamental to the endeavor. The first of these assumptions is that sense perception is generally reliable. Without this assumption, science could not proceed because the researcher would be unable to place any confidence in his ability to accurately observe the facts of nature. If that were true, it would be pointless to try to collect facts. Another way to say the same thing, is to say that the collection of facts is foolish if no confidence can be placed in the validity of the resulting data. This is not to say that the senses cannot err, but merely that, on the whole, they provide generally trustworthy information. Second, it is assumed that human beings can trust their mental abilities, and that the rules of logical thought are valid. This is necessary so that the facts can be compared, contrasted, combined, and remembered, and so that inferences can be drawn from the data in a consistent and systematic fashion. If this were not true, how could a scientist arrive at, or deduce from the facts a relationship of them? It is, thus, inescapable that logical consistency is a necessary precondition for science. This is not to say that every scientist always proceeds in a perfectly logical fashion, for we know that this is not always true. Instead, it is merely to say that there is a real logical connection of the facts that can be deduced. Finally, it must be assumed that the universe operates in a cause and effect fashion. That is, it must be believed that every effect must have an efficient cause. Without this

---

[130] Charles Hodge, *Systematic Theology*, (Grand Rapids, Michigan: W.B. Eerdmans Publishing Company, reprinted 1993, vol. 1), pg. 1.

assumption, the scientist has no work to perform, for the very essence of the endeavor presupposes that such relationships can be established.

On the basis of these axioms, science proceeds by collecting facts. These facts cannot be manufactured, nor modified to suit the fancies of the researcher. Rather, they must be taken as they are. It is the job of the scientist to carefully collect them and then to deduce from them the laws by which they are determined. Once the laws are discovered, they may be applied beyond the limits of the actual observation, as long as like circumstances prevail. It is important to note that the laws or principles are not derived from the mind and then assigned to the objects. Rather, they are deduced from the facts themselves and then impressed upon the mind. It is a process of discovery and not of invention.

Another important point should be noted. Namely, the object to be studied and understood is not science. The object of study is nature itself, and it is nature that provides the facts from which the scientist must deduce the laws by which those facts are determined. As such, the potential for error is great. The researcher may collect the facts without the necessary care needed to make an adequate assessment of them. Or, after having made a reasonable collection of the facts, the scientist may deduce the underlying laws or principles incorrectly. Finally, intellectual dishonesty may obscure the underlying reality as scientists suppress or pervert the facts because they do not adhere to their favorite theories. For all of these reasons, science will always provide an imperfect understanding of nature. Nevertheless, the pursuit can advance the depth of our knowledge about the world, and a better understanding of nature can be used to promote human well-being.

III. The Development of Modern Science

With this understanding of the scientific method in mind, consider how inquiry developed in the early modern period. The main obstacle to the advancement of science before the modern period was that state power was used to promote the official position of the Roman Catholic Church. That is, state power was used to advance the Roman Catholic understanding of the Christian religion. This impacted science, because there was a logical link between philosophy and theology. Prior to this era, bad science became intertwined with some of the official doctrines of the church. This created a problem for the conscientious scientist because the government used its power to execute people whose opinions were at odds with those of the church. As a result, there was a very real impediment to scientific advancement during the Middle Ages. The would-be scientist who might have advanced human understanding of the natural order of this world always ran the risk of being labeled a heretic and being burned at the stake. In fact, some scholars were so treated. Thus, the relationship of the religious and the secular authorities posed a formidable obstacle to scientific inquiry.

Nevertheless, the movements of the Renaissance and the Reformation, which tended to undermine the authority of the Latin Church in Europe, opened the door for more scientific investigation. Early modern scientists were not free of the threat of persecution that might accompany their work, but they were allowed a greater latitude to explore and speculate about the nature of things.

A. Nicolaus Copernicus (1473-1543)

One of the first individuals of importance that we should consider is Nicolaus Copernicus, who lived during the sixteenth century. He was a contemporary of the Protestant reformers, although he remained loyal to the Roman Catholic Church throughout his life. While Copernicus was not the only individual to pursue an invigorated scientific inquiry during this era, he was, nevertheless, an important investigator and a prime example of what a scientist did. His academic efforts provided the seminal work upon which our current understanding of the solar system was developed. His attention to the facts and his careful deductions from them, provided a tremendous leap forward in human knowledge about the order of the cosmos. Regrettably, it took many years for people to accept the truth of the matter.

Copernicus was born in Poland in the town of Thorn. His father died when he was ten years of age, and his uncle took charge of the family and provided for the education of the children. At the age of eighteen, Copernicus began his college studies at the University of Cracow where he prepared for the priesthood. His uncle arranged a church appointment for him which was to begin upon his completion of studies at Cracow. But, Nicolaus sought and received a leave of absence to continue his academic pursuits in Italy. He traveled to Italy and there entered into the study of mathematics, astronomy, and physics at the University of

Bologna. It was there that one of his professors exposed him to the heliocentric theory. The theory proposed that the earth was a planet that revolved around the sun, rather than the generally accepted view of his time that all heavenly bodies revolved around the earth. As he discovered, the theory was not new and had been presented in various forms by various individuals since the fifth century B.C. It had only recently been revived in Renaissance Italy.

After carefully examining the theory, Copernicus eventually concluded that it was a far more accurate explanation of the facts of nature. It was this conclusion that drove him to continue his academic work. After a brief return to Poland, Copernicus once again sought and received another leave of absence to pursue his studies in Italy and he enrolled in the University of Ferrara where he studied canon law and medicine. Yet, all the while, he also continued to consider the heliocentric theory. After completing his law degree, he returned to Poland to take up his church duties which he continued until his death in 1543.

Initially, he spent much of his spare time working on the heliocentric theory and by 1514 he developed a commentary that summarized the major findings of his work. He made several manuscript copies of these findings and began to distribute them to see what kind of reaction they might prompt. While there was little immediate threat from the Roman Church hierarchy, there was also little interest. His work was denounced by numerous theologians, both Catholic and Protestant, who regrettably misused Scripture to discredit the Pole's thesis. In 1530, Copernicus completed his work on the major manuscript that fully developed the theory. While he hoped that his work would be recognized as important, the lack of interest in it left him discouraged and he did not pursue its publication.

That might have been the end of the matter for quite some time had it not been for a young Protestant professor in Wittenberg by the name of Georg Rheticus. Rheticus read a copy of the earlier commentary and had become convinced of its truth. In 1539, he went to visit Copernicus and stayed with him in order to study the unpublished thesis. Afterwards, the young professor was even more enthusiastic than before and urged the aging priest to publish his work. As a result of Rheticus' persuasive efforts, Copernicus consented and the first copies were published in 1543, the same year the he died.

B. The Copernican Revolution

Copernicus' work touched off a dispute between scientists and ecclesiastics that was not settled until many years later. In fact, it was not until the immensely important academic work of Sir Isaac Newton (1642-1727) that the matter was settled. Among the other men who advanced the scientific inquiry necessary to resolve the matter were Tycho Brahe (1546-1601), Johann Kepler (1571-1630), and Galileo Galilei (1564-1642). Brahe was an astronomer who did not accept the Copernican theory, but whose recorded observations were of great value to Kepler. Kepler, in turn, was convinced by Copernicus' work and used Brahe's observations to make the Copernican system operable. Galileo was one of Kepler's contemporaries.

Galileo was born on February 15, 1564 in the city of Pisa. His father was an accomplished musician and became known for his innovative ideas about music. The family moved from Pisa to Florence when Galileo was ten years old, but he returned to Pisa to pursue an academic degree at the university there. He graduated in 1581 and continued his studies in several other areas of interest. Of particular importance during this time was his study of mathematics. Based upon his work in this area, Galileo was given the academic chair of mathematics at the University of Pisa in 1589. This position provided him the opportunity to begin his academic career. The thing that distinguished Galileo's work was his interest in deducing physical relationships on the basis of observation. At that time, Aristotle was assumed to be the foremost expert regarding cosmology and physics, and his speculations on these matters were generally accepted without debate. Yet, Galileo questioned many of the assumed relationships that his teachers attempted to pass on to him, because he did not believe that they were consistent with the plain facts of nature as he observed them to be. Galileo was able to show a number of errors in the Aristotelian physics that was so prominent in his day. In so doing, Galileo proved himself to be a scientist of immense talent and insight. It was his pursuit of accurate observation that led him to embrace the new Copernican astronomy. He noted that it provided a much better explanation of the facts as they could be observed. For his work in this area, he is often credited with establishing the surety of the Copernican theory when he published a monumental book on the subject in 1632.

This book offered the opportunity to rapidly extend human understanding of the cosmos. Unfortunately, it met with staunch resistance in the religious community. So great was the hostility to his work, that Galileo was forced to recant his position amidst a Catholic inquisition that followed the year after his book was published. The reason why so many religious authorities deplored the Copernican theory can be explained better if we understand how people of the time thought about the connection between nature and theology. As people popularly perceived the matter, the earth alone stood as the fixed point of reference for all else. Within this notion of the cosmos, the exact location of both heaven and hell were easily identified: hell resided at the innermost depths below the earth's surface while heaven was obviously located beyond the outermost sphere of the sky.[131] To accept the Copernican theory meant that people would have to alter their conceptions of the locale of heaven and hell if they were to continue to believe that they were real places. To do so seemed at odds with most everything that was generally believed to be true at the time.

Dante's *Divine Comedy* was an excellent illustration of the earlier understanding of the nature of things. In this work Dante took the reader on a journey down into the earth and into the pit of hell. He used his vast literary skills to provide vivid images all along the way. From hell, Dante then took the reader on through purgatory and into heaven following along a road map that was popular during his day. However, this assumed road map was not a map of the cosmos as it actually was. The Copernican understanding posed a serious threat to the well accepted view of the nature of things, and, in the minds of many theologians, it threatened the very essence of their religion. In truth, the fears of the theologians were unwarranted for the Scriptures never suggested that heaven and hell are located in this particular fashion. Therefore, their resistence to science proved to be quite unfortunate.

Nonetheless, the facts could not be suppressed forever and they eventually overwhelmed the false notion that the earth was a fixed object around which all other heavenly bodies moved. This happened amidst a great deal of strife and contention during the course of many years. The final acceptance of the Copernican theory for thoughtful men came with

---

[131] John Hedley Brooke, *Science and Religion: Some Historical Perspectives*, (Cambridge University Press, 1991), pp83-89.

the work of Sir Isaac Newton. Isaac Newton was born into a landholding family of modest means. He was born on Christmas day in 1642. His father died the same year almost three months prior to his birth. When he was three years old, his mother remarried. Newton's academic talents were recognized early in life, and owing to his family's efforts he was able to study at Trinity College, Cambridge. He excelled in his studies and proved himself to be particularly capable in mathematics. Newton is best known for his advances in scientific knowledge by using mathematics to discern scientific relationships. Of specific importance here was his use of mathematics to understand gravitational pull and the motion of the planets. Through this work he demonstrated once and for all the accuracy of the Copernican theory. From this point, the dispute was finally settled.

C. *The Relationship Between Theology and Science*

It was very unfortunate that so many theologians attached such strong significance to the geocentric theory, for in time the facts that undermined the theory also undermined the faith of quite a few individuals. The failure of the theory provided the enemies of the Christian faith with ammunition to attack Christianity itself. This attack made considerable progress, especially in the most recent times, but it was fundamentally of no account. It was, rather, a straw man constructed for the purpose of being attacked. Those who seek to attack the Christian faith today often hide behind the cover of science as if there were some natural conflict between science and religious faith. As Stillman Drake quite rightly pointed out, this need not be the case:

> The silencing and punishment of Galileo toward the end of a life devoted to scientific inquiry was an event of profound significance for our cultural history. Its full understanding requires much more than an assumption of inevitable conflict between science and religion. . . . If any simple explanation existed, it would. . . be in terms of the customary ruthlessness of societal authority in suppressing minority opinion. . . [132]

---

[132] Stillman Drake, *Galileo*, (New York: Hill and Wang, 1980), pg. v.

Christian faith need not be attached to the geocentric theory, nor to any other speculative philosophy for that matter. There is no particular reason to infer it from the Scriptures if one recognizes the fact that the Scriptures were written in the ordinary vernacular of the time and place of the individual authors. As such, they refer to natural phenomena with words and phrases that were common to the day in which they were written. For example, when modern reporters provide us with the time of the appearance of the sun on the horizon they do not say, "the sun will come into view today according to the earth's rotation in regards to our present position of orbit at 7:05 a.m." Instead, they simply say, "the sun will rise at 7:05 a.m." Certainly, no thinking person is confused about the relationship involved, but we still use such phrases as the sun's "rising" and its "setting" to describe such events. Likewise, the authors of the Bible used such ordinary phrases for communication purposes. They may not have understood the actual relationship, but that is hardly of any concern. Their intention was not to develop a scientific treatise for the purpose of explaining natural phenomena. In fact, the attempt to use Scripture in this way is to misuse it.

All of this brings to light an important consideration. Namely, it is important to reevaluate the proper relationship between theology and philosophy. Many modernists assume that there is a natural conflict between the two. Yet, that conclusion is not warranted by the facts; instead of abandoning their faith, many of the early scientists operated on the presumption of faith. As professor John Hedley Brooke has pointed out:

> The very possibility of a rational science of nature is usually considered to depend on a uniformity in the relations between cause and effect. In the past, religious beliefs have served as a *presupposition* of the scientific enterprise insofar as they have underwritten that uniformity. Natural philosophers of the seventeenth century would present their work as the search for order in a universe regulated by an intelligent Creator. A created universe, unlike one that had always existed, was one in which the Creator had been free to exercise His will in devising the laws that nature should obey. . . . When natural philosophers referred to *laws of*

nature, they were not glibly choosing that metaphor. Laws were the result of legislation by an intelligent deity.[133]

Thus, the reality was that the early scientists were religious men. The mistake made by the theologians was that they attempted to develop an understanding of creation on the basis of the Bible alone. Such an approach to theology and science cannot stand the test of time. In fact, attempts to decipher the natural order on the basis of Scripture alone resulted in both poor theology and a poor understanding of nature. As long as some theologians persisted in this perspective, they stood as obstacles to the advancement of science. However, as science progressed, the opposite error became prominent. When scientists pursued their speculative theories without regard to Scripture, they began to promote false theories of nature. In other words, theories were readily embraced even though they conflicted with God's Word. Such speculation served the purpose of leading people astray. They were attempts to find explanations of nature wholly apart from God. But, the notion of a world operating in a cause and effect fashion required an efficient cause. This created serious tension in the scientific community because the existence of God remained essential to the endeavor. He alone was the efficient cause. Therefore, since it was his good pleasure to reveal himself to us in the Bible, scientists ought to have considered that book before promoting speculative theories that were at odds with it.

The understanding being promoted here is that two revelations of God stand open before us. They are the "book of God's words" and the "book of God's works." Nature is God's creation, his "book of works", that he rules over and sustains according to the order of his choosing. In the study of theology, this is conceptually known as his providential rule. Interestingly, there can be agreement among people about this order even when some reject, or are not privy to, God's "book of words." Thus, Aristotle, Cicero, and others could arrive at a natural law understanding of the world without knowing or accepting the Scriptures as God's revelation. They viewed God as an impersonal force, while the Christians understood him to be both intelligent and personal, as well as orderly and rational. Still, both parties were able to observe the facts of nature and make deductive conclusions about the order that God designed, whether

---

[133] op. cit., pg. 19.

or not God was recognized as sovereign. What was necessary for agreement between these two groups of people was that both recognized the rule of law and that both deduced conclusions that were consistent with reality. Therefore, philosophy has always involved the collection of facts, the examination and classification of them, and the deductions that can be made from them. The actual understanding devised from science is only as good as its accounting for the facts as they are given by God. Thus, science is subject to improvement since there is yet much to learn about the connection of the facts of nature.

Likewise, God's revelation of himself in Scripture provides all the facts of theology necessary for the salvation of human souls. "The Bible is to the theologian what nature is to the man of science. It is his storehouse of facts; and his method of ascertaining what the Bible teaches, is the same as that which the natural philosopher adopts to ascertain what nature teaches."[134] It reveals certain truths about God, about his character, and about his attributes. Yet, as we have already discussed, it remains for the theologian to discern the relationship of each individual fact given in Scripture. For example, the Bible reveals God as both merciful and just. It is, therefore, a necessary part of theology to explain how these facts stand in relation to one another. For this reason, there will be better and worse theologies and theologians in much the same way that there are better and worse scientific theories and scientists.

The problems associated with an accurate theology are the same as those for developing an accurate science. Among the difficulties are a poor or incomplete gathering of the facts, a perversion of the facts for prejudicial reasons, and an inadequate induction from the facts in light of all of the evidence. Scientific speculation that is unsubstantiated by the facts has no value in increasing our understanding of nature. The same is true in theology. The conflict between science and theology arises for two reasons. First, some scientists promote speculative theories that are blatantly at odds with the clear teachings of Scripture and advance these theories even though there is no necessary reason to do so. This is both unreasonable and irreligious, especially when viable theories exist that are consistent with both the facts of nature and with Scripture. In modern times this error has become pronounced and consideration of how this

---

[134] Charles Hodge, *Systematic Theology*, (Grand Rapids, Michigan: William B. Eerdman's Publishing Company, reprinted 1993, vol. 1), pg. 10.

situation arose will be made. For now it is enough to state it as a possibility. Second, theologians may hold too strongly to their own interpretations of the Bible even when they are clearly at odds with scientific facts. Since nature is God's creation, such a stance is unwarranted and ultimately is a rejection of God's truth. This ought not to be done. This error is clearly illustrated by ecclesiastical hostility to the development of the Copernican heliocentric theory.

D. Vesalius

Scientific advances during the early modern era were by no means limited to astronomy. Investigators in many other areas were at work advancing human understanding of their fields of study. For this reason, it might be profitable to consider another individual whose work served to advance our understanding of human anatomy. His name is Vesalius.

Vesalius was born in Brussels in 1514. His family had many ties to the medical profession, so it is not surprising that he, too, had an interest in biology generally and anatomy in particular. Even as a boy Vesalius enjoyed dissecting animals. He received a good education, and when he came of age he studied at the University of Paris. There he studied anatomy as well as other subjects, and by the time he completed his work he had learned both Latin and Greek.

After finishing his studies, the young man made his way to Italy and began teaching anatomy at the University of Padua. His enthusiasm for his subject matter was infectious, and, as a result, he immediately became popular among the students and among other teachers and officials as well. In the early stages of his academic exploration he developed an immense interest in, and skill at, dissecting both animal and human cadavers. This skill, coupled with his careful attention to detail, led to his discovery of numerous errors in the traditional text that was used to teach anatomy at the time. Soon the errors were so numerous that Vesalius decided that it was incumbent upon him to write a book that would accurately correct for them. This he did and the subsequent work was published in 1543.

While Vesalius' work was quite an advancement in anatomy, it was not well received by his colleagues. He had exposed too many errors for their tastes and in recalcitrant style they refused to accept his work. Discouraged by the results, and perhaps pressured to do so, he resigned his position at Padua and became a physician for Charles V. Thereafter, he made no other contribution to the advancement of anatomy, but his book became the basis for future efforts. This case is a good example of how the prejudices of the men of science served to undermine the advancement of knowledge in their own field.

One insight that can be gained from Vesalius' experience is that it is not only false religious views that prevent the advancement of knowledge. Human pride and arrogance are also effective weapons against scientific advancement. Nonetheless, Vesalius and other scientists of the age worked to discover new things despite the obstacles and hindrances put in their way. In their example, we see an increased interest in the pursuit of knowledge about this world. It was the result of the efforts of these kinds of men, pursuing various courses of study, that bore the fruit of a marked expansion of human knowledge and understanding. It also served as the base upon which science has advanced in the modern era.

Study Questions

1. Discuss the nature of scientific inquiry and differentiate between the roles of deduction and induction.
2. What are the three basic assumptions that are fundamental to scientific inquiry?
3. What is the object of study in science? Why is this important to keep in mind?
4. What was the main obstacle to the advancement of science in the Middle Ages?
5. Explain how the Copernican discovery exposed a poor theological understanding of the Scriptures. How did this error provide religious skeptics an opportunity to expand their influence in the sciences?
6. What is the relationship between theology and science? How do modern scientists ignore this relationship? Why do they ignore it?
7. What was Vesalius' contribution to the advancement of science?

Chapter 16: Exploration and Trade

I. Introduction

During the early modern age there was a rise in intellectual curiosity, a proliferation of scientific advancements, the formation of nations, and a rise in religious conflict. It was also a time during which there were significant increases in trade and in geographic discovery. The expanded interest in trade served as one of the chief motivating factors for the numerous marine expeditions of the age which led to many important discoveries about the world. The discoveries about the size and shape of the world had profound ramifications and helped to shape modern Western societies. What is perhaps most fascinating, were the large risks taken by the adventurers who willingly ventured forth into the unknown. Their efforts opened the way for dramatic changes in the world and the lives that people lived.

II. *Exploration, Discovery, and the Commercial Revolution*

Prince Henry the Navigator was the younger son of John I who was the king of Portugal in the early fifteenth century. Henry was not in line for the throne and was essentially free to pursue his own interests. The thing that attracted his attention most was sailing, and he approached his fascination of it in a systematic way. In particular, perfecting the art of navigation became one of his chief desires. By advancing this art, he hoped to significantly expand the kinds of voyages that could be successfully undertaken. He believed that such voyages would achieve at least two ends. First, it would provide a means of bringing much of Africa, at least along the western coast, under Portuguese rule. In addition, such voyages could lead to the discovery of an alternative trade route to the East.

The importance of this latter task was clear, since the existing routes made use of the Mediterranean Sea and involved significant travel over land. The problems associated with these routes were obvious. First, ground transportation of products was far more expensive than water transportation. Thus, an all-water route would greatly reduce the costs and would provide a distinct economic advantage in trade to anyone finding one. Second, the main trading routes went through several Italian cities including Venice and Genoa. This resulted in a significant rise in the economic prosperity of the people living there. Such good fortune experienced by some is often the only motive needed to spur others on in their quest to reap similar gains by exploration or imitation. Finally, the rising power of the Ottoman Turks threatened to substantially disrupt the flow of trade by closing off the trade routes to the East.

The combination of these motives, coupled with Henry's love of sailing, led him to establish a school of navigation. The school attracted the top navigators, map makers, ship designers, and other experts from around Europe. Among the students who attended the school were Christopher Columbus and Vasco da Gama. During Henry's life, the school promoted his cause. Sailors from the school pushed down the coast of Africa far enough to get beyond the Sahara. There they found lush vegetation along with dark-skinned natives. The Portuguese captured some of these people for use as slaves. This marked the beginning of the African slave trade that lasted until the nineteenth century.

After Henry's death in the middle of the fifteenth century, the school continued to operate and new findings were produced. The efforts of the school's members were more and more focused on finding an all-water route to India. By 1482 the Congo River was discovered, and it was hoped that it might provide the desired passage. Additional exploration of it revealed that it did not, but that did not stop later expeditions from pushing still farther south along the West African coast. By 1488 the Cape of Good Hope, as the tip of Africa was named, had finally been rounded. To cap off this event, in 1497 Vasco da Gama left Lisbon on his historic voyage to India and arrived there ten months later. He brought back a load of spices that reportedly sold for about sixty times the actual cost of the trip. For the Portuguese, the economic prospects of trade with the East were immense. The economic fortunes of Portugal rose significantly as the country benefitted from trade via its all-water route to the East. Portuguese traders were able to sell their wares at prices far below those of the established merchants in Italy. As a result, the center of trade shifted westward to the open waters of the Atlantic and away from the Mediterranean. As business was lured away from the cities along the old trade routes they began to decline in size and importance.

While the Portuguese were focusing on finding an eastward water passage to India, one of the students of Henry's school, Christopher Columbus, had the idea that India might more easily be reached by sailing west. This was by no means a new idea, for others had advanced it over the years. In fact, most men of learning during this era believed that earth was round, making it possible to reach the East by sailing west. Unfortunately for Columbus, he thought the world was much smaller than it really was and never expected that the Americas would block his way. Nonetheless, based upon the facts as he understood them, he presented his ideas to the Portuguese who rejected the project. This prompted him to look elsewhere for support which he found in Spain.

King Ferdinand and Queen Isabella of Spain took an interest in Columbus' proposal and agreed to finance his expedition. With Spanish funds in hand, Columbus set out on a voyage that has since become the most widely known of any that was undertaken at the time. The immensity of the importance of what Columbus would discover on his voyage was not immediately obvious. In October of 1492, Columbus reached some barrier islands of the American continents. He thought that he had reached a group of islands beyond which he expected to find the East Indies and the rest of Asia. In an effort to realize his dream, he made three additional voyages. During these expeditions, the reality that his way was blocked by a previously unknown land mass became evident to Columbus. When he died, he believed that he had failed to achieve anything of value.

The Spanish, however, did not give up so quickly on how they might profit from the discovery. In the years that followed, many other Spanish expeditions were financed to explore and conquer the new territory for Spain. In addition, the Spanish crown kept alive the notion that an all-water route to the East could be found by sailing west, and in 1519 the expedition of Ferdinand Magellan was launched. Magellan had also sought Portuguese assistance, but like Columbus, his proposal had been rejected and he turned to Spain for help. He was granted five ships to find a western route to the East. Magellan's quest was to look for a southwest route around the Americas. After reaching the South American continent, the explorer made his way down the coast line looking for a passage through. He finally found one near the tip of the continent and sailed through a strait that bears his name today. After navigating the Straits of Magellan the expedition set out to cross the Pacific Ocean. The expedition was already over a year old when this journey began.

Crossing the Pacific took far longer than anyone had imagined. Many hardships were endured as the explorers looked for land of any kind. There was much relief when the sailors finally reached the Phillippines. However, in order to secure provisions, Magellan and his men had to agree to fight a neighboring tribe for a local chief with whom they were attempting to trade. During this conflict Magellan was killed. In the aftermath of his death, only one of the remaining ships sailed on. Finally, in September of 1522, this ship reached Spain after having circled the globe. It was one of the monumental feats in human history.

In order to profit from the new discoveries, numerous expeditions were funded to conquer land for Spain. Among the notable leaders of these expeditions were Ponce de Leon, De Soto, Coronado, Balboa, Pizarro, and Cortez. The Spanish concentrated their efforts of exploration and conquest on the more temperate climates of the Americas. In these locales they discovered and displaced several civilizations of people. In Mexico, Cortez conquered the Aztecs in the same year that Magellan's remaining ship reached Spain. In South America, Pizarro laid siege to the Incan civilization which he conquered shortly thereafter. The motive behind these conquests was to gain gold and silver for Spain. As Will Durant has accurately written:

> The Spanish who in this period conquered Mexico, California, Central America, and Peru were first of all adventurers, tired of poverty and routine at home, and facing with pleasure the perils of distant and alien lands. Amid the hardships of their reckless enterprise they forgot civilized restraints, frankly adopted the morality of superior guns, and accomplished an act of continental robbery, treachery, and murder.[135]

Their primary task was to gain a monetary return above the cost of the expedition. Looting and subjugating the native Indian civilizations

---

[135] Will Durant, *The Reformation*, (New York: Simon and Schuster, 1957), pg. 864.

was the easiest way to secure that end. As we have already seen from earlier times, plundering one's neighbors is always the most expedient means to obtain wealth. But, such action overlooks the long-run consequences because theft discourages production and reduces the prospects for future wealth. Nevertheless, the Spanish pursued this course of action throughout the sixteenth century and attempted to use the bounty they reaped from their conquests as a source of power to maintain their supremacy in Europe. However, the effort was largely a vain pursuit. By the latter part of that century, Spain had to face the reality that it was impossible for a nation to sustain itself by living off the booty gained from conquests. The nation's fortunes subsequently declined, and its dominance in the world was broken.

While Spain and Portugal stood to benefit most from the new discoveries, neither country fully seized the advantage. The main advantage they had was economic. If either country had focused its energies on securing and developing cooperative trading and production arrangements with the people they encountered, the face of the world would most likely be very different today. As it was, Spain seemed content to plunder the American Indian civilizations that its explorers found for all the gold and silver its boats could carry. Any serious trading activity was pursued as an afterthought, and even then it was very limited. As for Portugal, while the promotion of trade was at the heart of its early exploration efforts, and while Lisbon did develop rapidly into a prominent European trading center, the Portuguese did not maintain trade as their ultimate focus. In time, they turned their attention toward building and maintaining an empire in order to secure a monopoly over trade to the East. As more and more resources were devoted to this goal, rather than to further the development of trade itself, opportunities for others to profit from eastern trade grew.

To be sure, the other nations of the period were jealous of the Spanish and Portuguese positions. The French, English, and Dutch wanted their own rewards from new discoveries and, as a result, promoted their own expeditions. Since the Spanish and the Portuguese had established claims to certain territories in the New World, and to certain trade routes to the East, their expeditions focused on what they thought were other possible options. The most immediate goal was to find an alternative route to the East. Therefore, the early expeditions of the French, English, and Dutch sought to discover either a northeast or a northwest passage to the East.

It quickly became evident that no northeast passage would be possible, so the expeditions focused on finding the northwest route. The notable French explorers in this endeavor were Jacques Cartier, Samuel de Champlain, and Robert Cavelier de La Salle. Exploring for England were men such as John Cabot and Henry Hudson. Of course none of these men found what they were looking for, but they did explore a large amount of North America and laid claim to a great deal of territory for the countries they represented. In addition, a number of colonies were planted that were little more than wilderness outposts. Yet, these colonies attracted a number of Europeans who were willing to make their way in the wilderness in order to escape the religious persecution that was so prominent in Europe during that time.

It appeared that the efforts of these countries were a failure, but as professors Clough and Rapp have observed:

> The French, English, and Dutch were not, however, content to admit defeat. From the first they had coveted Portuguese and Spanish colonial wealth and had speculated on how they might encroach upon it. Needless to say, cerebration on the problem led them to identical conclusions, for the range of possibilities was extremely limited. First, they agreed that they might do well to trade in Latin America, second, that there would be profit in plundering Spanish galleons on their homeward voyages, third, that they themselves could go to the Far East via known routes and get the spices which the Portuguese were selling to them at such a profit, and fourth, that they should take some of the less well-defended and apparently fertile lands in Central and South America and bring them rapidly into production of things, like sugar, that Europeans wanted. They tried all four of these solutions.[136]

In terms of establishing their own trade with the East, it was the Dutch and the English who best seized the opportunity. They began innocently enough by purchasing goods in Lisbon and reselling them in

---

[136] Shepard B. Clough and Richard T. Rapp, *European Economic History*, (New York: McGraw-Hill Book Company, 3rd edition, 1975), pg. 134.

Northern and Western Europe. Antwerp and London became primary centers of this kind of trade. However, in the second half of the sixteenth century Spain was engaged in an effort to bring the Dutch territories to heel under Spanish rule. The English alienated Spain by siding with the Dutch, and when Spanish mercenaries sacked Antwerp in 1585, the English and Dutch were barred by the Spanish from Lisbon. Undaunted by the turn of events, the English and the Dutch sought to establish their own direct trade in the East, and both countries successfully began to develop their own presence there. They eventually began to compete aggressively against one another rather than against the Spanish and the Portuguese.

To facilitate the commerce, new business organizations were formed. The first joint-stock companies were created to raise the money needed to finance the buying and transporting of products. The governments of the various nations were heavily involved with these new companies and granted them official licenses or monopoly privileges to operate as sole providers of transportation services in particular areas. Two such companies were the Dutch East India Company and the British East India Company. The English government granted the exclusive right over trade with India to the British East India Company. This company was also given the right to rule over the portion of India that England controlled. The Dutch government gave a Dutch company the exclusive monopoly over any trade east of the Cape of Good Hope. The importance of these grants of privilege was that the trade which grew during this era was not open to all comers but only to a privileged few. This was not free trade, but was very much controlled by the political authorities. The system of political economy that developed during this period is referred to as mercantilism. It is important for us to understand this system because many of its assumptions are being used today to support political economic policies in many Western countries. Therefore, an examination of mercantilism will be presented in the next section. But before turning to that subject, let us consider some of the changes that the new trade produced.

One of the most important points of all of this is that the combination of discovering the Americas and of finding an all-water route to the East, resulted in many new commercial opportunities. The level of commerce increased so dramatically during this age that it is often referred to as the Commercial Revolution. Commerce is the facet of business that involves all the arrangements necessary for the interchange of goods. It does not involve the methods by which goods are produced nor does it generally involve the decision of which goods are produced in a given area. Yet, expanding commerce may provide new opportunities for production. In general, commerce can rapidly expand when the costs of communication and transportation are significantly reduced. The discoveries made during this era provided the kind of reduction in the costs of transportation that set off a dramatic rise in commercial trade. While the rise in commerce had little effect on the way in which production was carried out in the respective areas of the world, it did link peoples together more closely by the transport and exchange of many goods across a much larger region of the globe. On the production side of business, dramatic improvements would come later during the Industrial Revolution of the eighteenth, nineteenth, and twentieth centuries.

The new commerce resulted in the rapid expansion in the number and kinds of products that were generally available. Prior to the advancement in trade, some products could only be afforded by the very rich. But with the new means of transportation, the prices of these commodities dropped sharply and became available to people of lesser means. During the sixteenth and seventeenth centuries the supplies of spices, coffee, tea, sugar, tropical fruits, and fine textiles rose substantially throughout Europe. The result was a marked improvement in the material well-being of people generally. In addition to an increased supply of these kinds of goods, new commodities also flowed into trading centers from the Americas. Among the products introduced into Europe from the New World were potatoes, corn, tobacco, and chocolate.

To finance the substantial rise in trade, banking also expanded rapidly. One of the better examples of success in the development of a banking enterprise can be found in Augsburg with the Fugger family. The family's roots go back in that city to around 1380. Hans Fugger made a substantial fortune in the cloth industry in which he worked. He had evidently gained quite a reputation for delivering quality textile products to the marketplace and his son continued to build this business. In turn, the family business was passed on to Hans' grandsons. One of the grandsons was named Jacob, and it was mainly through his efforts that the family business emerged as an important banking enterprise. Jacob diversified the family business into mining and from there into large scale finance. The Fuggers went on to develop a large banking firm that accepted deposits and made loans at interest. While the earlier business endeavors had produced wealth, the family fortunes grew rapidly as their banks were among the largest and most prominent in Europe.

III. Mercantilism

As we have already seen, feudal ties were breaking up as nation-states developed. The rulers of the emerging European nations had steadily gained control over vast territories and were ruling over them with more or less absolute power. The declining influence of the Roman Catholic Church allowed political rulers to consolidate their positions more completely. This change in political power, coupled with the rapid rise in trade, set the stage for a new politico-economic system. The old feudalism of the Middle Ages was displaced by the rise of mercantilism.

Mercantilism was that system of economy built upon the assumed right of the king to rule absolutely over the economic affairs of the nation and its inhabitants. State control over commerce was thus fundamental to the system. "Mercantilism has been called by various historians or observers a 'system of Power or State-building' (Eli Heckscher), a system of systematic state privilege, particularly in restricting imports or subsidizing exports (Adam Smith), or a faulty set of economic theories, including protectionism and the alleged necessity for pilling up bullion in a country. In fact, mercantilism was all of these things; it was a comprehensive system of state-building, state privilege, and what might be called 'state monopoly capitalism'."[137]

In his book *Basic Economics*, Clarence Carson has accurately captured the underlying faulty premises upon which this politico-economic system operated. The first premise is the assumption that there is an exact relationship between the quantities of gold and silver held by a nation and the nation's wealth. The second assumption, that is closely tied to the first, is that it is necessary for a nation to maintain a favorable balance of trade in order to be successful economically.[138] The first of

---

[137] Murray Rothbard, *Economic Thought Before Adam Smith*, (Brookfield, Vermont: Edward Elgar Publishing Company, 1995), pg.213.

[138] See Clarence Carson, *Basic Economics*, (Wadley, Alabama: American Textbook Committee, 1988), pg. 276-277.

these, known as bullionism, is the notion that wealth consists solely of the amount of precious metals, such as gold and silver, that one possesses. It is natural enough to see how this assumption might have arisen in as much as gold and silver had become the common money of the period. As such, someone who possessed gold and silver in sufficient quantities could purchase commodities readily. The problem with this perspective is that it fails to realize that all trade ultimately depends upon the exchange of goods for goods. Therefore, real wealth consists in one's ability to produce a highly desirable good and trade it effectively for other things. In this sense, money is only an instrument to the ultimate end and not the end itself. Nevertheless, since having money in one's pocket does provide the immediate ability to consume, it is easy to see how it can be confused as the source of wealth itself. This error in thought is not exclusive to the early modern period, it is widely held in our own day.

The second faulty premise upon which mercantilism built was the notion that the nation had to maintain a favorable balance of trade. "The terms favorable and unfavorable balance of trade are basically mercantilistic concepts, though they are still very much in use in our own day. . . .Mercantilists favored a favorable balance of trade, that is, that their nation sell more in goods to other nations than they bought in return" for the purpose of increasing the nation's gold stock.[139] This premise is, therefore, very much an offshoot of the first. Nevertheless, it is important because it served to direct national economic policies that were decreed by the kings of that time. For example, one means of obtaining a favorable balance of trade was to promote the importation of raw materials while exporting finished products. The reasoning behind such a policy was the reality that finished goods command a higher price, stated in monetary terms, than the raw materials used in production. Therefore, if a nation were to focus its efforts on importing raw materials and exporting finished products, it would accumulate for itself a growing stock of gold and silver and thereby become wealthier. But this reasoning fails once it is realized that the premise upon which it depends is in error.

In addition to fostering a favorable balance of trade to increase the national stock of precious metals, kings also sought to expand their own holdings of gold and silver through more direct means. As commerce rose,

---

[139] Ibid, pg. 276.

one method of increasing the king's own store of gold was to sell monopoly privileges to certain individuals or groups. These privileges granted specific rights of certain kinds of trade allowed within the borders of the nation while simultaneously prohibiting all competition. This kind of policy served to restrict economic activity and limit economic prosperity generally while increasing the ruler's monetary holdings. It was a policy that benefitted the crown at the expense of the people under his rule. In addition to grants of special privilege to obtain precious metals, rulers also used a more direct method. They would simply use their power to take it by force from others. The inordinate desire for increasing one's monetary stock as a means for increasing one's wealth explains why the Spanish preferred to plunder the civilizations of America rather than establishing long-term trading relationships with the people they found there. Regrettably, their thinking was simply blurred by their own greed.

Whatever else might be said about mercantilism, it was a centrally planned economic system. It was a politico-economic system devised for the express interest of promoting the immediate interests of the crown and his chosen beneficiaries. Beyond the expansion of wealth that trade would produce, their specific betterment was also gained at the expense of most people living under their rule and at the expense of the peoples of other nations. In this latter regard, mercantilism was most certainly nationalistic and collective, and both anti-individualistic and anti-free enterprise. Trade was essentially viewed analogically as a kind of warfare. It was assumed that one nation's gain was another's loss. Thus, there was a failure to see that the expansion in commercial trade came about because it afforded mutual benefits to the participants in it. It is for this reason that the analogy of war is a wholly inadequate analogy in explaining the nature of what is transpiring in commercial trade. But this was largely unseen by the mass of people of the era and is still unseen by many today. In fact, in our own time there has been a revival of the underlying falsehoods that drove mercantilism. Strangely enough, many people today have succumbed to the false notions of the nature and source of wealth that undergirded that system. The importance of this is so significant that this will be a topic for later discussion.

Study Questions

1. What important discoveries launched the modern era?
2. How did the commercial revolution contribute to this process?
3. Even though they were positioned better than other nations to take advantage of the new discoveries, why did the fortunes of Portugal and Spain decline in the sixteenth century while those of England and the Netherlands rose?
4. What is mercantilism and how did it hinder economic progress?
5. What Christian teachings were essential to promoting the advancement of commerce that resulted in economic progress?

Section 4: The Modern Era: Conflicting World Views

In the sphere of religion, in particular, the present time is a time of conflict; the great redemptive religion which has always been known as Christianity is battling against a totally diverse type of religious belief, which is only the more destructive of the Christian faith because it makes use of traditional Christian terminology. This modern non-redemptive religion is called "modernism" or "liberalism." Both names are unsatisfactory; the latter, in particular, is question-begging. The movement designated as "liberalism" is regarded as "liberal" only by its friends; to its opponents it seems to involve a narrow ignoring of many relevant facts. And indeed the movement is so various in its manifestations that one may almost despair of finding any common name which will apply to all its forms. But manifold as are the forms in which the movement appears, the root of the movement is one; the many varieties of modern liberal religion are rooted in naturalism—that is, in the denial of any entrance of the creative power of God (as distinguished from the ordinary course of nature) in connection with the origin of Christianity.[140]

In the preceding paragraph, J. Gresham Machen captured succinctly the nature of an ongoing conflict that so readily defines the modern era. The rise of the scientific method of discovery led some people to assert that it was the only means of gaining knowledge about this world. As this idea spread, the whole notion of the existence of the supernatural or the transcendent was called into question. In time, the successful scientific discoveries that were made seemed to give credence to the growing view that the entire universe merely operated according

---

[140] J. Gresham Machen, *Christianity and Liberalism*, (New York: The Macmillan Company, 1934), pg. 2.

to some predetermined pattern. The idea emerged that everything, including mankind, operated in this fashion.

The spread of this idea, best called naturalism, has relentlessly driven religion from the various spheres of public life. The message, which began in the universities, spread to the other areas of life. As a result, religion in general, and Christianity in particular, were pushed from the public sphere. This is the reason why many people today think that the only legitimate place for religion is in the private lives of individuals. Indeed, any outward declaration that one's religious beliefs are true while others are false is viewed negatively. That is to say that any effort by one person to persuade others that his faith ought to be embraced is derided as being intolerant by the more vocal naturalists. In short, the anti-theistic religion of naturalism maintains that all theistic religions are irrelevant. Moreover, proponents of naturalism have been so aggressive in spreading their new faith that they have even attempted to subvert Christianity itself in an effort to expand the dominance of this viewpoint. To do this, liberal theologians have called into question the existence of miracles. This is significant because the very basis of Christianity rests on the supernatural resurrection of Jesus Christ. Since Western civilization is founded on Judeo-Christian principles, the spread of naturalism is undermining the foundational supports.

The ongoing battle between the traditional Judeo-Christian faith and the new faith in naturalism provides us with the best framework within which to understand our own age. The battle has moved progressively from one waged for human minds to a conquest for human hearts. As naturalism succeeded in gaining victory after victory, the battle affected the other spheres of human life. And, while it might appear today that there is no longer any room whatsoever for the traditional Christian faith, the reality is that naturalism contains, in itself, the seeds for its own destruction. Thus, while it may seem that it is nearly pervasive, the truth is that it is already beginning to unravel. The next four chapters chart the rise, and the early stages of the fall, of naturalism.

Chapter 17: The Battle for Human Minds

I.   Introduction

The modern era has been especially marked by the changes in the ways that people conceive of themselves and of the universe in which they live. For good or ill, there have been many different points of view in modern times. All the movements of the preceding ages served to shape the directions of change in human thought that have arisen in the past four centuries. Among the many elements leading to change that might be mentioned, the most notable factors are expanding educational opportunities, religious reform, the rise in science, and the economic progress obtained by taking advantage of new discoveries. The changes that developed in these areas provided an environment for an aggressive battle for the minds of men. The antagonists in this conflict have had as their aim the shaping of popular opinion.

This is not to say that persuasion had not existed beforehand. The art of trying to win another person over to one's own point of view has always been prevalent. Yet the modern era has many unanswered questions, and there is much debate among people in general. The reason for this substantial increase in argumentation was the result of the growing use of the scientific method itself. Throughout the Middle Ages, education was conceived of primarily as a means of handing down a known set of facts. In such an environment, knowledge was based most firmly on authority and experience tended to be discounted. The rise in scientific inquiry was largely the result of the questioning of the established authorities. Many of the advancements and discoveries that were made demonstrated that these sources had been in error. As a result, there was an increasing admiration among people generally for experience and experimentation.

Before getting into our discussion, it is important to note that both authority and experience have a place in learning. Considerable damage can be done by neglecting either one of these forms of learning. The acceptance of authority is fundamental. In regards to experience as a teacher, Benjamin Franklin said, "Experience keeps a dear school; the fool will learn in no other." The point that he was making is that it is a very foolish thing for an individual to totally discount the past experience of all other human beings and to presume that the only thing to be learned is what can be personally experienced. We know that we are better off not experiencing some things. For example, a child is much better off keeping his hands away from a hot stove than experiencing the burns that he will suffer if he touches it. In such cases, the knowledge embedded in the authority of his parents is much better than the knowledge gained by personal experience. Beyond this simple example, there are all kinds of other experiences that can only be had once and then there is no possibility of any future experience. Any experience that results in death will preclude the prospect for further investigation. As a result, authority in learning can never be abandoned totally even though there are those today that suggest that it should be.

On the other hand, authority alone is not a sufficient base for education and learning. The reason that this is true is that authority implicitly assumes that it is correct. But, if history teaches us anything about mankind it is that human beings are prone to error. Therefore, human authority is flawed and when it is it should be rejected. For this reason, experimentation to either confirm or reject past authority is often a worthy endeavor. Whether one should learn from authority or experience is a complicated matter. The trick is to know when it is wise to experiment and when it is wise to embrace the wisdom of the ages at face value. The difficulty in sufficiently answering this question has resulted in more than a little debate during the modern era. Yet throughout the debate, there has been a steady move toward the praise of experience and experimentation and against the acceptance of any authority whatsoever. So much is this the case, that even the authority of God has been called into question.

II. The Movement to Rationalism

As science succeeded in dispelling a number of widely held beliefs, a movement in thought, known as rationalism, developed. Rationalism is the belief that man can reason from the facts of nature alone in such a way as to produce completely satisfactory and comprehensive explanations of all possible questions that might be asked. Among the notable individuals who paved the way for the spread of rationalism was Rene Descartes (1596-1650). He lived through the turbulent religious upheaval that was spawned by the Reformation. While it is most natural to focus only on the conflict between the Catholics and the Protestants during the sixteenth century, in actuality there had always been a third party in this struggle–the religious skeptics of the day. Their importance to the times and to the shaping of the future should not be neglected. During this religious upheaval the skeptics made significant inroads in spreading their skepticism and in shaping the general perceptions of the times. Much of this success was perhaps due to the conflict between the Catholics and Protestants which had been particularly bloody. In light of such behavior on the part of men who professed Christian faith, it was an easy thing to point out the many errors being made. As a result, skepticism spread across the European landscape and became prominent by the dawn of the seventeenth century. It was in this atmosphere that Descartes grew to manhood and went off to college to learn the ways of the world.

Descartes enrolled in college with all the enthusiasm that might be expected of a young man in zealous pursuit of the truth. However, his college studies left him profoundly dissatisfied. As one writer put it, "Descartes, upon graduating from 'one of the most celebrated schools in Europe' in which he had expected to acquire 'a clear and certain knowledge of all that is useful in life,' found himself so involved in doubts and errors that he was convinced he had learned nothing but the depth of his ignorance."[141] He was so bothered by the prevailing skepticism of his day, that it moved him to ask himself whether or not there was any truth that could be known for certain. In the process of grappling with this question, he came to the conclusion that he could not doubt his own existence and that building from this conclusion alone, he could find truth. Descartes coined the Latin phrase, *cogito ergo sum*, which translates, "I think, therefore I am," as the basic truth upon which he wished to build.

Using this foundation as his starting point, he sought to use reason to find other certainties in life. Toward this end he became particularly

---

[141] Gordon Clark, *Thales to Dewey*, (Jefferson, Maryland: The Trinity Foundation, 2nd edition, 1985), pg. 308.

fond of mathematics whose proofs were so certain to his mind. It was this kind of thinking that led later writers to refer to Descartes as the Father of Modern Rationalism. Descartes' rationalism was not the same as that which is most prevalent today. It focused more on deductive rather than inductive reasoning. For this reason, he was primarily concerned with the use of systematic logic. Using this kind of reasoning one begins from some initial starting point to deduce his results instead of using empirical facts from which the researcher hopes to discern some principle. The latter method, called the inductive method, has become quite prominent today. Therefore, in a way, Descartes was a throwback to an age gone by. In many ways the deductive method used by Descartes linked him to the more traditional modes of thought. Nevertheless, his efforts did set off a quest to organize all truth by the use of the mathematical scale, and this set in motion a process that would eventually lead to a kind of rationalism that was the defining characteristic of the Enlightenment. As far as experimental science is concerned, Descartes was in favor of it ". . . for he believed that experimentation could 'suggest' many truths that logic would later prove."[142] But his stock and trade remained deductive reasoning based upon what he believed to be a foundational truth.

Later writers challenged Descartes' fundamental proposition of truth, as well as any notion of innate ideas or a priori starting points. Among the most prominent of these writers was John Locke (1632-1704). Locke was interested in examining three important issues of human knowledge. These included the existence of self, the existence of God, and the existence of the natural world. His study was primarily directed toward developing a cohesive understanding of human knowledge. In particular, he was interested in developing a rational conception of how the self, God, and the natural world can be known. He concluded that they can be known through intuition, demonstration, and sensation respectively. Within this context, Locke accepted the cosmological argument for God's existence, while arguing for a purely empirical method of approach.

Locke wrestled with the subject/object dilemma. This dilemma can be summed up in two questions. First, how does an individual person know objects external to himself? Second, how does a person know that

---

[142] Ibid, pg. 314.

his own individuality is not distorting or coloring his reception of the objective reality? The essence of the problem lies in individual perception. How does an individual know that reality is what he believes it is? Locke's struggle with these questions led him to propose the Correspondence Theory of Truth. This theory states that truth is subjective knowledge which corresponds to that which really is. Unlike Descartes, Locke ruled out the notion of innate ideas and the a priori mental abilities. Rather, he believed that the individual comes into the world as a *tabula rasa,* or a blank tablet, onto which experience is written. Using this as a starting point, he argued that all knowledge of the external world is a posteriori. This means that knowledge comes after one has experienced the world by way of his senses.

His theory worked in the following fashion. He assumed that after people are born, they immediately begin to have sense experiences, and these are recorded in our minds. He referred to these initial recordings as simple ideas. As more and more simple ideas are gathered, he reasoned that the mind works to develop these into complex ideas through the process of binding, relating, and separating the simple ideas. Locke affirmed that the external world is as we perceive it to be. He asserted that all objects are composed of primary and secondary qualities. While all individuals see the same primary qualities of an object, the perceptions of the secondary qualities will vary depending upon the person. As an example of a secondary quality, someone might comment that a pillow is soft. This statement may be disputed by someone else whose perception of softness is different from the first person's. But, no such disagreements could continue between rational persons in regard to primary qualities. For example, stating that a pillow is square is making a statement about a primary quality of the pillow. This statement is either accurate or inaccurate, given the definition of what it means for an object to be square.

These essential elements of Locke's philosophy set in motion efforts by other philosophers to describe the world apart from any revelatory aid from God. During this time there were a number of naturalists and deists who were eagerly working behind the scenes to develop a system of thought devoid of any theology whatsoever. Their efforts resulted in an era of thought that is often referred to as the Enlightenment, during which the analytical method was proclaimed as the only viable means of gaining knowledge. This method held that all that can be known is that which can be discerned from the facts of nature alone. By definition, this position discounted any value in divine revelation. This was something that the skeptics were eager to do. Their success in promoting such thinking was largely due to the many scientific discoveries that were being made about the natural world. Therefore, the skeptics used the occasion as a means of arguing against the Christian religion and against the authority of the Bible. The method itself was straightforward and nothing in it necessarily drives one to the conclusions of the skeptics. Rather, the skeptics sought to impose scientific method in areas of study for which it was not well suited. This method of investigation involves the collection of vast amounts of data from which the researcher attempts to determine the underlying principles that readily organize the data. As we have already seen, this kind of scientific approach, called induction, is extremely useful in determining the underlying principles that order nature. While induction is certainly an important tool, the defining step of the skeptics was the attempt to apply this method of study across the board to every conceivable area of study. They were so inclusive of the extension of this method that they applied it to the study of mankind and of religion as well as all other areas of human investigation. In other words, they argued that knowledge could only be gained in this fashion and, thus, rejected entirely the notion that knowledge could be gained from the revelation of God. This was a significant departure from the norm. Nonetheless, this conception of knowledge has sprouted, and has grown so pervasive that it has had a profound impact upon modern society.

Among the early promoters of this kind of thinking was David Hume (1711-1776). Hume was a very intelligent man. He was also opposed to Christianity and used his intelligence to devise a number of clever arguments aimed at undermining the Christian faith. Hume was a strong proponent of the empirical method of science and is famous for his critique of the classical understanding of causality. His criticism was put forth in the following way. He argued that a person cannot perceive a causal connection between events that are customarily related because all that can be observed is a series of events. In turn, the most that the observer is capable of concluding, Hume maintained, is that such a series is customary. Furthermore, he argued that just because they are customary, does not show any necessary cause and effect relationship in the events. In fact, there are clear cases where no cause and effect relationship is warranted. For example, if the rooster crows every morning just before the sun comes up, we cannot conclude that the rooster's crowing caused the sun to rise. Or, in his own famous illustration of billiards, Hume argued that we cannot conclude a cause and effect relationship in the game of pool as we observe the cue stick striking the cue ball, which subsequently strikes another ball, resulting in it rolling into a pocket on the table. Hume questioned how we could say that any cause took place.

In putting forth this argument, Hume was taking a highly skeptical position that would later call into question the possibility of any knowledge whatsoever. Hume seemed unaware of this prospect. He thought he was merely establishing a set of probability rules as the basis on which a practical kind of empirical knowledge could be secured. In addition, he thought his work would undermine the Christian faith which he sought to attack. In his attempt to refute causality, Hume argued that we can only be certain that we are having the sensation of causality and that we cannot be certain of causality itself. As a result, he believed that the wise course of action would be to accept as knowledge only that which experience shows to occur routinely enough to warrant some degree of confidence. On this basis, Hume attacked the Christian conception of miracles and argued that a rational person could not believe them.

Hume's attack went right to the heart of the matter, for if Christianity is to be reasonable, then miracles must be possible. We can understand this when we realize that miracles were often associated with those who claimed to speak for God. These miracles were acts that only God could perform and thus served as evidence that the spokesman was in fact speaking for God. The high point of this kind of evidence was provided by Jesus. During the ministerial period of his life, Jesus performed numerous miracles that could only be done by God himself. This he did to secure his position as God's spokesman. Furthermore, when he claimed to be God, he argued that people ought to believe him because of the vast evidence that was provided in the miracles that he performed. He affirmed this in John 10:38 when he said, ". . . though you do not believe me, believe the works. . . " This pattern of argumentation is found throughout the Bible. The apostle Paul affirmed it in his discussion of the very foundation of the Christian religion. In the fifteenth chapter of his first letter to the believers of Corinth, he argued that faith in Christ is vain unless Jesus has been raised from the dead. Therefore, Paul pointed to the resurrection as the foremost miracle upon which the validity of Christianity was secured.[143] Therefore, Hume believed rightly that if he could undermine confidence in miracles, he could undermine the Christian religion. In addition, Hume's work rightly pointed out the difficulty involved in accurately discerning cause and effect relationships by using naked empirical examination of the facts alone. In this regard Hume made a valuable addition to science by cautioning researchers not to jump too quickly to supposed cause and effect relationships.

Nevertheless, Hume's thinking was seriously flawed in his attack on the Christian religion. As Gordon Clark observed, ". . . it could be that Hume injured himself more than Christianity. . . . It is empiricism that is on trial. Can any knowledge be based on experience alone?"[144] The problem with Hume was that by focusing only on the routine, he did not allow for a first event. This was a crucial error since a series of the same kind of events must have a first occurrence. His fundamental problem can be seen in any of the inventions of the twentieth century. For example, consider the airplane. Before we could ever develop a probability measure of the likelihood of the successful flight of a particular airplane, we must have the first flight. But Hume argued that no one should believe that a plane can actually fly if none has ever been flown. Nor should anyone believe that one flew on the basis of the reports of the single experience. Therefore, Hume's position for knowledge based on experience alone is untenable. It is sort of like the ostrich that sticks his head in the sand to find refuge from predators, thus pretending he is safe as long as he cannot see his potential attacker. The problem with empiricism is that it cannot account for a rational world that is designed and sustained by a Creator. That the first flight occurred, and that countless flights have followed, happened precisely because some people looked beyond the probability quotients and looked to decipher the cause and effect relationships that make flight possible. The important thing in flying is that there are certain relationships that can be relied upon in designing airplanes that

---

[143] A complete discussion of miracles as the evidence securing the Bible as the Word of God can be found in R. C. Sproul, John Gerstner, and Arthur Lindsley, *Classical Apologetics*, (Grand Rapids, Michigan: Academie Books, 1984), pp.137-161.

[144] Op. Cit., pg. 391.

will fly whether or not a first flight has ever occurred. When considering Hume's attack against miracles, it is not the notion of miracles that is unreasonable, but Hume's rejection of them.[145]

In addition to his failure to adequately argue against miracles, he also failed to make an adequate case against causality. To be sure, the law of causality cannot be achieved on empirical grounds alone. On this point, Hume's argument is sound. Nevertheless, it must be noted that if human thought and human life are to be possible at all, the law of causality must be affirmed. Sproul, Gerstner, and Lindsley accurately dealt with this issue when they wrote:

> Causality is established on a more firm foundation if it is seen as an axiomatic corollary of the law of noncontradiction. In a sense the law of causality is merely an extension of the law of noncontradiction; it is a formal principle which is analytically true. Its definition is tautological: every effect must have a cause. The term *effect* carries within itself the notion of cause. Because we use the principle of causality to examine and evaluate observable phenomena does not mean that causality itself is a derivative of sense perception. It is a logically prior supposition necessary for the very discrimination of phenomena. . . . It is not enough to say that things exist in contiguous or customary relationships as Hume supposed. We must deal with the question of the *power* for such customary relationships. Questions may be raised about *which* power is causing being and change, but *that* some power is necessary is logically necessary.[146]

The point that the authors made is that explanations of any sort require us to assume that the universe in which we live operates in a cause and effect manner and we cannot give up the law of causality without giving up our minds. In the final analysis, Hume's attack on causality explodes. It leaves us with no means of knowing anything at all.

---

[145] Douglas Geivett and Gary Habermas have edited an excellent book on the subject of miracles. It is titled, *In Defense of Miracles: A Comprehensive Case for God's Action in History*, (Downers Grove, Illinois: InterVarsity Press, 1997).

[146] Sproul, Gerstner, and Lindsley, op. cit., pg. 83.

In fact, his attack amounts to an attack against logic itself. In the process of attacking Christianity, Hume committed intellectual suicide by eliminating the very bedrock of human thought. If human beings are to know anything, the principles of logical thought cannot be sacrificed. Therefore, the notion that the universe works in a cause and effect fashion must remain true if anything at all is to be known.

The importance of considering the work of Descartes, Locke, and Hume is to gain an understanding of the kind of ideas that were common during their lifetimes. During this era, it became fashionable among men of learning to reject the classic Christian faith and to embrace something else. Most were moved to a religious position known as deism. As a religion, deism recognized the order of the universe and understood the need for a designer. However, it rejected the notion of any further divine activity and opted, instead, for a purely mechanical understanding of nature. In this view, the universe operated according to established natural laws and God never intervened in the process. God was seen as if he were a watchmaker who finished his job and left the watch to function on its own impulse according to the features of its design. In other words, God was seen as being transcendent or above his creation, but not immanent or active in his creation. This was at odds with the traditional Christian position that held that God was both transcendent and immanent.

The difference in perspective about the nature of God led to numerous practical differences in religious views. For example, the Christian religion has always held that people were born into this world as sinners who were in need of redemption. Alternatively, deists held that human beings were a part of the natural order and were basically good. Furthermore, they believed that people could progress and seek perfection through their own efforts in life and required no additional divine aid in the process. In their minds, the problem of human beings living together arose because mystic religions imposed moral rules upon people that they could not live up to. The purpose of those rules was therefore seen as a means by which some people gained power and control over others. Therefore, they reasoned that what was needed was a reshaping of society to rid it of such religious excesses. In the context of this view, prayer was considered to have no value. Instead, those who embraced the deistic position believed that men ought to focus on individual or collective action to secure a better future, rather than depend upon the grace and mercy of God. In the eighteenth century, the proponents of such views were extremely optimistic about the future prospects of such beliefs. They believed that civilization was on the verge of gaining heaven on earth by employing the methods of science to investigate every area of life. As one writer put it:

> The utopian dream of the Enlightenment can be summed up by five words: reason, nature, happiness, progress, and liberty. It was thoroughly secular in its thinking. The humanistic elements which had risen during the Renaissance came to flood tide in the Enlightenment. Here was man starting from himself absolutely. And if the humanistic elements of the Renaissance stand in sharp contrast to the Reformation, the Enlightenment was in total antithesis to it. The two stood for and were based upon absolutely different things in an absolute way, and they produced absolutely different results.[147]

While the hopes of the deists were to be dashed in the course of time, it will be instructive to consider the life of Voltaire (1694-1778) before we consider the demise of rationalism. Voltaire was a man profoundly affected by the ideas of his age. He was born in France in the midst of the development of enlightened thinking and eagerly embraced the materialistic rationalism that was becoming so popular among certain segments of society. In the spirit of his day, Voltaire turned his immense writing talents to further spread the new ideas. He possessed a keen mind and a sharp wit and used these skillfully in the promotion of the enlightenment philosophy. He wrote poetry, drama, essays, and letters that became widely read. In these writings he made full use of his talents to extend the acceptance of the enlightened viewpoint. For his efforts, he was greatly esteemed by the skeptical intelligentsia of the time and remains highly respected by skeptics of our day.

Voltaire was particularly adept at using satire to get his point across. An illustration of this can be found in one of his most popular books, *Candide*. The book is a satirical novel about a young man who had

---

[147] Francis A. Schaeffer, *How Should We Then Live*, (Westchester, Illinois: Crossway Books, 1976), pg. 121.

been raised to believe that all things work out for the best. Voltaire cynically developed a plot that carried this young man through a series of adventures wherein he learned that this was not always the case. The main point Voltaire attempted to make in the novel, was that experience teaches that things do not always work out for good. Voltaire, no doubt, had in mind to poke fun at the apostle Paul who told his Roman audience "that all things work together for good to those who love God, to those who are called according to His purpose."[148] It is, of course, a fact that Paul never said that no ill would ever befall a believer in Christ Jesus. What he actually argued was that no matter what bad circumstances there were in one's life, they would ultimately serve to promote the individual's good if he were numbered among the elect in Christ. Voltaire, in rejecting Christianity, rejected this idea and made this world all that one should live for. For that reason, Christianity became one of his favorite targets, and he often sought to make fun of people of faith.

According to his deistic religion, Voltaire valued tolerance above almost everything else and preached it whenever he could. Like the other skeptics of his day, he thought rationalism would win the day and that it would bring about paradise on earth. Had he lived longer, he would have certainly had these hopes dashed as he would have had to witness the French Revolution first hand. During that dark span of time in France there was precious little tolerance, even though the Enlightenment philosophy was widespread. A thorough discussion of the French Revolution is a story for a later chapter. For now, it is enough to recognize the importance the arts played in extending the ideas of the Enlightenment.

Before continuing to trace the development of modern philosophical thought, one other point should be made. While it is true that the Renaissance movement played an important role in the development of modern science, it is also true that the Christian religion was no less important. By its nature, Christianity acknowledges that this world is the creation of an all knowing and all wise God. As such, one would expect to find underlying principles of order everywhere in the universe and would expect that these principles would point inevitably back to the Creator. This was in fact what many modern scientists

---

[148] Romans 8:28.

believed. Men such as Francis Bacon, Johannes Kepler, Galileo, Sir Isaac Newton, Blaise Pascal, and Michael Faraday were all professed Christians. They operated on the premise that God ordered his world according to a usual pattern and that the pattern could be discerned and explained on the basis of scientific laws. Nevertheless, they recognized that God could always intervene at any point that served his ultimate purpose in creation and so they acknowledged that the universe was an open system. Likewise, they recognized that man's ability to think, plan, and act set him apart from the rest of creation. Therefore, even though man was seen as part of creation in that he, too, was a creature who was subject to many of the same principles of this world, he was also over and beyond creation in that he was made in the image of God. However, the skeptics of the Enlightenment were pushing a new view of man and nature in which the system of nature was assumed to be closed. In this view, everything, including mankind, was seen as part of the natural order and, therefore, human beings were thought of as animals that function according to fixed principles that cannot be altered nor acted upon except in behaviorist ways. This difference in thought has immense importance in practice in many areas of life, as we will see in the pages ahead.[149]

III. Sowing the Seeds of Irrational Thought

The Enlightenment set off an intellectual quest aimed at finding purely natural explanations for everything. At first, enlightened thinkers were unabashedly optimistic that the goal of comprehensive knowledge could be found through unaided human reason. However, as each additional philosopher found flaws in the works of earlier writers, this optimism began to fade. In its place, pessimism developed concerning whether or not knowledge was possible at all. This pessimistic point of view was enhanced by real world events that spoke volumes about the depravity of mankind. Oddly enough, rather than admitting defeat in the presence of a satisfactory Christian alternative, the religious skeptics held firmly to their unbelief, in spite of the increasing pessimism and irrationality it caused. As a result, the nineteenth century was marked by the germination of the seeds of the irrationalism which have grown so

---

[149] Schaeffer, op. cit., has an excellent discussion of this in his book, pp. 130-143.

well in the twentieth century.

In the course of sowing the seeds of irrationalism, the first writer to be considered is Jean Jacques Rousseau (1712-1778). Even though he lived during the Enlightenment, he was not a part of it. Instead, his work actually attacked the proponents of rationalism. As a result, he set the tone for a growing romanticism that flourished during the latter part of the nineteenth century. This romanticism led to the abandonment of reason as the basis of human action in the twentieth century.

Rousseau's first notoriety came in 1750 when he won an essay contest with an article titled, *Discourse on the Arts and Sciences*. In this essay he argued that civilization was the source of human corruption. To arrive at this conclusion, he began with the rationalist's assumption regarding the fundamental goodness of mankind. From this premise he argued that science and the arts operated to promote evil among men. He reached this conclusion by watching closely the cosmopolitan society of Paris. He observed that the sophisticated people of the Enlightenment tended to be pompous, arrogant, and superficial and from this observation he concluded that their condition must have come about because of the advances in the arts and sciences. As a result, he put forth the notion that man is most noble in his most primitive state. For this reason, primal and undefiled nature were for Rousseau among his highest values.

Rousseau's work provided an important twist upon the readily accepted notions of the Enlightenment. While affirming the enlightened view that human beings were basically good, Rousseau turned the tables on the other rationalists of his day by using this idea to argue against the assumed value of progress. Instead, he argued that progress promoted man's ill-being rather than his well-being. In subsequent work, Rousseau expanded upon this theme as it applied to the various aspects of life in a social setting. In this examination, he concluded that the earliest civil code, which was established to secure property rights, served to undermine the equality of people and resulted in the proliferation of evil in the world. In his view, the establishment of property rights, which carried with it conceptions of justice and injustice, served to promote the greatest sorts of ill treatment of some men by others. He assumed that property came into existence only because communities developed laws that established it. By arguing in this fashion, he rejected the natural law understanding that property necessarily existed as a fact of nature. That is, he rejected the notion that since human beings are material creatures in need of material possessions to survive, property is a fact of life, whether or not communities seek to secure the individual's right to it by civil law.

By rejecting this understanding of property, Rousseau turned reason on its head in an attempt to make human emotions and feelings the primary source of knowledge. This set his position apart from both the common rationalistic position and the theistic position. In regard to property, both these groups reached similar conclusions about the rights of individuals. One might conclude that Rousseau advocated a return to the jungle and an every-man-for-himself ethic, but this was not the case. Rousseau never went to that extreme. Instead, he recognized the need to justify the existence of society in the context of his views of autonomous human freedom. Toward this end he developed the concepts of the "social contract" and the "general will." In Rousseau's view, people lived in community with others because they benefitted from such interaction. They were, therefore, willing to give up some of their autonomous freedom in order to gain civil freedom. As they did this, they entered into a social compact with others. Rousseau argued that while this compact was entered into by particular people with particular wills, the result of it was to form a collective whole that possessed a collective will. He called this the general will and gave it the status of being a public person that he often referred to as "the people" or the "State." Having posited the existence of such an entity, Rousseau proceeded to exalt it above the individuals themselves. He made the general will infallible and sovereign in the affairs of the individuals of the community. His position is concluded in the following fashion:

> In order that the social compact may not be an empty formula, it tacitly includes the undertaking, which alone can give force to the rest, that whoever refuses to obey the general will shall be compelled to do so by the whole body. This means nothing less than that he will be forced to be free.[150]

This was perhaps one of the strangest statements imaginable. In his effort to salvage some foundation for law and order in society after

---

[150]Rousseau, *Social Contract.*

arguing for the autonomous freedom of human beings, Rousseau was forced to radically change the common meaning of the words he used. If one were to take the statement as it stands in the common vernacular, it is clearly one of the most absurd statements anyone could ever make. If a person freely does something, then he is not being forced to do it. Moreover, if he is being forced to do it, then he is not free. Rousseau tried to avoid the inherent contradiction of his statement by using the term freedom in a new way. In the final analysis, however, he was left with a hodgepodge of strange propositions that led to conclusions that were irrational. Herein lies the foundation of the twentieth century's quest for utopia by way of state control that will be considered more thoroughly in a later chapter. For now it is enough to say that Rousseau's work marked an important break with rational thinking, and that his work was profoundly influential.

The flight from reason continued with the work of the German philosopher, Immanuel Kant (1724-1804). In 1781, he published a book entitled, *The Critique of Pure Reason*. This book dramatically changed the intellectual landscape. His work was so influential that it remains the backdrop upon which most of today's scholarship is presented. Kant was profoundly affected by the work of David Hume. After carefully considering and embracing the fundamental propositions of Hume's work, Kant sought to extend their implications. In developing these ideas, he "concluded that scientific knowledge, though highly useful, is not knowledge of the 'real' world but a construct of the human mind, drawn from bits of observation. While science thus provides only a restricted means of knowing about material things, it cannot even address itself to questions that go beyond them. On such issues as the existence of God, immortality of the soul, and moral responsibility, science is dumb."[151]

With this conclusion in mind, Kant set out to prove his point by attacking the traditional proofs of the existence of God. In so doing, Kant was attempting to divorce the human intellect from faith in God. "While it has always been realized that humankind could not comprehend God fully. . ., Kant was saying that humans cannot know Him even

---

[151] Thomas Greer, *A Brief History of Western Man*, (New York: Harcourt, Brace & World Inc., 1968), pg. 422.

partially."[152] Following the lines of thought prepared beforehand, Kant pieced together an argument that has been eagerly embraced by the scholarly world. Indeed, it remains the assumed bedrock of the academy.

But are Kant's arguments as compelling as is popularly thought? Or, are the traditional proofs of God's existence as compelling as they ever have been? If the correct answer to the latter question is yes, the acceptance of Kant has more to do with prejudice than persuasion. In fact, the contention made throughout this text is that the acceptance of Kant's position has been largely due to prejudice. Furthermore, this situation has, in turn, resulted in much confusion and in a great deal of irrational thought in the modern age. In reality, the validity of any human thought and the possibility that it provides knowledge, must be secured by some reference point. In other words, knowledge must have an ultimate source. It is inevitably linked to the existence of God who already knows everything there is to know. If this were not the case, then nothing could be known at all and no explanation for life or thought is possible.

Herein lies the essential problem that arises with Kant's work. Can anything be known for certain? If one follows Kant's system consistently, he must conclude that nothing can be known with any certainty. The restrictions that Kant attempted to impose on what might constitute human knowledge, actually serve to undermine the possibility of it altogether. At heart, Kant's argument amounts to an attack on the traditional Christian understanding of human knowledge. Traditional Christianity views human knowledge as analogical in nature. That is, even though human beings are finite creatures they can have real knowledge of the universe. To be sure, human knowledge is never complete, and human beings can and do err. Nevertheless, knowledge is still possible because God has infinite and perfect knowledge. The very essence of God's creating man in his own image secures the prospect that man can understand both nature and God in true but limited ways. Natural theology, which includes the proofs of the existence of God from the facts of this world, serves as the link between God's natural revelation and his divine revelation. Like all human thought, natural theology proceeds on the necessary prerequisites of the law of noncontradiction,

---

[152] Sproul, Gerstner, and Lindsley, op. cit., pg. 30.

the law of causality, and the general reliability of sense perceptions. On this basis, the proofs of God reveal to us certain characteristics about God. But this information alone cannot bring us into God's presence in the sense of providing salvation. It can only leave us with the certainty that God is not pleased with mankind.

The hope of salvation is, thus, left to the Scriptures. They stand alone in providing God's divine revelation of himself and of his plan of redemption. In this way, human knowledge is secure. It is secured in God's comprehensive knowledge. To reiterate, God's comprehensive understanding does not prevent people from making errors in their thinking, for people actually do err on many occasions for many reasons. Chief among these reasons is man's enmity with God. Human beings are prejudiced against God from the start and prefer to go it alone, so to speak, rather than to recognize their complete dependency upon their Creator. This is the fundamental prejudice that keeps people from using their God given faculties correctly. As a matter of course, people would rather suppress what they know must be true, rather than acknowledge the truth and submit to God as he really is.

Notwithstanding, Kant's work seemed to be the final piece needed for science to cut its relationship with theology completely. Theology, which is the study of God as revealed in the Scriptures, had been considered the queen of the sciences throughout the Middle Ages and remained more or less intact into the early modern age. It was taken for granted that a good scientist needed to know the teachings of the Bible as an indispensable aid in giving direction to his studies. The reason for this was clear to people of the time. If God was the author of both creation as well as the Bible, then there simply could not be any inconsistency between a proper understanding of the order of nature and a proper understanding of the teachings of Scripture. They did not believe that men possessed a proper understanding of either, but they did think that the facts properly interpreted were consistent and orderly. Yet, in the spirit of the Enlightenment, skeptics had been attacking this view. Kant's attack was seen as final, and the ready acceptance of his work served as a justification among skeptics to set aside any notion of revelation whatsoever.

But, in rejecting God's revelation, humans were left without a sufficient reference point on which knowledge could be secured. In the battle for the mind, modern man has been set adrift in an ocean of relativism. In the twentieth century, many storm clouds have formed that have tossed the boat of humanity to and fro on an endless sea with no port in sight. Despair over the prospect of ever knowing anything is so great, that some of the most irrational positions imaginable are embraced by people who live their lives in confusion. Among the irrational conclusions adopted, one suggests that individual human beings create their own realities according to their own thoughts. Nothing could be more absurd than this notion of self-creation. No one can live in accordance with such nonsense for long, because the reality of this world prevents it. While it is quite true that human beings possess a tremendous capacity to display creativity and imagination, it is, nevertheless, also true that they cannot in and of themselves alter the natural order that God created and sustains. When someone walks to a street corner, he knows quite well that he cannot create his own reality about the traffic conditions on that street. Everyone realizes that it is impossible to assume the ability to walk in front of moving vehicles without suffering some ill consequences. It is quite certain that the individual lives within the context of a larger order that ought to be studied, discerned, and respected. Nonetheless, having abandoned the sure foundations of knowledge, this is precisely what some profess to believe. Without an ultimate point of reference, human beings are left groping in the dark for anything that might give some legitimacy to their thoughts, no matter how much those thoughts are at odds with the order that is. The decline in rationality is a hallmark trait of the state of affairs at the end of the twentieth century. It is, therefore, worthwhile to trace some of the key movements in human thought as the irrational age has progressed.

While we might examine the work of many writers and philosophers in regard to the rising tide of irrationalism, it will suit our purposes here to focus only on the work of Friedrich Nietzsche (1844-1900). Nietzsche was a German philosopher who was inspired by the growing naturalism of his time and who sought to apply evolutionary concepts to the whole of life. "In a very profound sense Nietzsche can be called the philosopher of evolution; not only has the physical constitution of animals and men evolved, but religion, society, philosophy, and even logic are evolutionary products" according to his point of view.[153] On this

---

[153] Gordon Clark, op. cit., pg. 492.

basis, he tells his reader that all scientific theories are mere fictions imposed by human beings to make sense out of an otherwise incoherent universe. "Nietzsche tells us that the world itself is without order, intelligibility and purpose."[154] If this were true, then there would be no spiritual dimension to human life and no such thing as human souls. Copleston captured the essence of this point:

> When Nietzsche rejects metaphysics, he is thinking primarily of the contention that there is a reality other than this world, he is thinking of the metaphysician as a man who depreciates this world in favour of another and imaginary world, and who tries in this way to comfort and reassure the weak who are unable to accept the world as they find it, or find life too much for them.[155]

In essence, Nietzsche's aim was a complete assault on both traditional religion and traditional philosophy. Interestingly enough, in arguing along these lines, Nietzsche was merely pressing the inherent seeds of naturalism to a logical conclusion. Therein was a major problem that his own philosophy could not overcome. Namely, if all theories are fiction, is Nietzsche's theory fiction too? Or, does his theory tell us something that is ultimately true? Again Copleston's insights are helpful:

> But if this view is itself a fiction, Nietzsche obviously cannot claim to *know* that the world in itself is of this nature, while if he does claim to know it he cannot at the same time reject the correspondence theory of truth. For the statement that the world in itself is without order, intelligibility and purpose would be absolutely true because it corresponds with, or 'pictures', and actual state of affairs. . . . [Furthermore, if that were true,] on Nietzsche's own premises there can be no neutral criterion for deciding

---

[154] Frederick Copleston, *Philosophers and Philosophies*, (London: Search Press, 1976), pg. 121.

[155] Ibid, pg. 118.

between the view of the world which he recommends and any other view.[156]

Put bluntly, Nietzsche's philosophy fails. He began in classic style of other philosophers and questioned the popular assumptions of the philosophies of his day. He pushed the envelope by pressing these philosophies as far as they might be pushed. He had aimed at destroying all the older and more traditional ways of looking at the world in order to introduce newer and bolder ways of seeing things. He had hoped to open a philosophic door that would free people to determine realities for themselves. He called into question the notion of truth, but found that his attempt to do so was futile. Nevertheless, his influence remains as many people today continue to pursue the same kind of nihilism. But as Nash has written:

> Conceptual frameworks function like eyeglasses to bring the world into clearer focus. Naturally, a realistic view of the world–a view that is true to the way the world is–requires the proper conceptual framework. When someone views the world through the lens of an inaccurate worldview, the world may seem to make sense to that person. But the sense that person makes of the world will be wrong in important and potentially dangerous respects.[157]

In reality, naturalism was traveling an inevitable path from rationalism to irrationalism. Simply put, it is not possible to make sense out of the world in naturalistic terms alone. As we have seen from the outset of this book, reason presses us relentlessly toward the acknowledgment of that which is transcendent. In addition, humanity must have some relationship to this because of the very nature of our minds. In this sense, while human beings live in this world naturally, their minds transcend it. Not only this, but since we are limited transcendent creatures in need of explanation, we are driven to the conclusion that God must exist. Naturalism sought to undercut this conclusion; however, it only undercut the value of the human mind and the essence of what it

---

[156] Ibid., pg. 121 and 123.

[157] Ron Nash, *In Defense of Miracles*

326 • *The Essentials of Western Civilization*

means to be human.

Study Questions

1. How did religious skeptics continue to advance their cause in the early modern period? Explain their basic philosophy of life. What are the essential problems with this philosophy? How have these problems been exposed?
2. What is rationalism and how is it at odds with Christianity?
3. Explain the process that ultimately banned God and his revelation from the university. Why is this philosophy ultimately irrational?
4. Explain why empiricism cannot provide an adequate basis for human knowledge. In addition, explain why the knowledge of God is fundamental to all intellectual endeavors.
5. How is the spread of irrationalism contributing to the breakdown of Western civilization?

Chapter 18: The Battle for Human Hearts

I. The Rise of Romanticism

As was discussed in the previous chapter, the Enlightenment produced a growing naturalistic viewpoint that increasingly described the entire cosmos as if it were a machine operating solely on the basis of a set of mathematical principles. This idea was pushed so far that human beings were regarded as just another part of the machine. As this happened, there developed a growing irrationalism. Among the intellectual elite, there were those who began to doubt whether anything could be known at all. This led them to question the usefulness of the mind. Eventually, it led to the denial of the mind's existence. This set the stage for the rise of philosophical irrationalism. As part of the rising level of irrationality, romanticism developed. In the course of time, as rationalism failed to unravel the deep mysteries of existence, romanticists launched a new expedition. They aimed to construct paradise on earth by relying on one's feelings and sentiments as a guide to human action. While the rationalists thought that utopia could be realized by adequately employing one's mind, the romantics opted to use one's emotions.

Indeed, romanticism was a reaction to the inherent weaknesses of rationalism. But, instead of questioning the closed mechanical structure of naturalism, romanticism accepted the rationalist's approach uncritically. In truth, it merely pressed the naturalist assumptions to the inevitable logical conclusions embedded in them. Like rationalism, romanticism failed to account for the fullest expression of what it meant to be human. Furthermore, just like rationalism, it was profoundly antagonistic to Christianity. Judeo-Christian thought has always accounted for both the mind and the emotions. For example, when David was instructing his son, Solomon, prior to his death, he gave him these words of admonition:

> As for you, my son Solomon, know the God of your father, and serve Him with a whole heart and a willing mind; for the Lord searches all hearts, and understands every intent of the thoughts. If you seek Him, He will let you find Him; but if you forsake Him, He will reject you forever.[158]

In this admonition, David captured the essence of Judeo-Christian thought regarding both the mind and the emotions of the person. From David's perspective, both were created by God for the purpose of knowing God and for praising him. Therefore, in Judeo-Christian thought it would simply not be possible to reduce a person to only one aspect of what it means to be human without destroying his humanity. Therefore, according to David, as well as other biblical writers, the romanticist's approach is identified as one with much potential for misuse and one which will lead to certain disastrous consequences that accompany such thoughtless human action. The prophet Jeremiah put the matter this way, "The heart is more deceitful than all else and is desperately sick; who can understand it?"[159] That is, if someone only uses his feelings as a basis for deciding what he should do in this life, he will invariably deceive himself because of his own depravity. From the Judeo-Christian point of view, everyone needs to be informed by God's Word concerning the way that he should live, and this activity requires the person to make good use of his mind. This was the apostle Paul's point when he said, "And do not be conformed to this world, but be transformed by the renewing of your mind, that you may prove what the will of God is, that which is good and acceptable and perfect."[160]

But with the Enlightenment framework in mind, the romantics were not about to heed traditional Western wisdom. Instead, they sought to found a new approach that was free from the limitations of the mind and free from the limitations of the principles of nature as well. In their way of seeing things, while pure rationalism had ended in despair, it was possible to gain utopia by blind optimism. What they advocated was a

---

[158] I Chronicles 28:9

[159] Jeremiah 17:9

[160] Romans 12:2

"leap of faith" of sorts. However, unlike the Christian faith that has as its object Jesus, the faith of the romanticists was a faith in faith alone.

Romanticism not only abandoned the mind, it took a stand strictly against the mind. It was anti-rational. From the perspective of romanticism, the emphasis in life was placed upon the imagination and creativity of the person in an unbounded way. Such human expressions of ingenuity were to be seen as far more important than gaining any knowledge of the world in which we live. In fact, in the later post-modern expressions of this mental framework, the assertion has been made that there is nothing to be known. Moreover, proponents of post-modernity have argued that words have no particular meaning and are simply devices human beings use to implement their creative visions. But, using the same pattern of logical argumentation employed from the beginning of this book, such a position is simply not tenable. To make the assertion that all words are meaningless must mean that the words used to articulate the post-modern position are also meaningless. Therefore, if the theory were true it would be self-refuting.

By focusing on experimentation as the only means for gaining knowledge, naturalism promoted a wholly skeptical outlook on life that tended toward cynicism. Since romanticism was itself the final fruition of this approach, it was pessimistic with respect to the mind. The finality of this kind of thinking was to see life in a fragmented way. If nothing can be known, then knowledge itself is busted into a million dissonant pieces that bear no relationship to each other whatsoever. Likewise, humanity must be seen as being fragmented as well. Therefore, as these ideas have spread, so too has this disoriented way of looking at the world.

Francis Schaeffer captured the nature of the spread of this perspective when he wrote:

> Modern pessimism and modern fragmentation, have spread in three different ways to people of our own culture and to people across the world. *Geographically*, it spread from the European mainland to England, after a time jumping the Atlantic to the United States. *Culturally*, it spread in the various disciplines from philosophy to art, to music, to general culture (the novel, poetry, drama, films), and to

theology. *Socially*, it spread from intellectuals to the educated and then through the mass media to everyone.[161]

In terms of the social spread, we saw in the previous chapter the progressive character of naturalism as it tended to move toward irrationalism among intellectuals. In this regard, the title of Richard Weaver's book is apt, *Ideas Have Consequences*.[162] Eventually, the ideas developed by the philosophers were more and more adopted by the academicians, who, in turn, taught them to their pupils. These educated people then took those ideas and acted on them in the numerous different walks of life. It was in this way that irrationalism spread socially through the world.

As this happened, the irrationalist's perspective began to make its presence known culturally. One of the first pieces of evidence of this can be found in the work of the French impressionists. These painters used the technique of blurring the images of their paintings. Claude Monet's work is a particularly good example of this kind of effort. While the observer could still make out enough detail to identify the object painted, nevertheless the object itself was obscured and its reality was called into question. This departure was not significant enough to cause much concern since even Judeo-Christian thinkers understood the problem of seeing things as they really are. Indeed, the apostle Paul stated that in this world, we would "see in a mirror, dimly."[163] However, the underlying difference was that romanticism openly questioned whether or not there was any reality to finally see. As the irrationalist's ideas became more ingrained, so too did the distortion of the objects in paintings. In fact, art work became increasingly fragmented and twisted. Human images were eventually contorted into all sorts of shapes, sometimes nearly beyond recognition. The work of Picaso is a good illustration of this development.

It was not only the world of art that was affected by irrationalism and romanticism. The effects of such thinking were found in almost every

---

[161] Francis A. Schaeffer, *How Shall We Then Live?: The Rise and Decline of Western Thought and Culture*, (Westchester, IL: Crossway Books, 1976), pg. 182.

[162] Richard M. Weaver, *Ideas Have Consequences*, (Chicago: University of Chicago Press, 1948).

[163] I Corinthians 13:12

walk of life. From architecture to literature, to the methods of science itself, there was no place where the effects of this movement were not felt. In academic subjects, irrationalists twisted the very meaning of words which distorted communication. This was a particularly dangerous endeavor since the settlement of a debate cannot be relied upon simply because the same words are used. If a word can take on any meaning, then it does not mean anything and communication becomes impossible. Without some degree of certainty as to the plain meaning of words, communication tends to be stifled. This was most troublesome because as Paul Johnson told us, "the pursuit of truth in freedom. . . is the essence of civilization."[164]

One way that intellectuals subvert language according to Johnson, is to use it in such a way as "to scare or impress the less educated."[165] However, this kind of practice is essentially dishonest. It's very intention is to deceive the listener to gain the upper hand, either to appear more intelligent or to acquire some advantage. At the heart of it, "the creation of obscurity, if deliberate, is an offence against reason, and therefore against civilization; and if accidental, is a sign of incapacity."[166]

Beyond the mere absurdity of romanticism, it ought to be noted that a fundamental aspect of human nature is that people are valuing creatures. The human capacity to think about and reflect upon this world and about life's circumstances, leads inevitably to values. To put the matter another way, all people hold some things to be more important than others and, for this reason, develop affections for certain people, places, and things. Within the context of traditional Judeo-Christian thought, it is argued that people ought to value God above all else. Following this line of reason, they also ought to value his moral commandments. Likewise, within the context of natural law philosophy, it is argued that people ought to value the natural order of things and to coordinate their own activities to live in harmony with this order. But, within the context of irrationalism, there is no logical room for moral values of any sort. This inherent tension leads inexorably to attempts by

---

[164] Paul Johnson, *Enemies of Society*, pg. 145.

[165] Ibid, pg. 111.

[166] Ibid, pg. 112.

some to assert their own visions of what humanity ought to pursue. The social reform movement of the late nineteenth and twentieth centuries is largely a story of this effort.

II. Social Reform and the Growing Influence of Marxism

The social reform movement began in earnest during the middle of the nineteenth century. That is not to say that it did not exist beforehand. In truth, the French Revolution is best classified as this kind of effort as it was based in the philosophic romanticism of Rousseau. However, it was not until the development of Marxism in the middle of the nineteenth century that these ideas were spread around the world. To understand the social reform movement that has continued up to the present time, it is important to understand Marxism as developed by its originator, Karl Marx.

Karl Marx (1818-1883) was born in what is now Germany. He was the son of middle-class Jewish parents, though his father converted to Christianity in order to further his legal practice. At that time, a law was imposed that prohibited Jews from the bar. Therefore, on the basis of the evidence, his so-called conversion was a pragmatic act performed in response to a new law. This is a relevant point, since Karl would one day reject all religion and call it "the opiate of the masses." It was likely that his disdain for traditional religion was at least in part owed to the circumstances of his father's religious life.

When he was seventeen years of age, Marx began his college studies at the University of Bonn. However, his tenure at that institution was short-lived as he spent little time studying and more time pursuing pleasurable leisure activities. As a result, his father intervened in the situation and moved his young son to Berlin. At the University of Berlin, Marx came under the influence of naturalistic thinking. The work of Ludwig Feuerbach had considerable influence on him. Feuerbach was a naturalistic philosopher who argued in his book, *Essence of Christianity*, that all religions were the fulfillment of human desires for security in an insecure world. In particular, he argued that religion was fundamentally a human invention that enabled the weak willed people of the world to cope with life. This was an idea that Marx embraced and employed as the backdrop for his own work.

Marx had also been impressed by the work of Hegel. Hegel was a German philosopher who correctly saw the problem of irrationality that was inherently associated with naturalism. Since he understood this problem, he aimed to save rationality by founding the usefulness of the mind on the philosophical notion of the dialectic. The dialectic was essentially a description of the process of change in human thought. Hegel put the matter as follows. He asserted that for every thesis that might be proposed, there was also an antithesis. Since these were opposed to each other, the result was a tension in thought. Hegel argued that this tension inevitably led to some middle ground or compromise which he called the synthesis. Beyond the compromise, the process continued as the synthesis became the new thesis which spawned a new antithesis. This, in turn, resulted in a new tension. Thus, the process continued throughout time and knowledge is understood as being the product of evolution.

However, this philosophy does not allow for a thesis and antithesis which cannot be synthesized. For instance, if my thesis is that God exists, the antithesis is that God does not exist. In this case, there is no middle position between these opposites. Either God is, or he is not. God could not possibly be partially existent. Thus, there is an inherent weakness in Hegel's philosophy. Nevertheless, Marx seized upon Hegel's notion of dialectical change and sought to use it to explain the nature of social change.

Marx ended up promoting a theory that is referred to as dialectical materialism. The essential elements behind this phrase include the following ideas. First, the notion that the universe is a closed system made up solely of material stuff that operates in a machine fashion. Second, that social change occurs during the course of human history according to a dialectic pattern. Finally, that change is the result of an ongoing struggle between the various segments of any given society. In adding this last idea, Marx adopted the romanticism of Rousseau to develop a theory of class struggle and human exploitation that pretended to maintain some interest in human dignity even after all the logical reasons for that dignity were denied. The reason why this is so, is because it is simply not possible to provide an adequate explanation of why human beings are individually valuable beginning from a materialistic viewpoint. If people are only cogs in the wheel of some larger machine, then distinctions between right and wrong, between justice and injustice, and between moral and immoral are nonsense. Thus, Marx is best characterized as an irrational, romantic writer promoting social reform by urging people to make an irrational leap of faith. That leap requires the adherent to embrace the value of the collective as supreme over everything else. However, reason alone cannot provide an adequate explanation of why this value is legitimate or real. As already noted, on the basis of logic alone, if naturalism is true, then no value can be sustained rationally. Nevertheless, Marx asked his listener to adopt his collective value.

The cleverness of Karl Marx's work is that he attempted to provide humanity with a new moral imperative founded solely on naturalism. Having rejected Christianity (or any other theistic religion) and the high value it places on the individual person who is made in the image of God, Marx focused instead on the value of the collective. He thought of Jesus and his disciples as being immoral, because they taught that people needed to be reconciled to their Creator on an individual basis. From Marx's point of view this was wrong, because he thought that human beings are merely a product of nature. Therefore, in his view Christianity is exploitative. From his naturalistic perspective, what was important was to plan society beginning and ending with the notion that morality was achieved only by promoting the good of the collective alone. Thus, if a person needed to be sacrificed for the public good, that was merely a small, indeed negligible, price to pay. In this sense, it might be noted that Marx's philosophy is an extremely perverted and twisted sort of religious heresy. In essence, Marx was promoting a new religion of no religion.

On the basis of his analysis of social change, Marx advocated the revolutionary overthrow of existing cultural standards. He argued that private property was merely an institution created by some for the exploitation of others and, therefore, sought to destroy this institution. In addition, he aimed at destroying families to force people into communal living. The goal of his revolutionary proposal was essentially to collectivize human life to speed up the dialectic process. In essence, his thinking effectively destroyed the value of the individual by creating a fictional object which he deemed of higher value than the person. What he ended up with was akin to Rousseau's emphasis on the "general will" by a social contract. The only difference between the two was that the contract was viewed as unilateral from Marx's perspective. Hence, it was a contract that was to be forced upon all people by those using the power of revolution. Thus, the focal point of religious allegiance for Marx was no longer God, but the state.

While there have been a number of outright revolutions that aimed to bring the Marxist's utopia into being, such revolts have not occurred everywhere. But, Marx understood the difficulty of instigating revolt and, thus, provided details of how to bring about the change in the absence of a revolution by way of gradual change. In his *Communist Manifesto*, Marx provided a ten-point plan of action to secure the socialistic changes needed to undercut traditional moral values. These included (1) the abolition of property in land, (2) the imposition of a high and progressive income tax, (3) the elimination of the right of inheritance, (4) the confiscation of property of rebels and emigrants, (5) the creation of a central bank, (6) the establishment state control over transportation and communication, (7) the extension of state regulation over commerce generally, (8) the reduction of human beings to forced state labor, (9) the government direction of capital investments, and (10) the creation of free state schooling. While a revolution might achieve these ends directly, the ten-point plan was offered as a way to bring about the social reformation on a piece-by-piece basis. The aim of each piece was to undermine the human rights of the person in order to force him into submission to the collective. Indeed, being forced into the collective was the important task at hand, and that was to be accomplished either by an outright revolution or by gradual political change. In either case, Marx thought this would inevitably bring about paradise on earth.

III. *The Religion of No Religion: A Leap of Faith Beyond the Facts*

Rather than paradise on earth, Marxist revolutions have resulted in the creation of living hells. Furthermore, as we shall see, even the milder forms of socialism, result in the increase in tyrannical government, the limitation of human freedom, and the hampering of economic growth. The twentieth century is marked by a vast amount of experimentation with socialistic policies. In communist countries where revolutions took place, the ruling elites imposed a strict kind of governmental control that essentially aimed at destroying humanity. In the former Soviet Union it is estimated that between twenty to sixty million people were slaughtered by Stalin in his revolutionary efforts. The widespread killing of people for communist causes was not merely limited to Russia; Stalin's horrors have been played out elsewhere as well. Truly, in communism, the individual person was expendable if it supposedly served to bring about paradise on earth.

Beyond the horrors of communism, there has also been the gradual push toward socialism elsewhere in the world. These efforts, in turn, have created huge economic and political problems for the people who have been forced to live under these new rules. In the next two chapters, these problems will be developed more thoroughly. For now, it is enough to focus on how well Marx's new religion bears up under the facts of reality.

> That Marx's analysis was largely hogwash can now be stated with considerable assurance. Granted, there are enough half- or quarter truths in his historical analysis to give it at least an appearance of plausibility. The same could probably be said for his claims about a bourgeois ideology. But as for his vision for the future following the revolution it was nothing more than hokum. He had no political theory, for in his view the state would whither away. He had nothing more than a truncated economic theory, and that was of no use in the production or distribution of goods. Nor did he give any good reason for supposing that all conflict would end when and if the proletariat should come to power. He denied the reality of the spiritual, thus, leaving nothing to restrain man's base instincts and inclinations. Revolution was to be a universal solvent from which man would emerge purified, so to speak. The history of revolutions provides no substantial grounds for such unabashed faith. Revolutions typically loose the destructive in man which must be brought to heel by some strong man in power. Marxist revolution in practice has been no different; indeed, it has exaggerated the worst features of revolution.[167]

In fact, the experimentation with various socialistic practices in the twentieth century has resulted in widespread misery inflicted on human beings. This would cause us to wonder why proponents of various

---

[167] Clarence Carson, *Basic Economics*, (Wadley, AL: The American Textbook Committee, 1988), pp. 353-354.

Marxist positions continue to support this kind of social change? To answer this question, it might first be useful to consider the following story.

A man woke his wife early one morning to tell her that he was dead. As his wife became conscious enough to comprehend her husband's proclamation, she told him that he might actually die if he did not let her go back to sleep. Undaunted by the threat, the man continued to proclaim his death as his hapless wife attempted to refute all his arguments. Finally, after debating the matter for an hour, the wife phoned the man's physician to see if there was something that he could do. To the wife's relief, the doctor agreed to see her husband.

When the man arrived at the doctor's office, he continued to proclaim his departure from the realm of the living. In an effort to reason with the man the doctor began to show him numerous medical books which dealt with the state of deceased persons. In particular, the doctor pointed out the fact that dead men do not bleed. After showing the man his medical journals, the doctor took him to the morgue and proceeded to prick the toes of several cadavers. In each case he pointed out the absence of flowing blood.

Following the demonstration the doctor asked, "Are you convinced that dead men don't bleed?"

"Yes," the man responded resolutely, at which point the doctor took out a needle and pricked the man's finger.

As the blood began to stream down his finger, the doctor asked the man, "Well, what do you have to say now?"

The man replied astonishingly, "What do you know, dead men bleed after all!"

The significance of this story is to point out an unusual human propensity to abandon sound reason in order to promote what one believes is his own vested interest. This tendency has been manifestly prevalent during the twentieth century which has been marked by socialistic experimentation. Those who support these experiments argue that they are the very foundation for justice. In reality, they are little more than the means by which some benefit themselves at the expense of others.[168] Though human welfare has suffered generally, proponents of the socialistic experiments continually deny cogent economic reasoning and the incontrovertible facts of nature in order to maintain their positions. There are two kinds of proponents of socialism. First, there are those who promote socialism because they have been the predominant beneficiaries of it. Second, there are those who continue to support socialism because it expresses their religious beliefs.

The first group of socialists has had to face up to some hard economic facts lately; the long-run result of socialistic policies has been the destruction of the well-being of the beneficiaries, themselves. This is evidenced by the demise of the former Soviet Union and by the general failure of central economic planning wherever it is tried.[169] In the case of the Soviet Union, though the communist elite benefitted greatly, they did so at the expense of the general population. Eventually, the communist tyranny resulted in the economic collapse of the nation. One would think that this would be sufficient evidence to persuade people that socialism is inherently flawed. Nevertheless, there are still many proponents of socialism today. This can only be accounted for by the significant presence of the second kind of proponents of socialism. Namely, there must be a number of people who support socialism for religious reasons.

To understand the modern political and economic scene, it is important to recognize this fact. There are two competing religious views in Western societies. The Marxist view is the naturalistic one, and it is dominant. The Judeo-Christian view, which is the theistic one, is older and remains, but its influence has been significantly diminished. Interestingly enough, however, the first view leads to the destruction of wealth, while the other creates it. The Marxist view claims to be moral and at the same time abandons all morality; the Christian view teaches its adherents to engage in actual moral human behavior with regard to interpersonal relationships. Given these facts, it seems odd that so many people would abandon the view that provides for their present and future

---

[168] Clarence Carson provides an excellent treatise of this point in his book, *The World in the Grip of an Idea.*

[169] James Gwartney, Randal Holcomb, and Robert Lawson's paper, "Economic Freedom and the Environment for Economic Growth," *Journal of Institutional and Theoretical Economics,* addresses this very point. In that paper, they offer proof that the economic freedom is the primary factor that explains why some economies grow while others do not.

security to chase one that leads to their own destruction. To be sure, these two views are radically opposed to each other. In the modern era, the destructive religious view has made considerable progress in its spread around the world. Why has this occurred?

In the realm of economics, socialism offers a cheap imitation of the moral imperatives of Christianity. The Judeo-Christian tradition focuses the individual's attention on working hard to employ one's talents for God's glory and for the service of others, on planning for one's own future, and on the charitable giving to those in need. Alternatively, Marxist dogma reduces human beings to slavery by forcing them to produce for state purposes. Instead of planning for one's own future, Marxism destroys the plans of the individual and makes the person subservient to state plans. As for charitable giving, Marxism offers the pretense of charity by expropriating property and distributing it according to the state's discretion, rather than by the personal choices of actual individual people. However, this merely sets up a system of governmental favors and privilege, because it strips the individual person of his life, his liberty, and his property.

Even within the gradualist approach of democratic socialism, this is true. These favors and privileges arise in many forms. A few examples of government programs in which this is true are direct monetary transfer programs, in-kind transfer programs, business subsidization, and regulations aimed at providing special privileges or rights. On the revenue raising side of the ledger, socialism is making headway when graduated income taxes, inheritance taxes, estate taxes, gift taxes, tariffs, and special excise taxes are instituted, and where various other fees, penalties, and taxes are imposed based on one's ability to pay. Ultimately, the existence of socialism in society involves the disregard for human life and for property ownership. The tax policies aimed at paying for political favors can best be labeled public theft. To understand why this is the case, it is first useful to examine the nature of theft itself.

Human beings are born into this world with wants. To meet these wants, productive efforts are necessary to fashion the raw materials and partially finished materials at hand into forms useful for satisfying human desires. At any point in time, the sum total of all the resources which can be used in this process is limited, relative to the immensity of human want. This condition, in turn, necessitates choice and economy. The individual can either rely on his own production to provide for the satisfaction of his wants or upon someone else's. If he relies on the production of someone else, he can obtain the good desired by receiving it as a gift, as the result of a voluntary trade, or as a result of theft. In the latter case, the individual's aim is to take the desired property without permission either by force or by deception.[170]

On the surface, stealing would appear to be an extremely efficient means of providing for one's needs. It requires very little effort on the part of the individual to acquire things by stealing them from others. Yet it should be apparent that this fact cannot be used as a justification for the extension of that kind of human action. Such reasoning suffers from the logical fallacy of composition. Certainly, the individual thief gains much with little effort. But, the extent to which the thief forgoes some productive endeavor to engage in stealing as a means of his personal gain, is the extent to which there is that much less produced in the aggregate. That is, if the individual ceases applying his effort towards some production, he no longer has a product to consume directly or to trade with others for what he wants. If more individuals should engage in thievery, then total output falls below what it would have been otherwise. The larger the number of people attempting to live in this fashion, the greater will be the competition among thieves to steal the remaining output. Essentially, an increase in the practice of stealing to provide for one's desires makes the practice itself less effective. If all people choose this path, wants remain entirely unsatisfied because no one is left to produce anything of value.

The only conclusion that can be reached in this regard is that stealing destroys wealth. On this basis alone it should be rejected as a proper mode of behavior for the individual and for the group. Nevertheless, people often attempt to provide some rationalization for engaging in this activity. Theft is most pernicious when it is institutionalized in such a way that government becomes the vehicle through which the violation of property is accomplished. For example, the Romans contended that property was a legal convention rather than an indispensable fact of nature. The same argument is still common today. But, the question remains, does property exist prior to or because of

---

[170] Clarence Carson, *Basic Economics*, American Textbook Committee: Wadley, AL, 1988, pp 63-64.

human laws? The only plausible answer is that property exists as a matter of fact and not because of human laws. As Bastiat pointed out:

> In the full sense of the word, man *is born a proprietor*, because he is born with wants whose satisfaction is necessary to life, and with organs and faculties whose exercise is indispensable to the satisfaction of these wants. Faculties are only an extension of the person; and property is nothing but an extension of the faculties. To separate a man from his faculties is to cause him to die; to separate a man from the product of his faculties is likewise to cause him to die.[171]

In essence, given the fact that human beings are physical creatures in need of property to survive, property is merely a fundamental fact of nature and cannot be created nor destroyed by human laws. Human laws can only transfer property ownership and keep some property from ever coming into existence by depriving people of the means of pursuing a better standard of living. The legal code cannot destroy the reality of property itself.

Bastiat's argument is persuasive, and it is most reasonable to conclude that property rights exist prior to the social contract and legislative law. Good reason also suggests that people ought to respect and protect property rights. However, we find advocates for violating property in every age; they invariably deny sound reason in order to pursue legislation that is in opposition to the nature of property. Furthermore, while they often use lofty rhetoric to justify their actions, below the surface they are motivated by the desire to steal something from others by way of the legal granting of, or the protection of, some special privilege. Human history is filled with attempts to accomplish this very thing.

In the case of Rome, the contention that property was only a legal convention was needed to rationalize the use of slave labor to produce wealth for the ruling class. To admit that property preceded human law would have destroyed the position of privilege. Consequently, the Romans rationalized that the extent of property was merely the result of legislative

---

[171] Frederic Bastiat, "Property and Law", *Selected Essays on Political Economy*, Foundation for Economic Education: Irvington, NY, 1964, p. 99.

discretion in order to ease their consciences as they lived as plunderers of other people.[172]

In modern times, the violation of private property has been promoted by those seeking to redistribute it. These people have advocated the forced reallocation of property in order to obtain an equality of outcomes. This misguided sense of justice denies the very nature of property. Yet, the proponents of redistribution rationalize their position by assuming that the problem of production has been solved, and what is needed is a more equal distribution of resources.[173] Unfortunately, this assumption is wholly unfounded. The problem of production in an industrial society can only be said to have been solved if the matter is viewed from a static position. "That is, it has only been solved for today and a few more days, after which it will emerge once more if something is not done. Schemes to redistribute income, derive such plausibility as they have by abstracting a static picture from the situation as it momentarily exists."[174] Accordingly, all the schemes which have been employed to redistribute wealth fail to accomplish the purpose in mind and end up destroying the general welfare while only temporally benefitting some subset of society.

In both these cases the real problem is that rationalization leads to "legal plunder," the kind of government policy that undermines rather than protects the property rights of the individual. If this kind of rationalization is widely accepted, public theft can continue without troubling the consciences of very many people. The end result of such a situation would be the decline in the morality of the society. People would view it as a legitimate exercise to attempt to live off the produce of others by politically redistributing property.[175] As already pointed out, this decay invariably leads to the decline of civilization.

---

[172] Ibid, p. 101.

[173] See the work of J. R. Commons, John Kenneth Galbraith, John Maynard Keynes, and Thorstein Veblen for some examples of the various positions that such writers have taken.

[174] Clarence Carson, *The Flight From Reality*, The Foundation for Economic Education: Irvington, NY, 1969, p.216-217.

[175] Frederic Bastiat, "Justice and Fraternity", *Selected Essays on Political Economy*, The Foundation for Economic Education: Irvington, NY, 1964, p.134.

The failure of communism is an excellent case study of the problem of public theft and the human tendency to steal. The truth of this proposition was made clear in an article that appeared in *The Moscow Times*.[176] In that essay, written by Steve Liesman and titled, "Playground for the Political Elite", the author gave details of the opulence of a resort built exclusively for communist party officials. It was located at the base of the Zaliski Alatal mountain range. As the writer stated in his opening paragraph, "If you ever had any doubts that the Soviet Communist Party enjoyed luxury and privilege at the expense of the people, a visit to the Alatal Sanatorium will settle the issue once and for all." He went on to describe the magnificent features of the resort which, based on his description, rivaled some of the finest accommodations in the world.

Though the communist experiment promised a new egalitarian society, the reality was that the ruling elite lived lives of self-indulgence by robbing ordinary citizens. Communism collapsed because there was so little left to drain from the average person in society. The collapse was economically driven and can be understood by the analogy of the parasite. Such an organism can thrive successfully off its host so long as its host is alive. However, if the parasite should kill the host, then it too will die unless another suitable host is found. Anyone who visited a communist country in the Soviet block just before or just after the Soviet demise can attest to the impoverished conditions. One can also understand the continuing economic troubles facing the countries emerging from the Soviet rubble. Graft, crime, and corruption continue in countries like Russia today because the communists worked so hard there to destroy the rule of property law and to promote lawlessness among the people. Instead of promoting charity, communism bred hatred and discord. The simple fact is that the rule of property law is not like a light switch that can be turned on with the flick of a finger. It is rooted in a deeper religious and moral tradition that must first be embraced.

The future success or failure of each of the countries emerging from communistic control depends upon whether or not legitimate governmental structures can be implemented to foster the protection of life, liberty, and property since these are necessary to provide the atmosphere in which human beings can truly flourish. Only then can

---

[176] Steve Liesman, "Playground for the Political Elite", *The Moscow Times*, Friday, March 19, 1993, p. 16.

there be hope that trust between voluntary contracting agents will develop. However, for this to take place, real democracy, and not just political democracy, must develop. In a true democracy human action is controlled primarily by self-discipline within the context of a limited government. This form of society requires moral integrity and personal character on the part of the people while the government is constrained to operate within a limited sphere.

Regrettably, when the term democracy is used today, it is used predominantly to refer to a political system of majority rule. If democracy is merely understood as the rule of the majority by a vote of preference, then the system will degrade into a tyranny of the masses. If the people of former communist countries should confuse this type of political system with that which is based on self-evident human rights, then they will find that they have traded one form of tyranny for another since there will be no effective limitation of the possible actions which government might undertake. In this regard, James Madison made the following remark:

> In all cases where a majority are united by a common interest or passion, the rights of the minority are in danger. . . . We have seen the mere distinction of colour made. . . a ground of the most oppressive dominion ever exercised by man over man. . . . Debtors have defrauded their creditors. The landed interest has borne hard on the mercantile interest. The holders of one species of property have thrown a disproportion of taxes on the holders of another species. The lesson we are to draw from the whole is that where a majority are united by a common sentiment, and have an opportunity, the rights of the minor party become insecure.[177]

In the final analysis, should these countries embrace democratic socialism, their efforts will fail and little or no renewal in life will be had because the change in government is superficial. What is needed is true freedom. The prerequisite for this is the development of respect for the property and liberty of people generally. The Marxist vision must be jettisoned, and traditional morality must be embraced. For example, in

---

[177] James Madison, *Notes of the Debates in the Federal Convention of 1787*, Adrienne Koch, intro, Ohio University Press: Athens, Ohio, 1966, pp. 76-77.

the economic realm there needs to be a renewed respect for the property rights of others. In addition, people need to develop a willingness to keep their word so that a growing trust can develop that trading partners will in fact perform according to their contracts. The only help that government should provide in fostering this environment is to penalize anyone willing to lie, cheat, and steal in order to obtain the things that they desire. Disastrously, these are the very kinds of behavior fostered under communism and all socialistic governments. In fact, the ruling communist elite turned lying, cheating, and stealing into an art. Therefore, it will be very difficult for these countries to overcome the past and establish the kind of government necessary to facilitate the economic growth they desire in any widespread way.

Following the initial enthusiasm of gaining political freedom after communism collapsed, the obstacles to progress soon became abundantly clear. Though the opportunities for growth are tremendous, the burden of reaping the benefits remains because of the continued lack of trust in business relationships. This lack of trust stems primarily from a legal system which is largely unsuited for protecting property rights. If these rights were promoted by the law, they would tend to promote honesty among trading partners. However, to renew such personal rights politically will require a fairly widespread affirmation of traditional morality among the people. Herein lies the problem. The communists worked tirelessly for seventy years to destroy that morality.

Moral integrity is a fundamental prerequisite for the development of an orderly society in which human life can flourish. The government's role in this process is limited and negative; it must direct its efforts to punishing those who do wrong. People who lie, cheat, or steal for monetary gain ought to be punished. Likewise, those who murder other people ought to be punished as well as those who infringe upon the liberty of others. Also, the government should enforce contracts that voluntary agents have entered into for the purpose of fostering trust among trading partners. Finally, it should serve as the mediator of last recourse when contractual disputes cannot be resolved in any other way. When governments attempt to venture beyond this limited scope of activity, the results are disastrous, and more will be said of this in the next chapter.

The problem with Marxism is that it is wrong. Its anthropology is wrong, its moral imperative is wrong, its limited political theory is wrong, and its economic theory is wrong. These problems all derive from its naturalistic foundation. As a result, wherever its prescriptions of human action are followed, it invariably gives rise to the promotion of special interests at the expense of people generally. It has been well said that while socialists love humanity, they dislike actual people. All arguments which support socialism are really nothing more than rationalizations, since they all suffer from the logical fallacy of composition. Throughout human history, ruling elites, and now popularly elected government officials, have denied the obvious facts of the situation in order to promote their own agendas and those of favored special interests. The result of this behavior is not only the inevitable destruction of wealth, but the demise of society as well. Regrettably, in the face of the evidence, the proponents of these policies proclaim, "What do you know, dead men bleed after all!"

IV. The Subversion of Christianity

It is strange that nations which were predominately Christian and had embraced the best of the new scientific age should later succumb to the deceit of naturalism. Yet, that is what has happened. During the nineteenth century, naturalism made inroads into the Christian religion itself and sought to destroy it from the inside. That effort has continued up to the present day. Furthermore, the evidence suggests that such efforts have been widely successful.

To understand this process, it should be remembered that naturalism was the child of the Enlightenment of the eighteenth century. It spread rapidly in the nineteenth century. Since naturalism proposes the view that all there is, is nature itself, there is no room outside of nature for a transcendent God. At best the notion of God can only be conceived of within the terms of nature alone. That is, some naturalists think of God as being the mere summation of all that is present in nature. This view essentially strips God of his transcendence. In this view, God is no longer seen as a personal Creator who reigns as the majestic sovereign over the affairs of people. Instead, God is reduced to, at best, a system of mechanical, impersonal forces.

To be sure, a god incapable of thought, cannot choose to act unilaterally on his own terms. Therefore, naturalism found no place to even consider the fact that God would reveal himself to human beings through miraculous events that occurred at specific times and places in history. Within the religious perspective of naturalism, there is simply no room for the supernatural.

For this reason, naturalistic thinkers began to criticize Christianity. They rightly believed that if they could demonstrate scientifically that large segments of Scripture were mere fiction and at odds with sound science, that the Christian faith would be undermined. Therefore, a number of writers set out to do just that. This effort resulted in an exhaustive review of the Bible that aimed to demonstrate that the history provided within it could not be reconciled with other sources of information. In this way, these scholars sought to destroy the religion. Initially, this effort appeared to be particularly successful as these scholars pointed out a number of problems. However, as time has gone by, many of these have been cleared up by subsequent archaeological finds. Nevertheless, the Bible was increasingly held under the microscope of analysis by the religious skeptics who seized upon the slightest apparent discrepancy as a good reason for attacking the Christian faith.

Quite obviously, this situation made it very difficult for Christian thinkers. In the face of such work, there seemed to be only two alternatives. The Christians could either adequately address and refute the work of the critics to maintain the foundations of their faith, or they could accept as valid the criticisms being made and abandon their Christian convictions. Some Christians sought a third option: they accepted the criticisms lodged against the Bible on face value, but attempted to argue that the only important part of the religion was the principles that it taught. In retreating to this position, they asserted that it did not matter that there were problems with Scripture since the important thing was not the Bible, but the principles of life to be gained from it. This strategy, known as liberalism, has proved particularly ineffective against naturalism. Rather, it merely opened the door of the church for the naturalists to come in and spread their faith.

In following this compromised strategy, the liberal theologians surrendered the intellectual battle before it had ever begun. One cannot address the criticisms of others without a thorough examination of the evidence upon which they are lodging their attack. But, this kind of examination takes time and energy. Given the successes of the scientific method in making new discoveries, and given that these discoveries were leading to numerous inventions which were vastly improving the lot of the human race, the liberal theologians doubted the prospect that the

Bible could be adequately defended. As a result, they offered no defense and abandoned that field of battle. Regrettably, so too did a large number of conservative theologians who fell back to a dogmatic assertion that the Bible was valid without endeavoring to make their case. Their refusal to answer the critics with anything more than the mere assertion of its truth was taken by the opponents to mean that no answer could be given. This strategy was merely a refusal by Christians to provide a rational defense of their faith. That is not to say that no one attempted such a defense, but merely that they were relatively few in number. Things may be beginning to change, however. In recent times a number of Christian thinkers have risen to the task of addressing adequately the criticisms that have been leveled against the Bible.

The problem of liberalism is that in abandoning the validity of the Bible, these theologians have abandoned Christianity itself. This was the main point that J. Gresham Machen makes in his book, *Christianity and Liberalism*.[178] In that book, Machen examines the various doctrines of the Christian religion and demonstrates that when one abandons the Scriptures, one abandons the faith. Thus, what the liberal theologians of the time were doing was embracing a new religion; they were embracing the religion of naturalism. If someone accepts the naturalist critique, then clearly he must come up with some new explanation for all the miracles presented in the Bible. The foremost of these miracles is the resurrection of Jesus from the dead. This is no trifling matter. The apostle Paul made this point central to his profession of the Christian faith. In his first letter to the Corinthians he told them, "And if Christ is not risen, your faith is futile."[179] Therefore, one simply cannot say one is a Christian and deny miracles. They are central to the story.

It is true that modern science has made possible an incredible amount of material progress. However, the question remains: has science made it impossible to maintain one's faith in the Christian religion? Or, is the substance of the naturalist's attack against Christianity grossly exaggerated? Throughout this text, the position taken is that the substance of the attack is grossly exaggerated so that there is still good

---

[178] J. Gresham Machen, *Christianity and Liberalism*, (New York: The Macmillan Company, 1934).

[179] I Corinthians 15:17.

reason for the Christian faith. These reasons have been repeatedly pointed out. That is not to say that every possible argument that a skeptic might raise has been adequately addressed here, but merely that there is enough evidence available for us to think that real answers can be found for all such attacks. Nevertheless, the acquiescence of liberally minded church thinkers to naturalism has opened the door in many Western societies for the advancement of "the religion of no religion" which is best known as naturalism. Moreover, this move carried a heavy price culturally.

To end this discussion of the battle for the human heart, it is worthwhile to consider a lengthy quote from Machen's book, since he so succinctly captured the cultural price that has been paid:

> The improvement appears in the physical conditions of life, but in the spiritual realm there is a corresponding loss. The loss is clearest, perhaps, in the realm of art. Despite the mighty revolution which has been produced in the external conditions of life, no great poet is now living to celebrate the change; humanity has suddenly become dumb. . . .
>
> This unprecedented decline in literature and art is only one manifestation of a more far-reaching phenomenon; it is only one instance of that narrowing of the range of personality which has been going on in the modern world. The whole development of modern society has tended mightily toward the limitation of the realm of freedom for the individual man. The tendency is most clearly seen in socialism; a socialistic state would mean the reduction to a minimum of the sphere of individual choice. Labor and recreation, under a socialistic government, would both be prescribed, and individual liberty would be gone. But the same tendency exhibits itself to-day even in those communities where the name of socialism is most abhorred. When once the majority has determined that a certain regime is beneficial, that regime without further hesitation is forced ruthlessly upon the individual man. It never seems to occur to modern legislatures that although "welfare" is good, forced welfare may be bad. In other words, utilitarianism is being carried out to its logical conclusions; in the interests of the physical well-being the great

principles of liberty are being thrown ruthlessly to the winds.

The result is an unparalleled impoverishment of human life. Personality can only be developed in the realm of individual choice. And that realm, in the modern state, is being slowly but steadily contracted. The tendency is making itself felt especially in the sphere of education. The object of education, it is now assumed, is the production of the greatest happiness for the greatest number. But the greatest happiness for the greatest number, it is assumed further, can be defined only by the will of the majority. Idiosyncrasies in education, therefore, it is said, must be avoided, and the choice of schools must be taken away from the individual parent and placed in the hands of the state. The state then exercises its authority through the instruments that are ready to hand, and at once, therefore, the child is placed under the control of psychological experts, themselves without the slightest acquaintance with the higher realms of human life, who proceed to prevent any such acquaintance being gained by those who come under their care. . . .

Place the lives of children in their formative years, despite the convictions of their parents, under the intimate control of experts appointed by the state, force them then to attend schools where the higher aspirations of humanity are crushed out, and where the mind is filled with the materialism of the day, and it is difficult to see how even the remnants of liberty can subsist. Such a tyranny, supported as it is by a perverse technique used as the instrument in destroying human souls, is certainly far more dangerous than the crude tyrannies of the past, which despite their weapons of fire and sword permitted thought at least to be free. . . .

God grant that there may come a reaction, and that the great principles of Anglo-Saxon liberty may be rediscovered before it is too late![180]

---

[180] Machen, op. cit., pp.10-15.

Study Questions

1. What is romanticism and how did religious skepticism contribute to its spreading through Western civilization?
2. Why is romanticism fundamentally anti-rational?
3. How are romantic conceptions expressed in the arts and sciences?
4. How did religious skepticism contribute to the social reform movement?
5. Discuss Karl Marx and his communist ideology.
6. In what ways has his philosophy impacted the political and social institutions of the Western nations?
7. Why are property rights so important to the continuation of Western civilization?
8. In what ways has the Christian church been affected by the social reform movement?

Chapter 19: The Battle for Political Control

I. Introduction

Different conceptions of the world in modern times spilled over into different conceptions of the role of government in society. While the notions of human liberty and equality developed most fully in this time, the meaning of these terms tended to vary depending upon the underlying philosophy one held. On one hand, they meant that people ought to be free to speak their minds and to be protected equally by the law. In this sense, the idea was growing that aristocrats were subject to the same laws as the average person and that it was incumbent upon the government to promote the equal treatment of people under the law. This notion stood in stark contrast to the absolutist mentality that had dominated earlier times. While it emerged as an expression of the Christian concept that all people are created in the image of God, it was also affirmed by those thinkers who remained committed to a natural law perspective of the world.

Alternatively, words such as freedom, liberty, and equality are somewhat illusive and can be taken to mean something else depending upon the overall perspective about the nature of this world and of life in general. From the growing Enlightenment perspective and its increasing irrationality, equality, liberty, and justice came to mean something quite different. In this framework, the idea fermented that political power might be used equally by any who seized it. In addition, proponents of this view believed that liberty and freedom ought to mean the use of political control to achieve the equality of outcomes in life rather than the equality of one's treatment under the law. Such use of these words radically changed the direction of governmental action in society. Moreover, a growing number of secularists began to embrace the notion that it might be possible to develop the perfect form of government in order to secure paradise on earth.

II. A Judeo-Christian View of the Purpose of Government

To understand the ongoing battle for political control, we must first understand the purpose of government. Thus far in the study of civilization, one point that can be made is that some sort of government control was exercised wherever communities of people developed. Even in tribal communities there were means of governing relations among the members of the tribe. Thus, the notion that government is a necessary part of life is rarely questioned today. However, the purpose of government and the means of control have been a matter of much debate. Western civilization has been marked by an increasing regard for the value of the individual person. This has happened because both the Christian religion and the natural law philosophy tended to promote this value.

Natural law theorists supported this value on the basis of logical deduction. From this perspective, the argument begins by recognizing that each person is aware of his own existence in this world. As such, he is also aware of his own ability to think, to plan, and to act. Since this is true, and since he is free to act, he reasons that he is at liberty to do so according to his own nature. However, since he is not alone in this world, he must extend this same logical conclusion to all other persons who are likewise capable of the same mental activity and the same human action. Therefore, the natural law theory concludes that each person possesses fundamental human rights as part of a natural endowment that others ought not violate. Following this line of reasoning, these human rights include the right to one's own life, the right to choose one's own course in this life, and the right to own and possess property.

The right to property arises because human beings are physical creatures in need of material substances for survival; a person needs food, shelter, and clothing. In addition, there are other needs and wants that can only be satisfied by the possession and consumption of material goods. However, these goods do not come into existence apart from productive human efforts. Therefore, it has generally been recognized that each person is responsible for meeting his own needs. To meet one's needs, his property ought not be violated by others because to do so would be to attack his means of living. As the French statesman, Frederic Bastiat, put the matter in the nineteenth century, "life, liberty, and property do not exist because men have made laws. On the contrary, it was the fact that life, liberty, and property existed beforehand that caused men to make laws in the first place."[181]

It turns out that this natural law perspective coincides well with traditional Judeo-Christian thought. God's commandments prohibit murder, stealing, and lying and are consistent with the conclusions of natural law theorists. In practice, these commandments recognize the value of the individual person, his liberty, and his property. Therefore, as Christian thinkers have continued to ponder the practical applications of their theology, many have found themselves in agreement with others who recognized the natural order of things without necessarily acknowledging the validity of Christianity.

The recognition of individual human rights gives rise to the need for government, but what kind of government would be best? To answer this question we must first define what it means to govern. The word means to direct or control the actions and conduct of men. Therefore, in light of fundamental human rights, the best kind of government is self government. In other words, the best government would prevail when each individual manages the day to day affairs of his own life in conjunction with others, so that he does not infringe upon his neighbor in the course of his own activity. Certainly, this would be the best kind of government possible.

Regrettably, this is not the way people actually act towards each other. If history teaches us anything, it is that people are more than a little willing to violate the rights of others if it serves to promote their own interests. While people do not always behave in this manner, and while some people have demonstrated an incredible amount of love and affection toward others, nevertheless the bulk of human history provides substantial evidence that most are quite willing to rationalize the imposition of hardship on others if it serves their interests.

This is not surprising. "As an infant, man is observably self-centered, concerned only with his own desires and gratifications. Only slowly, and often painfully, does the child learn more sociable and thoughtful behavior, and if enlightened self-interest replaces self-centeredness as an adult, considerable progress has been made. In truth, man is subject to strong emotions, to fits of temper, may become violent,

---

[181] Frederic Bastiat, *The Law*, The Foundation for Economic Education: Irvington, NY, 1987, p.6.

aggressive, and destructive. . . . It is these potentialities in the nature of man. . . that make government necessary."[182]

The fact that men do not exercise a perfect form of self government, gives rise to the need for other forms of government if civilization is to exist in this world. The first and most important institution in this regard is the family. Whether we approach the matter from a natural orientation or from a religious one, the family is the first institution in this world whose purpose is to exercise governmental control. All children are born into this world by means of a family. In addition, all children are born with the propensity to pursue their own ends at the expense of others. All good evidence suggests that children have a natural bent to justify their uncivil behavior simply because they are pursuing what they want. Therefore, it is the parents' responsibility to teach children that such behavior is wrong and to instruct them in self discipline. By doing so, parents help their children grow to maturity so that they are better fit to live in community with other people.

> In wisdom, Providence has organized nature in such a way that, like it or not, parents bear the responsibility of training their children. Since human beings are what they are, it is incumbent upon parents to exercise their authority so as to train their children to respect others. When parents actively discipline their children, experience suggests that they will learn empathy for others and will be more prone to consider how their actions affect other people. As a result, people who were raised in homes where thoughtful discipline was applied tend to be able to demonstrate high degrees of self-discipline later in life. On the other hand, parents who shirk their responsibility, and rarely if ever exercise parental control, fail to teach their children respect for other people. In such cases, children are left more or less to raise themselves and often grow up reinforcing the self-centeredness they were born into. Throughout history, parents have ranged from being loving and generally

---

[182] Clarence Carson, *Basic Economics*, (Wadley, AL: American Textbook Committee, 1988), pp.20-21.

responsible, to being disinterested and undependable, to being abusive and capricious.[183]

Since self government is not an automatic human condition at birth, it is not surprising that some parents are better and some are worse in accomplishing the task at hand. If everyone were born into this world perfectly self governed, there would be little need for parents to exercise control over their children, since children would automatically conform themselves to their parents' authority and recognize its legitimacy. Likewise, parents would never abuse their positions of authority over children. But this is not the case. Rather, failures of legitimate submission to authority and abuses of power are common. The many failures on the part of all individuals involved gives rise to the need for other forms of government. In this regard, societies have many other institutions that provide governing structures that tend to guide human behavior. Extended families, churches, schools, and other associations are each important in aiding the work of parents in raising their children and teaching them to respect the lives of others. But these fail to achieve the goal of promoting perfect self government.

Therein lies the main problem of civilization and, thus, the reason why an institutional government is needed. A state government is needed as the final means of protecting the human rights of the people attempting to live in a particular community. When all other means aimed at promoting civilization fail, the government is the agency charged with the task of punishing the worst of the transgressions against human rights in order to secure the order and peace of society. As the apostle Paul said in his letter to the Christians in Rome,

> Let every soul be subject to the governing authorities. For there is no authority except from God, and the authorities that exist are appointed by God. Therefore whoever resists the authority resists the ordinance of God, and those who resist will bring judgment on themselves. For rulers are not a terror to good works, but to evil. Do you want to be unafraid of the authority? Do what is good, and you will

---

[183] Paul Cleveland, "Government: the Good, the Bad, and the Ugly", *The Journal of Private Enterprise*, Fall 1997, vol. 13.1, pp. 84-85.

have praise from the same. For he is God's minister to you
for good. But if you do evil, be afraid; for he does not bear
the sword in vain; for he is God's minister, an avenger to
execute wrath on him who practices evil.[184]

In this passage, Paul recognized the problem of human depravity.
He argued that depravity prevents human beings from relying upon self
government as the sole means of securing order in society. He realized
that such an effort was futile. Therefore, he understood the development
of state government as being God's institution of securing the peace so
that an orderly society could be maintained. According to Paul, the
fundamental purpose of government is to punish wrongdoers to secure
order. Since societal order is primarily achieved when interpersonal
relationships are maintained in good standing, it would tend to indicate
that the primary purpose of government is to punish those wrongdoers
who significantly violate the human rights of others.

III. *The Misuse of Government Power*

One of the fundamental problems of government is that it is
founded and administered by human beings. The reason that this is a
problem is that the people who wield government power are of the same
sort as any other people. That is, they are prone to depravity. Therefore,
the very reason why governments are necessary in the first place, is also
the occasion for their failure in practice. Namely, government power can
be used by state authorities for evil ends rather than virtuous ones.

Throughout human history, there are countless examples of the
abuse of government power. For instance, we can recall the Assyrians
who used their military wherewithal to plunder their neighbors in order
to secure their own means of living. Or, we might point to the Romans
who employed slaves to mine for precious metals which were then used
as their primary means of buying goods and services throughout the
empire they created. In each case we find an example of this fundamental
problem that is inherent to institutional government.

In his classic essay titled, *The Law*, the French statesman, Frederic
Bastiat, argued that the law "is the collective organization of the

---

[184] Romans 13:1-4.

individual right to lawful defense."[185] Bastiat argued, in essence, that since God created people as they are, they naturally have the right to defend themselves from the attacks of others. In short, he affirmed the natural law argument and noted that self defense is a legitimate means of maintaining basic human rights. He then went on to argue that governments, and the legal codes they create, are nothing but the collective right of self protection. As he put the matter:

> The law is the organization of the natural right of lawful defense. It is the substitution of a common force for individual forces. And this common force is to do only what the individual forces have a natural and lawful right to do: to protect persons, liberties, and properties; to maintain the right of each, and to cause *justice* to reign over us all.[186]

After he defined the legitimate purpose of government, Bastiat went on to point out that there is a fatal tendency in the human makeup. He noted that there is always a temptation among people to prosper at someone else's expense because work is necessary in order to satisfy human desires in this life. Furthermore, he pointed out that the most efficient means of plundering the material wherewithal of others is to use government power as the instrument of force to accomplish the task. When government power is used in this way, it is diverted from its legitimate purpose to an illegitimate one. In essence, argued Bastiat, the government can easily be used as a means by which one group victimizes another. As Bastiat wrote:

> Thus it is easy to understand how law, instead of checking injustice, becomes the invincible weapon of injustice. It is easy to understand why the law is used by the legislator to destroy in varying degrees among the rest of the people, their personal independence by slavery, their liberty by oppression, and their property by plunder. This is done for

---

[185] Frederic Bastiat, *The Law*, (Irvington, NY: The Foundation for Economic Education, 1987), pg. 6.

[186] Ibid, pg. 7.

the benefit of the person who makes the law, and in proportion to the power that he holds.[187]

All of this is not to say that government officials behave as badly as they possibly could in regard to practicing injustice. In fact, there have been rulers who made it their aim to render justice by faithfully executing their positions of authority. On the other hand, it is quite safe to say that there has never been a government that has been perfect in this regard and some rulers have practiced outright immorality as they pursued their own selfish ends at the expense of the people they ruled over.

IV. From Rousseau to Marx to Hitler: The Political Catastrophes of Romanticism

A. France

During the modern era, French, Russian, and German history provide ample evidence of the political disasters wrought by romanticism. To begin an examination of the recent histories of these nations we should consider the social reform movement in France. In the latter part of the seventeenth century, absolutism rose to its zenith in France under the rule of Louis XIV. He asserted his presupposed divine right to rule France as God's viceregent. His claim to power was pervasive. Few other rulers beforehand had thought to claim such a lofty position of authority as their divine right. Under his direction, the grand palace of Versailles was built as an expression of his own grandeur. The exorbitant cost of constructing, finishing, and furnishing the palace imposed a heavy toll on the nation. To finance his excesses, the crown imposed an enormous tax burden on the people. This set in motion the seeds for political strife that eventually broke forth into the French Revolution which occurred at the end of the next century.

By the time of the reign of Louis XVI, the financial condition of France had deteriorated so much that the state was virtually bankrupt. In an effort to raises taxes even higher, in 1787 the king called together the various representatives of the populace to gain approval for new impositions. However, times had changed significantly. The ideas of the

---

[187] Ibid., pg. 11.

Enlightenment, coupled with the romanticism of Rousseau, provided the conditions ripe for political strife. In fact, that was what happened. Many of those present thought the occasion was right to gain freedom from the king. In their minds, feudalism and absolutism were no longer tenable and the new forms of rationalistic and romantic thinking provided the framework for contemplating a new kind of French government. As such, they made their demands known.

To hold on to his power, the king responded by using military force against his political enemies. However, that action failed to put down the growing rebellion. On July 14, 1789, an angry crowd of people stormed a military fortress in Paris in search of weapons. The fortress had previously been turned into a prison, and, for this reason, had little by way of weaponry to offer the attackers. Nevertheless, the mob moved violently against the military garrison stationed there and overcame it. The result of this action was that rebellion gained momentum. France still celebrates the occasion each year as a holiday known as Bastille Day which is so-called because of the name of the prison.

Law and order quickly broke down in France as the warring factions positioned themselves against each other. A revolutionary government was put together amid the turmoil and pronounced its Declaration of the Rights of Man and the Citizen. While this document was somewhat analogous to the American Bill of Rights, it differed from it in that it adopted Rousseau's notion of the social contract as its foundation for state action. With its emphasis on the importance of the "general will," the citizen's responsibility to the state was made supreme. Hence, the value of the individual was made subservient to the value of the state. The rally cry of the French Revolution, "liberty, equality, and fraternity," had a much different meaning in France than it would have had in America. To put the matter simply, the French Revolution was largely informed by the socialistic ideals of romanticism.

Maximilien de Robespierre emerged as the leader of the new revolutionary government. He was a devoted follower of Rousseau and ruled France as a virtual dictator from 1792 to 1794. Robespierre had thousands of people executed for the crime of treason in what has been called the Reign of Terror. The new government was so heavy handed that it began its rule by deposing and executing Louis XVI. It spread from Paris to all of France, and thousands of people were executed for so-called crimes against the state. Whenever the authorities believed that such actions were needed to secure control, heads quite literally rolled.

Not only was the government's protection of life compromised, but its protection of liberty and property as well. In the case of liberty, Robespierre launched an assault against the Christian religion. He planned to ban the religion entirely and replace it with a form of deism. In this effort, he went so far as to introduce a new calendar based upon dates that were related back to the revolution. In addition, he sought to eliminate Sunday from the week altogether. Thus, as a result of the French Revolution, religious liberty sank to a new low. Rather than securing religious freedom, the revolution resulted in greater religious oppression. Likewise, the new regime undercut the property rights of private citizens for what government authorities claimed was the "public good." One example of such expropriations of property was associated with the revolutionary government's attack against Christianity. As the new government established and implemented its laws, it took the property of churches for state use and forced the churches to close.

As more and more power was consolidated by the revolutionary authorities, personal security waned. Not even members of the revolutionary party felt safe. In truth, many feared that the slightest misstep on their part would land them on the guillotine. A growing hatred for the revolution grew among the people. In July of 1794, Robespierre and his radical revolutionaries were overthrown. While he intended its use on others, Robespierre himself ended up on the guillotine along with his co-conspirators. But, this action merely left France open for yet another kind of political experimentation.

Napoleon Bonaparte rose to prominence in France between 1795 and 1799. Napoleon was born in 1769 on the island of Corsica. At an early age he was sent to a military academy in France. His small stature and Italian accent made him the subject of a good bit of childish humor which may have played some role in his larger than life aspirations. Whatever the case, he was commissioned into the French army as a second lieutenant and assigned to an artillery unit.

Napoleon was profoundly affected by the Enlightenment. He became a devotee of Voltaire and of other rationalist thinkers. He was also fond of the classics and fancied that he would eventually rule the world. He was, therefore, very much interested in the study of Rome and the rule exercised by Caesar. In addition to all of this, he maintained a considerable degree of admiration for the work of Machiavelli.

When the revolution got under way in France, it caused a stir throughout Europe. The nobilities of other European nations were very much afraid that the French Revolution would spill over into their own countries. Therefore, they banded together for the purpose of restoring monarchial rule in France. This provided Napoleon the opportunity to demonstrate his own military genius on the field of battle. His successes on the battlefield caused his fortunes to rise. After Robespierre's execution, the struggle for control provided Napoleon with an excellent opportunity to make a mark for himself in the minds of the French people. As an excellent military strategist, he entered the conflict on the side of what remained of the existing revolutionary government. This defense of the government proved successful and Napoleon's prominence increased.

Over the course of the next few years he busied himself with other military exploits and waited for an opportunity to seize control of France. That time came in 1799. On November 9th of that year, he overthrew the existing government and declared himself the ruler of France. He quickly moved to consolidate his control. Internally, he dispatched his military forces to restore law and order in a nation that had become essentially lawless. He also moved rapidly to secure a temporary peace with other nations. Thirdly, in what he always thought was his crowning achievement, he supervised the development of a Civil Code that aimed to eliminate a vast number of discrepancies in the laws that governed the nation. In this endeavor, he thought of himself as a modern Justinian. Finally, he made peace with the Roman Catholic Church. While Napoleon himself, was a religious skeptic and a cynic about such matters, he recognized the practical importance of maintaining some kind of positive relationship with the Catholic Church, because of its immense influence on the French people.

In truth, if Napoleon had stopped with these changes, it is likely that he would have been hailed as a great leader for securing the peace of France after a particularly violent and bloody era in the nation's history. However, Napoleon's ambitions did not stop with France alone. He aimed to rule the world and after securing France, he set about the task of conquering the rest of Europe. In this endeavor he had enormous success early on. However, Great Britain maintained its dominance of the seas and this ultimately led to his undoing. That coupled with his own vanity resulted in a number of stinging defeats. Napoleon's reign finally came to an end in June of 1815 when the Duke of Wellington defeated him at Waterloo. This loss marked the end of his political career and he died of stomach cancer six years later.[188] France itself has continued to toy with numerous socialistic policies and operates today as a social democracy. As with all socialism, these policies have prevented the French people from enjoying the material prosperity that might otherwise have been achieved. Nevertheless, Napoleon's changes to the legal code have been generally maintained despite these socialistic tendencies.

B. Russia

As already discussed, Marxism provided the impetus for the spread of a social reformation around the world. In its revolutionary form, perhaps no example of such efforts is better than Russia. Russia was a nation very much behind the times, so to speak. While monarchial rule had been successfully challenged throughout much of Europe, it remained strong in Russia during the nineteenth century. In fact, Russia remained a more or less feudal society.

This reality prevented the nation from enjoying the prosperity that was occurring because of the Industrial Revolution. More will be said of this prosperity in the next chapter, but for now it should be noted that the discoveries of modern science had led to numerous inventions that in turn promoted large economic gains. These gains were most readily secured in areas where people enjoyed a higher degree of personal freedom. Since such freedom was largely held in check under feudalism, Russia lagged far behind other nations in its material fortunes. As a result, Russia became more and more a backwater of sorts.

Nevertheless, in an age of alliances and other political maneuvering, Russia remained important. It allied itself largely with the French and the English in the late nineteenth century and against the Germans and the Austro-Hungarians. This alliance was crucial when World War I erupted in 1914, because it forced the Germans to fight the war on two fronts. However, Germany had previously built up its military strength, and was a formidable foe. The result was that Germany was able to inflict a great deal of suffering and hardship on its enemies. By 1917,

---

[188] An excellent summary of Napoleon is available in John Harrison and Richard Sullivan's book, *A Short History of Western Civilization*, (New York: Alfred A. Knopf, 1960), pp. 481-491.

Russia was struggling to survive against this German onslaught.

Among the intellectuals in Russia at the time, the notions of socialism had made considerable progress. Given the situation, and given the ineffective leadership provided by Czar Nicholas II, the opportunity arose to depose the monarch and to set up a republican government. At that time, a number of the more hard core revolutionaries who had been either imprisoned or exiled from Russia rose to prominence. One of them was Vladimir Lenin. Lenin had been living in exile in Switzerland. The Germans helped him get back to Russia in hopes that he would further destabilize the political situation there, which, in turn, would force Russia to exit the war. That was, in fact, what happened.

Lenin was a hard-core communist, a clever strategist, and an effective organizer. When he returned to Russia in April of 1917, he set about securing his position in the new government and looked for an opportunity to press his own cause. That opportunity arose in November of the same year. It was then that the Bolshevik Revolution took place and Lenin seized control as the nation's communist dictator. He immediately used the power of his position to implement his prized socialistic reforms. To do this, he sought and secured peace with Germany. He then moved to put down a counter-offensive that aimed to reestablish a more moderate government. Finally, he moved to seize control of the economy and to direct it in a centrally-planned fashion. Along with this, he sought to eliminate the existence of the Christian religion by seizing control of church property in much the same way that it had been done during the French Revolution.

Of course, the economy, which was largely agricultural, had been devastated by war. As a result, Lenin's efforts to take control of farming proved disastrous. In truth, since socialism is implemented by way of destroying property rights, it is most effectively implemented when there is something to steal. In situations where little or no property remains, there is nothing to expropriate and use for state purposes. This reality forced Lenin to back off of his socialistic agenda. To secure his control over the nation, he adopted the New Economic Policy (NEP) which allowed people to keep some of their property rights and which allowed for some market transactions. The effect of this policy was that the economy began to turn around as enterprising peasants engaged in productive activities according to the incentives allowed. Nevertheless, Lenin imposed strong regulations over this activity.

When Lenin died in 1924, a struggle ensued over who would reign as dictator in his place. Joseph Stalin emerged as Lenin's heir. He was a particularly ruthless man who used the power of his office in arbitrary and capricious ways. He was also a committed communist. Therefore, he aimed at implementing the purest form of communistic rule in Russia. To do this, he formulated a series of five-year plans. Each of these plans had a list of socialist goals that he aimed to achieve. The first of these plans aimed to wipe out private property almost entirely. In the agricultural area this meant the elimination of private farming that had been allowed by the NEP. Instead of relying on the private efforts of peasant farmers, crops were to be grown on large collectives. In addition to this change, Stalin aimed at promoting numerous large scale capital projects to make Russia an industrial power.

Stalin's heavy handedness was not well received by the peasants; kulaks as they were called. Their lives improved somewhat under Lenin's more lenient policy and they saw no reason to change. However, the reality was that Lenin's policy was essentially an acknowledgment that private property was necessary in order to secure economic progress. From the perspective of any good communist, as Stalin clearly was, this simply could not be allowed to continue. Therefore, he used all the power of the state that he could muster for the purpose of eradicating private property. This included consigning some people to forced labor camps, exiling some to bitterly cold regions of Siberia, and the outright murder of dissidents. His policies were so ruthless that it has been estimated that Stalin is responsible for the deaths of as many as sixty million of his fellow countrymen in his zealous efforts to establish the worker's paradise of communism. If this number is correct, it would be the equivalent of murdering about a quarter of the population of the United States today. In the communist paradise people were expendable if it served to promote the greater cause of Marxism.

It is a fact that communism operates on the premise of political tyranny. In truth, it could not operate otherwise because all people by definition are made servants of the state. Therefore, for communism to be implemented, personal liberty and freedom must be denied. That was exactly what happened in Russia. People were no longer free to associate with each other for private causes nor were they free to speak their minds. Rather, every act that was seen as undercutting the purposes of the state was summarily punished. The motivating factor by which state officials sought to achieve their goals was fear. Namely, the communist used the fear of state power as a means of controlling the nation's citizens. State power was used to overcome any obstacles that were in the way of the state's purpose, even if it meant the annihilation of human beings.

In this form of government an immense amount of power was deposited with those holding political control. The ruling elite used their positions of power strategically to gain the advantage over others. People, being what they are, rose through the ranks of power in the communist party by eliminating their political enemies. Thus, it became virtually impossible for anyone to really trust anyone else. Instead, a perverse system of favoritism developed. Positions of authority were valued, because they might be used for personal gain. If someone needed an authority's approval to act in a particular way, the government official in charge might gain personally by agreeing to grant permission for a fee. Such bribes were common place in Russia. In this way, bribery became the chief means by which people generally sought to get the things that they desired. Moreover, beyond the system of bribery, everyone was fearful of being visited by the secret police who might accuse them at any time of violating the cause of communism.

The reality was that communism was (and is) a corrupt political system that employed tyranny as its means of control. As time went on, Russia became more corrupt as bribery spread. That was not surprising. From the start, the government was run by individuals who acted like mere gangsters. They used power the same way any maffia boss would. Namely, they achieved their ends by threatening the lives and property of others. Yuri Maltsev accurately captured this reality in the following story:

> A young man from a peasant family I knew had heard that market activity was legal, and decided to raise a pig to sell in the market. For six months, this hopeful entrepreneur devoted his time and money to caring for it and feeding it, hoping he would earn twice his money back by selling it. Never was a man so happy as when he took the pig to market one morning. That night I found him drunk and depressed. He was not a drinker, so I asked him what happened. When he arrived at the market, a health inspector immediately chopped off a third of the pig. The inspector said he was looking for worms. Then the police

came and picked the best part of it, and left without even saying thank you. He had to pay bribes to the officials in charge of the market to get a space to sell what was left. And he had to sell the meat at state prices. By the end of the day, he earned barely enough to buy one bottle of vodka, which he had just finished drinking.[189]

The hard reality of communism in particular, and of socialism in general, is that it tends to suck the humanity right out of people. Its aim is to destroy their individual dreams and their individual hopes. Its aim is to take from people all that they possess and make them subservient to someone else. Its hope is to destroy the religious faith of people and, thus, rob them of any spiritual life whatsoever. It treats human beings as if they were merely cogs in a social machine, and as if their only purpose in life is to serve the ends of the political elite. Instead of offering the prospect of worshiping God with one's life and work by employing one's talents to the greatest achievement possible, the socialist prescribes the worship of the state. This has been, and remains, the living hell created by communists and various socialists around the world during the twentieth century.

C. Germany

By the end of the nineteenth century, Germany had become a formidable nation. In an era of intense national pride, perhaps no people were more patriotic to their own country than were the Germans. The German people had built for themselves an impressive military force, and made it known to their adversaries that they would use that force if it were necessary to achieve their ends. It was this willingness to use force that brought about World War I. During that war, the strength of Germany's military was made fully known. In fact, it appeared that the Germans would gain the final victory up until the end of the war. Nevertheless, that was not to be.

Instead, the allied forces won the war and forced Germany to surrender. The terms of peace were forced upon the Germans. Even

---

[189] Yuri Maltsev, *Requiem for Marx*, (Auburn, AL: Ludwig von Mises Institute, 1993), pp. 22-23.

though they saw the agreement as a miscarriage of justice, they had no real choice but to live within the confines of that settlement. Part of the agreement required the Germans to adopt a democratic form of government even though the people had no experience with it. It was this aspect of the Treaty of Versailles that eventually opened the door for the rise of the Nazi party, and for World War II. To be sure, both the German leadership at the time and most of the German populace desired to revenge its loss. However, it was not entirely clear that Hitler would have been successful in rising to power without the democratic structures that were forced in place by the allies at the end of the first world war. The fact that the general sentiment of the Germans inclined in the direction of revenge alone might not have secured Hitler's rise to power. However, when it was coupled with a new democratic government, it almost insured the likelihood of a dictator's success.

Adolph Hitler had a delusional personality. Like Napoleon, Hitler maintained visions of his own glory. Beyond his delusions of grandeur, he was neurotic and developed an intense hatred of Jewish people. In and of themselves, these character traits would not seem to be those that would catapult someone to a position of national prominence. He probably would not have risen to that place, had it not been for his ability to work a crowd. He developed his ability to influence people in the bars. Hitler was a rabble rouser, so to speak. He was able to play upon the passions and emotions of others in order to ferment their anger and to channel it in a particular direction. In the time after the first world war, Hitler found plenty of malcontents in the bars he visited and was able to play upon their sense of loss.

In the 1920s, Hitler organized the National Socialist party, better known as the Nazi party, and began the process of trying to gain political power within the context of the newly formed democratic government. Hitler played upon the German's deep sense of national pride in order to achieve success in this arena. The party grew slowly during the latter part of the twenties. It got a boost when the great depression hit in 1929. Feelings of discontentment rose when this economic downturn hit, and this fact provided new opportunities for Hitler to refocus that frustration.

By a series of successful political maneuvers, Hitler finally gained the chancellorship in Germany. He then quickly moved to secure dictatorial control over the nation. After accomplishing this, he turned his attention to implementing his socialist vision for the German nation.

Like others before him, he aimed at nothing short of world domination, and set out to accomplish that end. He began by abolishing the personal freedoms of speech, of the press, and of assembly. He used the media for the purpose of spreading propaganda. His aim here was to confuse the people and to spread fear among them so that no one would question his policies. Finally, as other social reformers had also done, he eliminated those people he deemed unwanted. He did this by practicing euthanasia on those who were permanently disabled. This practice was quickly extended to the Jews. From the policy's initial implementation to the end of World War II, it is estimated that six million Jewish people perished in German gas chambers and concentration camps. As Hitler began to act upon his global ambitions, Germany instigated a war with much of the rest of the world. Once again, the allied forces gained the final victory.

Because of the horrible experiences of France, Russia, and Germany, one might think that all rational people would abandon socialistic ideals forever. That has not happened. The same socialism that gave rise to Robespierre, Lenin, Stalin, Hitler, and to a host of other social reformers who have likewise caused great harm, has not been abandoned. There are still plenty of socialists who think that the past failures were largely the result of poor leadership on the part of earlier reformers. They do not think that the problem is with socialism itself.

V. The Struggle for Limited Government

Throughout history, political power has been misused. The socialistic perversion of government power is just another form of corruption. Nevertheless, the reality of oppressive government action has also given rise to an ongoing struggle to limit government power so that it operates within its appropriate domain. Nowhere was the struggle more successful than in England. As was already discussed, more than other peoples, the English people fervently struggled to secure their human rights against the arbitrary dictates of kings. From the signing of the Magna Carta in 1215 by King John to the later revolutions, the king's power was increasingly limited by the identification of a higher rule of law. Since England had been profoundly affected by the Reformation, that higher law was more and more seen as that which issued forth from God's commands as given in the Bible.

Samuel Rutherford (1600-1661) wrote a book that was published in 1644 titled, *Lex Rex*, which means that the law is king, as a statement of this position. In that book he argued that all men, including kings, stand under the government of God's law. As such, not even a king should dictate laws that go against God's law. Thus, in writing this book Rutherford identified the Bible as the final authority in a classic example of Reformation thinking.[190]

The ideas of Rutherford and other like minded thinkers had a profound impact upon the thinking of the founders of the United States of America. In truth, American culture was largely English anyway. As one writer stated:

> One of the major elements in the complex of experience and background which the Americans brought to their founding activities was their English heritage. The majority of the colonists were of English lineage, and they were preponderantly British in origin, since the latter designation would include those of Scotch and Irish descent. What the Americans constructed when they got the opportunity were mainly alterations and reshapings of their English heritage.[191]

Since this was the case, the American Revolution cannot be thought of as a revolt against everything that was English. Rather, it was spawned by the notion that the governors of England had failed to rule within the legitimate confines of government. As a result, the Americans believed that they were justified in their refusal to continue to live under English rule and declared their own independence in response. An excellent example of this can be found in John Witherspoon's sermon which he delivered in 1776 in support of the revolt against England. In it he said:

---

[190] See Francis A. Schaeffer, *How Should We Then Live?: The Rise and Decline of Western Thought and Culture*, (Westchester, IL: Crossway Books, 1976), pp. 105-110.

[191] Clarence Carson, *The Rebirth of Liberty*, (Irvington, NY: The Foundation for Economic Education, 1976), pg. 23.

If your cause is just–you may look with confidence to the Lord and entreat him to plead it as his own. You are all my witnesses, that this is the first time of my introducing any political subject into the pulpit. At this season however, it is not only lawful but necessary, and I willingly embrace the opportunity of declaring my opinion without any hesitation, that the cause in which America is now in arms, is the cause of justice, of liberty, and of human nature.[192]

It was, on the basis of this kind of thinking, that Americans fought for and gained their independence from England. In establishing their own order, the founders opted for a written constitution. This was largely due to the overwhelming Protestant thinking that shaped the manner of government that was to be adopted. Since Protestants were so strongly attached to the Bible as the final authority in matters of religion, they also wanted a written document that would establish the limits of the authority of government and would, hence, provide the final word in political matters. "By analogy, the English constitution was like the Roman Catholic Church in relying on tradition; the United States Constitution is Protestant like in being the written word."[193] Either way, both cultures saw good reason to secure the fundamental rights of the individual, and moved to do so by limiting the power of government.

All of this is not to say that all the founders of America were Protestant Christians. That would be a mistake. In truth, the Enlightenment in Europe had affected the thinking of quite a few gentlemen in America as well. Nevertheless, the deistic tendencies among these men tended to be of a natural law variety that coalesced well with that of the Protestants and they were able to agree on the essential elements of a limited government whose charge was to protect the life, liberty, and property of the citizens of the new nation.

During the nineteenth century, both American and English citizens enjoyed the greatest degree of personal liberty that had ever prevailed. There were, of course, plenty of examples of government abuse

---

[192] John Witherspoon, "The Dominion of Providence Over the Passions of Men," *The Patriot's Handbook*, edited by George Grant, (Elkton, Maryland: Highland Books, 1996), pg. 107.

[193] Carson, op. cit., pg. 37.

of power in both countries. There were also examples of government authorities who failed to faithfully carry out the execution of their offices to secure the peace by promoting justice. But, on the whole, both societies enjoyed a large measure of justice, peace, and prosperity.

One of the most glaring miscarriages of justice in the United States was slavery. The French statesman, Frederic Bastiat saw slavery as one of the two primary issues that "endangered the public peace."[194] The reason why he argued this, was that this practice stripped the slaves of their liberty. Moreover, since the legal code was thus used to deny some people of their liberty, it made them victims of the law. As Bastiat pointed out:

> Men naturally rebel against the injustice of which they are victims. Thus, when plunder is organized by law for the profit of those who make the law, all the plundered classes try somehow to enter–by peaceful or revolutionary means–into the making of laws. According to their degree of enlightenment, these plundered classes may propose one of two entirely different purposes when they attempt to attain political power: Either they may wish to stop lawful plunder, or they may wish to share in it.[195]

This was particularly insightful and even prophetic since it was written before the Civil War. While the issue of slavery came to a head with that conflict, the settlement was achieved by compromising a part of the Constitution. Up to this time in America, it had been assumed under the terms of the Constitution that each state had the right of secession. But, to resolve the issue of slavery, while maintaining the union of the states, force was used. This resulted in ceding more power to the federal government than had originally been extended to it. While such action seemed justified in light of the circumstances, in time this allowed for later compromises as federal government power was extended over more and more details of daily life. It was in this way that socialism made its way in the United States.

---

[194] Frederic Bastiat, *The Law*, (Irvington, NY: Foundation for Economic Education, 1998), pg. 15.

[195] Ibid, pg. 7

The Marxist religion, with its high value placed on the collective and its subordination of the individual to the public good, never played well in America. After all, Americans proclaimed the value of individual initiative and of personal freedom. Therefore, for socialism to advance in America, as well as other places where the individual person is prized, something else was needed. Namely, there needed to be some way to overcome the prevailing commitment to the natural rights of the person. Utilitarianism served that purpose.

In the early part of the nineteenth century, Jeremy Bentham, an English philosopher, began promoting a new view of morality. Bentham railed against the existence of a natural law which was the dominant view in England and America. He argued that there were no such things as natural human rights and promoted instead the notion that the morality of one's actions or of public policy rested solely in whether or not such action served to enhance the general level of happiness. At the time, economists were using the word utility to capture the notion that people buy and sell goods in the market on the basis of the usefulness they find in them. Bentham seized this term as a proposed way of measuring happiness. On the basis of this view, he thought that decisions ought to be made by employing a hedonistic calculus. Therefore, he promoted government action that increased the total amount of happiness. In his terms, a public policy was good as long as the amount of happiness in society rose no matter who suffered loss. Likewise, on this basis, if an action reduced the sum total of happiness, then it ought to be rejected. If a person adopted this view, then the protection of private property could be argued as being worthwhile so long as it served to promote the general happiness. To the extent that it did not do so, or it was argued not to do so, then property could be violated from the utilitarian's perspective.

"Bentham did not invent the principle of utility: what he did was to expound and apply it explicitly and universally as the basic principle of both morals and legislation."[196] In this regard, Bentham was merely a social reformer who adopted the naturalistic assumptions that were being promoted during his day. Bentham based his reform on the observation that all people seek pleasure and avoid pain. What was new with

---

[196] Frederick Copleston, A *History of Philosophy*, (London: Burns and Oates Limited, 1966, vol. 8), pg. 4.

Bentham was that he attempted to make this fact the essence of moral action. Thus, he attempted to equate pain with evil and pleasure with good in a moral sense.

Traditional moral philosophies emphatically rejected this idea. Rather, traditional Judeo-Christian thought held that ultimate pleasure was to be had by living a moral life. In this sense, morality was not defined by the immediate pleasure or pain that resulted from a moral act. Therefore, one could not say that a moral life would be free from all hardship and suffering. The opposite was more likely to be true. In fact, traditional morality admonished a person to endure the suffering that might come from living a moral life because it would secure the greatest ultimate reward. From this perspective, the notion that morality and pleasure were linked together as if they were one and the same thing was just plain wrongheaded.

In truth, there are plenty of examples of why this is true. For instance, the wisdom and prudence of traditional moral thought always held that one ought to plan for one's own future by way of saving resources. Therefore, it has been traditionally thought that the fool consumes all he possesses today and gives no thought to what might happen tomorrow. Alternatively, the wise man endures the pain associated with controlling his desires for the good purpose of securing his future. Bentham's moral philosophy turned this wisdom on its head, so to speak. In Bentham's world, prodigality might be justified if one argued that he ought to be able to plunder his neighbors in order to finance his own prodigality because he would experience more happiness by doing so than the pain his neighbors would experience in their loss. Notwithstanding the blatant nonsense of such a statement, Bentham remained committed to his new morality.

Bentham's philosophy suffers from a number of inherent problems. First, and perhaps most destructive of it, is the fact that one would have to be able to accurately measure happiness in order to employ utilitarianism. But how is this possible? Suppose a parent offers an ice cream cone to two children and both immediately respond that they would like to have the treat. Would it be possible for the parent to give the ice cream cone to the child that would be made the happiest to get it? It is sheer folly and nonsense to think that such a matter could be resolved in that way. Both children would make emphatic cases about how much happier they would be to have the treat. There would be no possible resolution to the matter on the basis of utilitarianism. Edmund Opitz comments well on this matter when he says:

> Words like pleasure happiness, or satisfaction are what might be called "container words." They are words needing a content, like the word "assistant." When someone tells you he is an assistant, you are told nothing about his actual job. All you know is that he is not an executive. To make it specific, the job of being an assistant needs some entity to hook up with. Similarly, happiness or pleasure. There is no such entity as pleasure or happiness; these are mental states which may be associated with many different things.[197]

In spite of its inherent problems, the new moral philosophy of utilitarianism spread in England and in the United States. This occurred in conjunction with the growing romanticism of these cultures. It was in this way that the door was opened for the spread of socialistic policies and the subversion of government. As Opitz rightly pointed out, utilitarianism ignores the spiritual dimension of human life. Rather, it simply "asserts that men are bound together in societies solely on the basis of a rational calculation of the private advantage to be gained by social cooperation under the division of labor."[198] However, this results in a very serious problem. Since theft was the first labor saving device, the utilitarian principle will inevitably lead to the collective use of government power for the purpose of redistributing property to achieve the supposedly valid goal of obtaining the "greatest happiness" in society. This in turn will serve to promote the notion that people are justified in their use of political power as a means of taking what they want from others. But, such behavior is really nothing more than a self-serving rationalization for theft. "Utilitarianism, in short, has no logical stopping place short of collectivism."[199] Once again, we find ourselves in the situation where the value of the individual is made subservient to the collective. This was the

---

[197] Edmund A. Opitz, *Religion and Capitalism: Allies, Not Enemies*, (Irvington-on-Hudson, NY: The Foundation for Economic Education, 1992), pg. 128.

[198] Ibid, pg. 131.

[199] Ibid, pg. 132.

essence of Marxism. It is also essential to democratic socialism and utilitarianism. In truth, Bentham's moral philosophy asserted that there was no place for the individual person nor for natural human rights.

Utilitarianism could not have spread widely without some help. It found that help from church liberals who had abandoned the Bible, but desired to maintain something of the Christian religion. Throughout the Scriptures, the reader is admonished to treat other people with charity and mercy. One of the fundamental marks of a believer is that his behavior is supposed to be of this kind. The true believer in Christ is instructed to treat others with charity as a clear testimony that he recognizes the mercy that God has shown to him in Jesus.

This religious emphasis on charity provided the proponents of social reform the opportunity to sell their scheme to churchmen who were becoming increasingly illiterate in regards to biblical instruction. They played upon the individual sympathies and the biblical notions of philanthropy in order to suggest that the government had a larger role to play in extending such mercies. However, as we will see, such government action was void of the essential part of true charity which makes such action virtuous.

To understand this, it must be noted that the government cannot give anything away that it does not take from someone else. All governments are dependent upon some form of taxation as a means for funding its operations. In a representative government, when the legislators move to enact some law, they necessarily intend to enforce that law by way of using taxpayers' money. There is simply no other way to do it. The legislators only pay for the programs they enact to the extent that they themselves are taxpayers. Thus, when they pass a law that provides some benefits for a designated group of people they are in essence transferring the ownership of property from one group to another. The question is, is this charitable?

Frederic Bastiat wrestled with this question and began his discussion of the matter by defining charity. He argued that charity is, *"voluntary sacrifice determined by fraternal feeling."*[200] Following from this definition, Bastiat then pondered whether or not it made any sense for the government to be involved in the enterprise of showing mercy toward

---

[200] Frederic Bastiat, *Selected Essays on Political Economy*, (Irvington, NY: Foundation for Economic Education, 1995), pg. 133.

others. His examination of this matter is worth our consideration.

> If you make of fraternity [or charity] a matter of legal prescription, whose acts are set forth in advance and rendered obligatory by the industrial code, what remains of the definition? Nothing but sacrifice; but involuntary, forced sacrifice, exacted by fear of punishment. And honestly, what is a sacrifice of this nature, imposed upon one man for the profit of another? Is it an example of fraternity? No, it is an act of injustice; one must say the word: it is a form of legal plunder, the worst kind of plunder, since it is systematic, permanent, and unavoidable.[201]

Clearly, Bastiat's argument cuts right to the central issue. It is not possible for a government to secure justice and at the same time be the instrument of mercy in society. To pursue the latter goal, it must violate property, and if it chooses to protect property, then it cannot extend special favors. Nevertheless, the spread of utilitarian ethics, coupled with an increasing willingness to compromise the Constitution to achieve certain practical goals, led to a growing welfare state in the United States. In England, all that was necessary was the spread of utilitarianism since it had no written constitution. In this way, socialism has spread around the world, even in societies that had traditionally embraced human freedom and liberty.

The path taken by societies in the twentieth century reminds one of the children's book, Pinnochio. In that book, the naive wooden boy is enticed to visit a place known as Pleasure Island. On the island, the boys can have anything their hearts desire. They are able to play freely and to indulge their every whim. Unfortunately, their fun on the island comes with a high price. It seems that all boys who come to the island to have fun are eventually turned into donkeys and then sold into slave labor. This is exactly what is happening as result of the spread of the welfare state. More and more, people are being enslaved to the state government which presupposes its right to intervene even in some of the most intimate details of private life.

---

[201] Ibid, pg. 133.

Study Questions

1. In what ways have religious skeptics undermined culture by redefining words?
2. Compare and contrast a Judeo-Christian conception of the purpose of government with that embraced by naturalists.
3. In what ways has government power been misused in the modern era?
4. Why are political catastrophes an inevitable result of embracing the naturalist notion of the purpose of government?
5. What is limited government and why is it so important to the continuation of Western civilization?
6. How has limited government been undermined in the United States and England?

Chapter 20: The Battle for Economic Control

I. The Industrial Revolution

The Industrial Revolution refers to an era during which there was a rapid increase in the mechanized production of products in England. This movement spawned the adaptation of the new methods elsewhere, especially in British colonies. It is loosely dated to the hundred years from 1750 to 1850. Indeed, during this span of time, inventors of various sorts acted upon the new scientific discoveries by inventing new machines to accomplish various tasks in many different production processes. The main results of this movement were the rapid improvement of the economic fortunes of people on average, coupled by a rapid rise in the population of those countries most affected by the new mechanized means of production.

The changes made in textile manufacturing, provide an excellent illustration of industrialization. In 1733, John Kay invented the flying shuttle. This new kind of shuttle doubled the speed of weaving cloth. That is, one person could weave twice as much cloth in the same amount of time using the device. This represented a sharp rise in productivity and meant that people no longer needed to spend as much time in this activity to obtain the same amount of output. In addition to this invention, others followed. These included James Hargreaves' invention of the spinning Jenny which set in motion other improvements in the process of spinning thread for the purpose of making cloth. Likewise, Eli Whitney's invention of the cotton gin greatly improved the process of removing lent and seeds from cotton so that it could then be spun into thread. All these devices served to expand the amount of output that could be had from the same amount of labor. The result was, less labor was needed for the purpose of manufacturing cloth. This freed up resources so that they could be employed in other areas of production. In turn, new inventions elsewhere greatly improved those processes and the result was the rapid rise in the availability of low-priced goods.

Another important feature of the mechanization of production, was the development of the factory system. Many of the machines being invented were large and required a number of people to run them. Therefore, they had to be housed in a central location under one roof. As a result, instead of labor working in their homes to produce items on a piece-by-piece basis as they had previously, the new method required them to come to work at the factory where the capital was housed. This resulted in the migration of people from the countryside to the city and the development of low cost housing in which these people lived. The rising concentration of the poorest segments of society in such close proximity, made the problem of poverty more apparent than it had ever been before. Prior to industrialization, it was possible for those of better fortune to have little or nothing to do with the poorest segments of society. The new means of production changed that situation.

While there were general gains from industrialization, those rewards were not shared evenly. The people who saw how to employ the new technologies most effectively gained far more than the average wage earner. Still, the average wage earner was better off than he was beforehand, but not as much as the entrepreneur who purchased the capital and managed the successful factory. Nonetheless, it was the fact that the gains were uneven that gave plausibility to the argument that was being made by the social reformers of that day that the mechanization of production was exploitative of labor. To add substance to their argument, social reformers also pointed to the new city slums as evidence that the poor wage earner was being exploited for his labor and forced to live a life of poverty for the benefit of the rich capitalist. However, this story does not fit well with all the facts of the matter. For example, rather than return to the countryside, the poor people living in the city slums and working in the factories chose to remain there of their own accord. That is, they chose to endure the conditions of the factories and the slums instead of fleeing back to the countryside from whence they came. Why did they do this?

The social reformers had painted an idyllic picture of what life had been like for these poor people before they moved to the city. They presented the notion that these people lived more or less carefree lives in the country before they were herded, man, woman, and child, into the city. That is, they pictured the lives of these people as if they lived in quaint cottages scattered here and there, with an abundance of food ready at hand, and with an ample amount of leisure time available to romp and play with their children. Given this picture of what they imagined life had been like, they then began to describe the relatively horrid conditions of the factory which was open for anyone to view. To be sure, those conditions were harsh. The reformers went on to argue that these people were being treated as if they were slaves.[202] In fact, Marx seized upon these images as the basis for his theory of a class struggle, a struggle between the bourgeoisie capital owners and the proletariat workers that he argued would bring down the free market.

But as F. A. Hayek has pointed out:

> The actual history of the connection between capitalism and the rise of the proletariat is almost the opposite of that which these theories of the expropriation of the masses suggest. The truth is that, for the greater part of history, for most men the possession of the tools for their work was an essential condition for the survival or at least for being able to rear a family. . . . The amount of arable land and of tools handed down from one generation to the next limited the total number who could survive. To be left without them meant in most instances death by starvation or at least the impossibility of procreation.[203]

Therefore, the reality of the situation was that people who might have perished otherwise, lived. "It is a distortion of the facts to say that the factories carried off the housewives from the nurseries and the kitchens and the children from their play. These women had nothing to cook with and to feed their children. These children were destitute and starving. Their only refuge was the factory. It saved them, in the strict sense of the term, from death by starvation."[204] Not only did they live, but

---

[202] For an excellent series of articles on this subject, see Burton Folsom, editor, *The Industrial Revolution and Free Trade*, (Irvington, NY: Foundation for Economic Education, 1996).

[203] F. A. Hayek, "Economic Myths of Early Capitalism,"*Industrial Revolution and Free Trade*, edited by Burton Folsom, (Irvington, NY: Foundation for Economic Education, 1996), pg. 68.

[204] Ludwig von Mises, *Human Action*, (New Haven, CT: Yale University Press, 1949), pg. 615.

for the first time they were able to afford to raise their own families. Beforehand, it would have simply been impossible for them to do so. Their lives in the countryside had been those of even greater hardship than those that they now endured in the city. However, there was one marked difference. In the city, there was the hope of a better future, if not for oneself, maybe for one's heirs. This was why the population of England rose so rapidly during the Industrial Revolution.

That is not to say that there were no problems that occurred during this span of time. One social problem that was prominent was that children from government-sponsored orphanages were forced to work in the factories. In this case, local government officials would round up pauper children and place them under the control of the state. State authorities would then enter into contracts with private factory owners and agree to provide them the child labor they needed to operate their plants. In this way some children were reduced to slave labor. But this was done by the government and its officials in a way that cannot be condoned based upon the assumptions of a free market. Nevertheless, reformers used this situation as evidence of the need to abandon free trade and to institute greater regulatory control.

In addition to this, it should also be noted that people from time immemorial have sought to gain their advantage in life by political rather than economic means. That was just as true in England during this span of time as it has been anywhere else. Indeed, there were numerous special privileges and favors that were granted to some people by governing authorities. However, as we saw in the previous chapter, in England and America, the rule of law had made considerable progress. As a result, the amount of such favoritism was less in these nations than it was in the rest of the world. In fact, it was this reality that allowed for the Industrial Revolution to take place. In turn, the economic gains made provided the evidence needed for academicians interested in this area of study to advocate a more thoroughgoing free enterprise.

II. The Meaning of Free Trade

While he was certainly not alone, Adam Smith (1723-1790) is perhaps the person best known for supporting the elimination of government privilege. Smith was born in Scotland. He demonstrated his intellectual abilities at an early age and, on this basis, was able to obtain an excellent education. In fact, he was a book worm of sorts and enjoyed his studies throughout his life. After completing his own formal education, he pursued a teaching career. "At the University of Glasgow and later at Oxford, Smith lectured on natural theology, ethics, jurisprudence, and political economy."[205] His early reputation was made in the field of moral philosophy. In fact, his initial fame was developed after he published a book titled, *The Theory of Moral Sentiments*. In that book, Smith aimed at developing a natural argument that would explain the origin of morality. In that regard, he argued that people will adopt a pattern of moral behavior to the extent they sympathize with the plight of others. This was certainly a work that was in keeping with his times.

In actuality, Smith turned to the issue of economics as an area where his original notions of morality might be expanded. There was at that time a very real interest in the extension of personal liberty, and Smith aimed to analyze whether or not that liberty might promote or hinder the material prosperity of a nation. In his most famous book, *Inquiry into the Nature and Causes of the Wealth of Nations*, published in 1776, Smith came to the conclusion that economic freedom was the single most important factor that explained why one nation was rich while another one was poor. As Smith saw the matter, all people were naturally driven to pursue their own material interests in this world. And, if they were merely kept from violating the property rights of others, then they would invariably serve the interests of others even as they pursued their own ends. That is, if a person's sole aim in this life was to amass for himself wealth, and if the government vigorously protected the property rights of all people, then the person's best means of achieving his goal was to produce something that was beneficial to other people.

Smith stated his premise this way:

> It is not from the benevolence of the butcher, the brewer, or the baker that we expect our dinner, but from their regard to their own self-interest. We address ourselves, not

---

[205] Robert B. Ekelund, and Robert F. Hebert, *A History of Economic Theory and Method*, (New York: McGraw-Hill Book Company, 1975), pg. 58.

to their humanity, but to their self-love, and never talk to
them of our necessities, but of their advantages.[206]

The argument that Smith was making in this passage, was that the
butcher was engaged in his enterprise fundamentally for the purpose of
gaining a living for himself and his family. He was not primarily concerned
with whether or not his customers were well fed. However, if he was
actually going to be able to accomplish his own self-interest, then in fact
his customers would be well fed.

This is an important insight and ought not be ignored or scorned.
Smith knew that people acting out of pure self-interest alone would not
make for a good society. He well understood that a good society was one
in which people embraced virtuous living and one in which people valued
other people. But Smith was also very realistic. He knew that human
beings have the propensity to ignore others in their decisions to act.
Therefore, taking people just as they were, he began to examine the
conditions that would be necessary for the general well-being to be
promoted even when the people making up the community acted in
thoughtless ways. What he discovered was that people would tend to
promote the interests of others as long as they pursued their own interests
by way of voluntary trade. To be sure, it would be much better if people
voluntarily pursued the interests of others in combination with their own.
But, before we could ever hope for that, the protection of property rights
must be the first line of defense against those who would pursue their self-
interest at the expense of others. This was the significant point that Smith
was making.

Smith's work provides a guidepost for government policy in the
economic realm. Namely, the primary function of government is to
protect the fundamental property rights of all the participants. If it
pursues this objective, then it will tend to secure the conditions in which
wealth can flourish. This was a marked departure from the mercantilistic
economic policies of his day. To be sure, the mandate to protect property
is easier said than done. For example, in modern times the issue of air and
water pollution has arisen because the property rights of air and water are
difficult to define. Therefore, a struggle between competing factions has
ensued. Nevertheless, Smith's directive gives us a guideline on how to

---

[206] Adam Smith, *The Wealth of Nations.*

resolve even these kinds of difficult issues in life. That guideline admonishes us to seek a solution to these problems by way of extending the rule of property law.

This brings us to the point where we ought to define what is exactly meant by the phrase free trade or free enterprise. There is a great deal of rhetoric today that tends to obscure our understanding of the subject and which leads to needless arguments. Therefore, we need to have a clear and concise idea about what free enterprise is.

> Free enterprise entails the freedom of persons to use their minds, faculties, and materials to produce and dispose as they will or choose, subject only to such obligations, responsibilities, duties, and restraints as they may have contracted or as inhere in their undertaking. A man who has married, for example, has contracted an obligation to provide for his wife according to his means. As a corollary of that, he is responsible to help look after and provide for children born from this relationship. His duties may extend to aged or infirm parents, to the repayment of his debts in a timely fashion, and to support the government which protects him in the enjoyment of life and property. The most obvious restraint is that he may not use his faculties and property so as to do demonstrable injury to others. . . . Nor does it entail the use of fraud, deceit, or damage to the reputations of others. All this is a way of saying that freedom is always counterbalanced by responsibility. . . . Free enterprise is the logic of private property.[207]

It is important to keep this definition in mind because social reformers are want to pin some of the most fundamental abuses of power on free trade. To do this, however, they must misrepresent the fundamental nature of what it is. The very basis of the free market is to insure that people are protected in their essential human rights. Free trade does not mean that there is no rule of law. Just the opposite is true. There is a rule of law, but its scope is limited. If the policy of free trade is supported, then the government is limited. In this case, the government

---

[207] Clarence Carson, *Basic Economics*, (Wadley, AL: American Textbook Committee, 1988), pg. 294.

is not at liberty to extend special privileges to some citizens at the expense of others since this would violate basic human rights. Alternatively, it is to vigorously and equally punish everyone who would violate the basic human rights of life, liberty, and property. That is, free trade assumes that everyone is treated equally under the law. In this way, government's role is to protect the property of its citizens no matter how little or how much of it the individual citizen actually owns.

The happy consequence of the government's general protection of human rights is that the economy tends to grow in such a way that the average standard of living rises. In other words, when people trade freely amongst themselves, unrestricted by government bureaucrats, wealth tends to be created. Not only this, but it is also the case that the ordinary person can rise to a position of prominence in society simply by serving the wants and needs of others better than his competitors. In this sense, free trade undercuts the class system of government privilege that has been evident throughout human history. Anyone with the right kind of foresight and motivation can achieve material success in a free market economy.

The rise in the general well-being of people comes about in this process of trade because those people who desire to improve their own financial positions, do so by focusing their efforts on the efficient production of products that are widely demanded by willing and able customers. The reason that this is true, is that a private business enterprise can make far more money for itself by selling a larger number of units of its product if it stands to clear some given margin on each unit. Or to put the matter simply, if a business makes one dollar in profit for each unit of output it produces and sells in the market, it will make more money selling ten million units than it would make selling ten thousand units. Therefore, wise business decision makers always seek to produce and sell products that have wide appeal. Moreover, in a world of voluntary choice, businesses are always encouraged when they find a large number of willing and able customers.

In this way, free trade has resulted in the proliferation of goods and services that have literally transformed the way of life for those fortunate enough to have lived and worked in that context. In an environment of freedom, the entrepreneurial spirit present in all human beings is released so that people seeking to better themselves have developed new products and new techniques for making products in order to gain an advantage in the market and to attract customers. In the United States of America, which has been more or less committed to a system of free trade, the average person enjoys certain amenities that provide a standard of living even higher than what would be considered rich in countries where strict class boundaries are maintained by the legal code. The widespread availability of refrigerators, automobiles, air conditioners, and a host of other conveniences in countries marked by a relative commitment to free trade provide the evidence of this fact.

All of this is not to say that the existence of a free market eliminates all social problems and all human suffering. Certainly, that is not true. As Edmund Opitz has rightly surmised about free trade:

> The market is not an omnicompetent contrivance; it is not a kind of magic mill through which all sorts of problems may be run for instant solutions, or all sorts of questions for perfect answers. It is not a superhuman thing at all. The inherent frailties and shortcomings of the market follow from a definition of it: The market consists of people in free, voluntary exchange of goods, services, and ideas. It is nothing but that and people are fallible. People are fallible, not only when they have shaken off the delusion that coercion is a fruitful source of social good, but always. They are fallible when they are neither being coerced nor coercing; even when they are acting peacefully, with the best will in the world, and on the fullest information available, they fall into error. It follows, therefore, that the market will exhibit every shortcoming men exhibit in their thinking and peaceful acting, for–in the broadest sense–it is nothing else but that.[208]

For this reason, social problems and human suffering will remain. For instance, the market alone will not be the sufficient condition necessary to insure that each participant adequately plans his own material future. To be sure, human depravity being what it is, there will be no shortage of spendthrifts and prodigals who foolishly pay no heed of tomorrow. They will be present in society. However, what the market

---

[208] Edmund Opitz, *Religion and Capitalism: Allies, Not Enemies*, (Irvington, NY: Foundation for Economic Education, 1992), pp. 79-80.

does tend to insure is that the negative consequences of depravity fall most heavily upon those who engage in it. Put simply, prodigals will suffer the primary consequences of their own folly when the material needs of the future arrive. Therefore, because of the foolishness present in all human beings, there will remain numerous social and human problems in this world. Within free enterprise, these conditions give rise to opportunities for charitable ministries.

Notwithstanding the fact that social ills will continue to plaque human civilization in the free market, the reality that the foolish person suffers most from his own actions does tend to motivate people, generally speaking, toward self restraint. That is, the individual's commitment to self preservation is typically ample motivation to learn from one's mistakes in order to secure one's own material well-being. In the case of prodigality, the fool that suffers hardship because of his own poor planning is likely to remember that hardship when his fortunes change. In this way, he is likely to begin the process of saving for his own future. And, if not the prodigal himself, then certainly anyone familiar with the hardships of the prodigal will have sufficient evidence that it is wise to make material provisions for the whole of one's life. In this way, the free market gives rise to the accumulation of capital which provides the wherewithal for economic advancement.

III. The Socialist Mentality

Given the abundant evidence of the material success of free enterprise and the subsequent improvements that were made for the general lot of mankind, one would think that everyone would eagerly embrace that kind of economic system. However, that is not what has happened in the modern era. Rather than developing a deep commitment to the underlying tenets of the free market, there has developed a widespread commitment to socialism. The oddity of this turn of events needs some explanation.

To understand why this has happened, we ought to consider the very nature of socialism itself. The central idea behind socialism, is the notion that economic success might be had more readily if human action were organized according to some central plan. In these terms, proponents of socialism argue that the problem of the free market is that it is unplanned and, therefore, people are acting in discordant ways.

Socialists argue that, economic prosperity could be better achieved if the economy were planned from the top down. To achieve that end, central planners argue that control over property must ultimately fall to the government. This could be achieved either by way of the government's outright ownership of property or by way of its regulatory control over property.

The development of the socialist thinking coincided with the Enlightenment. The first socialists were French utopian thinkers who vainly imagined paradise on earth. Their socialism fit well with the spreading philosophy of naturalism that aimed to understand the universe in purely mechanical terms. When that understanding included all phenomena including mankind, it seemed to make abundant sense that the economic order ought to be orchestrated according to some kind of overarching central plan. Therefore, socialism was the economic system that tended to be embraced by naturalists.

Therein is the fundamental problem of socialistic thinking. Namely, it fails to take account of human nature as it really is because it rests on naturalistic thinking. Human beings are thinking, planning, and acting creatures. All people possess the ability to reflect upon their situation and to devise plans that they think will move them from the situation they are in, to a more desirable one. And, given the fact that people are made in the image of God, they also possess creative abilities. Human ingenuity, coupled with the capacity to gain a better understanding of the natural order, serves as the basis upon which people can achieve greater levels of material prosperity in this world. Socialism ignores this fact. It discounts the validity of human action.

It is certainly true that all human plans are not created equal. Some people make better plans than others. Some plans are moral and some are immoral. Some plans are well-conceived and some are ill-conceived. And, some plans will succeed when implemented while others will fail. However, it is not necessarily the case that we can distinguish between good and bad plans before they are implemented. To be sure, apart from some difficult ethical issue, it would be possible to embrace or reject a plan on its moral basis. But apart from the issue of morality, it is often extremely difficult to know what new plan might succeed. Throughout history, inventors and entrepreneurs have typically been ridiculed by others when they went a different way. However, if and when they were successful, the rest of society quickly adopted the new way of doing things they developed because it resulted in material progress. This was the beauty of the Industrial Revolution.

Socialist thinkers, on the basis of their naturalistic assumption alone, deny the essential importance of human action as the main ingredient which explains economic change. Having given up on the mass of humanity, they presume that the best innovations are to be had by relying on a central planning authority. Having rejected the notion that individuals might have their own legitimate insights, they think that state planners are best situated to determine which economic course of action ought to be taken. By so reducing the value of the individual person, they disregard the creative nature of people generally. As a result, they also disregard the importance of the underlying incentives that arise when socialistic policies are pursued.

In the case of free enterprise, the inventor or entrepreneur aims at discovering and taking advantage of a new opportunity because of his own values. He has some underlying incentive to do so. That incentive may be reduced to a simple desire to show the world that his perspective about reality is correct, or it may be the desire to reap some economic advantage, or it may even be the desire to serve the rest of humanity. Whatever the underlying desire might be, the reality is that it is the entrepreneur himself who takes the risk of failure. If others find the results of his work valuable, the entrepreneur's economic fortunes increase. If not, then his efforts will be deemed a failure. In this way, the free market accounts for human valuation and the underlying incentives that motivate people to act.

Alternatively, socialists ignore the values of the bulk of the people that make up society, or at least assume that only the values of the central planning authority matter. That is, they presuppose that central planners can accurately discern the best plans before they have ever been proven successes or failures in the minds of the people that make up the community. In other words, central planners inherently presume that they are the best economic planners. They presuppose that their own values are better than anyone else's.

F. A. Hayek referred to this mentality as, *The Fatal Conceit*.[209] In essence, it is as if the socialist were proclaiming himself to be omniscient.

---

[209] F. A. Hayek, *The Fatal Conceit*

But the reality is, no mere human being possesses this kind of knowledge, nor can any single person or planning authority successfully force everyone else to live in accordance with some central plan. Such an effort is utter folly. It is the natural instinct of human beings to secure their own plans. Socialism is merely the attempt by some to force their plans upon the rest of humanity. It invariably collapses because people will naturally undercut the central plan. Within the context of socialism, this process will take place by way of a growing level of immorality as each person attempts to make himself better off by way of political action rather than by economic means. This results in economic stagnation and an increasing level of hardship instead of the promotion of economic progress.

As an illustration of this fact, the policies of Mikhail Gorbachev provide excellent examples. Yuri Maltsev recounted a number of those policies in the book he edited titled, *Requiem for Marx*.[210] One of those he mentioned is well worth our consideration. Gorbachev rose to the top ruling position in the former Soviet Union because he was a good socialist. That is, because he believed in socialism. As he saw it, the economic problems that were present in Russia during his tenure in power were largely the result of a population that was made up of too many drunkards. Therefore, in Gorbachev's mind, what was needed was a central policy aimed at severely cutting the production and availability of alcoholic beverages. But, the policy did not produce the desired effect. As Maltsev related:

> The Party bosses did not anticipate what happened next: sugar, flour, aftershave, and window cleaner immediately disappeared from the shelves. Using these products, the production of moonshine increased by about 300 percent in one year.
>
> The predictable result was a heavy loss of life. From 13,000 to 25,000 people died from drinking poisoned surrogate alcohol.[211]

---

[210] Yuri Maltsev, editor, *Requiem for Marx*, (Auburn, AL: Ludwig von Mises Institute, 1993), pp. 14-28.

[211] Ibid., pg 17.

Clearly, the centrally planned cure was worse than the disease. No matter what one might think about the wisdom of consuming alcoholic beverages, the reality is there has always been a healthy demand for those products. As such, it is simply not possible for government officials to ban the production of such products without producing some unintended consequences. As Bastiat admonished the reformers of the world, "Ah, you miserable creatures! You who think that you are so great! You who judge humanity to be so small! You wish to reform everything! Why don't you reform yourselves? That task would be sufficient enough."[212]

The underlying problem at hand is, how can individuals coordinate their actions in order to promote economic prosperity? The answer is, by letting people freely implement their own plans. The wise person will quickly abandon an activity that no one else finds valuable. No one will engage in the economic activity of producing a good which other people do not find sufficiently useful. That is, no one will continue to produce a product that he continually loses money on. People will only engage in economic activities in which a profit can be made. In this way, prices serve as the signals to decision makers about the wisdom of their plans and about how well those plans fit with those of other people. In this way, the free market is self-coordinating and the task of planning can and ought to be left up to each individual person. Moreover, economic success and failure provide an immediate assessment on the value others place upon one's actions. That is not to say that people naturally value the best things in all circumstances, but merely to say that in the realm of material interchange, coordination of effort is best had in a free market.

This fact gives rise to another reason why some people support socialism. Namely, socialism is also attractive to those who do not fare well in the free market. As Ludwig von Mises has aptly said:

> What makes many feel unhappy under capitalism is the fact that capitalism grants to each the opportunity to attain the most desirable positions which, of course, can only be attained by a few. Whatever a man may have gained for himself, it is mostly a mere fraction of what his ambition has impelled him to win. There are always before his eyes

---

[212] Frederic Bastiat, *The Law*, (Irvington, NY: Foundation for Economic Education, 1987), pg. 55.

people who have succeeded where he failed. There are fellows who have outstripped him and against whom he nurtures, in his subconsciousness, inferiority complexes. Such is the attitude of the tramp against the man with a regular job, the factory hand against the foreman, the executive against the vice-president, the vice-president against the company's president, the man who is worth three hundred thousand dollars against the millionaire and so on. Everybody's self-reliance and moral equilibrium are undermined by the spectacle of those who have given proof of greater abilities and capacities. Everybody is aware of his own defeat and insufficiency.[213]

Therefore, envy, jealousy, and greed, which are passions embedded in human hearts, naturally incline people to socialism. Rather than to enjoy the material blessings of a free market economy, people generally tend to support socialism because free enterprise inevitably exposes one's own inadequacies. Thus, in a perverse sort of way, the socialist idea is adopted because it helps its proponents save face even though it comes at the price of a lower general standard of living. That is, the socialist mentality is that greater relative poverty is a small price to pay for not having one's shortcomings exposed.

Finally, it should be reiterated again, that the spread of socialism during the nineteenth and the twentieth centuries is also a result of the desire to make charity a matter of state provision. It arises because of the inequality in talents and abilities of people generally. In this case, the market is thought to be unjust because some people are simply not as gifted as others. In addition, through no fault of their own, some people suffer from various calamities of misfortune or from a host of disabilities that have rendered them unable to succeed in a market economy. For this reason, it is often argued that socialism is needed to insure that such people are taken care of. However, as we have already seen, this is a misguided notion of charity. It presumes that charity can be mandated by the legal code. But such efforts eliminate the volitional nature of true charity.

This last reason for the spread of socialism can be clearly seen in

---

[213] Ludwig von Mises, *The Anti-capitalistic Mentality*, (South Holland, IL: Libertarian Press, 1972), pp. 12-13.

the development of the welfare state. The experience with such policies in the United States provides good evidence of the foolishness of presuming that it might be possible to eliminate poverty by governmental mandates. While every new welfare program in America was developed with the intention of easing the economic burden of some at taxpayer expense, the actual result was to extend the economic burden of taxpayers specifically and to hinder economic progress generally. Year after year these programs put added stress on government budgets. In turn, government officials have had to look feverishly for new ways to increase tax revenues to maintain the funding of these programs. The main problem with them, is the problem that economists call moral hazard.

The problem of moral hazard occurs when there is a third party who agrees to pay for a good. For example, suppose that a person purchases insurance coverage that will more than repay the value of his home should it be destroyed by fire. In this case, the homeowner need not worry as much as he might otherwise about conditions around his home that would actually result in his home burning down. In other words, the fact that the insurance company is underwriting the risk, allows the homeowner to be less concerned about it. For this reason, it is quite common for insurers to add provisions to their contracts that require the policyholders to take some minimum steps to cut the risk of loss.

In the case of welfare, when the government begins to provide for the economic needs of certain classes of people the same problem arises. For instance, if the government is going to provide unemployment compensation if a person should be fired from his job, that individual need not worry as much about doing his job well because he will not suffer the full cost of his failure. Or, if the government provides a retirement program that will pay people in their old age, there is less interest in saving for one's own future. In each of these cases, an incentive is provided to ignore the consequences of being foolish because such behavior no longer subjects the person to the brunt of the burden brought forth by his action. Given human nature is what it is, welfare programs invariably tend to grow with the only restraint being government's ability to secure the necessary resources by taxing the productive segments of society. At some point, taxpayers will eventually lose heart and opt to seek government assistance themselves.

It was in this way that the size and scope of the federal

government of the United States of America grew in the twentieth century. Stephen Moore has demonstrated the magnitude of this growth in his article, "The Growth of Government in America."[214] In that article, Moore shows that the federal government has grown exponentially over the course of the twentieth century. After adjusting for inflation, Moore found that federal expenditures increased from $8.3 billion in 1900 to $1,450 billion in 1992. This is a staggering increase that cannot be washed away even when it is put in per capita terms. The reality is that the federal government has assumed for itself roles in society that would have been unthought of at the founding of the nation. Nevertheless, this growth has taken place and it represents the success of socialistic ideas as they have spread through American society.

The constitutional form of government created by the founders set a new standard in human affairs. It gave the average individual the greatest latitude of freedom ever known, while simultaneously promoting the rule of law that allowed market transactions to flourish. It was the best representation of what Adam Smith had in mind when he wrote *The Wealth of Nations* and advocated a laissez faire form of government. However, it is clear that the United States government has loosed itself from the chains of the Constitution in many perverse ways.

As one writer has noted:

> In the broadest sense, government has been out of control in the United States in the last half of the 20th century. . . because it is no longer effectively under the control of the Constitution. Formally, of course, the government operates under the Constitution. Most of the forms are rigorously observed, such as, age and residency requirements for various offices, length of terms of elected officers, times for holding elections, and so on. But in substance and spirit, the written Constitution no longer controls by limiting and restricting the government to those powers authorized by it. The Constitution may not be a dead letter, but it has been stretched completely out of shape, ignored, and evaded so

---

[214] Stephen Moore, "The Growth of Government in America," *The Freeman*, (Irvington, NY: Foundation for Economic Education, April 1993), pp. 124-136.

as to produce a Leviathan whose justification can be found
nowhere in the letter or spirit of the written Constitution.[215]

There are several ways in which the government has loosed itself
from the substance and spirit of the Constitution. In particular, the
federal government's fiscal and spending policies, its increasing
bureaucracy, and its inattention to punishing actual criminals who violate
the fundamental rights of others are all evidence of the government's
departure from Constitutional restraints. By failing to adhere to the
Constitution, a good deal of hardship has resulted.

In terms of imposing taxes and spending the revenues on various
programs, a number of economic effects are well documented. For
example, the creation of the welfare state has resulted in a long list of
entitlement programs. Once established by law, spending on any
particular program continues to escalate as more and more individuals
become beneficiaries. But the beneficiaries of a program will always
remain a special class of citizens. Thus, the essence of welfare programs
and their proliferation is to create many special interest groups who
benefit at the expense of other individuals. These programs destroy the
individual recipient's incentive to develop his skills, to employ his
resources for the good of others, and to save his resources for future
needs. In short, entitlement programs promote prodigality and undermine
economic growth and development

As the government has assumed a larger role than that established
for it by the Constitution, it has established a huge bureaucracy aimed at
regulating and controlling all types of human endeavor. This expansion
has occurred on the basis of the mythical notion that government can
provide for the needs of life. Bastiat once again offered good insight into
the fundamental flaw of this type of thinking.

> I demand nothing better, you may be sure, than that you
> should really have discovered outside of us a benevolent
> and inexhaustible being, calling itself the state, which has
> bread for all mouths, work for all hands, capital for all
> enterprises, credit for all projects, ointment for all wounds,

---

[215] Clarence Carson, *Basic American Government*, (Wadley, AL: American Textbook
Committee, 1993), p. 442.

> balm for all suffering, advice for perplexities, solutions for all problems, truths for all minds, distractions for all varieties of boredom, milk for children and wine for old age, which provide for all our needs, foresees all our desires, satisfies all our curiosity, corrects all our errors, amends all our faults, and exempts us all henceforth from the need for foresight, prudence, judgment, sagacity, experience, order, economy, temperance, and industry.[216]

However, the reality is that such policies fail to take account of the underlying economic costs. The creation of government bureaus to carry out congressional legislation leads to the proliferation of all types of rules of conduct. The government bureaus create these rules at a rate of ten regulations for every law passed. Individuals who violate these rules are penalized just as if they had in effect violated the laws themselves. The problem most people face is that it is quite impossible to know and abide by the rules that have been created. This fact, coupled with the reality that they are often arbitrarily applied, fosters an atmosphere of fear for the potential entrepreneur. Even a well meaning person cannot be sure that he is handling the affairs of his life in accordance with the nation's law. This creates a general fear in people which leads to inaction. Thus, entrepreneurship, which is the very lifeblood of economic growth and development, is hampered.

> It might have been that Americans when confronted with constitutional amendments which posed the question of whether or not to increase the power of Congress, the President, and the Federal courts would have rejected such amendments by considerable majorities. That is not how the questions were posed, however. They were asked if they would like for government to bring social justice to them and punish their adversaries. Everyman cares very much about how his shoes pinch him, and he can sometimes be persuaded that the fault lies with others. Thus, many can be persuaded that it would be good to use government to help them and bring their opponents to heel. So it is, and by way

---

[216] Frederic Bastiat, "The State", *Selected Essays on Political Economy*, Foundation for Economic Education: Irvington, NY, 1964, p. 142.

of example, the poor may be persuaded to tax the rich and have their wealth divided among the "needy." . . . Farmers will vote to have industrialists give them their "fair share" of the national wealth. The aged will vote to have the young taxed to support them. Parents can often be attracted by the notion of having those without children assist in educating theirs. There is something irresistibly attractive to many people about others being penalized and themselves presumably benefitted by government programs.[217]

Beyond the mere economic costs of the government's abandonment of the Constitution, is the cost of losing civilization. Robert Bidinotto has noted that, "Since 1960, per capita crime rates have more than tripled, while violent crime rates have nearly quintupled. By any measure, we live in a nation much less safe than that in which our parents grew up."[218] Bidinotto argued that the increase in crime was the result of a sociological mind set that assumed that individuals commit crimes against others only because of socioeconomic factors such as poverty and illiteracy. As this view gained acceptance, the governmental system of justice was hindered in its efforts of punishing genuine criminals. This was especially true because numerous actions taken by federal judges made it very difficult for state and local law enforcement officers to apprehend and actually punish thieves and murderers. For example, between 1967 and 1977, convicts found guilty of committing capital offenses could not be executed. Moreover, even after ruling that such actions were not unconstitutional, federal rules made it extremely difficult to execute someone even when he was guilty of committing a particularly heinous crime.

This neglect was a failure to operate within the framework of the Constitution. It resulted in large economic costs which included increased spending on goods whose sole purpose was to provide individual protection and the loss of production from individuals who would have been deterred from their crimes by the efficient use of collective force.

---

[217] Clarence Carson, *Basic American Government*, pg. 403.

[218] Robert J. Bidinotto, "The 'Root Causes' of Crime", *The Freeman*, (Irvington, NY: Foundation for Economic Education, June 1995), p. 371.

There are, then, certain conclusions that can be immediately drawn. First, there is a fundamental role for government to play if there is hope for the marketplace to flourish. That is, property rights must be protected and voluntary contracts must be enforced. Without a referee of sorts to insure appropriate human behavior, to protect the life, liberty, and property of the individual, mob rule would quickly develop and free market trade would be severely diminished. However, if the government punishes murderers and thieves, then self-interested human nature will tend to be directed toward cooperation and voluntary trade even though any particular individual may be only concerned with promoting his interests. The invisible market force of competition would tend to motivate individual human action to promote greater excellence and better products which would in turn enhance the well-being of the general community.

The second conclusion is that there will never be a perfect from of government instituted by human beings. If human nature is flawed, and man's base disposition prompts him to participate in unjust actions to promote his own interests above those of others, then nothing could be more certain than the fact that he will always attempt to use the institution of collective force to accomplish his self-interested ends. As a result, governments throughout history have been, and always will be, more or less perverse. Among people who realize the need for moral behavior with regards to respecting one's neighbor in order to establish an atmosphere within which economic well-being and prosperity are fostered, is the task of forming a government which not only punishes wrongdoers, but which cannot be readily used for the purpose of wrongdoing.

To date, the most successful effort at establishing a government which more nearly promotes justice alone is in the United States which founded its state upon a constitution. The breakthrough of constitutional government was the creation of a written document whose sole purpose was to severely limit the actions of government. The potential weakness of this form of government did not escape its framers as has been seen from the words of George Washington who warned the nation to be on guard against special interest groups and associations which "are likely in the course of time and things to become potent engines by which cunning, ambitious, and unprincipled men will be enabled to subvert the power of the people, and to usurp for themselves the reins of government, destroying afterwards the very engines which have lifted them to unjust dominion." Indeed, the very fear he called all Americans to be wary of, has taken place in the twentieth century. Unprincipled men and women have gained control of the political structures and have shown an utter disregard for the spirit and content of the Constitution. As a result, the tyranny of government has escalated.

Study Questions

1. How did the industrial revolution contribute to the improvement to the general well-being of people?
2. What argument did social reformers promote against the free market and industrialization? What is wrong with that argument?
3. What is the meaning of free trade and why is it fundamentally connected to Western civilization?
4. Will a free market cure all social ills? Why or why not?
5. How is the socialist mind set hopelessly romantic and irrational?

Chapter 21: Epilogue

To conclude our consideration of Western civilization, it is important to summarize some of the key essentials of that civilization that can be gleaned from our study. There are a number of key issues. Some of these can be seen by an appeal to the highest expressions of Western civilization that have developed thus far. The examples of England and of the United States are the best expressions thus far in human history of Western civilization. Within the context of the histories of these countries we find that a number of issues of civilization were handled especially well. Perhaps the first among them involves religion. Truly, religion has played an important role in all of the various human societies that we considered. The question is, therefore, what is the fundamental role of religion in sustaining Western civilization?

We can note from the outset that Western civilization has been defined by the pervasive influence of Christianity. In fact, Christianity was for a long time the only legally recognized religion in the West. On this basis, it might be argued that Western civilization hinges upon the dominance of Christianity if it is to be sustained. Furthermore, in light of this fact, some might think that the only way to revive Western culture is to once again establish Christianity by law.

However, this is not necessary. While England sought to maintain its religious heritage by such a legal approach, the United States opted to do so by promoting religious freedom. In the modern era, Christianity has been vigorously attacked in both settings. However, the prospect for a revival of traditional Christianity is most likely to occur in the air of religious freedom. In truth, what we discovered from the history of this matter is that the establishment of a governmentally recognized religion tends to undermine civility. When people are forced to proclaim a particular religious creed as being true regardless of their own beliefs, discontentment is bread amongst the people. Instead of promoting civility, such mandates tend to undercut it. This friction is typically bad not only for individuals who are forced to submit to some particular doctrine apart from their consciences, but it is also bad for the religion itself. In time, the religion tends to be changed in order to promote politically expedient ends. To be sure, faithful members of the Church of England continue to struggle to maintain the purity of their religious faith in a secularized world. As for the United States, the problem has arisen only recently and that mainly due to the new religion of no religion that is taught in America's government schools. The problem in the United States is due to the near monopoly that government holds on available schooling. Given its control over the nation's main means of education, statists use the system as a means of indoctrination and this has led to its assault on the Christian religion.

The reality is that neither Christianity, nor any other theistic religion, will be held by everyone living in any particular community. To be sure, there will be communities with more Christians and those with fewer. However, it is highly unlikely that there will ever be a community where everyone is a Christian. But that is not necessary to secure the minimal conditions for the continuation of Western civilization. What is necessary is that there should be a pervasive acceptance of theism.

Civilization cannot survive apart from some degree of Judeo-Christian morality. The existence of morality depends upon the existence of God who has established and sustains the natural order of things. In this regard, people might disagree very much in regards to their religious creeds, and even about all the facets of what moral life might entail, but still be able to affirm together a minimal set of general moral standards of behavior. The minimal affirmation that must be made to sustain Western civilization is that people are endowed by God with the fundamental human rights of life, liberty, and property. If people of all faiths maintained this view towards their neighbors, it would certainly result in a great deal of civility.

There have certainly been people in history who were not Christians, but who nevertheless attempted to proclaim the need to live in accordance with certain moral standards. Both Socrates and Cicero are examples of this fact. Each of these men was theistic in his outlook and acknowledged the presence of the natural law. For this reason, these men where often admired by the founders of the United States. Therefore, the first essential of Western civilization is that there should be an affirmation of this minimal set of moral standards of behavior that would guide interpersonal relationships.

Regrettably, the affirmation of this minimal moral standard has been eroded in the United States as the social reform movement gained momentum. As a result, those most affected by the Enlightenment and the subsequent irrationalism it spawned departed from the basic agreement made in the Constitution regarding the role of government in society. As Charles Colson observed, "When the republic was founded, the biblical tradition and the Enlightenment–two distinct and often antagonistic understandings of the world–seemed to find a patch of common ground."[219] Both groups affirmed that certain human rights were fundamental and should be left alone in the course of the political affairs of state government. These rights were rooted in a common moral understanding and necessarily established a limit to government action. The Enlightenment rationalists reasoned to this common ground by way of the natural law, while the Christians observed it as being part of God's commandments. "The subsequent experiment in 'ordered liberty' was achieved because, while some saw their liberty secured by God and others by their status as human beings alone, all agreed to be bound together for the sake of that liberty. . . . [However,] if one party [no longer agrees to the contract], that party has breached what lawyers call a 'condition precedent': the essential promise by which the other party's agreement was secured."[220] As a result, the nation has more and more been cut off from the explicit terms of the Constitution which limit government action. This, in turn, has alienated a large portion of the populace from their own country and this has resulted in the decline of civilization in America. The question at hand is, what, if anything, can be done to salvage the contract and, hence, to save the American experiment of limited government and ordered liberty?

Intertwined with the first essential, is the affirmation of the need for limited government. In chapter nineteen we examined the role of government in society and saw that its primary function is to secure the peace. That is, it is the last line of defense in promoting the necessary minimum standards of moral behavior. One of the problems that has been associated with government is that it has always tended to overstep its

---

[219]Charles Colson, "Kingdoms in Conflict," *The End of Democracy?*, (Dallas, TX: Spencer Publishing Company, 1997), pp. 41-52.

[220]Ibid., pg. 48.

bounds. The tendency has been for governments to use power for immoral purposes rather for the purpose of securing the essential moral order.

One reason for the decline of Western civilization in America, is that people expect the government to do more than can be reasonably expected of it. Indeed, as the ideas of social reformers have been intermingled with those of classical times, the notion has developed that the government is the primary means by which all civility is to be gained. It is increasingly thought that government can educate all the citizenry, that it can provide the most modern health care for all its people, that it can secure the best form of progress in life, and that it can even make people like each other. But the more people have sought for government solutions to their problems, the less civil society has become. The reason that this is true, is that it makes all the issues of life political and, hence, it makes busybodies out of all people. If everyone is attempting to find a solution to the problems of life by way of political action, then everyone will think he has a vested interest in everyone else's business. In turn, the political action that will necessarily result from such a situation is that everyone will attempt to impose his will upon everyone else.

In the Declaration of Independence, Thomas Jefferson wrote, "We hold these truths to be self-evident, that all men are created equal, that they are endowed by their Creator with certain unalienable Rights, that among these are Life, Liberty, and the pursuit of Happiness." At first glance it would seem odd that Jefferson chose to use the phrase "the pursuit of Happiness" rather than the term "Property" in his list of the three fundamental natural rights that the signers of the Declaration affirmed. On the surface of things, it might appear that Jefferson was a sort of Benthamite who embraced utilitarianism.

However, that is not an accurate assessment of what he was doing. Jefferson well understood the reality that happiness was not something that was gained immediately, but was gained from a life well-lived. But, a life well-lived is one that is chosen by the individual who lives it. Therefore, by using this phrase, he was merely broadening the scope of the protection of property in order to point out the fact that people must be free to use their resources and their liberty according to their own values as they pursue meaning in this world.

This is what people do. All people desire to be happy. No one wishes to be miserable. As a result, all people pursue the things that they think will ultimately result in happiness. That is not to say that everything people pursue in this quest will actually bring about their happiness. In truth, many things that people think will increase their happiness do not end up securing it. For instance, the drug user begins using drugs believing that the pleasure gained from it will promote his happiness. Only later in time, does the drug addict realize that he has been bitten by the devil. Likewise, the spendthrift expects that his happiness is just one purchase away. But with every new possession gained, such people become increasingly disenchanted with this world.

Notwithstanding the immense variety and scope of the errors people make in living worthy lives, the reality is that a life that is truly well-lived does produce happiness and that is Jefferson's point. In the context of freedom, there will always be people who will give themselves to a particular vocation because they believe that God has called them to it. One might think of a person who sacrifices the prospects of a better material situation for himself in order to operate an orphanage for children, or of someone else who gives up similar material prospects to become a missionary as examples of this truth. In each case, the material sacrifices are not considered as valuable as accomplishing the good of the vocation. In truth, at the end of life, such people are typically immensely happy. But this happiness comes about as a matter of personal choice. It was for this reason that J. Gresham Machen instructed his reader that the authentic personality is always refined in "the realm of individual choice." It is simply impossible for a government to direct the affairs of men to promote the authentic personalities of the people who reside under it. That activity is a personal pursuit. Therefore, if such human flourishing is to be had at its greatest level, then the government must not interfere with the fundamental human rights of its citizens.

As was already said, this will not result in a society that is paradise on earth. Instead, there will always be people who seek happiness in the wrong places. There will be people who are religiously misguided. There will be drunkards and drug addicts, spendthrifts and misers, as well as a whole host of others who miss the way to real happiness. In fact, as Jesus said, the way to happiness is a narrow gate. It often involves the endurance of quite a bit of pain before the rewards are ever realized. Nonetheless, lives that are truly well-lived produce immense satisfaction and those lives provide good guidance to the rest of us. But the fullness of those lives will only become as much as they might be in the context of free choice.

That brings us to another essential–free trade among people is necessary. This actually goes hand-in-hand with limited government for as we saw, free enterprise is the logic of the protection of private property. Indeed, one of the chief ways that we use our God-given talents, is to employ them in the production of some good that can be traded in the marketplace. In fact, this is one of the primary ways by which we might serve the needs of others. Therefore, when people are free to own and trade property, the contextual conditions are established for human beings to flourish according to their God given talents. To be sure, some will not flourish and this is certainly the occasion for mercy ministries. However, others, most likely the large majority, will more nearly reflect the image of God. Robert A. Sirico, a Catholic priest, has rightly concluded the matter:

> So the question turns on the kind of community that is appropriate to free, rational human beings. The alternatives are manifold: There is the community of the hive, in which individual dignity and rights are not given proper consideration. Alternatively, there is the community of the prison, in which human freedom, right of association–or nonassociation, for that matter–and individual creativity are not important. However, a community suitable for free individuals, which is progressive in the best and truest sense, and which encourages economically productive cooperation among its members, dramatically differs from the communities of the hive and the prison–it is what we call civilization.[221]

Study Questions

1. What are the essentials of Western civilization?
2. Is it possible to revive Western culture and fend off the massive attack against it that has been mounted by the naturalists? If so, how is this to be accomplished?

---

[221] Robert A. Sirico, *Toward a Free and Virtuous Society*, (Grand Rapids, MI: The Acton Institute, 1997), pp. 9-10.

Index